P9-DVV-660

DISCOVERING THE GLOBAL PAST

A Look at the Evidence

Volume I: To 1600

DISCOVERING THE GLOBAL PAST

A Look at the Evidence

Merry E. Wiesner
University of Wisconsin—Milwaukee

William Bruce Wheeler
University of Tennessee, Knoxville

Franklin M. Doeringer
Lawrence University

Melvin E. Page
East Tennessee State University

HOUGHTON MIFFLIN COMPANY   Boston   New York

Senior Sponsoring Editor: Patricia A. Coryell
Assistant Editor: Jeanne Herring
Project Editor: Christina Horn
Senior Production/Design Coordinator: Jennifer Waddell
Manufacturing Manager: Florence Cadran

Cover Design: Len Massiglia
Cover Image: Jacob with his son Joseph on their way to Egypt. Mss. 1411, World Chronik by Rudolf von Ems, Toggenburg Bible, fol. 62V. Kupferstichkabinett, Berlin/AKG, London

Printed in the U.S.A.
Library of Congress Catalog Card Number: 96-76976
ISBN Student Text: 0-395-69986X
ISBN Examination Copy: 0-395-844029
123456789-QM-00 99 98 97 96

CONTENTS

Biological adaptations of early hominid competitors.   Chimpanzee and *homo habilis* dentition.   Very early *hominid* tools.   Lava flake tools from Africa.   A prepared core and flake tool.   Bone and antler tools.   Stone toolmaking techniques.   How early *hominid* toolmakers may have worked in the east African savannas.   *Homo sapiens neandertalensis* toolmaking and tool use.   How stone tools may have been used to work other materials.   The core and flake toolmaking technique for complex early *homo sapiens* toolkits.   Possible *hominid* tool use.   Electron microscope views of carnivore tooth marks and *hominid* stone tool marks on mammal bone.   The significance of fire.   The early discovery and use of fire.   *Hominid* and early *homo sapiens* tool-using techniques.

Aerial photograph of pre-Roman city in Italy.   Major ancient levees identifiable in LANDSAT imagery.   Water-lifting devices.   Hammurabi

CHAPTER TEN
Romances and Behavior in Aristocratic Japan and Italy
(1000–1350)   253

CHAPTER ELEVEN
Medicine and Reproduction in the Middle Ages
(1000–1500)   282

PREFACE

In 1919, Dean Harry Carman of Columbia University instituted a new course for undergraduates entitled Contemporary Civilization. Intended to broaden students' knowledge about the Western world as the United States emerged from its isolation to become a world leader, "C.C." (as the students quickly named it) spread to other colleges and universities and evolved into what became known as the introductory Western Civilization course, the staple of historical instruction for generations of college students.[1]

The Western Civilization course continues to be important in the shaping of student thought and in the imparting of valuable knowledge. From its inception, however, the course contained a number of inherent problems, chief among them its almost inevitable Eurocentrism—an implicit emphasis on the evolution and progress of the West and a corresponding overlooking or omission of the history of the rest of the globe. Attempting to correct this imbalance, a number of colleges and universities inaugurated courses in World History; in some cases this new course supplanted the Western Civilization course and in others stood side-by-side with it. Responding to the emergence of the "global village" and the increasing diversity of the United States's population, more and more colleges and universities have embraced this global perspective. As with its ancestor, Columbia's "C.C." course, the goal of World History is to provide students with an important introduction to the political, economic, social, and intellectual environment in which they live.

Students in World History courses are often overwhelmed by the amount of material presented, and we as instructors can lose sight of the fact that history is not simply something one learns about; it is something one does. One discovers the past, and what makes this pursuit exciting is not only the past that is discovered but the process of discovery itself. This process can be simultaneously exhilarating and frustrating, enlightening and confusing, but it is always challenging enough to convince those of us who are professional historians to spend our lives at it.

---

1. Ideas about such a course had been circulating in various American colleges and universities as early as the 1870s, but they got a special boost with the United States's entry into World War I. See Gilbert Allardyce, "The Rise and Fall of the Western Civilization Course," *American Historical Review,* 87 (June 1982), pp. 695–725; and Lawrence W. Levine, *The Opening of the American Mind: Canons, Culture, and History* (Boston: Beacon, 1996), especially pp. 54–74.

The primary goal of *Discovering the Global Past: A Look at the Evidence* is to allow students enrolled in world history courses to *do* history in the same way that we as historians do—to examine a group of original sources to answer questions about the past. The unique structure of this book clusters primary sources around a set of historical questions that students are asked to "solve." Unlike a source reader, this book prompts students to actually *analyze* a wide variety of authentic primary source material, to make inferences, and to draw conclusions in much the same way that historians do.

The evidence in this book is more varied than that in most source collections. We have included such visual evidence as coins, paintings, statues, literary illustrations, historical photographs, maps, cartoons, advertisements, and political posters. In choosing written evidence we again have tried to offer a broad sample—eulogies, wills, court records, oral testimonies, and statistical data all supplement letters, newspaper articles, speeches, memoirs, and other more traditional sources.

In order for students to learn history the way we as historians do, they must not only be confronted with the evidence, they must also learn how to use that evidence to arrive at a conclusion. In other words, they must learn historical methodology. Too often methodology (or even the notion that historians *have* a methodology) is reserved for upper-level majors or graduate students; beginning students are simply presented with historical facts and interpretations without being shown how these were unearthed or formulated. Students may learn that historians hold different interpretations of the significance of an event or individual or different ideas about causation, but they are not informed of how historians come to such conclusions.

Thus, along with evidence, we have provided explicit suggestions about how one might analyze that evidence, guiding students as they reach their own conclusions. As they work through the various chapters, students will discover not only that the sources of historical information are wide-ranging, but that the methodologies appropriate to understanding and using them are equally diverse. By doing history themselves, students will learn how intellectual historians handle philosophical treatises, economic historians quantitative data, social historians court records, and political and diplomatic historians theoretical treatises and memoirs. They will also be asked to consider the limitations of their evidence, to explore what historical questions it cannot answer as well as those it can. Instead of passive observers, students become active participants.

Each chapter is divided into six parts: The Problem, Background, The Method, The Evidence, Questions to Consider, and Epilogue. Each of the parts relates to or builds upon the others, creating a uniquely integrated chapter structure that helps guide the reader through the analytical process. "The Problem" section begins with a brief discussion of the central issues of the chapter and then states the questions students will explore. A "Background" section follows, designed to help students understand the historical context of the problem. The section called "The Method" gives students suggestions for studying and analyzing the evidence. "The Evidence" section is the heart of the chapter, providing a variety of primary source material on the particular historical event or issue described in the chapter's "Problem" section. The section called "Questions to Consider" focuses students' attention on specific evidence and on linkages among different evidence material. The "Epilogue" section gives the aftermath or the historical outcome of the evidence—what happened to the people involved, the results of a debate, and so on.

Within this framework, we have tried to present a series of historical issues and events of significance to the instructor as well as of interest to the student. We have also aimed to provide a balance among political, social, diplomatic, intellectual, and cultural history. In other words, we have attempted to create a kind of historical sampler that we believe will help students learn the methods and skills used by historians. Not only will these skills—analyzing arguments, developing hypotheses, comparing evidence, testing conclusions, and reevaluating material—enable students to master historical content; they will also provide the necessary foundation for critical thinking in other college courses and after college as well.

Because the amount of material in global history is so vast, we had to pick certain topics and geographic areas to highlight, though here too we have aimed at a balance. Some chapters are narrow in focus, providing students with an opportunity to delve deeply into a single case study, while others ask students to make comparisons among individuals, events, or developments in different cultures. We have included cultural comparisons that are frequently discussed in World History courses, such as classical Rome and Han China, as well as more unusual ones, such as peasant family life in early modern central Europe and Southeast Asia.

Discovering the Global Past is designed to accommodate any format of the World History course, from the small lecture/discussion class at a liberal arts or community college to the large lecture with discussions led by teaching assistants at a sizable university. The chapters may be used for individual assignments, team projects, class discussions, papers, and exams. Each is self-contained, so that any combination may be assigned. The book is not intended to replace a standard textbook, and it was written to accompany any World History text the instructor chooses. The Instructor's Resource Manual, written by the authors of the text, offers further suggestions for class discussion, as well as a variety of ways in which students' learning may be evaluated and annotated lists of recommendations for further reading.

A note on spellings: Many of the sources presented in this book were originally written in a language other than English, and often in an alphabet other than the Western (Roman) one. Over the centuries translators have devised various means of representing the sounds of other languages, and these conventions of translation have also changed over time. In general, we have used the most current spelling and orthographic conventions in our discussions and have left spellings as they appeared in the original translation in the sources. This means, for example, that Indian, Arabic, and Japanese words often have diacritical marks in the sources but not in our own material. For Chinese, in our own text we have used the pinyin system developed by the Chinese in the 1950s, with pinyin spellings indicated in brackets in the sources, most of which use the older Wade-Giles system.

We would like to thank the many students and instructors who have helped us in our efforts. We extend our gratitude to the following professors, who read and criticized the manuscript throughout its development:

Charles M. Barber, *Northeastern Illinois University*

Charlotte L. Beahan, *Murray State University*

Norman R. Bennett, *Boston University*

Matthew Ware Coulter, *Collin County Community College*

Linda T. Darling, *University of Arizona*

Steven C. Davidson, *Southwestern University*

L.T. Easley, *Campbell University*

Alexander Grab, *University of Maine*

Laird Jones, *Lock Haven University*

Carol Loats, *University of Southern Colorado*

Francisco A. Marmalejo, *Irvine Valley College*

Marilyn Morris, *University of North Texas*

Jim Rice, *Central Washington University*

Robert M. Seltzer, *Hunter College of the City University of New York*

Thomas C. Tirado, *Millersville University of Pennsylvania*

In addition to our colleagues across the United States, we would like to thank especially our colleagues at the University of Wisconsin—Milwaukee; the University of Tennessee, Knoxville; Lawrence University; and East Tennessee State University. Merry E. Wiesner wishes especially to thank Barbara Andaya, Judith Bennett, Mark Bradley, Holly Brewer, Martha Carlin, Jean Fleet, Marija Gajdardziska-Josifovska, Faye Getz, Michael Gordon, Abbas Hamdani, Anne Hansen, Jean Johnson, Jeffrey Merrick, Sheilagh Ogilvie, Jean Quataert, and Jane Waldbaum. Bruce Wheeler would like to thank Thomas Burman, Robert Bast, Todd Diacon, J. Daniel Bing, Owen Bradley, Palmira Brummett, W. Wayne Farris, Yen-ping Hao, and Vejas Liulevicius.

[xv]

Franklin M. Doeringer wishes to thank all of his colleagues in the Lawrence University Department of History for their support and interest in this project. J. Michael Hittle and Edmund M. Kern deserve particular mention for reading over portions of manuscript and offering helpful comments. He also expresses his gratitude to Jane Parish Yang and Kuo-ming Sung in the Department of East Asian Languages and Cultures for their suggestions on material pertaining to China and East Asia. Finally, he extends special thanks to Peter J. Gilbert of the Lawrence library for his unflagging help in tracking down elusive sources and obscure references. Melvin E. Page would like to thank particularly the following colleagues and students: Steve Fritz, Jim Odom, Shannon Vance, Nancy Roy, Tim Carmichael, Julie Lind, Scott Bailey, and Grady Eades.

Finally, we would like to thank Jeanne Herring, Christina Horn, and the rest of the staff at Houghton Mifflin for their support.

M.E.W.
W.B.W.
F.M.D.
M.E.P.

CHAPTER ONE

CLAIMING THE EARTH:

THE TECHNOLOGICAL CHALLENGE

OF PREHISTORY (TO CA. 10,000 B.C.E.)

THE PROBLEM

Every generation, it seems, faces some sort of technological watershed. Sometimes these turning points have involved new ways of accomplishing tasks that people had previously found perplexing, onerous, or time-consuming. At other times they have been new capacities for human beings that have changed our outlook on the world. For example, pivotal changes accompanied the coming of cinema and the automobile, reshaping both our social relationships and our sense of time and place. More recently, atomic power and the ability to send humans beyond earth's gravitational pull into outer space have set new, revolutionary benchmarks.

In our own time, perhaps the most important technological challenge has been the rapid advance in computer technology. Not only can we play fascinating games and trust machines to correct our spelling and grammar, but we can communicate almost instantaneously with people all over the world. Through the technological marvel of the Internet we can quickly and easily find information on countless topics, a challenge not only for students but also for their teachers and librarians.

In the last few decades it has often seemed as if technology was changing faster than we could adapt to it. A little over twenty-five years ago, even before the introduction of personal computers, sociologist Alvin Toffler described this problem as "future shock." His concern was that changes—and especially technological changes—were coming so rapidly that human beings would increasingly have difficulty adapting to them.[1] At times, all of us seem to feel in "shock" that way, and so have many generations of our ancestors.

1. Alvin Toffler, *Future Shock* (New York: Random House, 1970).

Chapter 1

Claiming the

Earth: The

Technological

Challenge of

Prehistory (to

ca. 10,000 B.C.E.)

One famous example of technological backlash was the early-nineteenth-century movement opposing economic changes brought on by the Industrial Revolution in Europe. Known as Luddism after the mythic English labor leader Ned Ludd, those all-too-real workers' protests were often aimed at literally demolishing the industrial machines that seemed to be displacing working men and women. Similar protests greeted early urban railways, and later automobiles, in the United States. You no doubt recognize similar opposition among people you know to today's technological explosion.

Yet we are also acutely aware that technology has aided human beings in many ways. Few of us would want to return—certainly not permanently—to a world without electricity, railroads, or even animal-drawn wagons. The work required of us would be overwhelming, and our chances for survival greatly diminished. Envisioning a time without tools, or even with only simple implements to work with, seems almost impossible. Contemplating such a possibility does, however, help us visualize an extremely distant historical past, a time when the earliest ancestors of human beings had no tools to aid them in their lives and work.

Hundreds of thousands, perhaps even millions, of years ago the first *hominids,* as those ancestral humans

2. "A *hominid* is a primate of the order *Hominidae,* which includes modern humans, earlier human subspecies, and their direct ancestors"—Brian M. Fagan, *The Journey from Eden: The Peopling of Our World* (New York: Thames and Hudson, 1990), p. 15.

are now known,[2] lived in the savanna grasslands of eastern Africa. There they had to compete with many other species for survival. Fortunately, that environment was comparatively rich in food and other resources, making survival much easier than would seem possible looking at that stark landscape today. For thousands of years, those grasslands seem to have allowed several varieties of these early *hominids* to exist side by side with many other creatures.

Well before our time, human beings—*Homo sapiens sapiens*—emerged from that setting, spread throughout the rest of the world, and came to have distinct survival advantages not only over other *hominids,* but also over a wide variety of other living creatures. Humans came to dominate the natural world in ways that no other species could even contemplate. Yet we are sometimes in awe of the abilities, powers, and characteristics of many of those beings with whom we share the earth and compared to whom we may sometimes seem to be inferior. Elephants are certainly stronger, horses faster, rabbits more prolific, butterflies probably more beautiful. What is it, then, that sets human beings apart from all these other creatures?

Indeed, this is the key to the problem set forth in this chapter. How were humans able to spread, more readily than other creatures, over the whole earth? Why were our ancestors able to survive outside that relatively advantageous environment found in eastern Africa so long ago? What legacies did these achievements leave for their successors?

BACKGROUND

Scholars who study the distant human past—paleontologists, archaeologists, and anthropologists, along with historians—generally agree that the earliest traceable origins of human beings are in Africa. Beyond that basic point, however, their agreements are few. Their differing interpretations and honest disagreements stem largely from the limited amount of evidence at their disposal. Granted, many discoveries and theories about human origins appear from time to time in newspapers and on television, but few such "breakthroughs" are based on more than a handful of recovered ancient bones, stones, or other limited pieces of evidence.

Most of this material comes from Africa, and much of it from the eastern portions of the continent stretching from the Awash Valley in Ethiopia and the shores of Lake Turkana in Kenya, southward along the Great Rift Valley through Olduvai Gorge in Tanzania, and on to northern Zambia and Malawi. Other African evidence has been found south of the Zambezi River, especially in South Africa. These artifacts consist primarily of skeletal remains and sometimes rock and bone fragments that appear to have been broken to make tools. In addition, there is occasionally evidence of bones from other creatures—various antelope and other mammals, for example— found in the same areas with the *hominid* remains. And in one case, at Laetoli in Tanzania, preserved footprints show that *hominids* may have walked upright over 3 million years ago.

In all these places, the evidence has been discovered either through systematic archaeological excavations or by discoveries made on the surface after the erosion of water and wind on the exposed edges of eastern Africa's Great Rift Valley. Most of the sites, as they are known, pose formidable problems for scholars trying to interpret the evidence. Obviously, the erosion that has revealed the artifacts may also have moved materials from one place to another, shuffling the original patterns. Moreover, this disturbance might well have happened thousands of years ago in areas only recently excavated. It is also likely that bones and stones were moved from one place to another either by *hominids* themselves or perhaps by other creatures, including canine and feline scavengers. Such effects mean that the limited available evidence must be treated with even further caution.

Similar concerns also apply to the other evidence of *hominids*, although from much more recent times. This is especially true concerning evidence of early *Homo sapiens*, which has also been found in Africa, as well as in Europe and Asia. These more widespread remains have led the scholars who study this part of the human past, which we often call prehistory, to develop two fundamentally different ideas about how *Homo sapiens sapiens*—whom archaeologist Brian Fagan has called "the clever person"[3]—came to populate the vast reaches of the

3. Fagan, *The Journey from Eden,* p. 11.

Chapter 1

Claiming the

Earth: The

Technological

Challenge of

Prehistory (to

ca. 10,000 B.C.E.)

entire earth. Both versions acknowledge that it is likely one particular group of *hominids,* known as *Homo erectus,* migrated out of Africa to various parts of Europe and Asia beginning as early as 1 million years ago, a time when today's extensive Sahara Desert was in fact much smaller and much less a barrier to human movement. Beyond that acceptance of a common root, there is little agreement.

Some archaeologists' ideas suggest that within the scattered populations of *Homo erectus* in Europe, the Middle East, and far eastern Asia, various biological and cultural transformations led to the independent appearance of human beings in each of those areas. The other approach, supported by controversial genetic evidence, argues that the first *Homo sapiens sapiens* appeared only in Africa and, from there, spread outward to other parts of Eurasia as recently as about 100,000 years ago, also a time when the Sahara was more hospitable to human movement. Both arguments acknowledge the importance of the African evidence, but they disagree about how to understand the somewhat later *hominid* remains found in both Europe and Asia.

This latter evidence involves not only the skeletal remains of *Homo erectus* populations found in Europe, Asia, and the Middle East, but also that of other *hominids,* especially *Homo sapiens neandertalensis,* more commonly known as Neandertals (named after the cave in Germany's Neander Valley where the first specimens of this type were discovered in the nineteenth century). Almost none of the experts believe that the Neandertals are direct ancestors of human beings, but rather represent populations that did not survive competition with new human beings, whether they first appeared locally or as a result of migration from Africa. Conflicting dates of various Neandertal remains can be used to reinforce both conceptions about how human beings spread over the earth. Thus knowledge about the Neandertals does not help much in interpreting the other data.

Obviously, analyzing and interpreting—and sometimes even just describing—this evidence is very difficult. None of the bones comprise complete skeletons, and few are even of complete skulls or other major skeletal parts. One of the most complete *hominids* ever discovered was that of a single female of a type often called *australopithecus afarensis.* This amazing discovery was made at Hadar in Ethiopia by Donald Johanson, although he and his colleagues were able to recover only about 40 percent of her skeleton. Nicknamed "Lucy" by her discoverers, she lived perhaps as many as 3 million years ago. As is commonplace in paleontology, the remainder of her bone structure was inferred and recreated from what *was* found; in recent years such reconstruction efforts have come to rely more and more on computer simulations.

Similarly, stone and bone fragments, even if found in proximity to *hominid* remains, are also incomplete and open to a variety of interpretations. Making decisions about just how the stones and bones came to be in the places where they were found is exceedingly difficult. Scientists must try to determine if the stones were simply broken through natural processes, accidentally chipped, or shattered by animal (including *hominid*) activities, or purposely broken by some creatures, most likely *hominids*. Broken bones offer similar puzzles. They might have been broken in natural occurrences, by the teeth of some carnivore, or by tools wielded by *hominid* predators or scavengers.

Working within these limitations, it is remarkably significant that scholars remain convinced of the African origins of ancestral human beings and the spread of those creatures, and humans themselves, from Africa to the rest of the world. Critical to this consensus is a resolution to the problem posed in this chapter: Why was it that human beings migrated out of Africa and came to dominate the earth? The answer surely is more complex than the changes in the climate of the Sahara. Something about *Homo sapiens* and their *hominid* predecessors must have given them an ability to survive where other crea-

tures could not and to extend their survival capacities at the expense of those same creatures.

Most assuredly, the answer must involve intelligence, a growing ability to use what was—if the paleontologists are correct—an increasingly larger brain capacity found in successive *hominid* groups. Yet we know that brain size, or even intelligence alone, does not guarantee success. Much more is required, often what we call "common sense," or the ability to apply ideas to solve problems. And that is what the early *hominids* had to do. At least once, and perhaps twice, their East African environment changed, becoming less hospitable. The desert to their north was gradually shrinking, permitting movement out of Africa, but at the same time requiring new adaptations in the migration process. Maintaining their existence in the newly opened lands of Asia and Europe demanded further adaptations. Discovering how they were able to do so is the question you are to consider in this chapter.

THE METHOD

In several ways, this chapter is different from much historical study. First, it extends to the distant past of prehistory, a time for which we have no written records. Yet it still is of great concern to historians. Understanding how human beings spread over and came to dominate the earth may offer insights into later human development. Just as some historians have

studied the political history of Greece, Rome, and other societies in an effort to better understand early political developments in the United States, other scholars expect that patterns of *hominid* behavior in prehistory may help explain social, economic, and even technological changes in later human history.

A second difference you may notice is the absence of clear dates for much of the evidence, something that historians generally try to establish

Chapter 1

Claiming the

Earth: The

Technological

Challenge of

Prehistory (to

ca. 10,000 B.C.E.)

with great care. In most of these cases, the dates would at best be estimates, derived from stratigraphy—the placement of objects in the layers of soils at the sites of their discovery—or from complex scientific tests of the *hominid* remains or objects found with them. Therefore, only very general dates are occasionally given for your scrutiny, although we have tried to be cautious in making sure the evidence is identified as clearly as possible in the chronological sequence of human development and the spread of *Homo sapiens* over the earth.

Yet another difference in this chapter is the mix of both primary and secondary sources, both of which scholars use when considering prehistory. The primary sources are the artifacts themselves, the bones and stones from archaeological excavations. In this book, of course, you will only be able to see these as photographs and drawings. Yet much additional evidence can be derived from these artifacts when they are subjected to a variety of scientific tests. The results of those tests are found here as secondary sources, in analytical descriptions and interpretations of the tests themselves. Sometimes scientists also create secondary sources by trying to replicate precisely the artifacts they have found. This distinction between secondary sources (of both kinds) and primary sources is an important one.

Historians always seek primary sources whenever possible. Yet in dealing with prehistory (and with other historical periods and situations as well) historians frequently use the secondary descriptions or creations of scientific (and other) experts because they are better able to interpret and replicate the primary sources, such as test results, than historians themselves. In doing so, historians acknowledge a reliance on someone else's informed opinion or professional skill, one step removed from the original evidence. That distance is why such accounts and replicas are called secondary sources.

Your task will be to use both the primary and secondary sources presented here, as do historians, to understand some of the earliest patterns of human adaptation and technological development. You too will need to interpret this evidence. To assist you, we have included some questions to consider and propositions to think about as you study each piece of evidence. Use these suggestions to formulate additional questions about what you see and read; then make notes of both your deliberations and your conclusions. As mentioned earlier, do not be overly concerned in this chapter with specific dates. Pay more attention to the processes of change over time than to the particular times when those changes occurred.

The first pieces of evidence (Sources 1 and 2) are drawings and descriptions of various animal adaptations, distinctive biological structures that allowed certain creatures to survive in the environment of prehistoric eastern Africa and elsewhere. As you study these drawings, try to envision what the particular biological adaptations allowed these animals to do in their quest for survival: to hunt, forage for, and process food; to protect themselves; to carry and store food. Also consider other animal adaptations you are aware of, such as the dual stomachs of cattle, the water storage capacity of camels, the distinctive tusks and feet of elephants, and the night vision of feline and other animals. Then look at Source 2 carefully, comparing the dentition of a chimpanzee with that of a very early type of *hominid* known as *Homo habilis*. What biological advantage might the chimpanzee (whose very similar ancestors lived at the time of *Homo habilis*) have had over *hominid* contemporaries?

The next group of sources (3 through 6) presents examples of *hominid* and *Homo sapiens* stone tools found in Africa and Europe. The first two photographs (Source 3) are of perhaps the earliest stone tools known, from Olduvai Gorge in East Africa and estimated to be 2 million years old. Their discovery established the great antiquity of toolmaking. These are followed by an archaeologist's drawing of similar African stone tools for a slightly later period (Source 4); note both the front and side views of each tool. Next, Source 5 is a photograph of what is known as a "prepared core" and a "flake tool" (top) made from it. This is not an ancient piece of evidence. It is, instead, a modern replica of the sorts of stone tools found in association with human beings' *hominid* ancestors. What similarities do you see between this replica and the previous stone tool artifacts? Some modern scholars have used such recreations as evidence that the type of broken rocks found in sites with *hominid* remains

are almost certainly tools made by those creatures. The last of these, Source 6, shows bone tools from a somewhat later period, discovered in both Asia and Europe.

You may wonder how these tools, especially the stone tools, were made by human ancestors so very long ago. The next group of sources (7 through 10) illustrates how anthropologists have reconstructed *hominid* toolmaking techniques. The first (Source 7) depicts the making of a prepared core and detaching a flake tool from it; this is the type of tool reproduced in Source 4. Next you will find an anthropological description of the principal stone toolmaking techniques (Source 8), followed by an illustration of these specific techniques (Source 9). Try to imagine how early human ancestors might have used these techniques in practical ways to create tools for specific tasks. Then compare your image of the practice of early toolmaking with that of Kathy Shick and Nicholas Toth, two of the leading scholars in this field (Source 10). How realistic do you find their vision to be? Does it help you see what adaptations *hominids* made to ensure their survival on the savanna of East Africa?

Certainly most anthropologists who study *hominids* and human ancestors believe that by the time of *Homo erectus* and the first *Homo sapiens*, tools had become much more than occasional implements for very specialized use. The increasing complexity of toolmaking and tool use among such early *Homo sapiens* as Neandertals is described by archaeologists in Source 11, as are the limita-

Chapter 1

Claiming the

Earth: The

Technological

Challenge of

Prehistory (to

ca. 10,000 B.C.E.)

tions of that Neandertal technology. Yet by the time of the first *Homo sapiens sapiens,* stone tools were used with increasing frequency to work other materials, such as skins, bone, and wood, likely in ways similar to the archaeological drawing you see in Source 12. The variety and complexity of *Homo sapiens* tools and the multiplicity of uses to which they were put have led anthropologists to describe them collectively as a "toolkit." In what ways might such toolkits allow for further adaptations by *Homo sapiens* to their surroundings?

The drawings and diagram in Source 13 suggest one way such collections of tools might have functioned among some of the earliest human populations. Notice the modern tool sketched in the bottom right corner of this source. What does this suggest to you? How might a comparison between the stone, bone, and wood tools of our early human ancestors, and the compact, present-day tool collection shed light on the adaptations of the first *Homo sapiens* to new and perhaps hostile environments? Such a comparison is sometimes referred to as an analogy; historians may use such analogies—even across great time periods—in trying to better understand how humans and their ancestors functioned in particular situations.

How the early *hominid* tools were actually put to use, of course, we can only imagine today. Anthropologists Shick and Toth, in addition to their portrayal of toolmaking in Source 10, also offer an intriguing scenario (Source 14) of how early tools might have been employed by a group of

hominids not only to support themselves but also to gain advantages over other creatures, their potential competitors. In such a case, how did these anthropologists determine that it was *hominid* scavengers, and not hunting carnivores (such as hyenas), who were responsible for the dissection and butchery of the wildebeest? Look at the next two sources (15 and 16), electron microscope enlargements of markings made by modern carnivore teeth and replicated stone tools on mammal bones. Can you see the differences described in the captions? How might such techniques be used with archaeological discoveries of bones in *hominid* and early *Homo sapiens* sites to learn more about early tool use? Could such knowledge reveal how *hominids* made adaptations to better deal with the challenges posed by other creatures?

The next two sources consider a tool of a somewhat different kind used by ancestral human beings: fire. These descriptions were written by anthropologists drawing conclusions from a wide variety of archaeological investigations. Both concern the use of fire by *Homo erectus* and early *Homo sapiens.* Source 17 indicates the significance of fire to our human ancestors, particularly as it first came under the control of *hominids* (rather than other creatures). How this happened— a process of domestication—is described more fully in Source 18. You should consider how fire, along with other tools, might have been associated with the spread of *hominids* out of Africa into Europe and Asia. What impact did fire have on the abilities of our human ancestors to control their environments and deal with the other creatures with whom they shared their surroundings?

The final bits of evidence you will find in this chapter (Source 19) are illustrations that summarize many of the uses of the tools and technologies, including fire, associated with our human ancestors in their long path to domination of the natural world. As you study these drawings, recall the array of evidence you have reviewed in this chapter of adaptations by both *hominids* and other creatures. Can you think of other examples of early technologies that *hominids* created to assist them in their struggles for survival? Would the gradual development of a complete toolkit, as opposed to individual tools, have given them with any additional ad-

vantages? You might especially compare these *hominid* tools and technologies with the biological adaptations of other creatures you reviewed in Source 1. Do any of these biological or technological adaptations provide particular advantages for one creature or group over another? Once you have considered that question, you may be in a better position to answer the central questions of the chapter: How were humans able to spread, more readily than other creatures, over the whole earth? Why were their ancestors able to survive outside of that relatively advantageous environment found in eastern Africa so long ago? And what legacies did these achievements leave for their human successors?

THE EVIDENCE

Source 1 from Kathy D. Shick and Nicholas Toth, Making Silent Stones Speak *(New York: Simon & Schuster, 1993), pp. 184–185. Courtesy of Kathy D. Schick and Nicholas Toth, CRAFT Research Center, Indiana University.*

1. Biological Adaptations of Early Hominid Competitors

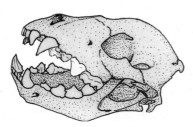

Hyena bone-crushing teeth and jaws.

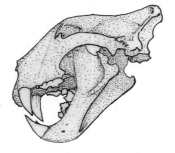

Carnivore flesh-cutting carnassial teeth.

Chapter 1
Claiming the
Earth: The
Technological
Challenge of
Prehistory (to
ca. 10,000 B.C.E.)

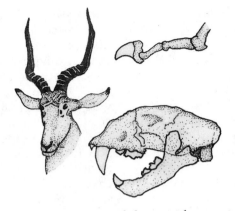

Carnivore canines and claws; antelope
horns.

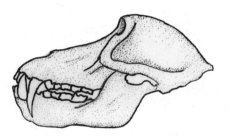

Baboon nut-cracking cheek teeth.

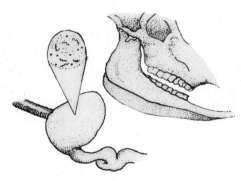

Herbivore jaws and teeth; stomach with
microorganisms to aid in consumption and
digestion.

Source 2 from Richard G. Klein, The Human Career: Human Biological and Cultural Origins *(Chicago: University of Chicago Press, 1989), p. 144. Reproduced with permission of University of Chicago Press.*

2. Dentition of Chimpanzee and *Homo habilis*

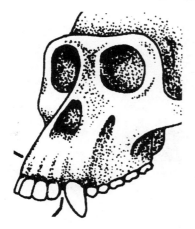

Chimpanzee upper jaw.

Homo habilis *upper jaw.*

Source 3 from John E. Pfeiffer, The Emergence of Man, *3rd ed. (New York: Harper & Row, 1978), p. 79.*

3. Very Early *Hominid* Tools

Pebble tool.

Chopper.

Chapter 1

Claiming the

Earth: The

Technological

Challenge of

Prehistory (to

ca. 10,000 B.C.E.)

Source 4 from Kenneth Oakley, Man the Tool-Maker, 6th ed. (London: British Museum, 1979), p. 76. Reproduced with permission of British Museum Publications.

4. Lava Flake Tools from Africa

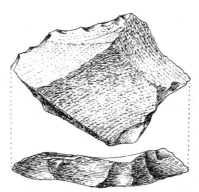
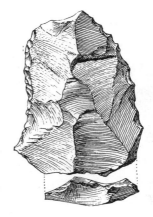

Front view.   Side view.

Source 5 from American Museum of Natural History. Photograph: Willard Whitson.

5. Replica of Prepared Core and Flake Tool Detached from It

Source 6 from Kenneth Oakley, Man the Tool-Maker, *6th ed. (London: British Museum, 1979), p. 16. Reproduced with permission of British Museum Publications.*

6. Anthropological Drawing of Bone and Antler Tools

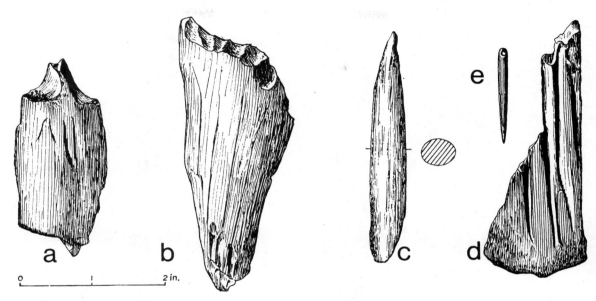

a, b. *Broken animal bones chipped for use as tools, "Sinanthropus" deposits near Pekin.*
c. *Awl of polished antler, Upper Paleolithic, Torbryan caves, Devon.* **d.** *Cannon-bone of horse from which slivers of bone have been gouged out for needles, Magdalenian, Grotte des Eyzies (Dordogne).* **e.** *Polished bone needle, Magdalenian, Bruniquel caves (Tarn-et-Garonne).*

Chapter 1

Claiming the

Earth: The

Technological

Challenge of

Prehistory (to

ca. 10,000 B.C.E.)

Source 7 adapted from Ian Tattersall, The Human Odyssey (Englewood Cliffs, N.J.: Prentice-Hall, 1993), p. 121.

7. Making a Prepared Core and a Flake Tool from It

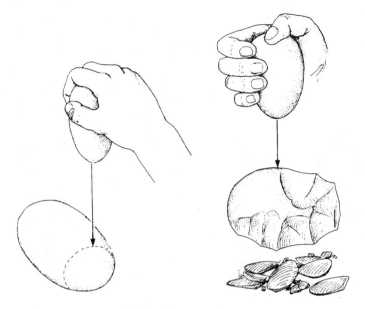

Making the prepared core.

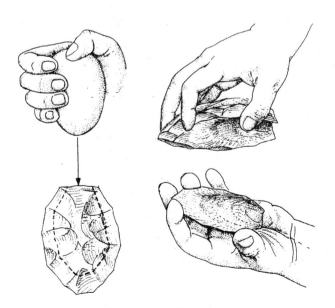

Detaching the flake tool.

Source 8 from Richard G. Klein, The Human Career: Human Biological and Cultural Origins *(Chicago: University of Chicago Press, 1989), p. 419.*

8. Anthropological Description of Stone Toolmaking Techniques

The process of flaking stone is called *knapping.* Three fundamental techniques exist: (1) *direct percussion,* (2) *indirect percussion,* and (3) *pressure flaking.*

Direct percussion can take two basic forms. In the most common variant, the knapper uses a *hammerstone* to strike a *flake* from a *core.* For best results, the hammerstone should be softer than the core, so that the core bites into it and slippage between the two pieces is minimized. If the core is flint, quartzite and certain kinds of volcanic rock generally make good hammerstones. Limestone is usually too soft. A wooden or bone rod (billet, or "soft hammer") may be substituted for the hammerstone if the goal is to detach relatively long, thin flakes—for example, in the final shaping of a hand ax. . . .

Wooden or bone rods were almost certainly used to finish some finely made late-Acheulean hand axes from Europe, dating from between about 400,000 and 200,000 years ago.

In the second basic, but less common, variant of direct percussion, the core is mobile and the hammerstone is stationary. The knapper strikes the hammerstone with the core to remove a flake. The hammerstone in this instance is called an *anvil.*

In indirect percussion, a third object, such as a wooden or antler rod, is interposed between the core and the hammerstone. This gives the knapper fine control over the point where the hammer blow enters the core. Indirect percussion was invented later than direct percussion, and it was probably rarely practiced before the emergence of Upper Paleolithic and related "cultures" about 50,000–40,000 years ago.

In pressure flaking, the knapper removes a flake by pressing a pointed antler rod or other hard object against the edge of a core. Alternatively, the object to be flaked can be forced against a stationary compressor. Like indirect percussion, pressure flaking was practiced mainly by Upper Paleolithic and later people, who used it mostly for modifying (retouching) the edges and surface of a flake rather than for primary flake production.

Chapter 1
Claiming the
Earth: The
Technological
Challenge of
Prehistory (to
ca. 10,000 B.C.E.)

Source 9 adapted from Jacques Bordaz, Tools of the Old and New Stone Age *(New York: American Museum of Natural History, 1970), p. 14.*

9. Stone Toolmaking Techniques

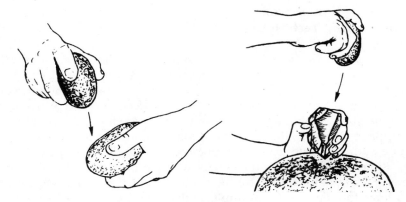

Direct Percussion.

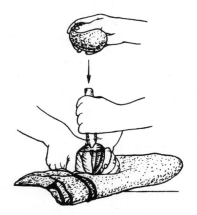

Indirect Percussion.

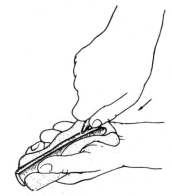

Pressure.

Source 10 from Kathy D. Shick and Nicholas Toth, Making Silent Stones Speak *(New York: Simon & Schuster, 1993), pp. 225–227.*

10. Anthropological Re-creation of How Early *Hominid* Toolmakers May Have Worked in the East African Savannas and Surrounding Areas

In the volcanic hills overlooking the plains and distant lake there is little vegetation: shrubs and tufts of grass work their way through the rocks here and there, and an occasional thorn tree stands defiant in the coarse rubble. Small lizards dart for safety as the bipedal figure approaches; the uneven black terrain is hot underfoot. Amid the giant rocks of the lava highlands, a figure searches for the ideal size and shape of boulder to use as a core for making his handaxe blanks. He picks up a somewhat smaller stone, raises it above his head, and hurls it violently against the boulder on the ground. The sharp, glassy ring of basalt is heard as a large flake is detached from the boulder core. He hears nearby, but out of sight, the sounds of other members of his group flaking boulders, the distinctive cracks echoing through the rugged hills.

Once this first flake is removed, his core is now ready for serious work. He selects a large cobble of lava as his hammer stone. After positioning the boulder core on top of smaller rocks, he begins striking many large flakes from the core, holding the hammer in his right hand and helping to steady the core with his left. He strikes down hard with the hammer, and he emits a deep grunt as the hammer hits the core a few inches from its edge. After two blows a large flake is removed from the underside of the core and falls on the ground with a dull thud. Three more great flakes are quarried before the hammer stone accidentally splits in half. It is replaced by another large cobble found nearby.

The boulder core is slowly worked down by further flaking blows, repositioned repeatedly as flaking proceeds, until there is very little weathered cortex left on its surface. It is abandoned as a large discoid core, dark bluish gray in color, with bold scars on both sides from flake removals. Spread around on the ground are about a dozen large flakes, as well as hundreds of smaller flakes and fragments, the inevitable waste from such an operation. The hominid's dark, muscular body is glistening in the late morning sun from the exertion of constantly reorienting and bracing the massive core against his powerful blows. His right shin and one of his fingers are bleeding from cuts, a common hazard of this quarrying.

Chapter 1
Claiming the
Earth: The
Technological
Challenge of
Prehistory (to
ca. 10,000 B.C.E.)

He then selects the best flake blanks from which to make handaxes. Some of the large flakes are too thick, too thin, or too narrow or exhibit the telltale hairline fracture of a fatal, internal flaw. The flakes he chooses are about a foot long, at least six inches wide, and about two to four inches thick. One roughly rectangular flake has a sharp, straight edge along one end. He selects it as a blank for a cleaver.

Carrying five of these blanks, and picking up another, smaller lava cobble for a hammer, he moves into the cooler shade of a lone acacia tree, sitting on his haunches and leaning back against the trunk, where he is joined by several of his fellow tool makers. He now concentrates more on his craft, removing flakes from first one face of the blank and then the other, paying special attention to thinning the large striking platform and bulb of percussion, until slowly an irregular oval form is created, with a sharp edge zigzagging around the circumference of the piece.

He reaches into his large tortoiseshell container and removes his favorite stoneworking tool, a dense giraffe ankle bone bearing the telltale wear marks of having been used as a soft hammer. He deftly strikes it against the edge of the handaxe, detaching longer, flatter flakes, which begin to thin the piece and give it a more even edge and a symmetrical teardrop shape. The final task is carefully thinning and shaping the curved tip and making sure its edge is less sinuous and very sharp. The entire process has taken about twenty minutes. After holding it up for closer scrutiny, he shows the finished tool to his compatriots, sets it down with a contented expression of self-approval, and reaches for another blank.

In a little more than an hour he completes one more handaxe, almost identical to the first, as well as a cleaver. The latter he shapes by removing flakes around most of its circumference to make a U-shaped profile, which will serve as the handle, leaving the natural flake edge at the other end as a straight, sharp, cutting bit. Two other attempts at fashioning handaxes lead to failures: one specimen breaks early because of an invisible flaw in the stone that splits the piece in two, and a forceful, misplaced blow with the lava hammer takes off the entire tip of the other. On both occasions he snorts with displeasure.

He places the bone hammer and the three finished forms in the tortoiseshell container, wedging a wad of coarse grass between each tool to cushion their sharp edges during transport. A natural water hole in the highlands, formed from massive column-shaped walls of basalt, provides refreshment and cooler shade. Within the hour the rest of his group has joined him, each adult with his or her own large cutting tools of surprisingly similar sizes and shapes, while those of most juveniles are much cruder and more irregular. Then they begin their slow descent from the lava highlands to the plains.

Source 11 from Rick Gore, "Neandertals," National Geographic, 189, no. 1 (January 1996): 25, 28–29.

11. Description of *Homo sapiens neandertalensis* Toolmaking and Tool Use

From studies of the tools Neandertals did use, researchers have begun to fill in the details of their technological skills. This is one of the few windows into the Neandertal mind. . . . We know they had fire to keep warm. Some cave floors are made almost entirely from compressed layers of ash many feet thick. . . . They probably wore unsewed hides. They left no tools for stitching, like the bone needles of early modern humans. . . .

To the uninitiated, Neandertal tools—mostly sharp-edged flakes of stone that can be held in the hand—look as if they had been casually knapped off a piece of convenient rock with another stone. Not so. Neandertals might have traveled many miles to procure just the right pieces of flint. Sometimes they would carry their kill to sites near those rock sources.

"You need a lot of brains for flint knapping," says Jacques Pelegrin of the French Center for Archaeological Research. "It would be like playing chess for us. You have to plan and organize how you are going to flake off each piece from the core rock ahead of time. Rocks are never standard. You have to adjust to the differences. Flint breaks under certain conditions. You have to learn those. It takes months, if not years, to learn to do it well. I have worked flint for 15 years now and can say that the techniques used by the Neandertals are no less difficult than those used later by modern humans."

In the Vézère Valley of southwest France, where many classic Neandertals have been found, Jean-Michel Geneste, an archaeologist with the Ministry of Culture in Bordeaux, [displays] a hand ax discovered there. . . . [I]t has notches for . . . thumb and fingers, as if it were an extension of [the] hand.

"This was a multipurpose tool," [Geneste] says. "Different edges of it were used for different purposes—cutting, butchering, scraping, defleshing. It was the Swiss army knife of its day. We get lots of information out of these. We might detect 300 scars on an ax, each made during its shaping. We know how to read the scars and then reconstruct how the ax was made. If I have only the by-products flaked off a piece of rock, I can tell you what kind of tool was made."

. . . [However], Neandertal technology may have been [limited]. "They were unable to conceive of projectiles; we don't know why," says . . . Geneste. Thrusting—rather than throwing—spears put hunters in harm's way.

Chapter 1

Claiming the

Earth: The

Technological

Challenge of

Prehistory (to

ca. 10,000 B.C.E.)

Source 12 from Earl Swanson, ed., Lithic Technology: Making and Using Stone Tools (*The Hague: Mouton, 1975*), *p. 188. Redrawn with permission of Mouton de Gruyter, a division of Walter de Gruyter & Co.*

12. How Stone Tools May Have Been Used to Work Other Materials, such as Wood and Bone

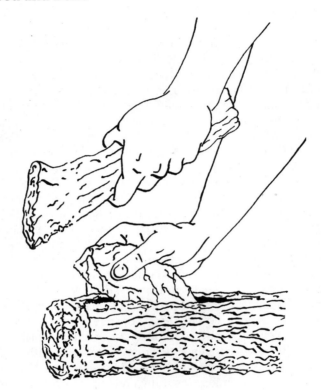

Source 13 from Brian M. Fagan, The Journey from Eden: The Peopling of Our World *(New York: Thames and Hudson, 1990), p. 157. Reproduced with permission.*

13. The Core and Flake Toolmaking Technique Applied to the Creation of Complex Early *Homo sapiens sapiens* Toolkits

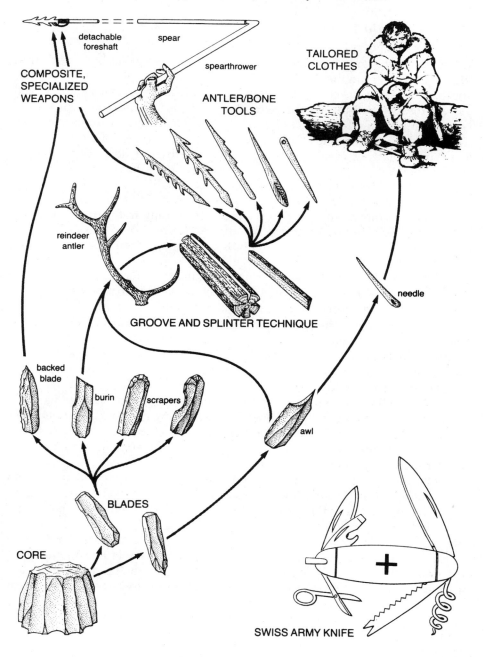

COMPOSITE, SPECIALIZED WEAPONS

detachable foreshaft

spear

spearthrower

ANTLER/BONE TOOLS

TAILORED CLOTHES

reindeer antler

GROOVE AND SPLINTER TECHNIQUE

needle

backed blade

burin

scrapers

awl

BLADES

CORE

SWISS ARMY KNIFE

Chapter 1

Claiming the

Earth: The

Technological

Challenge of

Prehistory (to

ca. 10,000 B.C.E.)

Source 14 from Kathy D. Shick and Nicholas Toth, Making Silent Stones Speak *(New York: Simon & Schuster, 1993), pp. 147–149.*

14. Anthropological Recreation of Possible *Hominid* Tool Use

The wildebeest is grazing mindlessly on the edge of the water hole, away from the rest of the herd in the afternoon. From downwind the pack of hunting dogs approaches, using the cover of the tall grass and shrubs to conceal their small piebald figures from the eyes of their intended prey. In a flash they converge.

The hominids are foraging along the river when an adolescent female hears a low-pitched bellow. She climbs a nearby fig tree and sees the dust; flailing legs; small, darting carnivore bodies; and, finally, red flesh. She excitedly gives a food call and gestures in the direction of the kill. Several other hominids, adult and immature, climb the same tree, perching on adjacent limbs to view the carnage. One drops down, picks up a few cobbles with one hand and a large fallen branch with the other, and starts running in the direction of the kill. Others follow suit, until there is an irregular phalanx of adult males, and adolescent males and females, with adult females and their infants and juveniles bringing up the rear.

The hunting dogs are distracted from their kill by the flapping wings of several vultures that have been patiently watching and waiting several meters from the kill. The source of their disturbance is the group of advancing bipeds, who are brandishing sticks and branches and begin to throw stones, yelling and whooping aggressively. The dogs bristle and snarl their bloodied muzzles but are finally chased away by the hominid interlopers; a well-placed pitch of a lava rock strikes one of the retreaters in the flank, accelerating his speed of departure with an angry yelp.

The dead wildebeest stares vacantly, its tongue clenched between its teeth. The body cavity has been ripped open by the hunting dogs and most of the internal organs consumed. Otherwise the carcass is still fairly intact. A strong smell of blood, viscera, fresh meat, and musk fills the air, which buzzes with an ever-increasing number of flies attracted to the kill.

The hominids surround the wildebeest and with excited vocalizations scan the landscape to make sure there are no hyenas or lions nearby to steal their new spoil. A number of them squat down with rocks in their hands and begin to crack them together.

Several large lava flakes are struck off a core, and the sharpest one, with a smoothly curved, convex edge, is selected as a butchery knife. As one hominid grasps the rear ankle of the wildebeest and pulls the hind limb taut, another starts cutting through the skin and muscle of the leg, exposing red meat and, underneath, the white bone of the joint. Through the parting flesh he glimpses the round end of the thighbone partially hidden in the circular socket of the pelvis. The grating sound of a stone knife edge against fresh bone can be heard. After numerous cuts at this joint, the hind limb is wrenched free from the body.

Two adult females are working at the other end of the carcass. One pulls the left forelimb taut while the other cuts into and around the shoulder area, which easily removes the entire forelimb from the body with the shoulder blade attached.

Soon the entire carcass has been portioned into easily carried units and is being hauled off on the heads, in the arms, or over the shoulders of the hominids as they make their way toward the shady grove of trees along the tributary that flows into the larger river. This grove is well-known to the hominids. Many half-buried stone artifacts and fragmented animal bones are scattered on the ground. The grove is open enough for the hominids to see any approaching pack of hyenas or pride of lions that might be hungry enough to challenge them for their booty, in which case they will make a hasty retreat up the trees with as much of the carcass as possible. Today, however, there is no contest.

Under the shade of the acacia and fig trees, several of them take their lava cores and strike off some more flakes. Then they start cutting the flesh off the individual limb bones, clenching the meat between their teeth and cutting with a stone flake where the muscle attaches to the bone.

There is much bickering, for there are twenty-odd hominids and only nine dismembered portions of the wildebeest: the two hind limbs, the two forelimbs, the head, the pelvis, the two sides of the rib cage, and the backbone, all still covered with meat. The dominant members of the group have first access to prime parts such as the limbs and begrudgingly share portions with other individuals who sit nearby in anticipation and occasionally abscond with a chunk if attention is diverted. Rarely is there an actual melée, however, unless food has been very scarce and hunger overcomes the established social hierarchy.

Consumption of the wildebeest proceeds rapidly and with much clamor, with satisfied grunts and belches. Mothers occasionally give pieces of meat to their weanlings, who are not yet old enough to use the stone tools.

One individual places a femur against a large root protruding from the base of the huge fig tree. She repeatedly strikes it sharply along the shaft with a rock until long cracks form in the surface of the bone and it finally splits open, breaking into many fragments and splinters and exposing the greasy marrow inside. This is scooped out with the index finger as far as it will reach, then fished out with a twig and swallowed. Finally the ends are smashed, exposing the red, spongy bone, which is sucked of its fatty contents. Some walk down to the river, crouch down, and drink from the cool flowing water.

Chapter 1
Claiming the
Earth: The
Technological
Challenge of
Prehistory (to
ca. 10,000 B.C.E.)

Soon only scatters of broken bone fragments and discarded stones are left, some of them covered with drying blood, meat, and fat. Ants begin to swarm over these. After a brief rest in the shade, with some grooming among adults and play and wrestling among the young, they begin to rise. Slowly, one by one, the hominids resume their foraging, halfheartedly, as no strong pangs of hunger gnaw at their insides. They spread out in open search of anything edible—fruits, berries, shoots, roots, insects, lizards, small mammals, birds' eggs, and such fare—along the strip of forest on their side of the river. As the afternoon progresses they begin to make their way to a cluster of fig trees that they climb, building their sleeping nests in the sturdier boughs.

The shadows lengthen on the plain as the reddish-orange sun sets behind the shimmering volcanic ridges on the horizon. As twilight turns quickly to night, the nearly full moon rises over the eastern highlands, splashing pale light on the reclining figures in the trees as it beams through the gently swaying foliage.

Source 15 and 16 from Kathy D. Schick and Nicholas Toth, Making Silent Stones Speak *(New York: Simon & Schuster, 1993), p.178; p.179. Courtesy of Kathy D. Schick and Nicholas Toth, CRAFT Research Center, Indiana University.*

15. Photograph of Electron Microscope View of Carnivore Tooth Marks on Mammal Bone

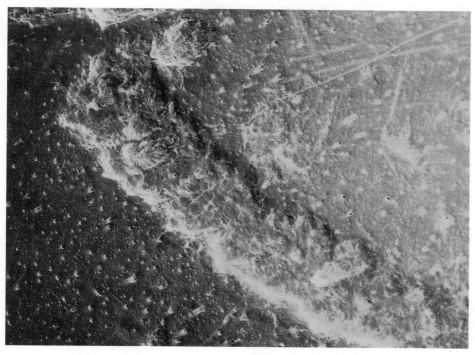

Carnivore calling card. Scanning electron microscope picture of a carnivore tooth mark on another bone from an early Stone Age site dating to approximately one million years ago. Tooth marks tend to be smoother and broader relative to depth. Magnification approximately 14x.

Chapter 1

Claiming the

Earth: The

Technological

Challenge of

Prehistory (to

ca. 10,000 B.C.E.)

16. Photograph of Electron Microscope View of *Hominid* Stone Tool Marks on Mammal Bone

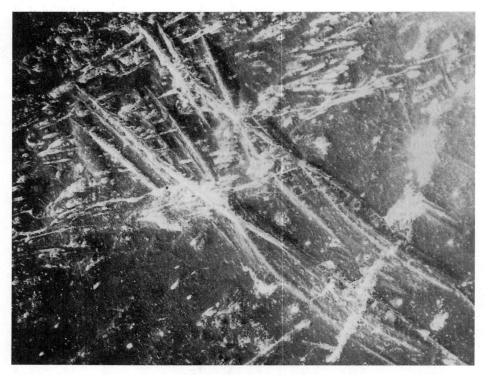

Hominid calling card. Scanning electron microscope picture of prehistoric cut marks made by a stone tool and found on a mammal bone from a million-year-old Stone Age site. Cut marks tend to be narrower than tooth marks, with multiple striations in the main groove. Although most cut marks appear as single grooves, irregularities on the edge of the stone knife that made these marks (probably a retouched flake) have produced a characteristic X-shaped "signature" from this tool when it cut through the bone, repeated twice on this fossil specimen. Magnification approximately 14x.

Source 17 from Ashley Montagu, Man: His First Million Years, *rev. ed. (New York: New American Library, 1962), p. 46.*

17. Anthropological Description of the Significance of Fire

The control of fire was presumably the first great step in man's emancipation from the bondage to his environment. Warmed by the embers, man could endure cold nights, and could thus penetrate into temperate and even arctic regions. The flames would give him light at night and allow him to explore the recesses of sheltering caves. Fire would scare away other wild beasts. By cooking, substances became edible that would be indigestible if eaten raw. Man is no longer restricted in his movements to a limited range of climates, and his activities need not be entirely determined by the sun's light.

But in mastery of fire man was controlling a mighty physical force and a conspicuous chemical change. For the first time in history a creature of Nature was directing one of the great forces of Nature. And the exercise of power must react upon the controller. The sight of the bright flame bursting forth when a dry bough was thrust into glowing embers, the transformation of the bough into fine ashes and smoke, must have stimulated man's rudimentary brain. What these phenomena suggested to him is unknowable. But in feeding and damping down the fire, in transporting and using it, man made a revolutionary departure from the behavior of other animals. He was asserting his humanity and making himself.

Source 18 from John E. Pfeiffer, The Emergence of Man, *3rd ed. (New York: Harper & Row, 1978), pp. 131–133.*

18. Anthropological Description of the Early Discovery and Use of Fire

The first force of nature to be domesticated, fire gave human beings a new degree of independence. By bringing fire to the places where they lived, they created zones of warmth and light in the darkness, halo spaces, caves of light. The wide wilderness became a little less wild and less lonely. They achieved a way of keeping the night and nighttime prowlers at bay and the freedom to explore new lands with harsh climates.

Judging by the evidence at hand, still largely negative, our ancestors first put fire to work on a regular basis to keep themselves warm somewhere along the route out of Africa across the Sahara and into Europe. Hominids must

Chapter 1

Claiming the

Earth: The

Technological

Challenge of

Prehistory (to

ca. 10,000 B.C.E.)

have been familiar with fire in Africa. They lived with it, and perhaps died by it, during volcanic upheavals associated with the formation of the African Rift Valley. They probably moved away when volcanoes were active, and returned when the earth became quiet again, being no less persistent than people today who keep returning to areas devastated by floods, earthquakes, and other natural disasters.

But no early hominid hearths have yet been found in Africa. Of course, most African sites may have been located in the open rather than in caves, and ashes and charcoal may have been scattered by winds blowing across savannas. On the other hand, early hominids presumably had no great need for fire in generally mild subtropical climates. In any case, ample evidence for fire exists in colder times and colder places, and [humans] wandered about as far north as they could at the time without starving and freezing to death. They were living where no normal primate should be, nearly within the shadows of alpine glaciers.

Fire was probably first obtained ready-made from natural sources. (The first sign of artificial fire making is an iron-pyrites ball with a deep groove produced by repeated striking to create tinder-igniting sparks; it comes from a Belgian site only about 15,000 years old.) The notion that Prometheus stole fire from the heights of Mount Olympus is not as widely believed as it once was. But Prometheus has a certain relevance if, as seems likely, volcanoes were a major source of fire in early prehistory. . . .[4]

Perhaps people camped near fire, a natural resource like game, water, and shelter. They may sometimes have left otherwise favorable areas when fires began petering out. If so, they had to take it with them when they moved away. It had to be kept burning like the Olympic flame, fed and nursed like a newborn infant. Each band may have had a fire bearer; perhaps one of its older members was responsible for carrying and guarding embers in a cup of clay covered with green leaves and breathed the embers into flame when the band found a new place to live.

Fire provided more than warmth. It soon became another factor in setting man apart from other species. With it he could move more freely, and instead of having to avoid other predators, they got out of his way. Fire must have kept cold weather as well as predators at a safe distance. On icy wilderness nights, big cats and other predators, attracted by the smell of meat and light, stayed outside the protective circle of the fireside. Perhaps people observed that on occasion the animals scrambled even further away when sparks flew at them out of the flames. They may have learned to produce the same effect by hurling glowing pieces of wood at animals' heads. In any case, they eventually began using fire more aggressively, in a shift from defense to offense.

---

4. Prometheus, one of the Titans in Greek mythology, stole fire from the top of Mount Olympus, residence of the gods, and gave it to humans along with instructions for its use. For this impertinence he was punished, eternally, by Zeus.

The earliest known hearths were located in caves, originally occupied by stronger and longer-established killers. Before fire people often had to be content with second-best sites, rock shelters, and overhangs and less effective protection. Fire, however, could help them drive other killers out. Bears, hyenas, and many other cave-dwelling animals shared the Durance Valley with early humans but stayed out of their caves. . . .

They also used fire to become more and more effective predators themselves, to stampede animals as they did in the Torralba Valley, and to produce more effective spears. The Australian aborigines charred the tips of their digging sticks lightly, a treatment which hardens the core of the wood and makes the outer part more crumbly and easier to sharpen.

Cooking is also believed to date back to these times, mainly on the basis of indirect but convincing evidence involving teeth, sensitive indicators of [biological] change.

Source 19 from Kathy D. Shick and Nicholas Toth, Making Silent Stones Speak *(New York: Simon & Schuster, 1993), pp. 184–185. Courtesy of Kathy D. Schick and Nicholas Toth, CRAFT Research Center, Indiana University.*

19. Summary Illustrations of *Hominid* and Early *Homo sapiens* Tool-using Techniques

Stone flake.

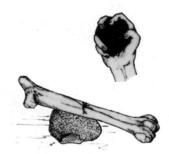

Hammer and anvil.

Chapter 1

Claiming the

Earth: The

Technological

Challenge of

Prehistory (to

ca. 10,000 B.C.E.)

Digging stick.

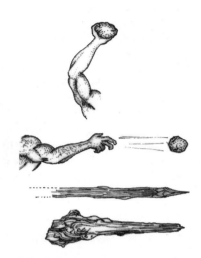

Missiles, spear, club.

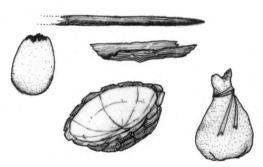

*Carrying devices and containers: wooden skewer,
bark tray, ostrich and tortoise shell, skin bag.*

Hammer and anvil.

Fire.

QUESTIONS TO CONSIDER

Over a half-century ago anthropologist Kenneth Oakley provided what then seemed a definitive assertion of the distinctiveness of human beings. His important book, *Man, the Tool-Maker*,[5] though revised several times, remains a powerful testament to that view. In reviewing the evidence in this chapter—and reflecting on your own lives—do you have any doubt that humans have, indeed, long been users and makers of an almost unlimited variety of tools? Even Oakley understood that other creatures use inanimate objects as tools. Yet today scientists studying animal behavior have observed ample evidence that other creatures also *make* tools; that is, they modify natural objects so as to utilize them for specific tasks.[6] Does this call into question Oakley's conclusion about the uniqueness of human beings?

As you consider that question, and as you review the evidence in this chapter, you may find it useful to organize your notes and thinking around three sets of questions. First, is this chapter only about the simplest of tools and the first of the forces of nature tamed by the predecessors of *Homo sapiens*? Does the evi-

dence also reveal how and why early *hominids* began to devise a variety of methods of adapting to their surroundings, of altering aspects of their natural world to solve some of the problems they faced? To what extent was this activity just an extension of the simple toolmaking process? To what extent was it something more? Were mental processes, the distinctiveness of *hominid* brain capacity, a critical factor in these developments? At what point did the process of toolmaking become one of technological innovation?

Second, as you work through the evidence in this chapter, you should also keep in mind the general patterns of *hominid* and *Homo sapiens* migration out of Africa and into the rest of the world, discussed in the Background section. To what extent did those migrations coincide with the development of technological alternatives by our human ancestors? Did these innovations provide them with any benefits in dealing with the other creatures they encountered in Africa? What advantages did technology afford to the first *Homo sapiens* as they spread northward in Eurasia (and later southward through Africa and eastward into the Americas)?

Finally, consider the impact that the development of technology may have had on human beings themselves. What did they learn from their successes? Do you suppose they encountered any setbacks? If, indeed, tools and fire gave *Homo sapiens* any distinct advantages over other living beings, what was the effect on the size of their population? Might their

5. Kenneth Oakley, *Man, the Tool-Maker*, 6th ed. (London: British Museum, 1979). The first edition of Oakley's classic was published in 1949.

6. The American anthropologist Marvin Harris has given considerable weight to animal toolmaking in his skepticism about the role of technology in human development; see Marvin Harris, *Our Kind* (New York: Harper & Row, 1990), pp. 26–33.

Chapter 1

Claiming the

Earth: The

Technological

Challenge of

Prehistory (to

ca. 10,000 B.C.E.)

new technologies have been put to any uses other than survival and extension into new lands? Were the technological advantages humans possessed likely to have been uniformly positive in their impact?

After thinking through all three groups of questions, you should turn your attention again to the key problems posed for this chapter. How were *hominids* and early *Homo sapiens*, rather than any other creatures, able to spread over the whole earth? And what legacies did this achievement leave for their human successors?

EPILOGUE

In studying the human past we often focus, perhaps more than we sometimes realize, on the technological changes that have occurred over the wide sweep of that history. The Industrial Revolution and the atomic age, to be sure, are marked examples of technologies reshaping human societies. So were the agricultural revolutions of a much earlier time. You can probably think of many other examples, both specific and general. Human history, however, can also be seen as actually beginning with a technological revolution, one that you have been studying in this chapter.

Some years ago Loren Eiseley gave eloquent testimony to the importance of this process. Humans, he wrote, "transferred to . . . machines and tools many of alterations of parts that in animals take place through the evolution of the body." Indeed, the human being "of today, the atomic manipulator, the aeronaut who flies faster than sound, has precisely the same brain and body [structure] as his ancestor of twenty thousand years ago who painted the last Ice Age

mammoths on the walls of caves in France" and who developed the most complex stone, bone, and wooden toolkits. "To put it another way," Eiseley concluded, "it is . . . [human] ideas that have evolved and changed the world about him."[7]

Certainly the development of ideas and the application of thought to solve problems, both the creations of *hominid* brains, resulted in perhaps the most significant step forward in the development of *Homo sapiens sapiens*. Mental capacity alone was insufficient. Nor was the first use of a tool the critical step. Rather it was the use of a variety of tools, each created for a specific task—including the capture and domestication of forces of nature such as fire—that marked the dawn of technology. This bringing together of human abilities and a variety of tools designed for specific tasks allowed *Homo sapiens sapiens* to solve increasingly complex problems related to survival.

Since that time long ago, human capacity to formulate technological solutions has only grown greater. It is impossible for us to know if any of

7. Loren Eiseley, *The Immense Journey* (New York: Vintange Books, 1959), p. 89.

the earliest *hominid* tool users were as frightened by their own technological inventions as some of their human successors. But despite the sometimes alarming pace and power of innovation, it is certainly true that only human beings have the capacity to make technological advances do our bidding, rather than being overwhelmed by our expanding abilities to create tools beyond the most fantastic imaginable by their earliest *hominid* ancestors.

CHAPTER TWO

THE NEED FOR WATER IN ANCIENT

SOCIETIES (2000 B.C.E.–500 C.E.)

The title of the course for which you are using this book is most likely some variation on "World Civilization." The meaning of *world* is self-evident, but why *civilization*? What distinguishes human cultures that are termed civilizations from those that are not? Though there are great differences among civilizations, all civilizations have a few features in common. The most important of these is the presence of cities; indeed, the word *civilization* comes from the Latin word *civis*, meaning "resident of a city, or citizen." Historians and archaeologists generally define a city as a place where more than 5,000 people live. Remains of the earliest communities of this size have been discovered in ancient Mesopotamia, or present-day Iraq.

Why should the presence of cities be the distinguishing mark of cultural development? It is not the cities themselves but what they imply about a culture that makes them so important. Any society in which thousands of people live in proximity to one another must agree in general to certain laws or rules governing human behavior. These may be either part of an oral tradition or, as they were in ancient Mesopotamia, written down. A city must also make provision to assure its residents of a constant supply of food, which involves not only transporting food into the city from the surrounding farmland but also storing food throughout the year and preserving stockpiles for years when harvests are poor. In addition to demonstrating that people could transport and store food effectively, the presence of cities also indicates that people were producing enough surplus food to allow for a specialization of labor. If the whole work force was devoted to farming, no one would have been available to build roads, produce storage bins, or enforce the laws on which the city depended. This specialization of labor eventually allowed some members of society the opportunity and time to build structures and produce goods that were not directly essential to daily survival. Urban residents in Mesopotamia began to erect large buildings and to decorate them with sculptures, paintings, and mosaics, to write poetry and history, and to develop religious and philosophical ideas, all of which we consider essential to a civilization. As the cities themselves grew, they needed greater and greater amounts of food, which led to further technological development.

The civilization of ancient Mesopotamia flourished in the valley of two rivers, the Tigris and the Euphrates, and other early civilizations were located in river valleys as well—the Nile in Egypt, the Indus in India, and the Yellow in China. In all of these areas, except perhaps the Indus Valley, the amount of natural rainfall is not enough to sustain the level of agricultural production required for urban populations; irrigation using river water is necessary. Rather than proving a block to further development, however, the need for irrigation in these river valleys may have been the very catalyst that prompted the growth of cities. We

may never be able to know this for sure, as irrigation systems were already in place before written records appeared, and because cities and irrigation expanded together. We do know that neither could have existed without the other in Mesopotamia; cities could survive only where there was a food surplus created by irrigation, and irrigation could be implemented only where there were enough people to construct and maintain ditches and other components of the system.

Supplying cities with water was not simply a technological problem, but one with economic, legal, social, and political implications as well. We can see this significance even in words themselves: the word *rival* originally meant those who shared, and quarreled over, the water in a *rivus,* or "irrigation channel." Your task in this chapter will be to use both visual and written evidence of ancient water systems to answer the following question: How did the need for a steady supply of water affect the technological, economic, political, and legal development of ancient societies?

BACKGROUND

Though the earliest of the world's civilizations all grew up in river valleys, the technical and organizational problems they confronted were very different because the character of the rivers differed tremendously. The Tigris and Euphrates flowed very

fast, carrying soil as well as water down from the highlands. This soil was extremely rich and created new farmland where the rivers emptied into the Persian Gulf. (The ancient Persian Gulf ended more than 100 miles north of its modern-day shoreline; all of that land was created as the rivers filled in the delta.) The soil also filled in the irrigation ditches,

Chapter 2

The Need for

Water in

Ancient

Societies

(2000 B.C.E.–

500 C.E.)

which meant they had to be cleaned out constantly. Every year this deposit was piled on the banks until they grew so high that the cleaning could no longer be accomplished easily. At this point a new ditch was cut and the old one abandoned, a process that entailed a great deal of work and required the cooperation of everyone whose land was watered by that particular ditch.

Mesopotamian farmers used several types of irrigation. They leveled large plots of land adjacent to the rivers and main canals, building up dikes around them in what is termed basin irrigation. During the spring and other high-water times of the year, farmers knocked holes in the dikes to allow water and fresh soil in. Once the sediment had settled, they let the water flow back into the channel. Workers also built small waterways between their fields to provide water throughout the year, developing a system of perennial irrigation. In the hillier country of northern Mesopotamia, farmers built terraces with water channels running alongside them. The terraces provided narrow strips of flat land to farm, and the waterways connected to brooks and streams.

Farmers could depend on gravity to bring water to their fields during spring and flood times, but at other times water-raising machines did the work. Technicians built many different types of machines, some of which are still in use in many parts of the world today. These solved some problems, but created others; for example, farmers with machines could

drain an irrigation ditch during times of low water, leaving their neighbors with nothing. How were rights to water to be decided? Solving this problem would be extremely important, and the first recorded laws regarding property rights are in fact rights to water, not rights to land. In Mesopotamia, land was useless unless it was irrigated.

Many of the irrigation techniques developed in Mesopotamia spread to Egypt, or were developed independently there. Egypt, because it received even less rainfall than Mesopotamia, was totally dependent on the Nile for watering crops. Fortunately, the Nile was much easier to use than the Tigris and Euphrates because it flooded regularly, allowing easy basin irrigation. The Nile was so predictable, in fact, that the Egyptians based their 365-day calendar on its annual flooding. The Egyptians also constructed waterways and water-lifting machines for perennial irrigation. Here as well, irrigation both caused and resulted from the growth of cities. Moreover, it contributed to the power of the kings, who the Egyptian people regarded as somehow responsible for the flood of the Nile.

The harnessing of the Yellow River in China was also closely related to the growth of centralized state power there. The Yellow is a very violent river and carries a great amount of silt—twelve times as much as the Tigris and Euphrates, and seventy times as much as the Nile. The silt, caused by deforestation and erosion in the highlands, raises the bed of the

Yellow River by three feet every century, necessitating either constant dredging of irrigation canals or the continual building of higher dikes to hold back the river. The violence of the Yellow River floods—which have continued into the twentieth century—has changed its lower course dramatically throughout recorded history and has always led to devastation and social upheaval. Engineers in the Yellow River Valley thus needed waterworks that would both protect cities and villages from flooding while at the same time irrigate fields; the earliest attempts to do both began in the seventh century B.C.E. In addition, states that developed in the Yellow River Valley received most of their taxes in the form of grain, which needed to be transported to the capital or to armies under state command. Along much of its course, the Yellow was too turbulent for transport, so canals were dug for grain barges. These three goals—flood control, irrigation, and grain transport—were not always compatible. In addition, competing armies often used waterworks as weapons, flooding the land of their rivals by building or destroying dikes. (Such tactics have also continued into the twentieth century; the dikes of the Yellow River were broken as a strategic move in 1938 during the Sino-Japanese War.)

Some of the earliest large-scale waterworks in China were the Hong Guo system of canals connecting the Yellow River with the Bian and Si Rivers, dating from the fifth or fourth century B.C.E., and the Zhengguo irrigation canal, first completed in 246 B.C.E. and still in use today. Branch canals dug from the major arteries created large irrigated areas, and farmers built water-lifting machines for the perennial irrigation of their plots. As in Mesopotamia, water rights were a contentious issue, and special officials charged with the regulation of water were appointed as early as the second century B.C.E.

Waterworks in the Indus River Valley took a slightly different form than those in Mesopotamia, Egypt, or China. Here the amount of rainfall, thanks to annual monsoons, was greater than in the other three river valleys, so that the river was more important as a bringer of fresh soil than of fresh water. Like the Nile, the Indus flooded regularly, and archaeological excavations have revealed embankments and flood walls dating from 2500 B.C.E. More impressive still are the systems of domestic and municipal drains and sewers unearthed in the ancient Indus cities of Harappa and Mohenjo-daro. Made of brick, these included drains leading from bathrooms in each house, and underground sewage channels with openings to allow repairs, much like those in today's cities. Not until the modern period would urban residents elsewhere benefit from such an elaborate system for waste control.

Though sewers were rare in the ancient world, pipes and conduits bringing water into cities and buildings were quite common in some areas. In China, earthenware pipes fitted together in sections have been excavated from as early as the second century B.C.E., and bamboo piping

Chapter 2

The Need for

Water in

Ancient

Societies

(2000 B.C.E.–

500 C.E.)

appears in illustrations from slightly later. The most extensive system for bringing water into cities in the ancient world was the one built for Rome. Like the four civilizations we have already discussed, Rome also grew up on the banks of a river, the Tiber, but substantial natural rainfall in the area made extensive irrigation for agricultural purposes unnecessary. Farmers did build drainage ditches, for much of the land around Rome was marshy and usable for agriculture only when drained. Rome's primary water problem was the lack of good drinking water; the Tiber was often brackish and unpleasant, or even unhealthy, to drink. The Chinese solved the problem of unhealthy drinking water very early by boiling theirs, but Romans instead learned from their Near Eastern neighbors and built aqueducts, covered or uncovered channels that brought water into the cities from pristine lakes and springs. The first of Rome's aqueducts was built in 312 B.C.E., and the system expanded continuously up to about 150 C.E. Over 300 miles of aqueducts served the city of Rome alone, with extensive networks in the outlying provinces as well. Roman engineers went to great lengths to avoid valleys but were occasionally forced to construct enormous bridges to carry the aqueduct across a gorge. Some of these bridges were over 150 feet high, and a few, such as that in Segovia, Spain, still serve to bring water to city residents. Roman construction techniques, such as the use of the arch and water-resistant cement, allowed them to build water systems undreamed of in Mesopotamia and Egypt. Legal problems were not as easily solved, however, and disputes about water rights occurred throughout Rome's long history.

THE METHOD

Historians use a wide variety of sources when exploring ancient irrigation and water-supply systems. Many of these systems were created before the development of writing, so archaeological evidence—the actual remains of ancient ditches, machines, or aqueducts—is extremely important, particularly when tracing technological development. Even when such evidence itself has completely disappeared, valuable traces remain. As you will discover in this chapter, modern landscapes often reveal the ancient uses of the land through patterns of depressions and discoloration.

The easiest way to see these patterns is through aerial photography. Analyzing aerial photographs can be difficult, for it takes a great deal of training to learn how to read ancient land-use patterns through the overlay of modern development. Occasionally the older patterns can be quite clear, however, and with only a bit of additional information, you can begin to decode them. Source 1 is an aerial photograph of the site of a pre-Roman city in Italy. Examine the picture carefully. Can you see the old grid pattern of drainage ditches, which shows up as light and dark marsh grass? The dark lines are ancient drainage ditches, the lighter squares ancient fields, and the white parallel lines superimposed on the top are part of a modern drainage system. To examine the ancient system, you will mentally have to strip away the modern system. What do you think the broader black strip at the top left is? Look at the flatness of the landscape. Would silting in be a problem?

A more sophisticated type of aerial photography involves the use of satellites, rather than airplanes. Satellites can take extremely detailed pictures of the earth's surface that reveal natural and artificially constructed features, both ancient and contemporary. The sharpest images are produced by high-resolution military satellites whose pictures are not available to the public, but low-power images produced by LANDSAT, the only U.S. commercial imaging satellite system, are adequate for most archaeological and historical purposes. Source 2 is a map of the major ancient irrigation ditches between the Tigris and Euphrates rivers identifiable in a recent LANDSAT image. What does the extent of the system reveal about Mesopotamian technology? What does the size of this network imply about the political systems in this area—that is, would you expect the cities in Mesopotamia to be politically unified? hostile to each other? New technologies such as LANDSAT imagery not only answer elusive questions, but also guide future research. How could you use this map to plan further investigations of irrigation systems?

Aerial photography provides visual evidence of entire irrigation systems, but not of specific tools and machines that lifted water to the fields. For these we must look to the remains of the tools themselves, or to depictions of them in tomb paintings, scrolls, mosaics, and pottery. Comparing such pictures with machines still in use today shows that many techniques for lifting water have not changed at all for thousands of years. Sources 3 to 6 show four different machines for raising water that we know were in use in ancient times: the shaduf, the saqiya, the square-pallet chain pump, and the noria. To assess their role and importance, you have to think about a number of different factors while you examine the four diagrams. Some of these factors are technical: How complicated is this machine to build? Does it have many moving parts to keep in good repair? How much water can it lift? How high can it lift it? Can it work with both flowing and stationary water? Some of the factors are economic: Does the machine require a person to operate it (thus taking a worker away from other types of labor)? Does it require a strong adult, or can it be operated by a child? Does it require the power of an animal, which must be fed and cared for? Some of the factors are both economic and political: Does the machine require more raw materials to build than one family might possess? Does it require any raw materials like metal that would have to be im-

Chapter 2

The Need for

Water in

Ancient

Societies

(2000 B.C.E.–

500 C.E.)

ported? (Such questions are political because someone has to decide which families get the raw materials necessary for their fields.) Some of the factors are legal: Does the machine raise so much water that distribution would have to be regulated? At this point, you may want to make a chart summarizing your assessment of the advantages and disadvantages of each machine; such a study aid will help you make your final conclusions.

We now turn from visual to written sources. Because water was so important, mention of water systems appears very early in recorded human history. The next five sources are written accounts of the construction or operation of water systems. Source 7 presents the sections from the Code of Hammurabi, a Babylonian legal code dating from 1750 B.C.E., that refer to irrigation. Source 8 is a description of the building of the Zhengguo [Chêng Kuo] canal in the third century B.C.E., written by the historian Sima Qian about 150 years later. In Source 9, the Roman historian Suetonius records the water-system projects undertaken by the Emperor Claudius during his reign (41–54 C.E.). Source 10 is a report of the activities of Shao Xinchen [Hsin-Ch'en], an administrator during the Han dynasty in China, dating sometime before 33 B.C.E. Source 11 is a discussion of some of the problems associated with Rome's water system, written

about 100 C.E. by Frontinus, who was commissioner of the water supply. Source 12 is a memorial dating from the first century B.C.E. by Jia Rang [Chia Jang], a specialist in flood control, answering an imperial decree that asked for opinions on river conservancy.

As you read these sources, notice first of all the technical problems each author addresses. What particular problems in controlling, tapping, transporting, and storing water are discussed? What solutions are suggested? Then look at legal problems, most clearly presented in the selection by Frontinus and the Code of Hammurabi. How were people misusing or harming the water systems? What penalties did they incur? Who controlled the legal use of water and decided how water was to be distributed?

The written sources also include information about political and economic factors in ancient water-supply systems that is nearly impossible to gain from archaeological evidence. Careful reading can give you an insight as to who paid for the construction of such systems and who stood to profit—financially or politically—from their use. What reasons other than the simple need for water led rulers to build water systems? What political and economic factors entered into decisions about how water was to be distributed?

THE EVIDENCE

Source 1 from Leo Deuel, Flights Into Yesterday: The Story of Aerial Archeology *(New York: St. Martin's Press, 1969), p. 236. Photograph: Fotoaerea Valvassori, Ravenna.*

1. Aerial Photograph of Pre-Roman City in Italy

Chapter 2
The Need for
Water in
Ancient
Societies
(2000 B.C.E.–
500 C.E.)

Source 2 from Robert MaC. Adams, Heartland of Cities; Surveys of Ancient Settlements and Land Use on the Central Floodplains of the Euphrates *(Chicago: University of Chicago Press, 1981), p. 34.*

2. Major Ancient Levees Identifiable in LANDSAT Imagery

Sources 3 through 6 adapted from sketches by Merry E. Wiesner.

3. Shaduf

4. Saqiya

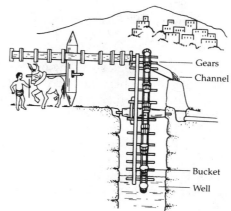

5. Square-Pallet Chain Pump

6. Noria

Chapter 2

The Need for

Water in

Ancient

Societies

(2000 B.C.E.–

500 C.E.)

Source 7 from Robert F. Harper, The Code of Hammurabi *(Chicago: University of Chicago Press, 1904).*

7. Sections from the Code of Hammurabi Referring to Irrigation, 1750 B.C.E.

53. If a man neglects to maintain his dike and does not strengthen it, and a break is made in his dike and the water carries away the farmland, the man in whose dike the break has been made shall replace the grain which has been damaged.

54. If he is not able to replace the grain, they shall sell him and his goods and the farmers whose grain the water has carried away shall divide [the results of the sale].

55. If a man opens his canal for irrigation, and neglects it and the water carries away an adjacent field, he shall pay out grain on the basis of the adjacent field.

56. If a man opens up the water and the water carries away the improvements of an adjacent field, he shall pay out ten *gur* of grain per *bur* [of damaged land]. . . .

66. If a man has stolen a watering-machine from the meadow, he shall pay five shekels of silver to the owner of the watering-machine.

Source 8 from Joseph Needham, Science and Civilization in China, *Vol. 4, Pt. 3 (Cambridge: Cambridge University Press, 1974), p. 285.*

8. Sima Qian's Description of the Building of the Zhengguo Canal, ca. 100 B.C.E.

(The prince of) Han,[1] hearing that the State of Chhin[1] [Qin] was eager to adventure profitable enterprises, desired to exhaust it (with heavy activities), so that it should not start expanding to the east (and making attacks on Han). He therefore sent the hydraulic engineer Chêng Kuo [Zhengguo] (to Chhin) to persuade deceitfully (the king of) Chhin to open a canal from the Ching [Qing] River, from Chung-shan [Zhongshan] and Hu-khou [Hukou] in the west, all along the foot of the northern mountains, carrying water to fall into

1. Han and Chhin were two states that bordered the Yellow River.

the river Lo in the east. The proposed canal was to be more than 300 *li*[2] long, and was to be used for irrigating agricultural land.

Before the construction work was more than half finished, however, the Chhin authorities became aware of the trick. (The king of Chhin) wanted to kill Chêng Kuo, but he [the engineer] addressed him as follows: "It is true that at the beginning I deceived you, but nevertheless this canal, when it is completed, will be of great benefit to Chhin. I have, by this ruse, prolonged the life of the State of Han for a few years, but I am accomplishing a work which will sustain the State of Chhin for ten thousand generations." The (king of) Chhin agreed with him, approved his words, and gave firm orders that the canal was to be completed. When it was finished, rich silt-bearing water was led through it to irrigate more than [667,000 acres] of alkali land. The harvests from these fields attained the level of [16 bushels] per *mou* (i.e. they became very abundant). Thus Kuanchung (the land within the passes) became a fertile country without bad years. (It was for this reason that) Chhin became so rich and powerful, and in the end was able to conquer all the other feudal States. And ever afterwards the canal (bore the name of the engineer and) was called the Chêngkuo Canal.

Source 9 from Naphtali Lewis and Meyer Reinhold, Roman Civilization (*New York: Columbia University Press, 1955), pp. 151–152.*

9. Suetonius's Description of the Water Projects Undertaken by Emperor Claudius (r. 41–54 C.E.)

The public works which Claudius completed were great and essential rather than numerous; they were in particular the following: an aqueduct begun by Caligula; also the drainage channel of Lake Fucine and the harbor at Ostia, although in the case of the last two he knew that Augustus had refused the former to the Marsians in spite of their frequent requests, and that the latter had often been considered by the deified Julius but given up because of its difficulty. He brought to the city on stone arches the cool and abundant springs of the Claudian aqueduct . . . and at the same time the channel of the New Anio, distributing them into many beautifully ornamented fountains. He made the attempt on the Fucine Lake as much in the hope of gain as of glory, inasmuch as there were some who offered to drain it at their own cost provided the land that was drained be given them. He finished the drainage canal, which was

---

2. 300 *li* = 100 miles.

Chapter 2

The Need for

Water in

Ancient

Societies

(2000 B.C.E.–

500 C.E.)

three miles in length, partly by leveling and partly by tunneling a mountain, a work of great difficulty requiring eleven years, although he had 30,000 men at work all the time without interruption.

Source 10 from Cho-yun Hsu, Han Agriculture: The Formation of Early Chinese Agrarian Economy *(Seattle: University of Washington Press, 1980), pp. 268–269.*

10. Activities of Shao Xinchen, Han Dynasty, before 33 B.C.E.

[Shao] Hsin-ch'en [Xinchen] was promoted to be grand administrator of Nanyang. . . . Hsin-ch'en was a person of energy and plans; he took an interest in creating benefits for the people and regarded it as his urgent task to enrich them. Crossing in and out of the fields, stopping and resting even at remote villages and cantons, and having very little time for quiet living, he personally encouraged farming.

As he traveled about, he inspected the waters and springs in the commandery. He dug canals and ditches and built water gates and dikes in several tens of places in all to expand the irrigated land, which increased year by year to as much as [500,000 acres]. The people obtained benefits from this and had a surplus of stores.

Hsin-ch'en formulated regulations for the people concerning the equitable distribution of water. They were inscribed on stones and set up at the boundaries of the fields to prevent disputes over the distribution [of water].

Source 11 from B. K. Workman, editor and translator, They Saw It Happen in Classical Times *(New York: Barnes & Noble, 1964), pp. 179–181.*

11. Frontinus's Discussion of Rome's Water System, ca. 100 C.E.

The New Anio[3] is drawn from the river in the district of Sinbrinum, at about the forty-second milestone along the Via Sublacensis. On either side of the river at this point are fields of rich soil which make the banks less firm, so that the water in the aqueduct is discoloured and muddy even without the damage done by storms. So a little way along from the inlet a cleansing basin was

3. An aqueduct completed under the emperor Claudius in 52 C.E.

built where the water could settle and be purified between the river and the conduit. Even so, in the event of rain, the water reaches the city in a muddy state. The length of the New Anio is about 47 miles, of which over 39 are underground and more than 7 carried on structures above the ground. In the upper reaches a distance of about two miles in various sections is carried on low structures or arches. Nearer the city, from the seventh Roman mile-stone, is half a mile on substructures and five miles on arches. These arches are very high, rising in certain places to a height of 109 feet.

. . . All the aqueducts reach the city at different levels. So some serve the higher districts and some cannot reach loftier ground. For the hills of Rome have gradually increased in height because of the rubble from frequent fires. There are five aqueducts high enough at entrance to reach all the city, but they supply water at different pressures. . . .

Anyone who wants to tap water for private consumption must send in an application and take it, duly signed by the Emperor, to the Commissioner. The latter must take immediate action on Caesar's grant, and enroll one of the Imperial freedmen to help him in the business. . . . The right to water once granted cannot be inherited or bought, and does not go with the property, though long ago a privilege was extended to the public baths that their right should last in perpetuity. . . . When grants lapse, notice is given and record made in the ledgers, which are consulted so that future applicants can be given vacant supplies. The previous custom was to cut off these lapsed supplies at once, to make some profit by a temporary sale to the landowners or even to outsiders. Our Emperor felt that property should not suddenly be left without water, and that it would be fairer to give thirty days' notice for other arrangements to be made by the interested party. . . .

Now that I have explained the situation with regard to private supply, it will be pertinent to give some examples of the ways in which men have broken these very sound arrangements and have been caught red-handed. In some reservoirs I have found larger valves in position than had been granted, and some have not even had the official stamp on them. . . .

Another of the watermen's intolerable practices is to make a new outlet from the cistern when a water-grant is transferred to a new owner, leaving the old one for themselves. I would say that it was one of the Commissioner's chief duties to put a stop to this. For it affects not only the proper protection of the supply, but also the upkeep of the reservoir which would be ruined if needlessly filled with outlets.

Another financial scheme of the watermen, which they call "puncturing," must also be abolished. There are long separate stretches all over the city through which the pipes pass hidden under the pavement. I found out that these pipes were being tapped everywhere by the "puncturers," from which water was supplied by private pipe to all the business premises in the area, with the result that only a meagre amount reached the public utilities. I can

Chapter 2

The Need for

Water in

Ancient

Societies

(2000 B.C.E.–

500 C.E.)

estimate the volume of water stolen in this way from the amount of lead piping which was removed when these branch pipes were dug up.

Source 12 from Cho-Yun Hsu, Han Agriculture: The Formation of Early Chinese Agrarian Economy *(Seattle: University of Washington Press, 1980), pp. 266–267.*

12. Memorial from Jia Rang, 1st century B.C.E.

[Jia Rang memorialized:] ". . . Digging canals has three benefits; not digging them has three detriments. When the people are constantly exhausted by preventing floods, half of them lose their livelihood. When the water overflows the land and when the accumulated moisture evaporates, the people are made ill by the humid atmosphere. All the trees rapidly rot away, and the soil, turning alkaline, does not produce grain. When the river breaks the dikes and overflows, destruction ensues, and [the victims] become food for fish and turtles. These are the three detriments.

"If there are canals for irrigation, then the salt is washed down to the marshy ground and the spreading of the silt increases fertility. Where formerly millet and wheat were raised, even nonglutinous and glutinous rice can be produced; the productivity is increased fivefold in the high-lying land and tenfold in low-lying land. Furthermore, there is the advantage of transportation by water. These are the three benefits."

[*Jia Rang next considers the possible types of irrigation projects, and proposes the building of large-scale dikes as the best policy. He describes two other alternatives to pursue if new dikes are not possible: digging new irrigation canals and repairing the old dikes. He assesses these two choices as follows.*]

"At present, the number of functionaries and conscript laborers for embankments along the Yellow River in each commandery is several thousand, and the costs of cutting and buying wood and stone are several tens of millions yearly [an amount] that is sufficient to dig canals and construct water gates. Furthermore, when the people benefit from irrigation, they will urge one another to make canals, and they will not be weary even if the work is strenuous. At the same time the people's fields will be cared for and the dikes on the Yellow River will be completed. This will indeed enrich the state, make the people secure, create profit, and do away with calamities, and it will endure for several hundred years. Therefore, I consider this a medium policy. Repairing the old dikes by means of increasing the height and thickness would cost limitlessly, and we would frequently encounter calamities. This would be the worst policy."

QUESTIONS TO CONSIDER

Now that you have looked at both visual and written evidence, you will need to compile and organize the information gained in each type of source to achieve a more complete picture. Because sources for the earliest periods of human development are so scant, we need to use every shred available and use them somewhat creatively, making reasonable speculations where there is no specific evidence.

Take all the evidence about technical problems first. Keeping in mind that the ancient world had no power equipment, and no tools more elaborate than axes, hammers, saws, and drills (the Chinese and Romans also had planes and chisels), what would you gauge to be the most difficult purely technical problem involved in constructing water systems? in keeping them operating? The four diagrams of the water-raising machines are arranged in the chronological order of their development, with the shaduf as old as 2500 B.C.E. and the other three introduced hundreds of years later. Looking at your chart of the advantages and disadvantages of each machine, how do the later machines improve on the shaduf? What additional problems do these improvements create? What types of

technological experimentation did the need for water encourage?

Technological advance is not always an unmitigated blessing. For example, water standing in irrigation ditches can become a fertile breeding ground for mosquitoes and other carriers of disease. Cities that depend on irrigation suffer food shortages and famine when ditches can not be kept clear or when river levels drop. Furthermore, the diversion of so much of their water makes rivers much smaller when they finally reach their deltas, which means the deltas become increasingly salty from sea water and eventually unable to support the kinds of plant and animal life they originally sustained. Judging by the aerial photograph and the LANDSAT map, would you expect any of these problems in ancient Italy or Mesopotamia? In the written sources, do you find evidence of problems in the Chinese or Roman water systems that were caused by technological advance? Are any suggestions made for solving these?

Now think about what you have learned about the economic issues associated with water systems. You have no doubt noticed that tremendous numbers of people were needed to construct irrigation ditches and aqueducts. Some of the written sources, such as Suetonius and Jia Rang, give exact figures as to the

[49]

Chapter 2
The Need for
Water in
Ancient
Societies
(2000 B.C.E.–
500 C.E.)

number of workers. The size and complexity of the systems depicted in all the sources also imply huge work forces, given the lack of elaborate equipment. The rulers of Mesopotamia and Rome did not view the need for mass labor as an obstacle, but rather as a solution to the problem of unemployment. Legend has it that the Roman emperor Vespasian, when offered a labor-saving machine, refused to use it on the grounds that it would put people out of work and lead to social unrest in Rome. You might approve of this concern for full employment, but it should also tell you something about the value of labor in ancient societies. What would you expect wages to be for construction workers? What class of people would you expect to find working on these water systems?

Large numbers of workers were needed not only in construction, but also in the maintenance of irrigation systems and the operation of water-lifting machines. What does this tell you about the value of labor? What would happen with a sudden drop in the population, such as that caused by a famine or epidemic? How would a loss of workers affect the available food supply?

The sources also reveal information about political factors associated with water systems. What does their construction indicate about the power of rulers to coerce or hire labor? How do rulers control the building and maintenance of machines and ditches? How might this affect the power and independence of local communities or of individual families? What can you surmise about the role water played in expanding centralized political power or in disputes between rival dynasties?

Finally, the sources provide evidence of legal changes necessitated by the search for, and limits of, water. Actions that had previously been unrestricted and unregulated now came under the control of public authorities, which meant that the number of enforcement agents and courts had to increase. What would this expansion of bureaucracy do to taxation levels? How did political concerns shape the regulations?

You are now ready to answer the question posed at the beginning of the chapter: How did the need for a steady supply of water affect the technological, economic, political, and legal development of ancient societies?

EPILOGUE

The irrigation and water supply systems of the ancient world required not only huge amounts of labor, but also strong central states to coerce or hire that labor and to enforce laws which kept the channels flowing. For example, each Mesopotamian city managed its own irrigation system, but the wealthy and advanced cities were attractive targets for foreign conquerers. The political history of ancient Mesopotamia was one of wave after wave of conquerers invading from the north—the Akkadians, Babylonians, Assyrians, Persians, Greeks, and finally Romans. Most of these conquerers realized the importance of irrigation, and ordered the vanquished residents to maintain or expand their systems. When the Moslems conquered the area in the seventh century, they studied Mesopotamian techniques and spread these westward across northern Africa and into Spain, where centuries-old Roman irrigation systems were disintegrating.

In between these powerful conquerers, however, and after the thirteenth century when the area was overrun by the Mongols, the irrigation ditches were often not maintained, and they silted in irreparably. The fertile farmland that had been built up in the delta became salinized from the salty waters of the Persian Gulf, making it useless for cultivation. Once the irrigation ditches were no longer functional, the cities could not survive. Centuries of irrigation combined with too little fertilization made even irrigated land less and less productive.

The benefits and problems brought by irrigation are not limited to the ancient world, however, but can be seen in many modern societies. A striking contemporary example comes from one of the parts of the world we have been studying in this chapter. Throughout the twentieth century, Egypt expanded the irrigation system fed by the Nile with a series of dams, culminating in the Aswan High Dam begun in 1960 to provide hydroelectric power and limit the free flow of water at the height of the flood season. The enormous reservoir created by the dam can also be tapped at low water times to allow for perennial irrigation. The dam does all of the things it was intended to do very well, but has also introduced some unexpected problems. The river's regular flooding had brought new fertile soil to the Nile Valley and carried away the salts that result from evaporation. Once the dam stopped the flooding, Egyptian fields began to need artificial fertilizer to remain productive, a supplement few farmers could afford. Because the soil of the Nile Valley contains much clay and so drains very slowly, the dam's steady supply of water makes many fields waterlogged and unusable. The large reservoir created by the dam sits in the middle of the Sahara Desert, losing tremendous amounts to evaporation and decreasing the total flow of water in the Nile significantly. The artificial lake also put many acres of farmland under water and forced the relocation of tens of thousands of people. The current drought in northern Africa has further lowered the level of the Nile, shrinking the amount of hydroelectric power the river can generate. Ending the flooding also allowed snails which carry bilharzia (schistosomiasis) to proliferate in the fields and irrigation ditches; bilharzia is an intestinal parasite that severely weakens its victims. Thus like the dikes in ancient China that could be broken by flood or foreign conquest, or the levees of the Mississippi that gave way

Chapter 2

The Need for

Water in

Ancient

Societies

(2000 B.C.E.–

500 C.E.)

in the floods of 1993, or the irrigation of the southwestern United States that is draining underground aquifers, the Aswan High Dam has proven a mixed blessing to modern Egypt.

As you reflect on what you have discovered in this chapter, you may want to think about problems associated with the distribution of water in your own area. How does the need for water affect the political and economic structures of your city or state? What technological solutions has your area devised, and how have these worked?

CHAPTER THREE
WRITING AND POWER: DEFINING
WORLD-VIEWS (1500–200 B.C.E.)

THE PROBLEM

According to Islamic tradition, when the angel Gabriel first revealed himself to Muhammad around the year 610, among the first words he spoke to Muhammad were these:

> In the name of the Lord who created all things. He has taught us the use of the pen. He taught us that which we know not.[1]

Although there is no record that Muhammad himself could either read or write, there is little doubt that the man who ultimately would be revered by Muslims as the Prophet understood the power that literacy held for those who could read and write, a power that literate people held over those who were not. Thoughts could be shaped, codified, and transmitted over both distance and time. Laws (whether political,

1. Qur'an (Koran), XCVI, 1–5.

economic, or religious) could be written down and interpreted or enforced by those who could record or read them. Perhaps more important, writing gave to some the power to bind a people together by giving them a shared history, a common literature, a united world-view, and even a shared *cosmology* (a branch of philosophy that deals with the origin, process, and structure of the universe). And while the oral traditions of nonliterate peoples could be powerful, effective, and in some ways even more "democratic" (in that all who heard could thereby participate in the carrying on of laws, religion, and history), writing possessed certain advantages over an oral tradition, not the least of which being that later historians from other cultures could gain access to the history, culture, and thought of peoples of the past.

Throughout history, virtually every culture possessed its own explanation of how the world was created (cosmology) and what place humans were meant to occupy in that world.

In addition to commercial information and law codes, a people's explanations of creation were one of the first things they wrote down, thus demonstrating the people's own belief in the superiority of written over oral transmission. By studying these written explanations of creation, historians can come to understand a particular people's value system, its view of itself, and the relationship of the people to the world, the universe, and to a god or gods. In addition, historians can gain an understanding of a people's own view of history. To a particular people, is history linear (resembling a straight line, from event to event), cyclical (circular, with patterns recurring), in another form, or formless (with events occurring purely at random, by chance)? In sum, by studying a people's accounts of creation, historians can learn a remarkable amount about how the people thought and even why they behaved as they did.

Your tasks in this chapter will require you to use all your analytical reading skills plus a good deal of historical imagination. In the Evidence section of this chapter you will find three written creation accounts—one from the Rig Veda of ancient India, one from the Yijing (or I Ching, the Book of Changes) of ancient China, and one from the Torah (the first five books of both the Jewish and Christian Bibles) of the Israelites. First, you must read each account to learn how each of these people sought to explain the creation of the world. Then, using your historical imagination, show what each creation account tells us about the people who thought it critical enough to write it down—their value system, their view of history, their relationship to the universe as well as to a god or gods. In essence, then, you will be studying the cosmologies of three ancient peoples, an extremely important exercise for historians.

BACKGROUND

Forms of "written" communication are nearly as old as humanity itself. Cave paintings and etchings[2] surely were intended to transmit simple messages as well as to provide means of self-expression. Message sticks (Australia), wampum belts (Native Americans), shell designs (Nigeria), knotted cords (Tibet, Polynesia, parts of Africa), bean patterns (pre-Inca Peru), and the like—all these were used to communicate uncomplicated messages.

Beginning about 6,000 years ago, however, people began to develop more complex and codified (systematic, with rules) forms of written communication. Evolving first among the Sumerians of the Fertile Crescent—the land between the Tigris and Euphrates Rivers—in approximately 3500 B.C.E., various types of writing on stone, clay tablets, and pa-

2. Carvings or etchings on cave walls are referred to by archaeologists as petroglyphs; cave paintings are called petrograms.

pyrus[3] emerged independently in Egypt, China, the Near East, Crete, Cyprus, and (by about 1000 B.C.E.) Central America. Ultimately, various cultures developed over two hundred written scripts, approximately eighty of which are still in use today.[4]

Wherever writing developed and whatever particular form it took, all types of writing can be divided into two general systems: *ideographic* and *phonetic*. Ideographic writing, known also as thought writing, evolved from using pictures to represent things or thoughts (Sumerian pictorials, Egyptian hieroglyphics, and Chinese pictographs, among others). The advantage of ideographic writing is that it is not tied to any particular spoken language and thus can be understood by peoples speaking a variety of tongues and dialects. The principal disadvantage of ideographic writing is that it requires the memorization of an immense number of different signs, or ideograms—four to six thousand, for example, for literate Chinese. On the other hand, in phonetic writing each sign (or letter, in our writing) represents a particular sound,

and signs are combined to make the sounds for particular words. For example, most Western Europeans employ a form of phonetic writing using the signs of the Roman alphabet. Regularized in the sixth century B.C.E., the Roman alphabet originally contained twenty-one signs (letters), later expanded to twenty-six.[5] The chief advantages of phonetic writing are that only a few signs need to be memorized and that these signs can be grouped in an almost endless number of sound combinations to make words and to create new words.[6]

Wherever writing developed, those who mastered this skill often wielded great power and commanded enormous respect. In Egypt, scribes were exempt from physical labor, taxation, and military service. As one scribe wrote, "Put writing in your heart that you protect yourself from hard labor of any kind." Scribes were likewise respected in Mesopotamia, among the Aztecs of Central America, and later in the nations of Islam. Most societies founded schools to teach royalty, nobility, and scribes the craft of writing, but in no early culture was universal literacy considered either necessary or desirable. This is because those in power quickly realized that those who could write possessed the capacity to shape the thoughts of those who could not. The illiterate would gather (or would be forcibly gath-

---

3. **papyrus:** a type of paper made from the inner stems of the papyrus plant that were pressed together with some form of adhesive, and developed by the Egyptians around 3100 B.C.E.; after being written on, the papyrus then was rolled into scrolls.

4. Of all the written scripts known to have existed, over twenty still are undecipherable. People who decipher ancient inscriptions or writings are known as epigraphers. For more on this exciting profession, see John Chadwick, *The Decipherment of Linear B* (Cambridge, England, 1958); Carol Andrews, *The Rosetta Stone* (London, 1981); Michael D. Coe, *Breaking the Maya Code* (New York, 1992).

5. The letters *W, J, Y, Z,* and *U* were added later.

6. An unabridged English dictionary contains approximately 500,000 words, and hundreds of new words are added to the language each decade.

ered) to listen to the readings of edicts, proclamations, laws, or religious texts and liturgies.[7]

As noted above, besides commercial agreements and legal codes, one of the first things a people committed to writing was their own explanation of the creation of the universe, the world, and human beings. Such creation accounts often bound a people together and formed a philosophical foundation for their thoughts and actions. In this chapter, you will be analyzing the creation accounts of the Indo-Aryans of ancient India (Rig Veda, written down in ca. 600 B.C.E., the Zhou dynasty of ancient China (Yijing, parts of which can be dated roughly at 1000 B.C.E., although the section you will be reading dates from around the third century B.C.E.), and the Israelites of ancient Israel (the Torah, traditionally first read publicly by the scribe Ezra in Jerusalem in 444 B.C.E.).[8]

The Indo-Aryans migrated to present-day India from the northwest around 1500 B.C.E., either conquering the earlier Indus civilization or moving in after its fall. Originally a warlike and pastoral people, the Aryans quickly adapted themselves to a sedentary, food-producing life. Politically, their Vedic society was divided into a strict caste system of priests (Brahman), warriors (Kshatriya), peasants (Vaishya), and serfs (Shudra). Although the original Aryan conquerors were illiterate, the preceding

Indus civilization had developed a writing system that was a mixture of ideographic and phonetic forms.[9] By roughly 700 B.C.E., however, Vedic society had developed its own form of writing known as Brahmi, apparently derived from a North Semitic script.

In Vedic society, writing was strictly controlled by the Brahman. Beginning around 700 B.C.E., the Brahman began collecting songs, hymns, histories, and other materials that had been passed orally from generation to generation into the Vedas.[10] Oldest among these was the Rig Veda, a collection of 1,017 hymns or songs divided into ten chapters or books. Some of these songs had been present in Vedic society at least since the Indo-Aryan migration to northern India in roughly 1500 B.C.E. It is here (Source 1) that the society's creation accounts can be found.

In China, the Shang dynasty (ca. 1523–1027 B.C.E.) was overthrown by the Zhou (Chou), once loyal dependents of the Shang whose military technology (including horse-drawn chariots) gave them the upper hand over their former masters. But the Zhou were wise enough to retain much of Shang culture, including its system of writing and its religious beliefs. A major part of those beliefs had to do with divination, the art of foretelling the future. Priests would take the bottom shell of a tortoise, pierce the shell with a small hole, ask a question and then apply heat to the hole in the shell. The resulting cracks

---

7. **liturgy:** a prescribed form for a public religious service; many religions have written down their liturgies in prayer books, or missals.

8. See Nehemiah 8:1–8.

9. The Indus script is one of those that is still a mystery.

10. **Veda:** "wisdom, or the path to wisdom."

in the shell formed various patterns that the priests could then interpret in order to predict future events. By around 200 B.C.E., the Yijing (or Book of Changes) had been completed and served as an interpretive guide that substituted eight trigrams (sets of three parallel lines) and sixty-four hexagrams (six parallel lines) for the cracks in the tortoise shell. The Yijing is less a religious book than it is a volume of philosophy and ethics, and it was considered important enough to escape the great book burning of 213 B.C.E. It is in the Yijing (Source 3) that the Chinese creation account can be found.

About the time that the Indo-Aryans were moving into India and the Shang dynasty was in the process of controlling the eastern half of the Yellow River Valley, in Mesopotamia and the Arabian peninsula groups of homeless nomads (referred to in Mesopotamian and Egyptian sources as "Habiru") wandered across the semi-arid landscape grazing their herds. One of these groups came to be known as "Hebrews," or "Israelites" or "Jews."[11] Sometime after 1550 B.C.E., the Jews voluntarily migrated to Egypt to escape a drought, but soon were enslaved by the Egyptians. Around 1200 B.C.E., the Jews either abandoned or escaped from Egypt. The decline of both the Egyptian and Hittite empires had left a power vacuum along the eastern coast of the Mediterranean Sea, and it was here that the Is-

raelites ultimately settled, fighting off Philistines and other peoples in order to seize and hold the land. Sometime after 925 B.C.E. (the traditional death of King Solomon), the Israelites broke into two kingdoms. The northern kingdom was destroyed by Assyrian invaders, while the southern kingdom (Judah) survived for another century and a half, until the Babylonian captivity.

Written Hebrew was one of the several offshoots of North Semitic script (another, as we have seen, was Brahmi), and was in use as early as ca. 800 B.C.E. The form of Hebrew writing known as Square Hebrew (for the rectangular shaping of the letters) traditionally owed its adoption to the scribe Ezra in the fifth century B.C.E. Like all Semitic scripts, Hebrew is consonantal—that is, phonetic with twenty-two consonant letters or sounds, but no vowels.

Similar to the early writings of other peoples, the Torah contains the Jews' creation account, history, and laws. Traditionally, authorship is credited to Moses, although a majority of biblical scholars assert that the Torah comes from more than a single source. According to ancient tradition, Joshua had the Torah "engraved upon the stones of the altar" of the tabernacle sometime before 1100 B.C.E., a claim that most scholars dispute as much too early (the fifth century B.C.E. is more likely). As with other peoples, the Israelites' explanation of creation (Source 2, from the book of Genesis, which began to be stabilized around 720 B.C.E.) tells historians a great deal about the Jewish people themselves.

---

11. At the time, "Hebrew" referred to a social category, whereas "Israelite" was used to describe all the people of the group; "Jews" derived from the southern kingdom's surviving tribe of Judah.

What does the creation account of each of the peoples excerpted in the Evidence section tell us about the people themselves? What can we discover about how they viewed the universe, themselves, the role of a god or gods, and the unfolding of history itself?

THE METHOD

Whenever people today consult the Rig Veda, the Torah, or the Yijing, most do so either as part of their religious worship or as an inspirational guide. Each of these writings, however, also is a historical document that can be examined and analyzed for what that document tells us about those who created it and who preserved and venerated it.

As you might expect, historians approach such a document in quite different ways than members of a group for which the document is an important part of their creed or philosophy. To begin with, whenever it is possible, historians prefer to read the document in its oldest version and in its original language. In that way, mistakes made in copying or translating, as well as purposeful additions to or deletions from the original text, will not lead the historians into errors of judgment. Second, it is important that historians know as closely as possible the date (or dates) of the document's creation. This information is valuable to historians because it enables them to study the context and understand more about the people who were living during that period, about the events taking place, and the ideas in circulation. Historians call this process learning about the "climate of opinion" of a particular time period. Unfortunately, very early documents (such as the ones you will be working with in this chapter) cannot be dated very precisely because they were written down only after a long period of oral transmission.

After completing these early steps, historians then are prepared to examine the document itself. When dealing with creation accounts, historians ask of each written account a series of questions. How does the account explain the creation of the universe, the world, and human beings? Is the creation divinely inspired; in other words, did a god or gods play an active role in the creation process, and for what purpose? Are human beings merely one among many objects of creation, *or* are human beings the pinnacle of the creation process? In return for creation and care, do human beings have any obligation to their creator? Finally, is the creation process in the account lineal (proceeding sequentially along a line from one event to another), cyclical (circular), in another pattern, or without pattern (formless)?

Having subjected each creation account to this series of questions, historians then are ready to ask what each document reveals about the people who created it. This will take some reading about the people under scrutiny in your text, as well as a considerable amount of historical imagination. For example, if each creation account can be seen as a life guide for those who venerate it, what does the account encourage or compel (or forbid) the true believers to do? Is the creation process *reproduced* in the lives of true believers (from birth to death)? What does that process tell you about the people who created it?

Finally, you are ready to compare the three creation accounts and the people who committed them to memory and later to writing. Historians call this process *comparative textual analysis,* and it is one of the most basic methods of investigation used throughout all the humanities (literature, philosophy, linguistics, history, and the like). As you compare these accounts and their creators, using the questions above as initial guides, be careful *not* to fall into the habit of thinking of certain cultures or peoples as "inferior" or "superior" because of how far or near a particular group is to your own beliefs or philosophy. This is a common trap, and you must make every effort to avoid it. After all, each of the creation accounts you will be examining and analyzing was preserved by a people or peoples for thousands of years, has

formed the foundation for one or more present religions or philosophies, and has been deemed satisfying by a group or groups for many, many generations. Historians, therefore, approach these sources with great sensitivity and respect.

The Rig Veda (Source 1) is the oldest of the sacred texts of modern Hinduism (733 million followers in 1992). The Torah (Source 2) is considered sacred to Jews (18 million), Christians (1.8 billion), and Muslims (971 million), all of whom are referred to by Muslims as People of the Book. The Yijing (Source 3) is one of the bases of Confucianism (195 million adherents is only a guess), a westernization of the name of the great teacher K'ung Fu-tze (551–479 B.C.E.).

As you read the Evidence, be sure to take notes. One effective way of organizing your thoughts is to divide your note pages into two parts. On the left side of the page, summarize the creation account you are reading. Then, on the right side, summarize your thoughts (and questions) about the value system, the view of history, the relationship between beings that you are able to infer from the creation account.

THE EVIDENCE

Source 1 from Franklin Edgerton, trans., The Beginnings of Indian Philosophy *(Cambridge, Mass.: Harvard University Press, 1965), pp. 60–61, 67–68, 73, 74.*

1. Excerpts from Book 10 of the Rig Veda

10.72[12]

1. We will now proclaim the origins of the gods to win applause (from any) who shall behold them in a later age, as the hymns are chanted.

2. Brahmanaspati (the Lord of the Holy Word) smelted them together, as a smith. In the primal age of the gods the Existent was born from the Non-existent.

3. In the first age of the gods the Existent was born from the Non-existent. After it (the Existent) the regions were born—(after) it, from the (World-mother) in labour.

4. The world was born from the (World-mother) in labour; from the world the regions were born. From Aditi Daksa was born, from Daksa likewise Aditi (was born).[13]

5. Aditi, verily, was born, who is thy daughter, O Daksa. After her the gods were born, the blessed ones, companions of immortality.

6. When, O gods, there in the flood you stood, holding fast to one another, then from you, as from dancers, thick dust arose.

7. When, O gods, like wizard-priests, you made the worlds to swell, then you brought forth the sun that had been hidden in the sea.

8. There were eight sons of Aditi, which were born of her body. She went to the gods with seven; the (Sun-)bird she cast away.

9. With seven sons Aditi went to the primal generation (of gods). She brought back the (Sun-)bird for alternate procreation and death.

---

12. The Rig Veda is organized into ten books totalling 1,017 hymns. The number 10.72 means hymn #72 of book #10.

13. Aditi "is Mother, is Father, is Son . . . is all that is born, that will be born" (Rig Veda, 1.89). Normally, however, Aditi is taken to mean the Great Mother from whom the world was born, as well as the mother of the gods themselves. Daksa is masculine and often referred to as the "primordial cause," the original power of wisdom. Daksa's personification fluctuates throughout the Vedas.

10.81

1. The seer who, in sacrificing all these worlds, took his seat as *hotar*-priest, our father—he, with prayer seeking wealth (i.e. sacrificing), concealing that which was first, entered into the later beings.

2. What, verily, was that resting-place (support)? What manner of thing did he begin from, and how vast was it, that from which the All-maker, the all-seeing, creating the earth, unfolded the heaven by his might?

3. With eyes and face in all directions, likewise with arms and feet in all directions, he welded (as a smith) them together with his arms, with fan-bellows, creating heaven and earth, the sole god.

4. What, verily, was the wood, what the lumber, from which they carpentered out heaven and earth? You wise ones, with your wisdom inquire into that, upon what base he rested, establishing the worlds.

5. These your highest places, your lowest also, and these that are your midmost, All-maker, teach to (your) friends at the oblation, O Self-mighty One. Yourself offer sacrifice, prospering your own self (thereby).

6. O All-maker, thriving on sacrifice, do you sacrifice for yourself (i.e. create, by the cosmic "sacrifice" of creation) earth and heaven. Let other people round about stray helplessly; for us here let there be a generous patron.

7. Let us summon today for aid at the (sacrificial) contest the Lord of Holy Utterance,[14] the All-maker, who inspires the intellect. Let him take pleasure in our offerings, being helpful to all, working surely unto our support.

10.90

1. The Purusa[15] has a thousand heads, a thousand eyes, and a thousand feet. He, encompassing the world on all sides, stood out ten fingers' lengths beyond.

2. The Purusa alone is all this universe, what has been, and what is to be. He rules likewise over (the world of) immortality (viz. the gods), which he grows beyond, by (sacrificial?) food.

3. Such is the extent of his greatness; and the Purusa is still greater than this. A quarter of him is all beings, three quarters are (the world of) the immortal in heaven.

14. **Lord of Holy Utterance:** the feminine version of the Lord of the Holy Word (see 10.72, verse 2), which were hymns composed by the Brahman (priests); the Brahman held contests to see who could compose the best hymns.

15. **Purusa:** man as a cosmic being, a sort of world-giant.

4. In his three-quarters the Purusa arose to the upper regions; a quarter of him, on the other hand, came to be here below. From this (quarter) he expanded manifoldly into the things that eat and those that do not eat (animate and inanimate beings).

5. From him the Shining One (the cosmic waters) was born, from the Shining One (was born likewise) the Purusa. Being born (from the Shining One) he extended beyond the world, behind and also before.

6. When the gods, with the Purusa as oblation,[16] extended (performed) the (cosmic) sacrifice, Spring became the butter for it, Summer the firewood, Autumn the oblation.

7. They consecrated on the sacred grass this sacrifice, (namely) the Purusa, born in the beginning. With him the gods sacrificed, the Sadhyas,[17] and the Seers.

8. From this sacrifice, offered as whole-offering, the ghee-mixture[18] (the juice that flowed off) was collected; it made these animals—those of the air, of the jungle, and of the village.

9. From this sacrifice, offered as whole-offering, the stanzas of praise (the Rigveda) and the melodies (Samaveda) were produced; the meters were produced therefrom, the sacrificial formulas (Yajurveda) were produced therefrom.

10. Therefrom were produced horses, and whatever animals have (cutting-) teeth on both jaws. Cattle were produced therefrom, therefrom were born goats and sheep.

11. When they divided the Purusa (as the victim at the cosmic sacrifice), into how many parts did they separate him? What did his mouth become? What his two arms? What are declared to be his two thighs, his two feet?

12. The Brahman (priestly caste) was his mouth, his two arms became the Rajanya (warrior caste); his two thighs are the Vaisya (artisan caste), from his two feet the Sudra (serf caste) was produced.

13. The moon sprang from his thought-organ, the sun was produced from his eye; from his mouth Indra (war-god and soma-drinker) and Agni (the Fire-god), from his breath Vayu (the wind) was produced.

14. From his navel arose the atmosphere, from his head the heaven evolved; from his two feet the earth, from his ear the directions. Thus they fashioned the worlds.

16. **oblation:** offering (to a deity).

17. **Sadhyas:** ancient gods or demigods.

18. **ghee:** a clarified butter, used in religious rituals.

15. Seven were his surrounding sticks (at the burnt-offering), thrice seven were made the pieces of kindling wood, when the gods, extending (performing) the (cosmic) sacrifice, bound the Purusa as the victim.

16. With offering the gods offered the offering; these were the first (holy) institutions. Verily these powers have followed up to heaven, where are the Sadhya-gods of old.

10.129

1. Non-existent there was not, existent there was not then. There was not the atmospheric space, nor the vault beyond. What stirred, where, and in whose control? Was there water, a deep abyss?

2. Nor death nor immortality (mortals nor immortals) was there then; there was no distinction of night or day. That One breathed without breath by inner power; than it verily there was nothing else further.

3. Darkness there was, hidden by darkness, in the beginning; an undistinguished ocean was This All. What generative principle was enveloped by emptiness—by the might of (its own) fervour That One was born.

4. Desire (creative, or perhaps sacrificial, impulse) arose then in the beginning, which was the first seed of thought. The (causal) connection (*bandhu*) of the existent the sages found in the non-existent, searching with devotion in their hearts.

5. Straight across was stretched the (dividing-)cord of them (i.e. of the following); below (what) was there? above (what) was there? Seed-bearers (male forces) there were, strengths (female forces) there were; (female) innate power below, (male) impellent force above.[19]

6. Who truly knows? Who shall here proclaim it—whence they were produced, whence this creation? The gods (arose) on this side (later), by the creation of this (empiric world, to which the gods belong); then who knows whence it came into being?

7. This creation, whence it came into being, whether it was established, or whether not—he who is its overseer in the highest heaven, he verily knows, or perchance he knows not.

---

19. A suggestion that the world was created by some sort of cosmic intercourse between male powers and female powers. But, as Edgerton suggests, verses 6 and 7 strongly imply that the poet feels that he has gone too far. See *Beginnings of Indian Philosophy*, p. 73. See also Abinash Chandra Bose, *Hymns from the Vedas* (New York: Asia Publishing House, 1966), pp. 303–305.

Source 2 from The Torah: A Modern Commentary *(New York: Union of American Hebrew Congregations, 1981), pp. 18–20, 29–30, 116–117.*

2. From the First Book of Moses, called Genesis

CHAPTER 1

1] When God began to create the heaven and the earth—2] the earth being un-formed and void, with darkness over the surface of the deep[20] and a wind[21] from God sweeping over the water—3] God said, "Let there be light"; and there was light.   4] God saw that the light was good, and God separated the light from the darkness.   5] God called the light Day, and the darkness He called Night. And there was evening and there was morning, a first day.

6] God said, "Let there be an expanse in the midst of the water, that it may separate water from water."   7] God made the expanse, and it separated the water which was below the expanse from the water which was above the ex-panse. And it was so.   8] God called the expanse Sky. And there was evening, and there was morning, a second day.

9] God said, "Let the water below the sky be gathered into one area, that the dry land may appear." And it was so.   10] God called the dry land Earth, and the gathering of waters He called Seas. And God saw that this was good.   11] And God said, "Let the earth sprout vegegation: seed-bearing plants, fruit trees of every kind on earth that bear fruit with the seed in it." And it was so.   12] The earth brought forth vegetation: seed-bearing plants of every kind, and trees of every kind bearing fruit with the seed in it. And God saw that this was good.   13] And there was evening and there was morning, a third day.

14] God said, "Let there be lights in the expanse of the sky to separate day from night; they shall serve as signs for the set times—the days and the years;   15] and they shall serve as lights in the expanse of the sky to shine upon the earth." And it was so.   16] God made the two great lights, the greater light to dominate the day and the lesser light to dominate the night, and the stars.   17] And God set them in the expanse of the sky to shine upon the earth,   18] to dominate the day and the night, and to separate light from darkness. And God saw that this was good.   19] And there was evening and there was morning, a fourth day.

20] God said, "Let the waters bring forth swarms of living creatures, and birds that fly above the earth across the expanse of the sky."   21] God created

---

20. Some Hebraic scholars point out that this phrase ("surface of the deep") echoes a "Mesopotamian creation story where it is told that heaven and earth were formed from the car-cass of the sea dragon, Tiamat." *The Torah: A Modern Commentary*, p. 18.

21. **wind:** also translated as "spirit."

the great sea monsters, and all the living creatures of every kind that creep, which the waters brought forth in swarms; and all the winged birds of every kind. And God saw that this was good.   22] God blessed them, saying, "Be fertile and increase, fill the waters in the seas, and let the birds increase on the earth."   23] And there was evening and there was morning, a fifth day.

24] God said, "Let the earth bring forth every kind of living creature: cattle, creeping things, and wild beasts of every kind." And it was so.   25] God made wild beasts of every kind and cattle of every kind, and all kinds of creeping things of the earth. And God saw that this was good.   26] And God said, "Let us make man in our image, after our likeness. They shall rule the fish of the sea, the birds of the sky, the cattle, the whole earth, and all the creeping things that creep on earth."   27] And God created man in His image, in the image of God He created him; male and female He created them.   28] God blessed them and God said to them, "Be fertile and increase, fill the earth and master it; and rule the fish of the sea, the birds of the sky, and all the living things that creep on earth."

29] God said, "See, I give you every seed-bearing plant that is upon all the earth, and every tree that has seed-bearing fruit; they shall be yours for food.   30] And to all the animals on land, to all the birds of the sky, and to everything that creeps on earth, in which there is the breath of life, [I give] all the green plants for food." And it was so.[22]   31] And God saw all that He had made, and found it very good. And there was evening and there was morning, the sixth day.

CHAPTER 2

1] The heaven and the earth were finished, and all their array.   2] On the seventh day God finished the work which He had been doing, and He ceased on the seventh day from all the work which He had done.   3] And God blessed the seventh day and declared it holy, because on it God ceased from all the work of creation which He had done.

4] Such is the story of heaven and earth when they were created.

When the LORD God made earth and heaven—5] when no shrub of the field was yet on earth and no grasses of the field had yet sprouted, because the LORD God had not sent rain upon the earth and there was no man to till the soil,   6] but a flow would well up from the ground and water the whole surface of the earth—7] the LORD God formed man from the dust of the earth. He blew into his nostrils the breath of life, and man became a living being.

8] The LORD God planted a garden in Eden, in the east, and placed there the man whom He had formed.   9] And from the ground the LORD God caused to grow every tree that was pleasing to the sight and good for food, with the tree

---

22. Many biblical scholars assert that humans and other animals were herbivores (exclusively vegetarian) until after the Flood, when they became omnivores (eating all kinds of food, including the flesh of other animals). See Genesis 9:3 and Isaiah 11:7.

of life in the middle of the garden, and the tree of knowledge of good and bad. . . .

15] The LORD God took the man and placed him in the garden of Eden, to till it and tend it.   **16]** And the LORD God commanded the man, saying, "Of every tree of the garden you are free to eat;   **17]** but as for the tree of knowledge of good and bad, you must not eat of it; for as soon as you eat of it, you shall die."[23]

18] The LORD God said, "It is not good for man to be alone; I will make a fitting helper for him."   **19]** And the LORD God formed out of the earth all the wild beasts and all the birds of the sky, and brought them to the man to see what he would call them; and whatever the man called each living creature, that would be its name.   **20]** And the man gave names to all the cattle and to the birds of the sky and to all the wild beasts; but for Adam no fitting helper was found.   **21]** So the LORD God cast a deep sleep upon the man; and, while he slept, He took one of his ribs and closed up the flesh at that spot.   **22]** And the LORD God fashioned the rib that He had taken from the man into a woman; and He brought her to the man.   **23]** Then the man said, "This one at last / Is bone of my bones / And flesh of my flesh. / This one shall be called Woman, / For from man was she taken."   **24]** Hence a man leaves his father and mother and clings to his wife, so that they become one flesh.

[*Disobeying God's command, Adam and Eve ate the forbidden fruit, were cursed by God, and were banished from the Garden. Their first two children were Cain and Abel. Out of jealousy, Cain murdered Abel and was even further banished. Adam and Eve had many more children. After several generations, humans had become corrupt, and God determined to punish them by flooding the land. He warned righteous Noah, who gathered his family and all species in an ark, which survived the flood. Many generations later, people attempted to build a tower to reach heaven, but were confounded by God who caused them to begin speaking different languages. Many generations later, God appeared to Abram, offering to make a covenant (contract) with him.*]

CHAPTER 17

1] When Abram was ninety-nine years old, the LORD appeared to Abram and said to him, "I am El Shaddai.[24] Walk in My ways and be blameless.   **2]** I will establish My covenant between Me and you, and I will make you exceedingly numerous."

3] Abram threw himself on his face, as God spoke to him further,   **4]** "As for Me, this is My covenant with you: You shall be the father of a multitude of

---

23. Given the fact that Adam did not die immediately on eating the forbidden fruit, perhaps a better translation might be "you shall lose your immortality."

24. **El Shaddai:** God Almighty.

nations.   5] And you shall no longer be called Abram, but your name shall be Abraham, for I make you the father of a multitude of nations.   6] I will make you exceedingly fertile, and make nations of you; and kings shall come forth from you.   7] I will maintain My covenant between Me and you, and your offspring to come, as an everlasting covenant throughout the ages, to be God to you and to your offspring to come.   8] I give the land you sojourn in to you and your offspring to come, all the land of Canaan, as an everlasting possession. I will be their God."

9] God further said to Abraham, "As for you, you and your offspring to come throughout the ages shall keep My covenant.   10] Such shall be the covenant between Me and you and your offspring to follow which you shall keep: every male among you shall be circumcised.   11] You shall circumcise the flesh of your foreskin, and that shall be the sign of the covenant between Me and you.   12] And throughout the generations, every male among you shall be circumcised at the age of eight days. As for the homeborn slave and the one bought from an outsider who is not of your offspring,   13] they must be circumcised, homeborn and purchased alike. Thus shall My covenant be marked in your flesh as an everlasting pact.   14] And if any male who is uncircumcised fails to circumcise the flesh of his foreskin, that person shall be cut off from his kin; he has broken My covenant."

15] And God said to Abraham, "As for your wife Sarai, you shall not call her Sarai, but her name shall be Sarah.   16] I will bless her; indeed, I will give you a son by her. I will bless her so that she shall give rise to nations; rulers of peoples shall issue from her."   17] Abraham threw himself on his face and laughed, as he said to himself, "Can a child be born to a man a hundred years old, or can Sarah bear a child at ninety?"   18] And Abraham said to God, "Oh that Ishmael might live by Your favor!"   19] God said, "Nevertheless, Sarah your wife shall bear you a son, and you shall name him Isaac; and I will maintain My covenant with him as an everlasting covenant for his offspring to come.   20] As for Ishmael, I have heeded you. I hereby bless him. I will make him fertile and exceedingly numerous. He shall be the father of twelve chieftains, and I will make of him a great nation.   21] But My covenant I will maintain with Isaac, whom Sarah shall bear to you at this season next year."   22] And when He was done speaking with him, God was gone from Abraham.

23] Then Abraham took his son Ishmael, and all his homeborn slaves and all those he had bought, every male in Abraham's household, and he circumcised the flesh of their foreskins on that very day, as God had spoken to him.   24] Abraham was ninety-nine years old when he circumcised the flesh of his foreskin,   25] and his son Ishmael was thirteen years old when he was circumcised in the flesh of his foreskin.   26] Thus Abraham and his son Ishmael were circumcised on that very day;   27] and all his household, his homeborn slaves and those that had been bought from outsiders, were circumcised with him. . . .

Source 3 from Cary F. Baynes, trans., The I Ching [Yijing], or Book of Changes, *3d ed.*
(Princeton: Princeton University Press, 1967), pp. 280, 283–287, 293–296, 328–335.

3. From Yijing, Commentary
on the Appended Judgments

Heaven is high, the earth is low; thus the Creative and the Receptive are determined. In correspondence with this difference between low and high, inferior and superior places are established.

Movement and rest have their definite laws;[25] according to these, firm and yielding lines are differentiated.

Events follow definite trends, each according to its nature. Things are distinguished from one another in definite classes. In this way good fortune and misfortune come about. In the heavens phenomena take form; on earth shapes take form. In this way change and transformation become manifest.

Therefore the eight trigrams succeed one another by turns, as the firm and the yielding displace each other.[26]

Things are aroused by thunder and lightning; they are fertilized by wind and rain. Sun and moon follow their courses and it is now hot, now cold.

The way of the Creative brings about the male.

The way of the Receptive brings about the female.

The Creative knows the great beginnings.

The Receptive completes the finished things.

The Creative knows through the easy.

The Receptive can do things through the simple.

What is easy, is easy to know; what is simple, is easy to follow. He who is easy to know attains fealty. He who is easy to follow attains works. He who possesses attachment can endure for long; he who possesses works can become great. To endure is the disposition of the sage; greatness is the field of action of the sage.

By means of the easy and the simple we grasp the laws of the whole world. When the laws of the whole world are grasped, therein lies perfection. . . .

The Book of Changes contains the measure of heaven and earth; therefore it enables us to comprehend the tao[27] of heaven and earth and its order.

Looking upward, we contemplate with its help the signs in the heavens; looking down, we examine the lines of the earth. Thus we come to know the circumstances of the dark and the light. Going back to the beginnings of things and pursuing them to the end, we come to know the lessons of birth

---

25. *The Book of Changes* is concerned primarily with understanding and predicting what appears to be constant and random change. ("Everything flows on and on like this river, without pause, day and night."—K'ung Fu-tze)

26. **displace each other:** an example of cyclical change.

27. **tao:** the way.

and of death. The union of seed and power produces all things; the escape of the soul brings about change. Through this we come to know the conditions of outgoing and returning spirits.

Since in this way man comes to resemble heaven and earth, he is not in conflict with them. His wisdom embraces all things, and his tao brings order into the whole world; therefore he does not err. He is active everywhere but does not let himself be carried away. He rejoices in heaven and has knowledge of fate, therefore he is free of care. He is content with his circumstances and genuine in his kindness, therefore he can practice love.

In it are included the forms and the scope of everything in the heavens and on earth, so that nothing escapes it. In it all things everywhere are completed, so that none is missing. Therefore by means of it we can penetrate the tao of day and night, and so understand it. Therefore the spirit is bound to no one place, nor the Book of Changes to any one form. . . .

When in early antiquity Pao Hsi [Baoxi][28] ruled the world, he looked upward and contemplated the images in the heavens; he looked downward and contemplated the patterns on earth. He contemplated the markings of birds and beasts and the adaptations to the regions. He proceeded directly from himself and indirectly from objects. Thus he invented the eight trigrams in order to enter into connection with the virtues of the light of the gods and to regulate the conditions of all beings.

He made knotted cords and used them for nets and baskets in hunting and fishing. He probably took this from the hexagram of THE CLINGING.

When Pao Hsi's clan was gone, there sprang up the clan of the Divine Husbandman.[29] He split a piece of wood for a plowshare and bent a piece of wood for the plow handle, and taught the whole world the advantage of laying open the earth with a plow. He probably took this from the hexagram of INCREASE.

When the sun stood at midday, he held a market. He caused the people of the earth to come together and collected the wares of the earth. They exchanged these with one another, then returned home, and each thing found its place. Probably he took this from the hexagram of BITING THROUGH.

When the clan of the Divine Husbandman was gone, there sprang up the clans of the Yellow Emperor, of Yao, and of Shun. They brought continuity into their alterations, so that the people did not grow weary. They were divine in the transformations they wrought, so that the people were content. When one change had run its course, they altered. (Through alteration they achieved continuity.) Through continuity they achieved duration. Therefore: "They were blessed by heaven. Good fortune. Nothing that does not further."

---

28. More commonly known as Fuxi (ca. 2953–2838 B.C.E.), who is credited with constructing the eight trigrams based on cracks on a tortoise shell, from which was developed the system of Yijing.
29. **Shennong:** the teacher of agriculture to humans.

The Yellow Emperor, Yao, and Shun allowed the upper and lower garments to hang down, and the world was in order. They probably took this from the hexagrams of THE CREATIVE and THE RECEPTIVE.

They scooped out tree trunks for boats and they hardened wood in the fire to make oars. The advantage of boats and oars lay in providing means of communication. (They reached distant parts, in order to benefit the whole world.) They probably took this from the hexagram of DISPERSION.

They tamed the ox and yoked the horse. Thus heavy loads could be transported and distant regions reached, for the benefit of the world. They probably took this from the hexagram of FOLLOWING.

They introduced double gates and night watchmen with clappers, in order to deal with robbers. They probably took this from the hexagram of ENTHUSIASM.

They split wood and made a pestle of it. They made a hollow in the ground for a mortar. The use of the mortar and pestle was of benefit to all mankind. They probably took this from the hexagram of PREPONDERANCE OF THE SMALL.

They strung a piece of wood for a bow and hardened pieces of wood in the fire for arrows. The use of bow and arrow is to keep the world in fear. They probably took this from the hexagram of OPPOSITION.

In primitive times people dwelt in caves and lived in forests. The holy men of a later time made the change to buildings. At the top was a ridgepole, and sloping down from it there was a roof, to keep off wind and rain. They probably took this from the hexagram of THE POWER OF THE GREAT.

In primitive times the dead were buried by covering them thickly with brushwood and placing them in the open country, without burial mound or grove of trees. The period of mourning had no definite duration. The holy men of a later time introduced inner and outer coffins instead. They probably took this from the hexagram of PREPONDERANCE OF THE GREAT.

In primitive times people knotted cords in order to govern. The holy men of a later age introduced written documents instead, as a means of governing the various officials and supervising the people. They probably took this from the hexagram of BREAKTHROUGH.

QUESTIONS TO CONSIDER

One of the first truths that historians come to appreciate is that people from different cultures not only think differently about various subjects (such as life, death, and cosmology) but also use different thought patterns when attempting to solve a problem. Thus we must not only determine *what* people of the past think, but also *how* they think.[30] Accounts or inter-

30. The same can be said about the study of writing itself. For example, fewer than half of the systems of writing that exist (or are known to have existed) begin at the top left of a page and move from left to right, then drop down one line and repeat the process. Some peoples' systems require writing right to left, some vertical (either top to bottom or bottom to top), some circular, and a few (like the Aztec script of Central America) have no particular form at all.

pretations of creation are excellent sources from which to deduce not only how a particular culture thinks about creation, but how it thinks in general.

The first thing that we discover about Vedic culture is that it has not one creation account but several. In Rig Veda 10.72, the creation of the universe is compared to the birth of a human child. Who is Aditi, and what function does she perform? But how was Aditi created (see verses 2–5)? Note that these verses have a cyclical pattern: Aditi is born and gives birth and in turn is born. This cyclical thought pattern would become a key component of Hindu philosophy (Westerners are most familiar with it in the Hindu doctrines of *karma* and reincarnation—see R.V. 10.81, verse 1).

R.V. 10.81 is interesting for two reasons. First, this creation account, unlike 10.72, is quasi-monotheistic (monotheism is belief in one god), in this case called the All-maker. But might that All-maker in fact be Aditi herself (both are feminine)? More interesting are the questions asked in verses 2 and 4. If originally there was nothing (10.72 called it the "Non-existent"), then where did the materials to make the world come from? Does the hymn's composer answer those questions?

In R.V. 10.90 the universe itself (Purusa) is masculine, and encompasses everything, including the gods. Note, however, the cyclical thinking again in verse 5, and in verse 6 in which Purusa (the universe) is himself sacrificed by the gods to create all other things. What is the implication about how humans are to honor this creation process? How does this creation account support and justify the Vedic caste system?

In R.V. 10.129, the author begins by emphasizing the nothingness that preceded creation. And then, mysteriously, That One was born. But what role (if any) did That One play in creation? What about the male forces and female forces? Where did those forces come from? What feelings does the author convey in verses 6 and 7?

The narrative of creation in the Torah is a familiar one to Jews, Christians, and Muslims, and is quite different from the accounts in the Rig Veda. Almost immediately, however, we see that we are confronted not with *one* creation account in the Torah but with *two*. Notice that Genesis 1:1 through 2:4 contains one account and immediately following, Genesis 2:5–24 is *another* account, in some ways markedly different. In your view, what are the principal differences between the two creation accounts in Genesis? Can you explain why there are two accounts? Why do you think that both accounts were included and have remained stable fixtures in Genesis for over 2,700 years?

In the Torah, it is extremely clear that the Israelites (and the later Christians and Muslims) were strict monotheists. Moreover, the one god of the Torah exhibits human traits: intent, desire, love, satisfaction, anger, and others, and is given a voice that speaks to many people. And even more important, God has made some specific promises to and demands on the humans He created, most especially the ancient Israelites (the "Chosen People," as explicitly stated in Genesis 17:2). What were those demands? What was the covenant?

As opposed to the Torah, the Yijing not only lacks an account of a divinely inspired or god-caused creation, but it also seems almost unconcerned about these questions at all. Gods do appear (Heaven, the high god, is most prominent), but more as abstract models for humans to emulate than as powers to worship or obey. Instead, the Yijing is a search for order, for patterns that can be discovered in the heavens and then later on earth—the patterns of birth and of life and of death.

How can The Creative and The Receptive be seen in the universe? Can any patterns be discerned and applied to the world? In this way "man comes to resemble heavens and earth, he is not in conflict with them." One can see day and night (and day again) in the heavens. To what could you compare that cycle on earth?

How is Pao Hsi (Baoxi) treated in the Yijing? Obviously, he was not a god, but was nicknamed "the inventor" by millions in later years. What did Pao Hsi "invent"? The remainder of the excerpt traces a line of creative leaders or sages. What were their contributions? How did they "discover" these things? What was the final (the highest) gift of the holy men? Finally, how did those who venerated the Yijing think about creation?

EPILOGUE

The development of writing held out many advantages for a culture. Important commercial agreements (water rights, real estate titles, merchant contracts, bills of sale) could be recorded and handed down with considerably more precision, often giving the ownership of property and goods more security and status. Laws and proclamations also could be codified, read in public, and enforced with more regularity. Finally, works of religion, philosophy, and literature could bind a people together, give them a sense of their past and of mission, and could shape and mold their collective thought.

For these reasons, a people's written accounts of creation were never merely interpretations of the origins of the universe, the world, and human beings. The Torah revealed the Jews' (and later Christians' and Muslims') belief in a purposeful deity who created humans for a specific purpose and made a covenantal agreement with Abraham and his descendants that required worship and obeying God's laws in return for God's blessing and protection. Not only did the Rig Veda strengthen Indian thinking about the cyclical laws that governed birth, life, and death, but it also legitimized the Aryan caste system of priests, warriors, peasants, and serfs. The Yijing called Chinese to meditation about the interrelationships of all things—past, present, and future. Indeed, these creation accounts as well as all others (and there are literally dozens) contain much more than a simple relating of origins.

Just as writing offered cultures that possessed it certain advantages, so also the ability to read and write elevated certain individuals, elite groups, and classes *within* a culture. To begin with, it was these people who had the power to make and enforce laws, to mold and sanction beliefs, and to exercise authority over the illiterate. As soon as a particular group had established a political or religious canon,[31] its next step often was to punish those who violated or opposed the established orthodoxy.

There is little doubt that literate elites tried to limit the spread of writing. But ultimately such restraint was almost impossible. The invention of the printing press in the mid-fifteenth century in Mainz (Germany) made it possible for writing to reach an almost limitless audience.[32] As a result, literacy in Western Europe increased dramatically. Once political and religious canons could be read by many, however, disputes erupted, often over their "proper" interpretation. Yet once Pandora's box had been opened, it was nearly impossible to close it again.

Ultimately, widespread literacy strengthened cultures in which it occurred and gave them great advantages over those in which literacy was more limited or confined. In the long run, near-universal literacy tended to support political stability and continuity, in part because of earlier political revolts and changes that, ironically, literacy often had instigated, and in part because literate cultures could develop and disseminate technology and economic systems that more often led toward economic abundance. It may be no accident that in the world's most prosperous economies (Germany, Japan, the United States, the Scandinavian nations, the United Kingdom, France, and the like) illiteracy is negligible and political stability is prevalent, whereas in the world's poorest nations (such as Chad, Niger, Afghanistan, and Bangladesh), illiteracy is rampant and political systems are extremely unstable.[33]

It would take centuries before the relationship between widespread literacy, economic abundance, and political stability would be fully understood. And yet as early as the prophet Muhammad, people appreciated the fact that writing meant power, and that the pen (or carving tool or stylus or quill or brush or whatever writing instrument) could be mightier than the sword.

31. **canon:** code of law.

32. In fact, printing, movable type, and paper all had been invented in China over five hundred years earlier.

33. 1980 statistics show Chad with an astounding 95 percent illiteracy, Niger with 94 percent, Afghanistan with 88 percent, and Bangladesh with 78 percent.

CHAPTER FOUR

REPRESENTING THE HUMAN FORM

(2600 B.C.E.–600 C.E.)

In the last chapter, you explored the role that writing and written texts played in shaping the world-views of several early civilizations. As important as they are, however, written texts are only one of the types of sources available for learning about early cultures. We can also use artistic and archaeological evidence, in the same way that we use such sources for information about preliterate cultures. Because so few people in early cultures were able to read, artistic evidence provides us with sources that were usually accessible to more people than written texts.

Artistic evidence has been used to answer a wide range of historical questions about early civilizations. Some of these are technical: What level of engineering skill in a culture would enable it to construct certain types of buildings? What chemical or other technological processes did a culture use in the production of writing materials, metal work, or other products? Some are economic: What proportion of a culture's wealth went into the production of what types of artistic products? Who paid for and benefited from artistic production? Some questions are aesthetic: How skillful were certain artists? How would one describe an individual artist's or a civilization's style, particularly in comparison to that of others? Some are cultural: Why were certain subjects depicted, and depicted the way they were? What did a civilization view as important enough to include in its permanent visual record?

The questions that we might term aesthetic or cultural are perhaps the most tricky for historians or art historians, particularly if they involve comparisons between civilizations. Assessing the skill of an artist requires not only appreciating the technical aspects of production, but also understanding ideas about the purpose of artistic products as well as the cultural context in which the artist worked. We may be able to say immediately that we "like" or "don't like" an artistic product, but we certainly need information on the culture in which it was created to assess its meaning and use it as historical evidence. It is often difficult to gain much understanding of a culture from a few pieces of artistic evidence, particularly when we view them, not where they were intended to be displayed, but on a gallery wall or in a museum case. Thus using artistic evidence is in some ways a circular process: we learn about a culture from the available written and artistic sources, then use that background to analyze a single piece of art, which may in turn make us change or refine our ideas about the written record or other artistic creations, and eventually may lead to new conclusions about the culture as a whole.

Analysis of individual pieces of artistic evidence is thus an important

tool for historians. It is often difficult to view pieces in their original setting—they may have been removed, or we may not be able to travel to distant lands—so our only access to such evidence is via museums or in books of reproductions. In this chapter we use such reproductions of sculpture and painting to investigate three different early cultures: Egypt in the Old and New Kingdom (2600–1200 B.C.E.), Archaic and Classical Greece (600–350 B.C.E.), and Buddhist India (200 B.C.E.–600 C.E.). In all three of these cultures, one of the most common subjects for artistic presentation was the human form. Our questions for this chapter, questions that are aesthetic and cultural, focus on this one subject: How do these cultures depict the human form? What do these depictions tell us about the values of these cultures?

BACKGROUND

Though most historians and art historians regard some knowledge of a culture as important for an understanding of its artistic products, there are those who discount such a prerequisite. Some people, though usually not art historians, assert that aesthetic judgments are not culturally or historically based, but derive from universal standards, so that "good" art, or at least a masterpiece, is recognizable to all. Others contend that knowing about a culture shapes one's impressions too strongly, making it

impossible to view an artistic product objectively. To them what is most important is seeing with a fresh eye, and they stress that to use visual evidence correctly, we must both sharpen our powers of observation, and also *unlearn* previous ideas about art.

You may agree with either or both of these arguments and may wish to test them with this chapter. To do this, turn immediately to the Evidence and look carefully at each sculpture or painting. Record your general impressions and also write down your initial responses to the central questions for the chapter. (This will enable you later to assess how much even a slight understanding of a culture may alter your viewing.) Do any of these impressions or answers come from what you already know about any one of these cultures, or do they come solely from looking at the art?

As we turn now to background information, we begin with characteristics common to all of the sources. For each of the three cultures, the sculptures and paintings are arranged roughly in chronological order, though they span different amounts of time. All the pieces served some sort of religious function and come from either tombs or religious buildings such as temples. All were created in cultures that believed in *anthropomorphic* gods; in other words, their gods were conceptualized in human form so that human form and divine power were linked. (The Egyptians had other gods that were thought of as animals or as part animal and part human.) In all three cultures, making an image of a god and honoring that image were seen as meritorious, and thus the creative process was linked to spiritual or religious values.

In ancient Egypt, art was an integral aspect of religion, with much of the art that has survived made not for human eyes but for the inside of tombs, part of the Egyptian cult of the dead. The Egyptians had an extremely strong belief in the afterlife, an afterlife that was very much like life in this world and that required both physical objects and funeral rituals to attain. In the Archaic Period and the Old Kingdom (about 3100–2200 B.C.E.), only the pharaoh was regarded as capable of achieving a full afterlife. Nobles built their tombs as

close to his as possible, pledging in carved inscriptions to continue their allegiance to the pharaoh after death; if he engaged their services, they, too, might achieve eternal life. By the Middle Kingdom (ca. 2050–1800 B.C.E.), eternal life was viewed as a hope for all, as long as the body was preserved through mummification and the spirit led to Osiris, the god of the dead, through the proper mortuary ceremonies. Funerary objects and statues or paintings of the deceased all helped lead him or her to Osiris by depicting the deceased in rituals that assured eternal life. Throughout all periods of ancient Egyptian history, the statue of a deceased person in a tomb or temple was regarded as a home for his or her *ka,* the spirit or immortal alter ego, which entered the sculpture during a funeral ritual. The *ka* within the sculpture made the deceased a participant in festivities held in the temple even after death. Though we might view this preoccupation with death and the afterlife as morbid and reflecting a rejection of life, it does not seem to have been so for the ancient Egyptians whose portraits and tomb paintings have been preserved; they enjoyed their life here on earth so much that they simply wanted to continue it after death.

Because most statues were regarded as substitutes for a particular deceased person, and paintings were to show the deceased involved in activities or rituals, it was extremely important that depictions be recognized as the correct individual. Egyptian artists achieved this objective not by individualistic portraiture of a physical likeness, but by painting or inscribing the name on the statue or painting. The portrait itself could then be used to depict stereotyped qualities: plumpness represented wealth and well-being; signs of age, maturity and wisdom; a trim build, confidence and vitality. Egyptian art also sought to link the impermanent individual clearly to the permanent office or occupation, so it was important to include unmistakable symbols of office—a scribe was always portrayed with a scroll, and the pharaoh with the crown of Upper and Lower Egypt and a crooked staff. By the Middle Kingdom there was some attempt to individualize facial features, but the bodies remained stock types and the faces continued to be idealized.

The emphasis on permanence emerges in many aspects of Egyptian art, most noticeably perhaps in the lack of change over thousands of years in the basic style of portraying the human body. The deceased was rendered motionless, in standardized standing or sitting poses, so that there was no indication of change. Throughout Egyptian history, the pharaoh was regarded and portrayed as divine, though there were slight variations on this, with the emphasis in wall paintings sometimes on his handling of earthly problems and participation in earthly activities, and at other times on his role as executor of divine will and participation in celestial ceremonies. After every period of turbulence and violence, such as an invasion or a civil war, there was a return to the old artistic styles, a deliberate *archaism.*

Egyptian artists did not attempt to portray scenes or figures as they appeared to the eye, but as they actually were, what we might call a depiction of their essence. Thus individual figures are not foreshortened or drawn from one particular vantage point, for one's vantage point might easily change; instead they are shown in a way that presents many sides or angles at once. The most famous example of this is the Egyptian way of depicting the human body, which you can see most clearly in Sources 2 and 4. The Egyptian way of setting elements in a scene is also one that does not reproduce a visual image, but reflects the content of what is being represented. Thus, artists use what is sometimes termed an *aspective* rather than a *perspective* approach, basing the size of the figures not on their placement in the scene, but on their importance in the social hierarchy.

Many of the earliest Greek depictions of the human form were also from tombs or temples, the male *kouros* and female *kore* figures. These were not portraits or ceremonial substitutes for the deceased the way Egyptian tomb sculptures were, but were rather erected in memory of an individual or by a living person to fulfill a vow to the gods. These large stone sculptures began to be made in Greece beginning in the mid-seventh century B.C.E., and many art historians have linked them stylistically with much earlier Egyptian statuary. Unlike in Egypt, however, the portrayal of the human body in Greece changed rapidly over the next two hundred years, with sculptors basing their work more and more on actual human anatomy. This concern with the way that the body actually looked can also be observed in Greek painting. Unfortunately most large-scale Greek paintings have been lost, but Greek pottery was frequently decorated with painted figures and scenes that allow us to see human forms in a setting.

Along with the kore and kouros figures, Greek statuary from the Archaic period (about 630–480 B.C.E) also portrayed gods and mythological heroes who are sometimes part divine and sometimes fully human. Because the gods bore no physical sign of their divinity, it is often difficult to tell exactly who is being depicted unless the subject is accompanied by a standard symbol such as the sea god Poseidon's trident or the hero Herakles' lion skin. Gods and heroes continued to be the most common subject matter for Greek sculpture in the Classical period (about 480–330 B.C.E.), with actual historical events shown only rarely, though mythological events appear frequently, especially in reliefs.

Like the Egyptians, the Greeks saw their gods as having all the bodily qualities that humans did, but qualities that were perfected because they did not die and did not require food or sleep to sustain their bodies. The gods feasted, but did not need to eat; they bled when wounded, but did not die. Gods could also change their bodily shape at will, and often disguised themselves either to achieve an end or to shield the radiance of their bodies from human observers (humans who looked on a god directly in Greek mythology generally died). The mythological heroes had died, but were thought to have joined the undying gods in a type of "eternity," an afterlife that consisted of eternal feasting and banqueting rather than the variety of activities characteristic of the Egyptian afterlife. Whether normal humans could aspire to such an afterlife is unclear, though at least those men who died in war were thought to have a chance. For most humans, the afterlife was a sort of shadowy existence in the underworld (Hades) neither good nor bad; correct funeral practices were important to allow one's psyche (usually translated as "soul" or "spirit") to go to Hades, but these were much less elaborate than those of the Egyptians and did not involve preservation of the body.

As mentioned above, Greek pottery often shows mythological scenes, but it also depicts everyday life—women weaving, men banqueting, people going in and out of doors. Some of its subjects are pornographic, showing men with prostitutes or gods and satyrs chasing nymphs. Because of such subject matter, pottery has traditionally been viewed as having no religious or ceremonial significance. This view has recently changed somewhat as scholars have recognized that, for example, the banqueting scenes depict not only the setting in which the pottery was actually used, but also envision a certain type of afterlife for those using it. The doors may not be simply entrances of houses, but also the gateway between this life and the next. The mythological scenes are not simply decorative, but are meant to reinforce cultural norms.

The Greek view of the human body was determined by philosophy as well as religion, particularly after the time of Plato (427–347 B.C.E.). Plato saw the human body as in some ways a microcosm of the universe (an idea that influenced Western thought until the time of the Renaissance), a universe that was itself a living creature. Both the body and the universe are material and perishable, but the soul is immortal, as is the perfect form of the universe and all that exists within it. For Plato these perfect forms, which are sometimes called "ideal types," were not simply mental constructs but had an existence somewhere and were actually more "real" than the transitory, material world around us. (The notion of ideal types, or idealism, has also been a long-lasting one in Western thought. It operates, for instance, in many people's understanding of such concepts as justice. Their concept of a just society comes not so much from observing societies that actually exist in the world as from abstract principles regarding what might be termed "ideal justice.") As a proponent of idealism, Plato scorned the attempts of the artists and sculptors who were his contemporaries to depict the human body based on visual observation. Plato thought the chief purpose of art was to represent eternal forms as understood by the soul, not to imitate fleeting external appearances. He praised Egyptian art for its elevated portrayals, and he regarded mathematical forms as the most beautiful because their beauty was absolute and not based on—or biased by—either intellectual or physical points of view.

In many ways, sculptors in India working within both Buddhist and Hindu traditions fit Plato's ideal better than did his Athenian contemporaries. Sculpture, in Indian religion and philosophy, is not to depict the physical body but to give concrete shape to an invisible spirit within the body. Indian artists sought to give visible form to the living principles within the body, conceptualized as breath (*prana*) and sap (*rasa*). *Prana* pushes against the walls of the body, making the skin appear taut and keeping the body erect, so that the muscles are less important. Indian sculpture does not aim to record the appearance or structure of the body, but instead to express the awareness of life within the body, of the breath that sustains and moves the body. Sculptors achieve this, not by looking at other bodies as models, but by feeling the breath and pulse of life within their own bodies and by meditating or contemplating. There is a link between the body and the natural world, which also has breath and sap. When a sculpture was completed, it was consecrated by a priest, given the breath of life. Then it was placed in a position within a temple where it could be seen, worshiped, and perhaps eventually copied, for the replication of images was considered auspicious.

Buddhist teachings did not reject earlier Indian ideas about art or the body, but built on them. The religious teachings generally termed Buddhism were first taught in India by

Siddhartha Gautama, a nobleman living in the sixth century B.C.E. who came to be known as the Buddha, or the Awakened One. Buddhist teachings are extremely complex, though at their heart is an emphasis on morality, meditation, and achieving wisdom. Part of the wisdom one strives to achieve is the understanding that there is nothing permanent, including the individual soul, and that the ideal state of being (*nirvana*) is a life that transcends individual desires. On achieving nirvana, an individual would become awakened to a transcendental eternal realm of being, that is, a buddha.

Over the centuries, many divisions developed within Buddhism, one of the most significant being a split beginning in the first century B.C.E. over how strictly one needed to follow the Buddhist path in order to achieve nirvana. Mahayana Buddhism taught that many people, not simply a small spiritual elite of monks, could become fully buddha, an idea that gave this branch of Buddhism a wide popular base. As it spread, Mahayana Buddhism absorbed a number of local deities, transforming them to fit with Buddhist ideas by turning them into guardians of the Buddha, or *bodhisattvas*. A bodhisattva is a being who has almost achieved nirvana but decides instead to turn away from this final, blissful, transcendental state to help others on their way to becoming buddha. Although bodhisattvas had human bodies, they were no longer subject to the physical limitations of human life and were often worshiped in their own right. Their

merits could be shared by their worshipers, and their intervention, combined with devotion, could allow the worshiper to achieve nirvana. The Buddha himself had been a bodhisattva in his earlier lives, and stories of his actions and exploits during these previous lives became an important part of Buddhist literature.

Though there was no explicit prohibition of portraying the Buddha as Buddha, there are no images of him until several centuries after his death; he was symbolized by an empty throne or a hemispheric mound containing a relic, termed a *stupa*. With the spread of Mahayana Buddhism, people became more devoted to Buddha's person and not simply his teachings, so they wanted physical likenesses. Images of the Buddha showed up first on coins and temple railings and, by the first century C.E., as free-standing sculpture. Sculptors adopted existing ideas about portraying the body to the portrayal of the Buddha's body, striving to produce a sacred image that both transcended and represented perfect human beauty. The links between the body and the natural world were stressed in the shapes of the Buddha's body parts, and a system of proportions was developed based on the height of the head or the breadth of the finger. These calculations for the correct proportions of the Buddha were based not on actual human anatomy, but on the magical properties of certain numbers, and they became the standard for images of the Buddha for centuries.

THE METHOD

The single most important method for using visual sources was stated at the beginning of the Background section—**look at them**. This may seem self-evident, and we may feel our "looking" skills are well-honed because of the visual culture of advertising and television in which we live. Too often, however, we view visual material as merely illustrations of a text (this is often how graphics are integrated into textbooks) and don't really look at the images themselves. To answer the first question in this chapter, turn to the Evidence (which you may already have done if you decided to do the pretest suggested in the Background section.) Look carefully at Sources 1 through 4, all of which present pharaohs and queens of Egypt. What do you notice most about these figures; in other words, what details stand out? What words would you use to describe the individuals as they are portrayed? How do their expression and stance sway your description? How would you compare the portrayal of humans with that of animals—for example, the birds in Source 2? How would you compare the portrayal of Queen Nefertari in Source 4 with that of the goddess Isis in the same tomb painting? How would you compare the depiction of the pharaoh Mycerinus in Source 1 with that of the pharaoh Ramesses II in Source 3? How is clothing depicted in these examples of Egyptian art?

Now look at the artistic evidence from Greece, Sources 5 through 9. What main differences do you see in the depiction of the human form in the kore and kouros figures from the early sixth century B.C.E., Sources 5 and 6? How would you compare these to the statues of the Egyptian pharaoh? Would you make any distinction in your comparisons between the body and the head? Judging by the vase painting in Source 7 and the sculpture in Source 8, what changes do you see in the representation of the human form over the next century? What differences do you see between the depiction of female and male forms in Source 7? Now look at Source 9, which is about one hundred years more recent than Source 8 and is one of the first depictions of the nude female form in Greek art. (Until this period, the only women depicted nude were prostitutes; even Aphrodite, the goddess of love and beauty, was shown clothed.) What words would you use to describe Aphrodite as she is shown here? Looking at Sources 8 and 9, what differences do you see in the way male and female bodies are depicted? How would you compare these depictions of the human body with those in Source 1?

Now look at the examples from India, Sources 10 through 13. What details stand out in these portrayals? How would you describe the body of the female deity (*yakshi*) in Source 10? How would you compare this with the female bodies portrayed in Egyptian and Greek art? Sources 11 and 12 show the Buddha. How does his body differ from the bodies in the other sources? How would you describe his expression and demeanor? How would you compare the treatment of clothing in these two sculptures with the treatment of clothing in Egyptian and Greek sculpture? Source 13 is a bodhisattva, usually identified as Vajrapani because he is holding a thunderbolt. (Bodhisattvas can often be identified only by items they wear or carry, for no names are inscribed on these sculptures. Both Egyptian tomb sculptures and Greek statues were mostly inscribed, but in Greece the inscriptions are often destroyed or missing, so that we identify them as well by their dress or other details.) How would you describe the bodhisattva's body? his stance? his clothing? How would you compare these with those of the Buddha? with those of a Greek male body such as the one in Source 8?

From looking at the Sources and considering questions like those suggested above, you can formulate your answer to the first question for this chapter: How do these three cultures depict the human form? The second question—what do these depictions tell us about the values of these cultures?—involves extrapolating from the sources and combining your observations with your previous knowledge of the cultures. Here you (or any historian) must be more speculative, for we generally can't know exactly how individuals living at the time a statue or painting was made looked at it, or how their view of the artist's intent differed from ours. We must also be especially careful, when using visual sources, to choose ones that are representative or typical rather than unusual. (On this issue you will have to trust our choice of evidence or do some further research in books of reproductions or museums in your area.)

These reservations apply, of course, just as much to historical arguments based on written sources as to those based on visual evidence, and in both cases the best method of historical interpretation is the same: stick as closely as possible to arguments that are based on the sources themselves. In this case, then, your exploration of the values of these cultures needs to be based primarily on the careful observations you have already made.

Think about your observations of the depiction of the body in Egypt. Whose bodies are shown? What does their stance or expression indicate were admirable qualities in such individuals? What does the similarity between the portrayals of the pharaoh over more than a thousand years indicate about Egyptian culture? What do the similarities between the depiction of Isis and Nefertari indicate about Egyptian ideas about the relationship between the human (or at least the royal) and the divine?

Next, think about the Greek art. Why might the depiction of the body become more anatomically accurate earlier than the head? Why might the Greeks have broken with the Egyptian pattern and portrayed men nude, even in scenes (such as the battle scene in Source 7) in which men were not normally naked? What might account for the differences in the portrayal of male and female nudes you noted in Sources 8 and 9? Though we generally think of nakedness as revealing, are there certain facts that nakedness obscures?

Now turn to the Indian art. What does Source 10 indicate about cultural attitudes toward the female body? How does this portrayal of a goddess differ from those of Egyptian or Greek female deities (Isis in Source 4 and Aphrodite in Source 9)? What does the Buddha's expression indicate about the qualities admired in a leader? How does this differ from the qualities suggested in the depictions of the Egyptian pharaohs and Greek heroes? What do the differences you have noted between the Buddha and the bodhisattva indicate about attitudes toward each of these revered individuals?

THE EVIDENCE

Source 1 from Harvard University–MFA Expedition. Courtesy, Museum of Fine Arts, Boston.

1. King Mycerinus and Queen Khamerernebti, from Funerary Temple near his Pyramid at Giza, ca. 2600 B.C.E.

2. Nebamum Hunting Birds, with his Wife and Servant, from his Tomb at Thebes, ca. 1400 B.C.E.

Source 3 from Hirmer Fotoarchiv.

3. Statues of King Ramesses II and his Wife, Queen Nefertari, at Luxor, ca. 1250 B.C.E.

The statue of Nefertari is much smaller than that of Ramesses; her head is just below his knee.

4. Wall Painting from Nefertari's Tomb near Thebes, ca. 1250 B.C.E.

The goddess Isis is holding an ankh—the symbol of life—to Nefertari's nostrils.

Source 5 from Archaeological Receipts Fund/National Archaeological Museum, Athens.

5. Anavyssos Kouros, Attica near Athens, ca. 525 B.C.E.

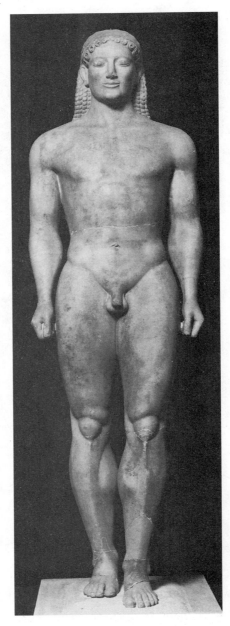

Source 6 from Archaeological Receipts Fund/Acropolis Museum, Athens.

6. Peplos Kore, Athens, ca. 530 B.C.E.

Source 7: Courtesy of the Trustees of the British Museum.

7. Theseus and the Amazons, from an Attic Red-figured Krater,[1] ca. 440 B.C.E.

1. **Krater:** a wide, two-handled bowl common in ancient Greece.

8. Polykleitos, *Doryphoros* or *"The Canon,"* ca. 440 B.C.E. (Roman copy)

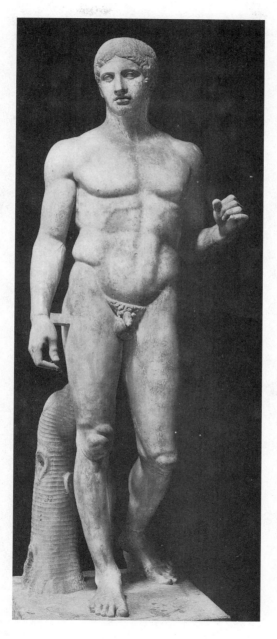

Source 9 from Biblioteca Apostolica Vaticana.

9. Praxiteles, *Aphrodite of Knidos,* ca. 340 B.C.E. (Roman copy)

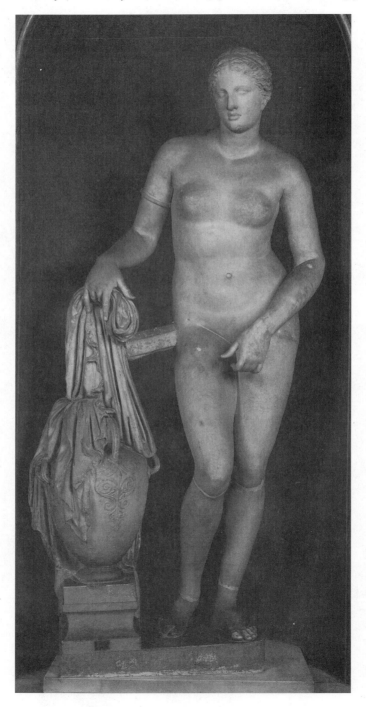

Source 10 from the Archaeological Survey of India.

10. Yakshi, from a Pillar at the Great Stupa of Bharhut, ca. 100 B.C.E.

Source 11: John C. Huntington.

11. Standing Buddha, from Gandhara, ca. 200 C.E.

Source 13 from the Metropolitan Museum of Art. L.1993.51.5. Lent by the Kronos Colletions.

13. Bodhisattva Vajrapani, Nepal, 6th or 7th century C.E.

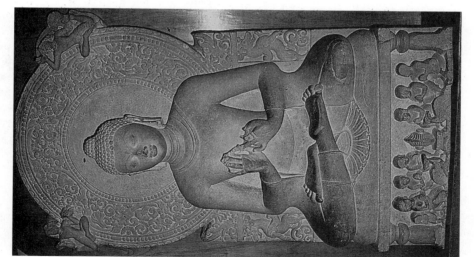

Source 12: Robert Fisher.

12. Preaching Buddha, from Sarnath, ca. 475 C.E.

QUESTIONS TO CONSIDER

As you examine the evidence for this chapter, you may be discovering that your viewing is shaped to a greater or lesser extent both by what you already know about one or more of the cultures and by your previous experience with sculpture and paintings of the human form. Some of the sources may thus seem very familiar, whereas others appear strange and exotic. This has caused some people who work with visual evidence to deny that we can ever view things with the "fresh eye" that other scholars deem indispensable. Does your experience in working with the evidence in this chapter lead you to support either side of this dispute? If you did the pretest, did your observations and impressions change after reading the Background section?

Though all of the evidence in this chapter depicts the human form, some of the portrayed individuals were regarded as fully human, some as fully divine, and many as both human and divine or as moving between a human and divine state. Do these differences affect the way these individuals are depicted? What does this tell you about the three cultures?

When making any sort of cultural comparison, it is often easiest to think in terms of similarities and differences. What similarities have you found in the depictions of the human body among the three cultures? Are there any words that you could use accurately to describe the bodies in all or most of the sources? Do any of these words suggest cultural values that may be similar? Do any two of the cultures handle representations of the human body in a similar fashion? What might this tell you about other ways in which these two cultures are similar? What do you see as the most important differences among the sculpture and painting from the three cultures? Are any of these the result of technological differences (such as differences in the material out of which the sculpture is made), or do they indicate cultural differences?

You are now ready to answer the central questions for this chapter: How do these three cultures depict the human form? What do these depictions tell us about the values of these cultures?

EPILOGUE

In all three of the cultures we have investigated here, a certain way of depicting the human form came to be accepted as the norm and was then copied extensively. Over many centuries after this norm developed, variations occurred from time to time, but these digressions were always followed by returns to the original standards (or what were perceived as the original standards).

In Egypt, this copying was largely internal, as the form developed in the Old Kingdom (Source 1) was repeated for thousands of years. There were occasional deviations from this, such as that under the pharaoh Akhenaton (ruled ca. 1372–1354 B.C.E.), who abandoned traditional Egyptian religion in favor of the worship of one god, the sun god Aton. Akhenaton supported an artistic style that was much more naturalistic, and paintings of him show him with narrow shoulders and a pot belly. As soon as he died, however, his new religious system was abandoned, and both art and religion returned to its traditional form. This artistic form was even adopted centuries after the fall of pharaonic Egypt by the Macedonian dynasty of the Ptolemies, who were established as rulers through the conquests of Alexander the Great. The most famous of the Ptolemies, Cleopatra (69–30 B.C.E.), the sister and wife to Ptolemy XII, had herself portrayed looking very similar to Nefertari in Source 4, using this archaic form to stress her link with the ancient pharaohs.

The way in which the human body was portrayed in fourth-century B.C.E. Greece (Sources 8 and 9) was even more influential than that of Egypt. These depictions came to be regarded by later Greeks and Romans as the ultimate standard of perfection, and these pieces were copied and recopied hundreds of times. (This is very fortunate, for the Greek originals have in many cases been lost, and what remains are Roman copies; Sources 8 and 9 are actually Roman copies of the originals.) The Roman historian Pliny (ca. 23–79 C.E.), in fact, noted that Polykleitos' sculpture of the athlete (Source 8) was "called the Canon by artists, who drew from it the rudiments of art as from a code," and judged Praxiteles' Aphrodite

(Source 9) the finest statue "not only by Praxiteles but in the whole world."[2] When Romans took or copied Greek images, they generally took them out of their religious setting as temple statuary and placed them in gardens, homes, or public squares. The statues thus lost their religious functions as objects of veneration and became secular objects prized primarily for their aesthetic appeal.

Greek style from this period, which has come to be called classical in the West, has been consciously emulated during many periods since, including the Italian Renaissance, the French Revolution, and the early decades of the United States. You need only to visit your state capitol or other local government buildings to assess the ways in which classical Greek standards still influence our portrayal of heroes and leaders.

Like Greek art, Buddhist art in India is generally regarded as having gone through a formative period and then achieved a level of perfection regarded as classical. Source 11 comes from the formative period, from an area of western India called Gandhara (now a part of Afghanistan) in which artists may have been influenced by Greek statues or sculptors. Sources 12 and 13 come from northern India or Nepal in the Gupta period (ca. 300–600 C.E.), a time during which the Gandharan merged with styles from other parts of India. The Gupta period was one of Indian cultural expansion into central and

2. Pliny, *Historia naturalis*, xxxiv, 55, and xxxvi, 20. Quoted in Gisela M. A. Richter, *A Handbook of Greek Art* (New York: Da Capo Press, 1987), pp. 120, 141.

southeastern Asia, and Gupta styles were copied over a very broad area. Just as in Egypt, there were periods of deviation followed by a return to the classical style for the Buddha and bodhisattvas. In areas of southeast Asia, such as Cambodia where the ruler was viewed as a god-king, the statues often looked slightly like the ruling king, though they still were not portraits in the modern sense. Unlike Greek statuary, Buddhist images did not lose their religious function, for they were copied because of their sanctity, not solely their artistic merit. Images modeled on those of Gupta India are still produced today for use in worship, particularly in areas where Buddhism is strong, such as Sri Lanka and parts of southeast Asia.

CHAPTER FIVE

THE EQUINE REVOLUTION

(3700 B.C.E.–100 C.E.)

According to Greek mythology, Athena, goddess of wisdom, and Poseidon, god of the seas, held a contest to determine the right name to name a new and beautiful Attican city in Greece. Whichever of the two who could give the city the gift that would be most useful to its citizens would win. For her part, Athena produced an olive tree, which had many uses. Poseidon then raised his trident[1] and struck the ground. From that spot emerged the first horse, who leaped up and galloped about. The other gods who were judges of the contest gasped in awe.[2]

The duel between Athena and Poseidon is not the only episode in which the horse figured prominently in ancient religion or mythology. Throughout central Asia, Egypt, India, the Middle East, Europe, and North America, humans frequently held the horse in such high regard as to approach veneration. In many cultures, rulers and warriors were buried with their horses beside them, and in several places the sacrificing of horses was considered to be among the most pleasing gifts to the gods. Alexander the Great ceremoniously buried his favorite steed, Bucephalus, on the banks of the Hydaspes River, and the city founded there was named Bucephala.

The prominence of the horse in ancient religion and mythology is evidence of how important the horse was to humans. Before the widespread domestication and expanded use of the horse—the so-called *equine revolution*[3]—travel, agriculture, warfare, and society were extremely different. Although dogs, cattle, and reindeer

1. **trident:** a three-pronged spear.

2. Because Poseidon made the mistake of emphasizing only the horse's advantages in warfare, Athena was declared the winner and, characteristically, named the new city for herself: Athens. As a consolation prize, Poseidon was named god of horses. But Athena's olive branch became the symbol of peace.

3. **equine:** pertaining to the horse.

had been domesticated earlier, people recognized that the equine revolution had brought about a revolution in their own lives as well.

Your task in this chapter will require a considerable amount of inference and imagination. From the evidence presented, you are to determine the impact of the equine revolution on humans. At one level, think of how the horse affected travel, agriculture, warfare, and general standards of living. And at a somewhat more sophisticated level, imagine how the horse would have affected social organization (including gender relations), thought, and perspectives.

Almost immediately you will recognize something very important.

Many present-day students of history assume that sedentary peoples, those who grew crops and built cities, were superior to more nomadic people, even to the point of viewing such nomads as barbarians who made no contribution to human development. Yet you will quickly see that several nomadic peoples (pastoralists, or nomadic or seminomadic herdspeople and shepherds) played a key role in the equine revolution—as domesticators, breeders, inventors of much of the equipage of the horse (bridles, saddles, horseshoes, stirrups, and so on), and as the first people to learn how to ride horses. Often ignored, pastoralists are important groups in the larger drama of human development.

BACKGROUND

Although historians are almost exclusively concerned with understanding the past of human beings, a study of *Homo sapiens* would be seriously incomplete if no consideration was paid to the changing environment in which humans developed. For example, the change from food gatherers to food producers undoubtedly was a major step in the dietary history of humankind—a turning point that led to humans' gains in height, weight, and perhaps intelligence. Contributing to this were the domestication of both dogs and cattle, both of which could be used for food as well as for labor and other needs.

But many ancient peoples believed that the taming of the horse was their most significant accomplishment. By the time that humans met horses, the

horse had gone through a considerable evolution, much of which was to humans' advantage.

The ancestor of the modern horse can be traced, through archaeological findings, to both North America and Europe roughly 50 million years ago. The "dawn horse" (Eohippus) was only around 15 to 20 inches tall at the shoulder (withers) and probably weighed no more than 100 pounds. Its front feet had four toes each, padded on the underside not unlike the feet of present dogs, and the back feet had three padded toes. The Eohippus primarily was a leaf eater, and its principal defense against its enemies was its impressive speed.

Over thousands of generations, the horse evolved into a creature quite different from its original ancestor. Most important perhaps, a change in the animal's teeth alignment turned it into a grass eater, a fact that probably added considerable height and weight. Foot pads gradually disappeared, and the toenails of the hooves became a thick and solid nail. The legs gradually grew longer and the muzzle became elongated. In North America, on the eastern slopes of the Rocky Mountains, the horse found sufficient grass for food.

In Europe, the Eohippus for some reason became extinct. But in North America, these larger and stronger horses began to migrate north and east, across the land bridge that at the time existed between present-day Alaska and Russia.[4] Indeed, it is probable that at the same time horses were migrating eastward across this land bridge, the ancestors of present-day Native Americans were migrating westward across this same route.

Sometime between 10,000 and 8,000 years ago, the remaining horses in North America became extinct. Their disappearance is something of a mystery. Many reputable scholars believe that the incoming humans butchered these animals en masse for food.[5] Other equally respected historians claim that a disease wiped out the horse population and, along with it, the mastodons, elephants, rhinoceroses, camels, and saber-toothed tigers that once existed in North America. Whatever the reason, the Western Hemisphere did not see another horse until Spanish conquerors (*conquistadors*) and settlers reintroduced the horse to the Americas in the sixteenth century.[6]

By the time that the migrating horse spread across Asia, southern Russia, and Europe, three distinct breeds had emerged. In Europe, the forest pony (*Equus abeli*) probably most resembled the horses that had migrated from North America. Short, squat, with a blunt muzzle, they were small (about 9 to 11 hands high)[7] and quick. In eastern Europe and the Ukraine, the tarpan (*Equus gmelini*) was somewhat larger and probably swifter. And in Asia, especially on the steppes of central Asia, emerged Przewalski's horse, strong and large (approximately 13 hands high).[8]

It was on the steppe that the horse began to reach its near-present development. The steppe is a vast, treeless grassland that runs 3,000 miles from the river valleys of China to the Carpathian Mountains of the Ukraine and eastern Romania. Unsuited to agriculture (unless expensively irrigated), the steppe provides exceptionally fine grazing, which permitted the horse almost to achieve its present size and weight. Because an adult horse needs 20 to 30 pounds of

4. Today the Bering Strait is only 180 feet deep. Thus, a lowering of ocean levels 250 to 300 feet deep (which was the case in the middle of the Pleistocene Age) would have exposed a considerable land bridge between Asia and North America.

5. See, for example, John Keegan, *A History of Warfare* (New York: Vintage Books, 1993), p. 156.

6. Native Americans of Central America called Cortes's horses "deer." See Miguel Leon-Portilla, ed., *The Broken Spears: The Aztec Account of the Conquest of Mexico*, trans. Lysander Kemp (Boston: Beacon Press, 1962), p. 30.

7. A hand is equal to 4 inches. Therefore, a horse that is 10 hands high would be 40 inches tall at the shoulder.

8. Przewalski's horse (alternative spelling Przevalskii) was named for Nikolai Przewalski (1839–1888), who "discovered" the horse in the wild in 1879. As a comparison, the present Arabian horse is approximately 14–15 hands high and the massive Clydesdale is 16–17 hands high.

vegetation each day, the horse needed to roam over fairly large territories, which the steppe provided.

Early humans encountered wild horses beyond the steppe. At first they probably thought of horses exclusively as food. At the base of a rock shelter at Solutré, France, the bones of around 40,000 horses have been found, dating back to about 25,000 years ago. Because horses had such strong bonding instincts, humans found that they could drive a few horses into canyons to be trapped there and the rest would follow. Then the butchering could begin.

It is not clear when (or where) humans first reasoned that they could domesticate horses for food rather than chasing wild bands over the steppe. Previous to the horse, the reindeer had been domesticated and bred in central Asia, and it probably was not long before peoples on the steppe were domesticating and breeding horses, probably for food. In sites along the lower Dneiper and Don Rivers in what is now the Ukraine, the number of bones from what were young and healthy horses seems far too high to reflect only animals killed in the wild. Those sites have been dated (using carbon dating of the horse bones) at around 3640 B.C.E. By 1000 B.C.E., the domestication of the horse had spread to Europe, Asia, and northern Africa, although wild horses existed until well into our own time.[9]

As with much of the history of the equine revolution, it is not clear precisely when humans began to ride

their horses. At the same archaeological sites noted above (dated at approximately 3640 B.C.E.), pieces of carved antlers and bones are thought to be the remains of bridle cheek pieces, which held cord or leather bits that were fitted into the horse's mouth to hold the two (left and right) reins. Similar cheek pieces and even some metal loops have been found in somewhat later sites from central Asia to eastern Europe, evidence that horseback riding spread quickly beyond its original homeland. Yet horseback riding was not done south of the steppe (in the lower Mesopotamia, the Indus Valley, or the Mediterranean region) until considerably later. The Scythians of Asia and southeastern Europe brought the horse to Greece sometime between the eighth and seventh centuries B.C.E.

In the 1960s, a magnificent archaeological find was discovered by Russian explorers in the high Ulagan Valley in the Altai Mountains west of Mongolia. Dated at around the fifth century B.C.E., the site was marvelously preserved by a series of climatic accidents that formed ice masses in graves that almost completely halted decomposition. Sixty-nine almost perfect horse cadavers were found, including hair, hide, flesh, and even stomach contents. The horses were very close to the modern horse (*Equus caballus*) in size and weight, and clear evidence indicated that they had been carefully bred for size and strength. The animals were light tan with black manes and tails. Some of the horses were geldings (castrated stallions), certain evidence that the horses' owners were breeding their animals. Sad-

9. Wild Przewalski horses were last sighted in Mongolia in the 1960s, and are thought now to exist only in zoos.

dles, saddlebags, and bridles were found as well, although no traces of breakable objects (like pottery) were discovered—evidence that the animals' owners were nomads. Thus the horse became valuable to humans not only as a food source, but also as an important means of transportation, one that would be critical to human movement until the development of the railroad in the nineteenth century and the automobile in the twentieth.

The use of the horse as a load puller came somewhat later, having to wait for technological innovations for the horse to be adapted to this work. Sumerians of the Fertile Crescent had developed both the two-wheeled cart and the four-wheeled wagon as early as 2800 or 2700 B.C.E., but these vehicles were designed to be hauled by oxen, not horses (which the Sumerians called "asses from the mountains" and considered of little practical value). With solid disk wheels and heavy carriages, these vehicles weighed up to a half-ton each. Moreover, the animals that pulled them were yoked, a device suitable for oxen but one that would almost surely choke a horse. To us these carts and wagons would be pitifully slow—traveling at only about 1.5 miles per hour (10 to 12 miles per day under the best of circumstances)—and would be almost immobile in hilly or wet terrain. Similar vehicles have been unearthed in the Middle East, the Indus Valley, and the regions now known as Armenia and Georgia (between the Black and Caspian Seas). And pottery models of similar oxen-drawn wagons have been found in graves as remote as Denmark. Most of these wagons

were used by sedentary peoples, for nomads would have found them far too slow and inefficient.

The key technological challenge, therefore, was to make these vehicles lighter and to devise a type of harness that would not choke a horse. The earliest evidence of spoked wheels comes from cylinder seals discovered in an Assyrian commercial outpost in what is now north central Turkey and dated at around the early nineteenth century B.C.E. The carts had been lightened considerably and another important technological innovation had been developed: wheel hubs allowed the wheels to revolve independently around the axle so as to allow sharper turning where inner and outer wheels spin at different speeds. A special neck yoke for horses, which put the pulling pressure on the horse's chest instead of its throat, soon followed.

Hittites or some other early people from the Caucasus Mountains or the Ukrainian steppe also developed the chariot (around 2000 B.C.E.), designed for the rapid transportation of humans rather than for freight. Between 1700 and 1600 B.C.E., the chariot spread throughout the Near East, North Africa, Europe, Iran, India, and even China. Originally ownership was confined to the very wealthy. Ancient records from both China and the Middle East indicate that chariots were eyed as one of the most prized gifts that rulers could bestow on their followers, and chariots became a great status symbol in those societies. Indeed, there is evidence that members of the elite had their chariots as well as their horses buried with them. In societies in which the great majority of people walked or rode donkeys or asses, the chariot was a sign of privilege and power. Of course, it was not lost on these people that, with their potential for great speed, chariots might have military value as well. Again, the Hittites probably led the way.

Thus from the steppe of central Asia and eastern Europe, the hunting, domesticating, breeding, riding, and harnessing of the horse as a draft animal together formed an equine revolution, a revolution that was arguably as important to human development as any other before or since.

THE METHOD

Your task in this chapter is to infer from the evidence the impact that the equine revolution had on humans—on travel, agriculture, warfare, standards of living (including diet, clothing, and other factors), social organization, gender relations, and even thought. Much of the evidence comes from archaeological discoveries and must be examined and analyzed (archaeologists would say "read") with considerable imagination.

As you examine the evidence, it would be extremely helpful to make a chart like the one shown below so as to organize your notes.

Once you have completed your chart, then use the evidence, the chart, and your imagination to add a fourth column to your chart (see the top of page 105). Be sure you leave enough space on your chart for each source, so that you can write down your thoughts fully.

Sources 1 and 2 are cave and rock paintings, respectively—Source 1 from France and Source 2 from Egypt. The animals in Source 2 may well be asses and not horses.

Source 3 is a Scythian frieze. A frieze is a decorative horizontal band,

Source Number	Description	Deductions
1	Cave painting from Lascaux, France, 15,000—10,000 B.C.E.	By painting them on cave wall, artist attached great importance to horse, probably for food.
2		

Source Number	Description	Deductions	Impact of the horse on humans
1	Cave painting from Lascaux, France, 15,000–10,000 B.C.E.	By painting them on cave wall, artist attached great importance to horse, probably for food.	Impact on diet; would decrease starvation, since horses could be eaten year-round (when fruits and berries were only seasonal). Good protein. Perhaps sped up use of fire to cook raw horsemeat.
2			

usually along the upper part of a wall but also found on urns and vases (in this case, a jar with a narrow neck). "Read" the bottom row of the frieze first, left to right, then move to the top row and repeat the process. What is being depicted here?

The map in Source 4 gives you a good idea of how horse breeding spread from the steppe to the east, west, and south. Source 5 is an Iranian-style portrait of a king and hunter. How would the horse have helped hunters?

Herodotus (Source 6), a Greek historian of the fifth century B.C.E., has been called the father of history because of his extraordinary work. This selection from his masterpiece *The Persian Wars* gives an interesting description of a group of mid-fifth-century B.C.E. nomadic warriors known to Herodotus as the Massagetae. How does Herodotus, a "civilized" Greek, view these horse people? In his view, how has the horse affected the lives of the Massagetae?

Sources 7 through 11 show the various ways humans used mounted horses. Sources 7 and 11 are reliefs (projections of figures from flat backgrounds), Source 8 is a felt appliqué, and Sources 9 and 10 are statuettes. What do these artistic representations tell you about the impact of the horse on human development?

Source 12 is a toy model of a Sumerian cart and a drawing of a Sumerian cart wheel; Source 13 is a sketch of a wagon dating from the second millennium B.C.E. that was found by Russian archaeologists in present-day

Armenia. These wagons could not have been drawn by horses (see above), whereas the wagons and chariots in Sources 14 through 16 and 18 clearly could have been. What were the differences between these two types of vehicles? How did wagons and chariots affect their human users?

Source 17 is a photograph of a grave from China's Shang dynasty, dated about 1700 B.C.E. What does the photograph tell you?

Source 19, a photograph of early Greek figurines, shows a representation of an early plow. Why would early cultivators have preferred oxen over horses to pull plows? What would be needed before horses could pull plows? Would there be any advantages in using horses instead of oxen?

THE EVIDENCE

Source 1: Jean Vertut.

1. Cave Painting, Lascaux, France, 15,000–10,000 B.C.E.

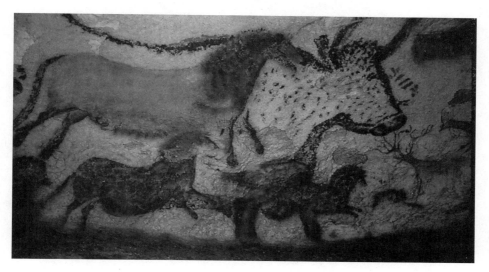

Source 2 from Anthony Dent, The Horse Through Fifty Centuries of Civilization *(New York: Holt, Rinehart & Winston, 1974), p. 11.*

2. Rock Painting, North Africa

Source 3 from E. H. Minns, Scythians and Greeks (Cambridge: Cambridge University Press, 1913). Reproduced with permission of Cambridge University Press.

3. Scythian Frieze on Silver Amphora

Source 4 from Miklos Jankovich, They Rode Into Europe: The Fruitful Exchange in the Arts of Horsemanship Between East and West, *trans. Anthony Dent (London: George G. Harrap, 1971), p. 26.*

4. The Migrations of Horse-Breeding People in Asia and Europe

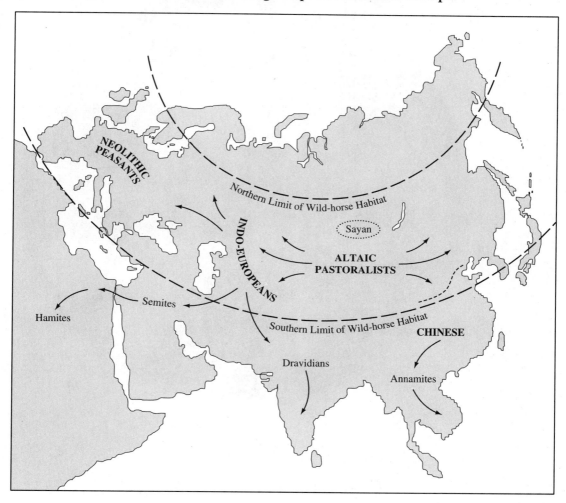

Source 5 from the Hermitage, St. Petersburg.

5. Iranian-Style Royal Portrait from Sasanian-Type Silver Plate

Source 6 from Herodotus, The Persian Wars, *trans. George Rawlinson (New York: Modern Library, 1942), Book I, Chs. 201, 215–216.*

6. From Herodotus, *The Persian Wars,* 5th century B.C.E.

201. When Cyrus had achieved the conquest of the Babylonians, he conceived the desire of bringing the Massagetae under his dominion. Now the Massagetae are said to be a great and warlike nation, dwelling eastward, towards the rising of the sun, beyond the river Araxes, and opposite the Issedonians. By many they are regarded as a Scythian race. . . .

215. In their dress and mode of living the Massageate resemble the Scythians. They fight both on horseback and on foot, neither method is strange to them: they use bows and lances, but their favourite weapon is the battle-axe. Their arms are all either of gold or brass. For their spearpoints, and arrow-heads, and for their battle-axes, they make use of brass; for head-gear, belts, and girdles, of gold. So too with the caparison[10] of their horses, they give them breastplates of brass, but employ gold about the reins, the bit, and the cheek-plates. They use neither iron nor silver, having none in their country; but they have brass and gold in abundance.

216. The following are some of their customs: Each man has but one wife, yet all the wives are held in common; for this is a custom of the Massagetae and not of the Scythians, as the Greeks wrongly say. When a man desires a woman he hangs his quiver in front of her wagon and has intercourse with her unhindered. Human life does not come to its natural close with this people; but when a man grows very old, all his kinsfolk collect together and offer him up in sacrifice; offering at the same time some cattle also. After the sacrifice they boil the flesh and feast on it; and those who thus end their days are reckoned the happiest. If a man dies of disease they do not eat him, but bury him in the ground, bewailing his ill fortune that he did not come to be sacrificed. They sow no grain, but live on their herds, and on fish, of which there is great plenty in the Araxes. Milk is what they chiefly drink. The only god they worship is the sun, and to him they offer the horse in sacrifice; under the notion of giving to the swiftest of the gods the swiftest of all mortal creatures.

10. **caparison:** a cover put over a horse's saddle or harness, usually for ornamentation.

Source 7 from Miklos Jankovich, They Rode Into Europe: The Fruitful Exchange in the Arts of Horsemanship Between East and West, *trans. Anthony Dent (London: George G. Harrap, 1971), opposite p. 48. Courtesy of the Trustees of the British Museum.*

7. Assyrian Horsemen, Relief from the Palace of Nineveh, ca. 639 B.C.E.

Source 9 from Anthony Dent, The Horse through Fifty Centuries of Civilization (New York: Holt, Rinehart & Winston, 1974) p. 85. Courtesy of the Trustees of the British Museum.

9. Parthian Mounted Archer, Etruscan Vase

Source 8 from the Hermitage, St. Petersburg.

8. Felt Hanging found at Pazyryk, Siberia, 5th century B.C.E.

[113]

Source 10: Seth Joel/Laurie Platt Winfrey, Inc.

10. Chinese Pottery Figures, 3rd century B.C.E.

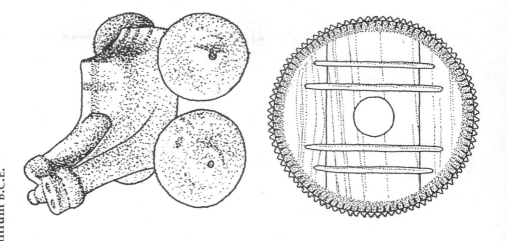

Source 12 from M. A. Litauer and J. H. Crouwel, Wheeled Vehicles and Ridden Animals in the Ancient Near East (Leiden, The Netherlands: E. J. Brill, 1979), Fig. 1. Wagon: After a photograph from the Ashmolean Museum, Oxford; Wheel: After de Mecquenem 1943, Fig. 89:1–2 and Pl. X:2. Reproduced with permission.

12. Toy Model of a Sumerian Wagon and Drawing of a Wheel from a Sumerian Cart, early 3rd millennium B.C.E.

Source 11 from Miklos Jankovich, They Rode Into Europe: The Fruitful Exchange in the Arts of Horsemanship between East and West, trans. Anthony Dent (London: George G. Harrap, 1971), opposite p. 48. Photograph: Landesmuseum Mainz.

11. Relief Tombstone of a Trooper of the Roman Auxiliary Cavalry Regiment Recruited in Noricum

13. Drawing of Caucasian Wagon and Cart, early 2nd millennium B.C.E.

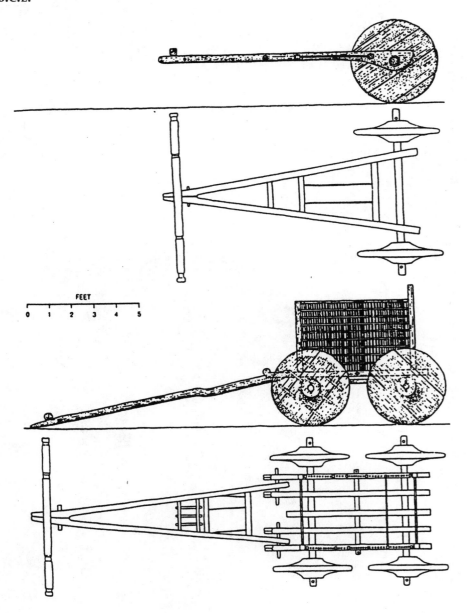

Source 14 from Miklos Jankovich, They Rode Into Europe: The Fruitful Exchange in the Arts of Horsemanship between East and West, *trans. Anthony Dent (London: George G. Harrap, 1971), opposite p. 48. Photograph: Hungarian National Museum, Budapest. Inv. Nr. 56.1900.*

14. Roman Wagon, from Roman Tombstone in Pannonia (in Modern Hungary)

Source 15 from M. A. Litauer and J. H. Crouwel, Wheeled Vehicles and Ridden Animals in the Ancient Near East *(Leiden, The Netherlands: E. J. Brill, 1979), Fig. 29. Photograph: The Metropolitan Museum of Art, Anonymous Gift, 1966.*

15. Anatolian Chariot, from Assyrian Seal, early 2nd millennium B.C.E.

16. Egyptian Chariot, mid-2nd millennium B.C.E.

This Greek drawing is based on an Egyptian relief.

Source 17 from Anthony Dent, The Horse through Fifty Centuries of Civilization *(New York: Holt, Rinehart & Winston, 1974), p. 20.*

17. Photograph of Gravesite from China's Shang Dynasty, ca. 1700 B.C.E.

Source 18 from the Monumenti Museii e Galerie-Pontificie.

18. Roman Triumphal Chariot

Source 19 from Anthony Dent, The Horse through Fifty Centuries of Civilization *(New York: Holt, Rinehart & Winston, 1974), p. 62. Photograph: Louvre © R.M.N.*

19. Early Greek Clay Figurines Depicting a Plow Team and a Chariot

On the left, oxen are yoked to a plow; on the right, horses pull a chariot.

QUESTIONS TO CONSIDER

Continue to work on your chart as the questions in this section prompt new ideas. At the same time, be willing to ask questions yourself; for example, in terms of using the horse for food, what advantages would there have been to capturing horses, putting them in corrals, and breeding them?

Source 1 is a painting made by Cro-Magnon people of the Magdalenian era, and many of these have been found by archaeologists and explorers, from France to North Africa (Source 2). Why do you think people painted images of the horse as often as they did? Most scholars theorize that the paintings were part of magic rituals conducted before hunts. If so, what might these hunters have been thinking?

Source 3, from a Scythian frieze, appears to show how Scythians domesticated horses. After catching the horse, it looks as if the man is trying to get the horse to kneel or bow before him (which actually was part of the Scythian domestication ritual). How would you explain this? At the top left, the forefeet of the saddled horse appear to have been bound, or hobbled, by the man. Why would he do this?

Source 4 represents the migration of people who bred horses. Note how far many of them traveled, and how they passed on their knowledge to other people, who in turn also moved. How would horse breeding have affected the horse? the people who bred them? Remember that the western

Asian horse was only between 10 and 11 hands high, whereas today's Arabian horse is roughly 14 to 15 hands high.

Source 5 is a representation of a mounted hunter. How would the horse affect the process of hunting (note that in Source 2, from ancient Egypt, the hunters are on foot)? How would that change affect the diet, dress, family life, and so on of nomadic hunters?

Source 6 is the historian Herodotus's account of the failed efforts of the Persians under Cyrus the Great to subdue the Massagetae, an Iranian-speaking group of Scyths or a kindred people who lived on the steppe east of the Caspian Sea. Although Herodotus obviously understood the value of mounted warriors, he also appreciated the fact that the horse played other important roles in the lives of the Massagetae. For example, Herodotus notes that the Massagetae "sow no grain." On what does he say they lived? The milk that he claims served as their principal drink undoubtedly came from mares, too. And horses also were important in the religious life of the Massagetae (why were horses sacrificed to the sun god?).

Sources 7, 9, and 11 demonstrate clearly the power of the mounted warrior. How did the introduction of cavalry change military tactics? How could nonmounted peoples defend themselves? How might weaponry and armor have changed, both for the mounted warriors as well as for foot soldiers battling against cavalry?

Source 8 is a fascinating wall hanging that comes from a grave in the

Altai Mountains. In the picture, the Great Goddess is shown holding a tree of life in her hand. What symbolism do you see?

Source 10, a pottery figure of an officer who served China's first emperor, Qin Shi Huangdi, tells us a great deal about the horse's effect on Chinese life. What is he wearing? This is not the traditional garb of the Chinese, who preferred loose-fitting robes, and so where did this type of clothing originate?

Sources 12, 13, and 14 show the evolution of the wagon that could be drawn by a horse, or by a team of horses. What were the drawbacks of the Sumerian wagon (Source 12)? How did the Caucasian cart and wagon improve on the Sumerian (Source 13)? What were the problems with the Caucasian vehicles? How did the wagon in Source 14 finally reach the desired goal? What effects on human lifestyles might the evolution of the horse-drawn wagon have had? Think about commerce, migration, the ability to move more breakable objects (pottery), the ability to carry adequate food, and other implications.

Undoubtedly the chariot spurred a revolution in warfare. The Assyrians would use massed vehicles in a frontal assault on an enemy while mounted archers attacked the enemy's flanks. The carnage, as you might imagine, could be ghastly. But the chariot had other important consequences as well.

Note the chariot in Source 18, obviously not a military vehicle but a ceremonial one. And think about why a man would have wanted to have been buried with his chariot and horses, slain for the occasion (Source 17). Think about the chariot not in terms of its functions but rather in terms of its status.

Source 19 is a photograph of Greek figurines depicting an oxen-drawn plow and a horse-drawn chariot. Why couldn't the horse have been used to pull the plow (recall what you learned earlier about problems with the first wagons)? What alterations would have to be made before the plow was compatible with horse power? One answer was to breed and raise larger horses (the Clydesdale, for example, weighs between 1,600 and 2,200 pounds and has enormous pulling strength). Were there other (easier) solutions?

The evidence has given you some very good clues about the impact of the horse on human diet, dress, transportation, and warfare. From those clues, you should also be able to infer ways in which the horse also affected religion, social organization and classes, gender roles, and even child-raising (for example, how would boys be raised differently from girls, and who would perform the child-raising functions for each). And you may be able to imagine other important effects as well.

EPILOGUE

The evolving relationship between horses and humans is far more than just a story of human ingenuity. At another level, it is the story of the interdependence of the earth's life forms and the interrelationships between human beings and other species in their environment. In one sense, the equine revolution is the history of two of those species—humans and horses—evolving together, each needing the other for its own particular evolution. Just as the original horse (Eohippus) is vastly different from the modern horse (*Equus caballus*), so also are humans today radically different from their Cro-Magnon ancestors who hunted horses and devoured them by the tens of thousands. The ways in which each has changed can be attributed in part to their relationships with one another. As human beings pave over pastures with asphalt and clear-cut forests for farmland, perhaps we should remember that earlier peoples owed their development—and perhaps even their own existence—to other species that today we threaten to eradicate.

Similarly, people today often regard their nomadic cousins as barbaric, forgetting that the nomads of the steppe of central Asia and the Ukraine were innovative and intelligent peoples, humans who tamed the horse, invented saddles, bridles, stirrups, and wheeled vehicles that gave people new possibilities and new visions. To be sure, some of those innovations were used for war and terror. Referring to the invading Chaldeans, the Israelite prophet Habakkuk wrote, "Their horses are swifter than leopards, more fierce than the evening wolves" (Habakkuk 1:8). And the Roman chronicler Ammianus Marcellinus, on observing the Hun horsemen in 392 C.E., noted that "because of their extraordinary rapidity of movement . . . you would not hesitate to call them the most terrible of all warriors."[11] For their part, the Aztecs of Central America in 1519 C.E. were terrified of Cortes's horses (they called them deer).[12]

But, as you have learned from the evidence, the impact of the horse on human beings was far greater than just as a military weapon. The equine revolution altered the ways in which people waged war, yes, but also the ways in which they ate, dressed, traveled, related to one another, raised children, and confronted strangers. Indeed, the equine revolution brought about a human revolution as well.

11. J. Otto Maenchen-Helfen, *The World of the Huns* (Berkeley: University of California Press, 1973), p. 202.

12. See Miguel Leon-Portilla, ed., *The Broken Spears: The Aztec Account of the Conquest of Mexico,* trans. Lysander Kemp (Boston: Beacon Press, 1962), p. 30.

CHAPTER SIX

HAN AND ROME:

ASSERTING IMPERIAL AUTHORITY

(300 B.C.E.–400 C.E.)

Shi Huangdi, the Chinese monarch who in 221 B.C.E. created the first truly imperial realm in East Asia, awed his advisers by the scale of his success. "Now your Majesty has raised a righteous army to punish the oppressors and bring peace and order to all under heaven, so that everywhere within the seas has become our provinces and districts," they told him, observing that this was a feat "which has never once existed from remote antiquity onwards."[1] In their eyes, he had conquered not a kingdom but a world. And because no one to their knowledge had ever done so before, they had trouble en-

visioning a state able to govern on such a vast scope. Half a world away, the leaders of Rome faced a nearly identical problem. Having wrested North Africa, present-day Spain, and southern France away from Carthage in 201 B.C.E. and then conquering Greece and Anatolia (contemporary Turkey) by 133 B.C.E., the city-state of Rome found itself in control of nearly all of the Mediterranean world.

Emerging almost simultaneously at opposite extremes of Eurasia, these two great empires welded their respective spheres together with such success that they initiated new stages of political development. No longer mere regional powers, they had become world states whose rule extended over many different peoples and cultures. As such they had to be redefined and justified in new and broader terms. Although their immense size made this endeavor somewhat unique, the Roman and Han empires were by no means the

---

1. These remarks appear in a biography of Shi Huangdi in the *Records of the Historian (Shiji)* by the historian Sima Qian. The version quoted here comes from Raymond Dawson's translation, *Historical Records* (New York: Oxford University Press, 1994), p. 84.

Chapter 6

Han and Rome:

Asserting

Imperial

Authority

(300 B.C.E.–

400 C.E.)

first to face such a task. Throughout history rulers have tried to secure the loyalty and obedience of their people by portraying their authority and the state through which they exercised it in the best possible light.

Such efforts to legitimize political power offer important insights into the way people in different times and cultures have viewed the state and political authority. Current states, for example, generally present themselves as embodiments of a single ethnic group or "nation" whose members share a common language and culture. According to modern beliefs, such national groups form a "people" with a "natural right" to self-rule. So governments today claim to derive authority from their people and to reflect popular opinion in their policies. The idea of popular sovereignty seems reasonable today because it accords with present assumptions about human nature and politics. But people of other times and places with different assumptions might well consider the concept absurd.

To presume, then, that the people of the Han or Roman empires un-derstood political authority much as modern people do courts problems. Conquerors of many peoples and cultures, these empires exemplified a very different kind of multinational state that had to be justified in terms of universality rather than exclusivity. Efforts to portray them as nation-states or even as ancestral forms of modern nations involve all sorts of anachronistic assumptions that project present ideas into the past. To overcome this danger, we need to discover how the builders of the Han and Roman states conceived of political authority within the constraints of their own political traditions. And that is the task facing you in this chapter. In the Evidence section, you will find two sets of primary materials dealing with imperial rule, one Roman and one Chinese. Investigate both to determine the answers to these questions: How did each of these peoples redefine political authority to suit a new level of world mastery? What do their views of imperial authority tell us about the ways in which they understood the state and its power?

BACKGROUND

Neither the Han nor the Roman empire emerged through sudden, unexpected revolutions. On the contrary, both evolved as final, logical outcomes of long processes of regional integration. Some general remarks about the origins of these empires, therefore, will provide a context for better understanding their transformation from regional to world powers. Tracing their rise will also provide insight into the political traditions to which they were heir. For though both innovated freely, they primarily shaped new identities by reinterpreting older, indigenous ideas and institutions. As a result, it would be difficult to understand how the builders of these empires conceived of them without reference to the historical circumstances out of which each evolved.

The Han state clearly owed a heavy debt to the past. For one thing, much of its institutional structure derived directly from the short lived Qin dynasty, officially inaugurated by Shi Huangdi in 221 B.C.E.[2] Despite that conqueror's boast that his dynasty would rule the new empire for ten thousand years, his early death little more than a decade later created a vacuum of power that brought its swift collapse. For a few years, civil war raged as rival provincial leaders restored local kingdoms and vied with one another for regional mastery. But finally one warlord, Liu Bang, overcame all other contenders and reimposed imperial unity. The Han dynasty, which he proclaimed in 202 B.C.E., proved a far more lasting regime than the one it replaced, surviving in its basic form for nearly four centuries until swept away by rebellion and mutiny in a series of upheavals that began in 184.

Despite the change of rulers, much of the basic structure of the Qin regime persisted under the Han, whose early rulers slowly modified its institutions to meet changing conditions. Throughout history, therefore, Qin and Han have often been linked together and deemed, as they will be here, but two phases of a single stage of imperial development. The fact that ancient records carefully distinguish between them, however, points up an impor-

tant difference between the Chinese political tradition and the European: in China, states were named in terms of dynasties, or ruling families, rather than in terms of territories, people, or institutional structures. Viewed from this perspective, Rome would appear to be not one but a series of different empires, each named after successive ruling houses like the Julian and Flavian lines.

Though novel in scope, neither the Qin nor the Han ascension marked an abrupt departure from earlier political patterns. Indeed, much of their imperial system evolved out of the efforts of territorially more limited kingdoms, some ethnically Chinese and some not, to create centralized monarchies during the preceding third and fourth centuries B.C.E. Qin was itself initially just one of a half-dozen or so of these kingdoms, which fought so incessantly with one another during these centuries that later ages termed the era the Warring States Period. Because it succeeded in centralizing faster than its rivals, Qin proved better able to mobilize its resources and so conquered them. But many of them, too, including Qin's chief contender for imperial mastery, a great southern kingdom called Chu, followed their own programs of centralization. Out of their collective experiments evolved many important, new institutions like autocratic kingship, centralized provincial administration, civil bureaucracy, mass military organization, and standardized legal codes, all of which the later Qin and Han empires adapted to their own purposes.

The Warring States era also supplied a diverse body of new ideas

2. Chinese terms appear in the modern *pinyin* system of romanization, with the often more familiar Wade-Giles spelling sometimes given in parentheses. The name Qin sounds approximately like the English word "chin," and the first emperor's title is pronounced something like *shur hwang dee.*

Chapter 6
Han and Rome:
Asserting
Imperial
Authority
(300 B.C.E.–
400 C.E.)

about the nature and purpose of the state. As in earlier times, Confucianism remained a significant intellectual force. A practical political doctrine developed from the ideas taught by Confucius (in *pinyin* Kung Fu Zi, ca. 551–479 B.C.E.), early Confucianism advocated government based on ethical principles rather than mere expediency or a ruler's whims. Confucius himself directed his followers to seek such principles in an old ruling house called the Zhou, claiming that its kings exemplified the highest ethical ideal, a rare quality called *ren*, translated variously as humanity, goodness, and benevolence. Later followers like the idealistic Mencius (Mengzi, ca. 371–288 B.C.E.) and the third-century B.C.E. rationalist Xunzi (Hsün Tzu) offered updated Confucian interpretations to suit the altered conditions of the Warring States Period. All, however, insisted that inherent human goodness made coercion unnecessary and argued that governments should rely on moral persuasion rather than force to win support. Only "sages," people endowed with extraordinary ethical virtue and intellectual ability, could in their view establish such regimes, and thus they claimed that rulers should turn government over to a well-trained, upright elite.

Other schools of thoughts, however, advocated different modes of sagely rule. Proponents of a political brand of Daoism (Taoism), a doctrine associated with a sixth century B.C.E. figure named Laozi (Lao Tzu), proposed a doctrine of paternalistic, *laissez-faire* rule. In their view, secretive sage rulers trusted in the great Way

(*Dao*) that orders the natural world to keep their people content and harmonious. And a group known as the Legalists propounded a theory of outright autocracy. Likening most people to unruly animals, they claimed that the only means to achieve any social order was to allow those few individuals who overcame their base emotions to serve as enlightened despots. Using a strict system of rewards and punishments, these elevated autocrats were then to train their fellow humans to behave in orderly ways much as dogs are trained.

Despite wide disagreement on how to achieve order and stability, all these schools of thought bequeathed a common legacy to later empires. First, all anticipated an end to the era of multiple kingdoms. Although they sharply differed about how unification of their cultural world would be achieved, none doubted its likelihood—or desirability. They thus spoke of a state including all *Tianxia*, or "Underheaven," that is, a state stretching across the entire earth. Their idea of a world-wide state, however, was colored by assumptions of cultural difference.

For they expected this realm to develop around a core area located in the Central Plains of north China, the homeland of ethnic Chinese, then known as the *Xia*. Much earlier at the start of the first millennium B.C.E., when united under the loose rule of the Zhou dynasty, this region had dominated regional politics. The collapse of Zhou power in the eighth century B.C.E. brought politically fragmentation and the loss of regional mastery. But the people of this area continued to enjoy high cultural status in the centuries that followed, winning their petty principalities recognition as the *zhung guo* or "central states." When arguing for regional integration, Warring States thinkers reinterpreted the meaning of this term, understanding it to mean a single Central State that could serve as the core of a greater world polity.

Advocates of integration also fostered belief that a world-state would be founded by the same kind of *sheng ren* or "sage" said to have founded the Zhou dynasty. Thus they encouraged a second assumption: that Underheaven would be united by a special kind of person. Unique to this tradition, the sage had no counterpart in Western thought. The figure may have evolved out of the semidivine forebears of ancient north Chinese clans to whom old foundation myths ascribe all sorts of wondrous powers. But by Warring States times, sages seem to have been seen as purely human geniuses who personally created all of human culture, including its social and political order. Already, a number of thinkers were advancing historical schemes in which a line of sages seemingly guided humankind out of barbarism and onto the path of civilization. These schemes encouraged the idea that all great changes, including the founding of new states, depended on the leadership of such an event-making figure.

Warring States thinkers introduced a third assumption about any future world-state. Caught up in a wave of recent cosmological speculation, many argued that a strict correspondence existed between natural and human order. In their opinion, all political shifts occurred in concert with larger changes in the natural world. Confucian writers developed a special version of this idea, claiming that a conscious power whom they called *Tian* or "Heaven" willed this correspondence. Borrowing from old apologists who had justified the Zhou monarchy's power in terms of Heavenly authority, Mencius claimed that Heaven gave true sages a special Heavenly Mandate or charge to found new regimes. He thus helped to revive an old Zhou belief that its kings were "Sons of Heaven," destined to serve as its agent among all humankind. From such concepts emerged a unique theory that universal states would rise and fall in dynastic cycles responsive to Heavenly bidding.

Rome, too, inherited a rich legacy from its Mediterranean forerunners. But it developed out of a very different milieu, one in which city-states rather than regional kingdoms dominated the political scene. The political tradition connected with such city-states celebrated the uniqueness and autonomy of small communities in which a select citizenry enjoyed special privileges. Even in imperial times, the Romans continued to identify with their own distinct origin as a small Latin "republic." Based on the idea of a *res publica*, or "public thing," held in common by a body of people, the ancient republic was a form of government in which authority was thought to reside in a group of citizens rather than in one family or one individual. Only those whom the citizens chose to represent them could

Chapter 6

Han and Rome:

Asserting

Imperial

Authority

(300 B.C.E.–

400 C.E.)

thus legitimately rule the community. In early Rome as in most Mediterranean city-states, only a small portion of the community actually possessed citizenship and could select rulers. Nonetheless, even this limited form of popular participation in government created a strong sense of communal identity that was lacking in East Asia. Compared to the highly standardized Qin–Han imperial system, in which provincial administrations tolerated no local deviation nor any form of communal power, the Roman Empire appeared more like a federation of semiautonomous cities and provinces than a fully integrated domain.

In its earliest stages, of course, the Roman Empire arose out of just such a league. Beginning as a small Latin city-state on the Tiber River in central Italy in the eighth century B.C.E., it gradually expanded through the conquest of neighboring cities until by 272 B.C.E. it controlled the whole of the Italian peninsula. Thereafter, the decline of Greek power to the east and the rise of a rival Carthaginian hegemony in the west drew Rome into a wider involvement in the Mediterranean world. Within less than a century and a half more, the Roman republic extended its rule over most of the Mediterranean basin. This imperial success, however, placed an enormous burden on Rome's republican institutions, creating a period of political crisis during the mid–first century in which factional strife and civil war threatened to destroy the state.

These strains encouraged a shift toward more autocratic rule during the last half of the third century B.C.E.

This process intensified when the chief republican institution, a patrician council known as the Senate, accorded Julius Caesar dictatorial powers so that he could carry out a program of comprehensive reform. Although out of deference to republican tradition Caesar rejected the outright title *rex* ("king"), he became a monarch in all but name in 44 B.C.E. when the Senate voted him a lifetime dictatorship. His assassination that year briefly halted the transition toward monarchial rule, but it resumed little more than a decade later when Caesar's grandnephew Octavian convinced the Senate to name him dictator, too. By a further act of the Senate in 27 B.C.E. Octavian became *imperator* or "emperor," and under the new title Augustus completed the transition from republic to monarchy. From then until the empire's disintegration in the early fifth century, Caesarian style emperors ruled over the Roman state.

Although an outgrowth of the Roman political situation, this monarchy increasingly reflected the influence of the Hellenistic[3] states of the eastern Mediterranean that Rome eventually absorbed. Most of these were monarchies still ruled by descendants of the followers of Alexander the Great, the Greek conqueror who in the fourth century B.C.E. briefly created the predecessor of a Mediterranean world-state by annexing the

3. **Hellenistic:** refers to the people of the eastern Mediterranean who after the time of Alexander the Great became Greek in their ways and outlook though not necessarily Greek in ancestry; it derives from the word *Hellene,* the name the ancient Greeks gave themselves.

Persian Empire to his own much expanded kingdom of Macedonia. Fascinated by Near Eastern forms of kingship, Alexander had himself declared a god like the Egyptian pharaohs and ruled in the autocratic manner of the Persian warrior kings. Although Alexander's empire broke apart after his death, successors in Egypt and Asia Minor kept alive the tradition of posing as god kings, bequeathing it in turn to their Roman conquerors in the first century B.C.E.

In other areas, too, Hellenistic culture and thought influenced Roman political life. Two Athenian philosophers of the fourth century B.C.E., Zeno and Epicurus, proved particularly influential on later Roman thought. Epicurus, a strict materialist, denied any purpose or meaning to the world other than what humans made of it. He thus counseled followers to seek a quiet life of simple human pleasures. Zeno argued an almost opposite position, contending that a divine spirit worked mysteriously through all things to manifest cosmic harmony. Humans, he felt, provided a special medium through which this spirit operated. He accordingly urged people to recognize human fellowship and to dedicate themselves to a life of service to others and, through it, to the purpose of the divine will. In speaking of a broader human fellowship united by a common purpose, Zeno gave the Mediterranean area a concept of world community that could replace the localism of the city-state. His doctrine, known as Stoic philosophy, thus promoted a more cosmopolitan outlook on the eve of Rome's great expansion.

These Hellenistic ideas helped prepare the way for Rome's creation of an empire by providing terms with which to envision a universal state. Hellenistic writers, especially the Stoics, popularized the idea that the Mediterranean basin formed a single cultural domain, called the "ecumene,"[4] because its inhabitants, whatever their language and ethnicity, shared a common legacy of Greek ways and Greek thought. Out of it developed the later concept of a single Western civilization made up of diverse peoples united by a common classical tradition. Hellenistic thinkers, however, wanted political as well as cultural integration. They thus encouraged hopes that a divine, or at least a divinely inspired, figure would emerge to unite the whole Mediterranean world and help humankind realize its oneness in a new kind of universal state. Rome's eventual conquest of most of this area naturally seemed a fulfillment of their prophetic desires. And Roman emperors easily came to equate their *imperium* or "rule" with an assumed divine mission to order the entire world, or *orbis terrarum* as they called it.

4. **ecumene:** from the Greek word *oikoumene* ("the inhabited world"); the term, like the Chinese "underheaven," signifies a worldwide or universal sphere.

Chapter 6
Han and Rome:
Asserting
Imperial
Authority
(300 B.C.E.–
400 C.E.)

THE METHOD

The problem at issue here—how the builders of the Han and Roman empires understood their imperial authority—certainly involves aspects of political and institutional history. Yet, it pertains more to what people thought than to what they did. The study of what people of the past thought falls largely in the realm of intellectual history, a branch of history that seeks to trace the development of ideas and their impact on society. For all that they may appear to lack the concreteness of political events and institutions, ideas too can be recovered, providing we tap the right kind of evidence.

Written materials, of course, yield the most information on complex political ideas, for they typically reveal them in the fullest detail. Government documents like degrees, announcements, and commemorative statements give evidence of the official perspective, whereas individual histories, critiques, memoirs, and letters reveal something of the private viewpoints of the time. But written materials by no means exhaust all possibilities. As any visitor to a modern capital city quickly discovers, buildings, monuments, and artworks also express public ideals in powerful ways. Unlike written documents, which make sense only to literate elites, materials of this sort "speak" to a broader segment of the population through the language of visual symbols. In earlier times of restricted education and literacy, they probably played a greater role than written texts in conveying basic notions of the state and political authority to the populace. For that reason, we include visual materials as well as written documents in the Evidence section of this chapter.

Evidence presented here on the early Chinese empire includes both sorts of artifact. Source 1 is a selection from a famous biography of Qin Shi Huangdi contained in an early Chinese history of the world called the *Shiji,* or *Records of the Historian.* Compiled in the late second century B.C.E. by the Han scholar Sima Qian, it incorporates a number of older documents along with the texts of certain stone inscriptions made at the first emperor's own order in 219 and 218 B.C.E. The photographs that serve as Sources 2 and 3 illustrate this emperor's tomb. Source 4 includes parts of essays written by Dong Zhongshu (Tung Chung-shu), a Confucian adviser to Han emperor Wudi (Wu-ti, r. 141–87 B.C.E.), and Source 5 is the text of a decree issued by Han emperor Wendi (Wen-ti) in 178 B.C.E. Sources 4 and 5 both reflect later views of the Qin-Han monarchy.

The Roman material, too, is visual as well as textual. Source 6, an excerpt from the *Res Gestae Divi Augusti,* or *The Achievements of the Divine Augustus,* sets forth the feats for which Rome's first emperor, Caesar Augustus (r. 27 B.C.E.–14 B.C.E.) wished to be remembered in his own words. Source 7, an excerpt from a work called *Roman History,* presents a different view of the accomplishments of Augustus by the third-century historian Cassius Dio. Source 8, a Roman coin, and Sources 9 and 10, a

Roman monument called Trajan's Column, present visual images of the monarchy intended to influence the less literate. Additional official statements by later Roman emperors comprise Sources 11 and 12, both inscriptions are carved on the walls of public temples in the eastern part of the Roman Empire.

As Sources 1 and 5 demonstrate, political ideas tend to be discussed most intensely when governments first emerge or when they undergo crisis. More apt to feel threatened and vulnerable at these times, leaders often take much greater pains than normal to explain their actions so as to consolidate their power. They issue special proclamations asserting their legitimacy and experiment with new guises through which to portray themselves and their power. Rivals, too, speak out more freely at such moments, whether to challenge authority or to voice alternate views. Material from such critical moments, therefore, provides an especially rich source of political ideas, and you will find a number of such items included here. But even the less intense level of political "talk" that continues in ordinary times may reflect important aspects of a political tradition. Governments, for example, often take advantage of routine statements to reaffirm basic ideals and conventional claims, as do private interests. The very repetitiousness of such messages may, in fact, prove more revealing of commonplace assumptions than more carefully authored statements.

In assessing the following materials, try to distance yourself from modern political assumptions and look for the unfamiliar. One way to do so is to pay special attention to the unique terms and images that appear with any frequency. In written sources, "keywords" or special terms that appear again and again and seem critical to an understanding of the text provide a useful starting point for analysis. Because their uniqueness makes modern translation difficult, many will appear in their original language like the Latin *imperium* or the Chinese *huangdi*. But even when translated, most should catch your eye because of their oddity if not frequency. Where in modern political discourse, for example, would you find people talking about "sages" or "ovations"? Write these words down and note any passages that offer hints to their meaning. You may have to work back and forth among several of these passages, using clues from one to illuminate others. But if you do so carefully for both sets of evidence, you should end up with a basic vocabulary list of important political terms for each of the two traditions. In a similar way, look for significant factors in the visual materials to add to your list, and ask yourself if they correlate in any way to the keywords.

An approach of this sort, which requires you first to identify the basic words and images of the evidence, will force you to respect the integrity of the evidence and enable you to confront it on its own terms. But doing so will not automatically give you an answer to the central question of this chapter—how did the builders of the Han and Roman empires conceive of and justify their political authority? To get to that point, you will

Chapter 6

Han and Rome:

Asserting

Imperial

Authority

(300 B.C.E.–

400 C.E.)

need to ask yourself what each set of key elements collectively indicates about the nature of imperial rule. Keeping a few fundamental considerations in mind at this point should help you piece the evidence together into a larger picture. First, ask yourself what in each case the state seems to embody. Is it a land, an ideal, a people, or something else? A second, closely related question to consider involves the purpose of imperial rule. Modern states, which usually claim to represent a nation, often cite securing the liberty and well-being of their people as their primary purpose. But throughout history other kinds of states have asserted different ends. Some, for example, have claimed to be embodiments of religious movements or churches with divine purposes to fulfill. Others have posed as bearers of cultural traditions, which they presume to defend or promote. Frequently they link this purpose to some higher order or power that thus bestows an ultimate sanction on their power. Logically, a third question to

consider, then, is who or what authorizes imperial rule.

Once you have reached some general conclusions about the way in which Han and Roman rulers each understood their imperial authority, compare the differences and similarities between them. Juxtaposing one against the other should highlight what is unique to each. You will no doubt remark with what distinct "voices" early Chinese and Roman sources speak; patterns of rhetoric and style differ as much, if not more, than basic political beliefs. Think what these differences imply about the gulfs between cultures and the difficulty of interpreting one in terms of the other. Yet, at the same time, note how similar some Roman and Chinese ideas of authority seem relative to the modern notion of popular sovereignty. How do you think people today would react to these ideas? Time, in this case centuries, creates gaps between people that are not easily bridged.

Source 1 from Raymond Dawson, Historical Records *(New York: Oxford University Press, 1994), pp. 63–70.*

1. From Sima Qian, *The Annals of Qin,* ca. second century B.C.E.

Now Qin for the first time had unified all under Heaven and instructions were given to the Chief Minister and the Imperial Secretary saying: "On another occasion the King of Hann offered us his territory and handed over his seal, requesting to become a frontier vassal, but having done so he turned his back on the agreement and formed a north–south alliance with Zhao and Wei to rebel against Qin, so we raised troops to punish them and took their king prisoner. I consider this to be a good thing since it practically brought an end to the fighting. . . . With my own insignificant person I have raised troops to punish violence and chaos and, with the support of the sacred power of the ancestral temples, the six kings have all admitted their crimes, and order is magnificently restored in all under Heaven. Now if the title is not changed there will be no means of praising these achievements and transmitting them to later generations. You are to discuss the imperial title."

Chief Minister Wang Wan, Imperial Secretary Feng Jie, Superintendent of Trials Li Si, and others all said: "In days of old the territory of the Five Emperors was 1,000 *li* square, and beyond this was the territory of the feudal princes and of the barbarians. Some of the feudal princes came to court and some did not, for the Son of Heaven was unable to exercise control. Now Your Majesty has raised a righteous army to punish the oppressors and bring peace and order to all under Heaven, so that everywhere within the seas has become our provinces and districts and the laws and ordinances have as a result become unified. This is something which has never once existed from remote antiquity onwards, and which the Five Emperors did not attain. Your servants have carefully discussed this with the scholars of broad learning and, as in antiquity there was the Heavenly August, the Earthly August, and the Supreme August, and the Supreme August was the most highly honoured, so your servants, risking death, submit a venerable title, and propose that the King should become 'the Supreme August.' His commands should be 'edicts,' his orders should be 'decrees,' and the Son of Heaven should refer to himself as 'the mysterious one.' " The King said: "Omit the word 'supreme' and write 'august' and pick out the title of 'emperor' used from remote antiquity, so that the title will be 'August Emperor.' The rest shall be as you suggest." And an edict was issued saying that it should be done. King

Chapter 6

Han and Rome:

Asserting

Imperial

Authority

(300 B.C.E.–

400 C.E.)

Zhuangxiang was to be posthumously honoured as "the Supreme August on High."

The Chief Minister Wang Wan and others said: "The states are newly defeated and the territories of Yan, Qi, and Chu are distant, so if we do not establish kings for them there will be no means of bringing order to them. We beg to set up your sons in authority, but it is up to the Supreme One alone to favour us with his agreement." The First Emperor handed down their suggestion to the ministers, and they all thought this would be expedient. But the Superintendent of Trials Li Si advised: "Only after an extremely large number of sons and younger brothers and people of the same surname had been enfeoffed by King Wen and King Wu did they win the adherence of the distant, and then they attacked and smote each other and behaved like enemies. And when the feudal states wrought vengeance on each other more and more, the Zhou Son of Heaven was incapable of preventing them. Now all within the seas has been unified thanks to Your Majesty's divine power, and everywhere has been turned into provinces and districts. And if your sons and the successful officials are richly rewarded from the public revenues, that will be quite sufficient to secure easy control. If there is no dissension throughout the Empire, then this is the technique for securing tranquillity. To establish feudal states would not be expedient." The First Emperor said: "It is because of the existence of marquises and kings that all under Heaven has shared in suffering from unceasing hostilities. When, thanks to the ancestral temples, all under Heaven has for the first time been brought to order, if states are reintroduced, this will mean the establishment of armies, and it would surely be difficult to seek peace in those places. The advice of the Superintendent of Trials is right."

So the Empire was divided into thirty-six provinces, and a governor and army commander and an inspector were established for each. The people were renamed "the black-headed people," and there were great celebrations. The weapons from all under Heaven were gathered in and collected together at Xianyang and were melted down to make bells and stands and twelve statues of men made of metal, each 1,000 piculs in weight, to be set up in the courts and palaces. All weights and measures were placed under a unified system, and the axle length of carriages was standardized. For writings they standardized the characters.

In the twenty-eighth year the First Emperor travelled eastwards through his provinces and districts and ascended Mount Zouyi. He set up a stone tablet, and after discussion with the various Confucian scholars of Lu an inscription was carved on the stone extolling the virtue of Qin. They also discussed the matter of the *feng* and *shan* sacrifices[5] and the sacrifices to mountains and rivers. So next he ascended Mount Tai, set up a stone tablet, and made the *feng*

5. *feng* **and** *shan* **sacrifices:** sacrifices to Heaven appropriate only to a supreme ruler.

sacrifice. As he descended and there was a violent onset of wind and rain, he rested under a tree, which was consequently enfeoffed as fifth-rank grandee. He made the *shan* sacrifice at Liangfu. The stone tablet that he had set up was inscribed with the following words:

When the August Emperor came to the throne, he created regulations and made the laws intelligent, and his subjects cherished his instructions.

In the twenty-sixth year of his rule, he for the first time unified all under Heaven, and there were none who did not submit.

In person he made tours of the black-headed people in distant places, climbed this Mount Tai, and gazed all around at the eastern limits.

His servants who were in attendance concentrated on following his footsteps, looked upon his deeds as the foundation and source of their own conduct, and reverently celebrated his achievements and virtue.

As the Way of good government circulates, all creation obtains its proper place, and everything has its laws and patterns.

His great righteousness shines forth with its blessings, to be handed down to later generations, and they are to receive it with compliance and not make changes in it.

The August Emperor is personally sage, and has brought peace to all under Heaven, and has been tireless in government.

Rising early and retiring late, he has instituted long-lasting benefits, and has brought especial glory to instructions and precepts.

His maxims and rules spread all around, and far and near everything has been properly organized, and everyone receives the benefits of his sagely ambitions.

Noble and base have been divided off and made clear, and men and women conform in accordance with propriety, and carefully fulfil their duties.

Private and public are made manifest and distinguished, and nothing is not pure and clean, for the benefit of our heirs and successors.

His influence will last to all eternity, and the decrees he bequeaths will be revered, and his grave admonitions will be inherited for ever.

In the twenty-ninth year the First Emperor made a tour in the east. When he reached Bolangsha in Yangwu, he was startled by bandits. They looked for them but did not find them, so he ordered a grand search throughout the Empire for ten days. He ascended Zhifu and had an inscription made on stone with the following words:

Chapter 6

Han and Rome:

Asserting

Imperial

Authority

(300 B.C.E.–

400 C.E.)

In the twenty-ninth year, the time being in the middle of spring, when the sunny season had just started,

The August Emperor made a tour in the east, and during his travels he ascended Zhifu, and his gaze shone upon the sea.

The servants who were in attendance observed him in admiration, recalled his blessings and glory, and reflected upon and sang the praises of what he initiated.

In creating the government, the great sage established the laws and regulations, and made manifest the guiding principles.

Abroad he taught the feudal lords, gloriously bestowing the blessings of culture, and spreading enlightenment by means of the principles of righteousness.

The Six States remained aloof, insatiable in greed and violence, and the atrocities and killings did not cease.

The August Emperor felt pity for the multitude, and then sent forth chastising armies, and displayed with determination his military power.

He made his punishments just and his conduct sincere, and his awesome glory spread around, and no one did not submit.

He wiped out the strong and violent, rescued the black-headed people, and restored order to the four quarters.

Everywhere he bestowed enlightened laws, and made warp and woof for all under Heaven, to provide a model for all eternity.

He has become great indeed, and within the whole universe we accept and obey his sage-like intent.

All his servants sing the praises of his achievements, and request to inscribe them on stone, so that they may be displayed and handed down as a constant rule.

He then proceeded to the east of Bohai, passed through Huang and Chui, did a complete tour of Mount Cheng, ascended Zhifu, and set up a stone tablet there extolling the virtue of Qin and then left.

He then went south and ascended Langye and, since he greatly enjoyed it, he stayed for three months. Then he moved 30,000 households of the black-headed people to the foot of Langye terrace, giving them tax and labour exemption for twelve years. When he built Langye terrace, he set up a stone inscription extolling the virtue of Qin, to make clear that he had achieved his ambition. It said:

In his twenty-eighth year, the August Emperor makes a beginning.

Laws and standards are corrected and adjusted, as a means of recording the myriad things.

Thus he clarifies human affairs, and brings concord to father and son.

With sagacity, wisdom, humaneness, and righteousness, he has made manifest all principles.

In the east he has pacified the eastern lands, and thus he has inspected officers and men.

When this task had been magnificently accomplished, he then turned towards the sea.

Through the achievements of the August Emperor, the basic tasks are diligently worked on.

Farming is put first and non-essentials are abolished, and it is the black-headed people who are made wealthy.

All people under Heaven, have heart and mind in unison.

Implements are given a uniform measure, and the characters used in writing are standardized.

Wherever the sun and moon shine, wherever boats and carts carry goods.

Everyone completes his destiny, and nobody does not get what he wants.

He makes things move in accord with the seasons, such is the August Emperor.

Source 2 from Cultural Relics Publishing House.

2. Grave Mound of Qin Shi Huangdi at Mt. Li

Source 3: Julian Calder/Tony Stone.

3. Flanking Pit of Excavated Tomb of Qin Shi Huangdi

Chapter 6

Han and Rome:

Asserting

Imperial

Authority

(300 B.C.E.–

400 C.E.)

Source 4 from William Theodore de Bary et al., eds., Sources of Chinese Tradition *(New York: Columbia University Press, 1960), pp. 178–179.*

4. From Dong Zhongshu (Tung Chung-shu), Essays on Kingship

HOW THE WAY OF THE KING JOINS THE TRINITY

Those who in ancient times invented writing drew three lines and connected them through the middle, calling the character "king" [王]. The three lines are Heaven, earth, and man, and that which passes through the middle joins the principles of all three. Occupying the center of Heaven, earth, and man, passing through and joining all three—if he is not a king, who can do this?

Thus the king is but the executor of Heaven. He regulates its seasons and brings them to completion. He patterns his actions on its commands and causes the people to follow them. When he would begin some enterprise, he observes its numerical laws. He follows its ways in creating his laws, observes its will, and brings all to rest in humanity. The highest humanity rests with Heaven, for Heaven is humaneness itself. It shelters and sustains all creatures. It transforms them and brings them to birth.

The ruler holds the position of life and death over men; together with Heaven he holds the power of change and transformation. There is no creature that does not respond to the changes of Heaven. The changes of Heaven and earth are like the four seasons. When the wind of their love blows, then the air will be mild and the world team with life, but when the winds of their disfavor come forth, the air will be cold and all things die. When they are joyous the skies are warm and all things grow and flourish, but from their wrath comes the chill wind and all is frozen and shut up.

THE THREEFOLD OBLIGATIONS OF THE RULER

The ruler is the basis of the state. In administering the state, nothing is more effective for educating the people than reverence for the basis. If the basis is revered then the ruler may transform the people as though by supernatural power, but if the basis is not revered then the ruler will have nothing by which to lead his people. Then though he employ harsh penalties and severe punishments the people will not follow him. This is to drive the state to ruin, and there is no greater disaster. What do we mean by the basis? Heaven, earth, and man are the basis of all creatures. Heaven gives them birth, earth nourishes them, and man brings them to completion. Heaven provides them at birth with a sense of filial and brotherly love, earth nourishes them with clothing and food, and man completes them with rites and music. The three act together as hands and feet join to complete the body and none can be dispensed with. . . .

[142]

Source 5 from Dun J. Li, The Essence of Chinese Civilization *(New York: Van Nostrand, 1967), pp. 116–117.*

5. Han Wendi (Wen-ti),
On the Eclipse of the Sun

I have heard that Heaven installs rulers to govern the people it creates and that it will warn a ruler with natural disasters if he has lost virtue or if his rule has become unjust.

On the eleventh month of this year there was an eclipse of the sun. No natural disaster can be more serious than this: Heaven has reproached me!

I have inherited the duty of protecting the temples of our imperial ancestors. A simple and insignificant person though I was, I was called to become the king of all people and scholars. I am solely responsible for all occurrences on earth, be they good or evil. In administering the vast empire, I am assisted by some of my closest minister-advisers.

I have lost my virtue indeed as my inability to take care of my people has aroused the wrath of the sun, the moon, and the stars. Let it be known that immediately after this decree is issued, all of you should think seriously about my shortcomings and inform me on happenings that I have not been able to hear and see myself. Report your findings to me directly! Moreover, you are urged to recommend to me the virtuous, the upright, the honest, and the outspoken so that I can benefit from their counsel and advice. Be it also decreed that all of you are to be diligent at your tasks and that you are to reduce taxes and corvée [enforced labor] duties among my subjects.

Source 6 from Res Gestae Divi Augusti *in Naphtali Lewis and Meyer Reinhold, eds.,* Roman Civilization: Selected Readings, *vol. 1 (New York: Columbia University Press, 1955), pp. 562–572.*

6. From Caesar Augustus,
The Achievements of the
Divine Augustus

Below is a copy of the accomplishments of the deified Augustus by which he brought the whole world under the empire of the Roman people, and of the moneys expended by him on the state and the Roman people, as inscribed on two bronze pillars set up in Rome.

1. At the age of nineteen, on my own initiative and at my own expense, I raised an army by means of which I liberated the Republic, which was oppressed by the tyranny of a faction. For which reason the senate, with honorific decrees, made me a member of its order in the consulship of Gaius

Chapter 6

Han and Rome:

Asserting

Imperial

Authority

(300 B.C.E.–

400 C.E.)

Pansa and Aulus Hirtius [43 B.C.E.], giving me at the same time consular rank in voting, and granted me the *imperium*. It ordered me as propraetor, together with the consuls, to see to it that the state suffered no harm. Moreover, in the same year, when both consuls had fallen in the war, the people elected me consul and a triumvir for the settlement of the commonwealth.

2. Those who assassinated my father I drove into exile, avenging their crime by due process of law; and afterwards when they waged war against the state, I conquered them twice on the battlefield [the two battles of Phillippi (42 B.C.E.)].

3. I waged many wars throughout the whole world by land and by sea, both civil and foreign, and when victorious I spared all citizens who sought pardon. Foreign peoples who could safely be pardoned I preferred to spare rather than to extirpate. About 500,000 Roman citizens were under military oath to me. Of these, when their terms of service were ended, I settled in colonies or sent back to their own municipalities a little more than 300,000, and to all of these I allotted lands or granted money as rewards for military service. I captured 600 ships, exclusive of those which were of smaller class than triremes.

4. Twice I celebrated ovations, three times curule triumphs, and I was acclaimed *imperator* twenty-one times. When the senate decreed additional triumphs to me, I declined them on four occasions. I deposited in the Capitol laurel wreaths adorning my *fasces* [an emblem of Roman authority] after fulfilling the vows which I had made in each war. For successes achieved on land and on sea by me or through my legates under my auspices the senate decreed fifty-five times that thanksgiving be offered to the immortal gods. Moreover, the number of days on which, by decree of the senate, such thanksgiving was offered, was 890. In my triumphs there were led before my chariot nine kings or children of kings. At the time I wrote this, I had been consul thirteen times, and I was in the thirty-seventh year of my tribunician power [14 C.E.]. . . .

6. In the consulship of Marcus Vinicius and Quintus Lucretius, and again in that of Publius Lentulus and Gnaeus Lentulus, and a third time in that of Paullus Fabius Maximus and Quintus Tubero [in 19, 18, and 11 B.C.E.], though the Roman senate and people unitedly agreed that I should be elected sole guardian of the laws and morals with supreme authority, I refused to accept any office offered me which was contrary to the traditions of our ancestors. The measures which the senate desired at that time to be taken by me I carried out by virtue of the tribunician power. In this power I five times voluntarily requested and was given a colleague by the senate. . . .

10. My name was inserted, by decree of the senate, in the hymn of the Salian priests. And it was enacted by law that I should be sacrosanct in perpetuity and that I should posseses the tribunician power as long as I live. I declined to become *pontifex maximus* in place of a colleague while he was still

alive, when the people offered me that priesthood, which my father had held. A few years later, in the consulship of Publius Sulpicius and Gaius Valgius, I accepted this priesthood, when death removed the man who [had] taken possession of it at a time of civil disturbance; and from all Italy a multitude flocked to my election such as had never previously been recorded at Rome. . . .

20. I repaired the Capitol and the theater of Pompey with enormous expenditures on both works, without having my name inscribed on them. I repaired the conduits of the aqueducts which were falling into ruin in many places because of age, and I doubled the capacity of the aqueduct called Marcia by admitting a new spring into its conduit. I completed the Julian Forum and the basilica which was between the temple of Castor and the temple of Saturn, works begun and far advanced by my father, and when the same basilica was destroyed by fire, I enlarged its site and began rebuilding the structure, which is to be inscribed with the names of my sons; and in case it should not be completed while I am still alive, I left instructions that the work be completed by my heirs. In my sixth consulship [28 B.C.E.] I repaired eighty-two temples of the gods in the city, in accordance with a resolution of the senate, neglecting none which at that time required repair. In my seventh consulship [27 B.C.E.] I reconstructed the Flaminian Way from the city as far as Ariminum, and also all the bridges except the Mulvian and the Minucian. . . .

26. I extended the frontiers of all the provinces of the Roman people on whose boundaries were peoples not subject to our empire. I restored peace to the Gallic and Spanish provinces and likewise to Germany, that is to the entire region bounded by the Ocean from Gades to the mouth of the Elbe river. I caused peace to be restored in the Alps, from the region nearest to the Adriatic Sea as far as the Tuscan Sea, without undeservedly making war against any people. My fleet sailed the Ocean from the mouth of the Rhine eastward as far as the territory of the Cimbrians, to which no Roman previously had penetrated either by land or by sea. The Cimbrians, the Charydes, the Semnones, and other German peoples of the same region through their envoys sought my friendship and that of the Roman people. At my command and under my auspices two armies were led almost at the same time into Ethiopia and into Arabia which is called Felix; and very large forces of the enemy belonging to both peoples were killed in battle, and many towns were captured. In Ethiopia a penetration was made as far as the town of Napata, which is next to Meroe; in Arabia the army advanced into the territory of the Sabaeans to the town of Mariba.

27. I added Egypt to the empire of the Roman people. Although I might have made Greater Armenia into a province when its king Artaxes was assassinated, I preferred, following the precedent of our ancestors, to hand over this kingdom, acting through Tiberius Nero, who was then my stepson, to Tigranes, son of King Artavasdes and grandson of King Tigranes. And afterwards, when this same people revolted and rebelled, after I subdued it through

Chapter 6

Han and Rome:

Asserting

Imperial

Authority

(300 B.C.E.–

400 C.E.)

my son Gaius, I handed it over to the rule of King Ariobarzanes, son of Artabazus, king of the Medes, and after his death to his son Artavasdes. When the latter was killed, I dispatched to that kingdom Tigranes, a scion of the royal family of Armenia. I recovered all the provinces extending beyond the Adriatic Sea eastward, and also Cyrenae, which were for the most part already in the possession of kings, as I had previously recovered Sicily and Sardinia, which had been seized in the slave war. . . .

34. In my sixth and seventh consulships, after I had put an end to the civil wars, having attained supreme power by universal consent, I transferred the state from my own power to the control of the Roman senate and the people. For this service of mine I received the title of Augustus by decree of the senate, and the doorposts of my house were publicly decked with laurels, the civic crown was affixed over my doorway, and a golden shield was set up in the Julian senate house, which, as the inscription on this shield testifies, the Roman senate and people gave me in recognition of my valor, clemency, justice, and devotion. After that time I excelled all in authority, but I possessed no more power than the others who were my colleagues in each magistracy.

35. When I held my thirteenth consulship, the senate, the equestrian order, and the entire Roman people gave me the title of "father of the country" and decreed that this title should be inscribed in the vestibule of my house, in the Julian senate house, and in the Augustan Forum on the pedestal of the chariot which was set up in my honor by decree of the senate. At the time I wrote this document I was in my seventy-sixth year. . . .

Source 7 from Cassius Dio, Roman History *in Naphtali Lewis and Meyer Reinhold, eds.,* Roman Civilization: Selected Readings, *vol. 1 (New York: Columbia University Press, 1955), pp. 557–559.*

7. From Cassius Dio, *Roman History*

POWERS AND TITLES OF THE EMPEROR

In this way the power of both people and senate passed entirely into the hands of Augustus, and from this time there was, strictly speaking, a monarchy; for monarchy would be the truest name for it, even if two or three men later held the power jointly. Now, the Romans so detested the title "monarch" that they called their emperors neither dictators nor kings nor anything of this sort. Yet, since the final authority for the government devolves upon them, they needs must be kings. The offices established by the laws, it is true, are maintained even now, except that of censor; but the entire direction and administration is absolutely in accordance with the wishes of the one in power at the time. And yet, in order to preserve the appearance of having this authority not through their power but by virtue of the laws, the emperors have taken to themselves all the offices (including the titles) which under the Republic possessed great power with the consent of the people—with the exception of the dictatorship. Thus, they very often become consuls, and they are always styled proconsuls whenever they are outside the *pomerium*. The title *imperator* is held by them for life, not only by those who have won victories in battle but also by all the rest, to indicate their absolute power, instead of the title "king" or "dictator." These latter titles they have never assumed since they fell out of use in the constitution, but the actuality of those offices is secured to them by the appellation *imperator*. By virtue of the titles named, they secure the right to make levies, collect funds, declare war, make peace, and rule foreigners and citizens alike everywhere and always—even to the extent of being able to put to death both *equites* and senators inside the *pomerium*—and all the other powers once granted to the consuls and other officials possessing independent authority; and by virtue of holding the censorship they investigate our lives and morals as well as take the census, enrolling some in the equestrian and senatorial orders and removing others from these orders according to their will. By virtue of being consecrated in all the priesthoods and, in addition, from their right to bestow most of them upon others, as well as from the fact that, even if two or three persons rule jointly, one of them is *pontifex maximus,* they hold in their own hands supreme authority over all matters both profane and sacred. The tribunician power, as it is called, which once the most influential men used to hold, gives them the right to nullify the effects of the measures taken by any other official, in case they do not approve, and makes their persons inviolable; and if they appear to be wronged in even the slightest degree, not merely by deed but even by word, they may destroy the guilty party as one accursed, without a trial. The emperors, it should be explained, do not think it lawful to be tribunes, inasmuch as they all belong to the patrician class, but they assume the power of the tribunes in its entirety, as it was at its height; and the number of the years of their rule is counted from the assumption of this power, the theory being that they receive it annually along with those who actually hold the office of tribune. These, then, are the institutions they have taken over from the Republic, each essentially in its traditional form and with the same title, so as to give the impression of possessing no power that has not been granted them. . . .

Thus by virtue of these Republican titles they have clothed themselves with all the powers of the government, so that they actually possess all the prerogatives of kings without the usual title. For the appellation "Caesar" or "Augustus" confers upon them no actual power but merely shows in the one case that they are the successors of their family line, and in the other the splendor of their rank. The name "Father" perhaps gives them a certain authority over us all—the authority which fathers once had over their children; yet it did not signify this at first, but betokened honor and served as an admonition both to them to love their subjects as they would their children, and to their subjects to revere them as they would their fathers. . . .

[147]

Chapter 6

Han and Rome:

Asserting

Imperial

Authority

(300 B.C.E.–

400 C.E.)

Source 8: Courtesy of the Trustees of the British Museum.

8. Roman Coin of the Reign of Emperor Nero (r. 54–68)

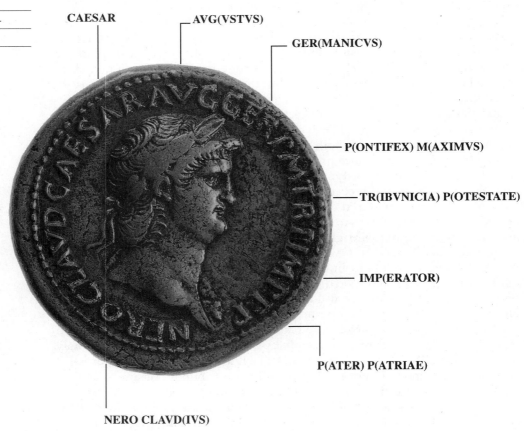

CAESAR

AVG(VSTVS)

GER(MANICVS)

P(ONTIFEX) M(AXIMVS)

TR(IBVNICIA) P(OTESTATE)

IMP(ERATOR)

P(ATER) P(ATRIAE)

NERO CLAVD(IVS)

Source 9 from Alinari/Art Resource, NY.

9. Trajan's Column, Rome

Chapter 6

Han and Rome:

Asserting

Imperial

Authority

(300 B.C.E.–

400 C.E.)

10. Detail from Trajan's Column

Source 11 from V. Ehrenberg and A. H. M. Jones, trans., Documents Illustrating the Reigns of Augustus and Tiberius, *1976, p. 72.*

11. Roman Temple Inscription in Myra, Lycia (Asia Minor)

Divine Augustus Caesar, son of a god, imperator of land and sea, the benefactor and saviour of the whole world, the people of the Myrians.

Marcus Agrippa, the benefactor and saviour of the province, the people of the Myrians.

Source 12 from E. M. Smallwood, trans., Documents Illustrating the Principates of Gaius, Claudius and Nero, *1967, p. 64.*

12. Edict and Speech of Nero to the Greeks

Imperator Caesar proclaims:

Since I wish to reward most noble Greece for its good will and piety towards me, I order that as many as possible from this province attend at Corinth on November 29th.

When crowds had gathered in convention, he delivered the following address:

Men of Greece, I bestow upon you an unexpected gift—though anything may be anticipated from my generosity—a gift of such a size that you were incapable of asking for it. All you Greeks who inhabit Achaea and what until now was the Peloponnese, receive freedom and immunity from taxation, something you have not all had even in your most prosperous times, for you have been slaves either to foreigners or to each other. I wish that I might have bestowed this gift when Greece was at her peak, so that more might enjoy my beneficence. For this reason I hold the times to blame for having reduced the size of my beneficence. But, as it is, I bestow the beneficence upon you not out of pity but out of good will and I reward your gods, whose constant care for me on land and sea I have enjoyed, because they have made it possible for me to bestow such great benefactions. For other principes have conferred freedom on cities, but only Nero has done so even on a province.

[*In response, the following decree of Acraephia was issued, proclaiming Nero a god.*]

Chapter 6

Han and Rome:

Asserting

Imperial

Authority

(300 B.C.E.–

400 C.E.)

The high-priest of the Augusti for life and of Nero Claudius Caesar Augustus, Epaminondas, son of Epaminondas, proclaimed (submitted by him for prior consideration to the council and people):

Since the lord of the entire world, Nero, pontifex maximus, in his 13th year of tribunician power, father of his country, New Sun that has shone on the Greeks, has decided to bestow beneficence upon Greece and has rewarded and shown piety towards our gods, who have stood by him everywhere for his care and safety; since he, Nero, Zeus the Liberator, the one and only greatest imperator of our times, friend of the Greeks, has bestowed the eternal indigenous, native freedom that had formerly been taken from the Greeks, he has shown his favour, he has brought back the autonomy and freedom of the past and to this great and unexpected gift has added immunity from taxation, quite complete, which none of the previous Augusti gave us. For all these reasons it has been decided by the magistrates and councillors and people to worship him at the existing altar dedicated to Zeus the Saviour, and to inscribe upon it "To Zeus the Liberator, Nero, forever" and to erect statues of Nero Zeus the Liberator and the goddess Augusta Messallina in the temple of Ptoian Apollo to share it with our ancestral gods, so that, when these things have been done, our city may be seen to have poured out every honour and piety upon the house of the lord Augustus Nero; it has also been decided to inscribe the decree on a column set beside Zeus the Saviour in the marketplace and on the temple of Ptoian Apollo.

QUESTIONS TO CONSIDER

As you read and studied the individual pieces of evidence looking for clues about the ways the builders of the Han and Roman empires conceived of and justified imperial authority, you probably noted some shifts of emphasis. Later rulers and their advisers often embellished the ideas of the founding emperors. The founder of the Chinese empire, Qin Shi Huangdi, based much of his claim to an exalted imperial position on his success in conquering "all lands within the four seas." But subsequent rulers, who did not themselves play the role of conquerors, needed to develop other justifications for their power. Do you detect a similar shift in the Roman materials?

The stone inscriptions in Source 1 probably best reflect Qin Shi Huangdi's own view of his authority. Though they hail his military victories and worldwide conquest, note the claim that he inaugurated a new age by unifying the Six States and standardizing all laws and norms "wherever the sun and moon shine." Note, too, the references to his sageliness, a quality reflected in the title *Huangdi* (*Huang-ti*), which he adopted. Both words compounded into this title, though often translated "August Emperor" as here, came from terms applied to ancient sages whom tradition portrayed as the creators of human civilization. What does "sage" seem to imply in the emperor's biography? Why do you think the first emperor identified himself with this figure?

In addition to setting up stone markers and other monuments to celebrate his accomplishments while alive, Shi Huangdi constructed a huge tomb out on a plain some fifty kilometers away from his capital city to preserve his fame in death. This practice, which Han emperors continued on a more modest scale, gave him another way to shape his public image. Revisit Source 2, the photograph of his burial mound at Mt. Li. Originally an earthen pyramid 47 meters tall, this mound stood within a 2 square kilometer enclosure that contained a virtual underground palace. As the detail of one of the excavations shows (Source 3), the area all around was honeycombed with pits filled with thousands of pottery figures. The overwhelming majority of these figures are soldiers like those shown here. What image of authority does this monument and its legions of clay figures imply? How does it compare with the images of conqueror, unifier, and sage presented in the biography?

Qin Shi Huangdi tried to link his rule with higher powers. These included his own deified ancestors and an impersonal cycle of cosmological forces believed to shape human events. But later Han emperors, who patronized Confucianism, elaborated this tendency further. In Source 4, Dong Zhongshu (Tung Chung-shu), a court Confucian adviser, explains how a ruler serves the higher moral power of Heaven, the deity with whom Confucians linked cosmic order. What

does his statement that "the king is but the executor of Heaven" imply about the nature of imperial authority? What purpose does it ascribe to the state? And what does it mean to say "the ruler is the basis of the state"? Source 5, a decree issued by the Han Emperor Wendi expresses the full development of the idea that Han emperors had a special mandate from Heaven to rule. But note that an emperor could lose this charge. Confucians argued that since Heaven gave ethical rulers mandates to rule, it could likewise withdraw authority from the unworthy. What according to Wendi's decree seems to bring Heaven's displeasure—and how does he expect Heaven to show it? Confucians used the doctrine of heavenly warnings to press for a professional bureaucracy schooled in their values as a check on arbitrary rule. Can you gather from this decree how the doctrine empowered imperial officials as well as emperors?

Source 6, *The Achievements of the Divine Augustus*, or *Res Gestae Divi Augustus*, issued by Augustus Caesar provides a comparable Roman counterpart to Qin Shi Huangdi's stone inscriptions. It, too, came to be inscribed on stone, as copies were carved on the walls of temples throughout the Roman Empire. More autobiographical and personal than Shi Huangdi's inscriptions, it nonetheless served much the same purpose: to explain Augustus's new titles and power. Notice, however, that despite the name of the work, Augustus himself makes no claim to divinity here. Nor does he presume to be a new kind of ruler by right of any transcendent

Chapter 6

Han and Rome:

Asserting

Imperial

Authority

(300 B.C.E.–

400 C.E.)

power, divine or natural. Although pointing out how he has enlarged the Roman Empire, he does not claim to be a world conqueror, much less the creator of a new state. Saying only that he "liberated the Republic, which was oppressed by the tyranny of a faction," he presents himself as a restorer not an innovator and carefully professes not to transgress "the traditions of our ancestors."

Yet, as Augustus notes, the Roman people not only elected him consul, the highest executive office in the Republic, the Senate voted him the extraordinary title of *imperator,* or emperor. Again and again he attributes his authority to these two sources. Their importance in the state was symbolized by the universal inscription S.P.Q.R., signifying *Senatus Populusque Romanus* ("The Senate and the Roman People"), borne on Roman standards and monuments. As the "sole guardian of the laws and morals with supreme authority" elected by the Roman Senate and people, what kind of imperial ruler did Augustus presume to be? In keeping with his elected offices, Augustus often preferred to use another title bestowed upon him by the Senate—*princeps,* meaning "first" among his fellow citizens. What kind of legitimization do these claims imply? In what sense did it qualify him to assume the title "father of the country," which he asserts so prominently at the end of this laudatory piece.

In his *Roman History,* the third-century historian Cassius Dio questions Augustus's pose as mere restorer of the Republic. In Source 7, an excerpt from this work, Cassius Dio argues that Augustus and subsequent Roman emperors actually wrested all power from the Senate and people and instituted an autocratic system of monarchy in which the *imperator* became an absolute ruler. Behind the façade of their republican titles, he charges, Augustus and his successors assumed "all the prerogatives of kings without the usual title." They not only absorbed all civil authority in this way, he says, but other authority, too. For they took the title *pontifex maximus,* or high priest of the official Roman pantheon of gods, along with their profane offices and honors. One of the few surviving statues of Augustus indeed portrays him in this priestly role. What support do you suppose he and his successors expected to add to their status through this title?

Later emperors continued to present themselves as high priest as well as civic father, chief executive, and, of course, heir to Augustus. Look at Source 8, a *sesterius* or bronze coin minted during the time of Emperor Nero (r. 54–68). Long accustomed to commemorating leading citizens on state coinage, the Romans found it natural to mint money bearing imperial portraits under the empire. These portraits and the legends accompanying them, of course, provided emperors with an excellent way to propagandize their public images. Notice all the names and titles appearing on the face of the coin reproduced here. Beginning at the lower left, the coin gives the emperor's personal name, Nero Claudius, then affirms his relationship to Caesar Augustus through his adopted father, Germanicus. Then around the rim follow abbreviated versions of his four most prized titles: PM for *Pontifex Maximus,* TRY for *Tribunicia Potestate* or tribuneship (an office supposedly representing the lower or plebeian class of the empire), IMP for *Imperator,* and PP for *Pater Patriae* or "father of the country." How do these titles compare with those assumed by Augustus?

Besides asserting civil and religious authority, a number of later emperors chose to portray themselves as military commanders and conquerors. Emperor Trajan (r. 98–117), who began his political career as a general, especially popularized this role. He not only commissioned statues of himself in full armor and minted coins bearing his image as a warrior, but raised a great column in Rome to depict his generalship. Source 9 shows this column. Although built primarily to hold aloft a huge statue of Trajan in military dress, the column also publicizes his most famous campaign, a war fought against the Dacians on the Balkan peninsula. Battle scenes like the one shown in Source 10 spiraled up its entire length, recalling a tradition of battlefield leadership going back to Alexander the Great and the Persian monarchs whom he imitated. Like similar monuments and victory arches raised in Rome by other emperors, Trajan's Column openly celebrates military conquest. What kind of imperial authority do these images evoke?

The image of a world conqueror closely parallels another theme that eventually affected the way Roman emperors characterized themselves and their authority: the tradition of world savior. In the eastern lands of the empire, rulers had often claimed not only to represent gods but to *be* gods in their own right. Rome's newly conquered subjects in this quarter, therefore, readily accorded the emperors divine status. Source 11, a commemorative inscription from the time of Caesar Augustus carved on a temple in Myra, a city on the Mediterranean coast in present-day Turkey, showed this trend well underway. Note how it characterizes the first emperor as "divine Augustus Caesar" and calls him "son of a god," implying that his adoptive father, Julius Caesar, was divine, too. And observe how it lauds him as "benefactor and savior of the whole world," far more than just a restorer of Roman liberties.

By the time of Nero, the cult of imperial divinity encouraged even more exaggerated claims like those in Source 12, an inscription from Acraephia. Issued by a priest in the service of the Augusti, or imperial cult, on the occasion of Nero's decision to grant many Greek cities special tax immunity, it equates Nero, "lord of the entire world," with the greatest of Greek gods, Zeus—here characterized as Liberator and Savior. By the end of the fourth century, Emperor Diocletian, who ruled from the eastern half of the realm, regularly equated himself with Zeus, or with his Roman equivalent, Jupiter. Contrast this form of divine monarchy with Augustus's own more modest view of sovereignty. How does it change the nature and justification of imperial authority?

Chapter 6

Han and Rome:

Asserting

Imperial

Authority

(300 B.C.E.–

400 C.E.)

As you compare this vision of a divinely led empire with the Han idea of a Heavenly ordained ruler, ask yourself why religious beliefs of this sort became so entwined with political institutions in both imperial traditions. How would people today react if their leaders claimed to have special divine or religious powers? Modern assumptions about the separation of state and religion make it difficult for us to understand why political supremacy might be equated with sacred power. But clearly this equation occurred in both ancient Rome and China. What other common features do you find in these two traditions that contrasts with modern practice or belief? Think for a moment about the gender implied in all of these images of imperial rule. How different would it be if the Han rulers had claimed to be "children" of Heaven or the Roman emperors proclaimed themselves "parents" of the country. What does the masculine nature of the expressions imply about ancient Roman and Chinese notions of power?

EPILOGUE

Although extremely powerful for a few centuries, neither Han nor Rome proved immune to eventual decay. Internal conflicts and divisions strained their administrative structures to the breaking point, and as central authority ebbed, their empires fragmented in the face of rebellions and invasions. To their subjects such collapse entailed far more than the end of political regimes. It meant the break-up of world order and the start of extended eras of change, turmoil, and insecurity at both ends of the Eurasian continent. Among other results, such change brought an end of regional unity and world-states.

The Han collapsed first following a generation of court intrigues and coups in the second half of the second century that allowed imperial power to drift away from reigning emperors into the hands of palace eunuchs who lacked any claim to virtue or legitimacy. Uncertain of the bureaucracy's loyalty, they hesitated in the face of a wave of popular insurrections that exploded in the Yellow River plain in 184 following a devastating plague. United by millenarian bands known as Yellow Turbans, pledged to found a revolutionary "Heavenly State of Great Peace," the rebels nearly toppled the Han. For lack of central forces, provincial governors and local elites had to organize their own resistance against the rebels. After quelling the rebellions, therefore, they refused to disband their forces and relinquish local control. Nervously building up their power, they became de facto warlords, who began to vie with each other for wider influence. Eventually one of their number, a general named Cao Cao, set himself up in the capital as protector of the impotent throne and used his armies to prolong nominal Han rule for a few decades more. But when his son deposed the last Han emperor in order to ascend the throne himself in 220, many provincial magnates refused to recognize his authority and partitioned the empire into warring fragments. Despite a brief reunification of their territories at the end of the third century, further civil strife soon broke out again, and all hope of imperial restoration crumbled as waves of invaders swept across the frontiers to engulf north China.

Imperial Rome lasted longer, but eventually it, too, fragmented. Although for different reasons than in China, rivalry around the throne weakened the monarchy. Left with inadequate resources, provincial leaders failed to deal with mounting domestic problems and frontier dangers. Emperor Diocletian (r. 284–305) and his immediate successors tried to overhaul the administrative structure of the empire and enhance imperial prestige. Constantine (r. 306–337) who shifted the capital away from Rome to his namesake city, Constantinople, enjoyed brief success. But the benefits of these belated reforms did not last long, and by the end of the fourth century, the decline had begun anew. Eventually the relentless pressure of German tribes along the Rhine and Danube frontier brought the empire's final collapse. Following the Gothic invasion and sack of Rome in 410, outsiders overran and divided up the empire's western half. With the loss of Rome and most of the Latin-speaking lands, the eastern half, ruled from Constantinople, began to evolve into a very different kind of Greek empire known as Byzantium.

Despite their fall, both empires left enduring legacies of institutions and ideas, including ideals of universal empire and imperial authority. After a lapse of nearly three and a half centuries, East Asians succeeded in resurrecting a great imperial state under the Sui and Tang dynasties of the sixth through the ninth centuries. Though altered in subsequent centuries, this imperial state essentially survived intact until 1911 when the last *huangdi,* or sage lord, abdicated in the face of the revolution that instituted a westernized Chinese republic. And to this day, the Chinese still call themselves in their own language *Han ran*—the "people of Han." In the West, the imperial ideal proved more elusive, and though Europeans tried on occasion to revive the Roman Empire, none of their endeavors fully succeeded. Justinian's effort in the sixth century to rebuild it from a Byzantine base failed, as did Charlemagne's ninth-century attempt to restore it from his Frankish kingdom. Yet the mystique of the Caesars persisted into modern times, leading the Germans and Russians to appropriate the name for their rulers in *Kaiser* and *Czar.* Napoleon, who rode to power in France on the first tide of modern nationalism, showed how powerful that aura remained at the start of the nineteenth century when he gladly abandoned republican scruples to grasp the old title *imperator* for himself. And both Mussolini and Hitler evoked it again in the twentieth century in the symbols of their authoritarian power. As many have observed, the papacy preserves a more benign version of the Roman monarchy into the present.

Chapter 6

Han and Rome:

Asserting

Imperial

Authority

(300 B.C.E.–

400 C.E.)

The lasting power of these imperial ideals suggests that they embodied some of the most deeply rooted assumptions and beliefs from within their respective cultural spheres. A final point worth considering, therefore, is the degree to which they may continue to influence contemporary political life. Some, for example, claim to see vestiges of assumed sagehood in the "great Helmsman" Mao Zedong (Mao Tse-tung) who, after all, proclaimed the advent of a new socialist age with global significance from a balcony overlooking Tiananmen Square in Beijing—a square whose very name, derived from the adjacent entrance to an old imperial palace, means the Gate of Heavenly Peace! And how many modern republics still revere a military figure who became "father of his country" by virtue of restoring the lost liberty of a people through some presumed divine grace?

CHAPTER SEVEN

INTERNATIONAL RELIGIOUS

COMMUNITIES (300 B.C.E.–800 C.E.)

THE PROBLEM

In the last chapter, we examined the growth of large empires in the ancient world, noting the technical and bureaucratic structures that enabled them to grow and flourish. In this chapter, we explore another way in which large territories were brought or held together: through allegiance to a set of religious ideas or a religious figure. Of the thousands of religions practiced in the world today, three claim large numbers of adherents throughout the world: Buddhism, Christianity, and Islam. Each of these began as a small group of followers around a single leader and then was transformed, slowly or quickly, into an international religious community. In the case of Buddhism and Christianity, this occurred several centuries after the lives of the initial leaders, Siddhartha Gautama, called the Buddha (ca. 563–483 B.C.E.), and Jesus of Nazareth (ca. 5 B.C.E.–29 C.E.). In the case of Islam, this growth

began during the lifetime of the initial leader, Muhammad (ca. 570–632 C.E.), and continued for many centuries after his death.

For each of these religions, the transformation from small sect to international community was accomplished by individuals who also had what we would term secular political power; in other words, they were political as well as religious leaders. In the case of Buddhism, the person generally regarded as dramatically expanding Buddhism both within and beyond the Indian subcontinent was the Mauryan emperor Ashoka (ruled ca. 273–232 B.C.E.). In the case of Christianity, the Roman emperor Constantine (ruled 306–337 C.E.), the first emperor to become a Christian, is usually seen as the key figure. In the case of Islam, Muhammad himself and the first four caliphs who succeeded him, termed the "patriarchal caliphs"—Abu Bakr (ruled 632–634), Umar (ruled 634–644), Uthman (ruled 644–656), and Ali (ruled 656–661)—spread Islam across Arabia and into Persia and

Chapter 7
International
Religious
Communities
(300 B.C.E.–
800 C.E.)

North Africa, setting the pattern for later, more extensive, expansion into Europe, Africa, and Asia.

In each of these cases, the individuals involved, or those close to them, have left us a record of these transformations and what they were attempting to accomplish. Your task in this chapter will be to use a variety of sources to answer these questions: How did political leaders within Buddhism, Christianity, and Islam encourage the growth of their chosen religious community? What differences and similarities do you see in their actions and in what they viewed as most important in the lives of these communities?

BACKGROUND

Studying the history of any religious movement can pose special problems for historians. We may have more trouble achieving unbiased assessments of the history of religion than of other historical topics because of our intellectual, spiritual, or emotional commitments to certain religious ideas. This does not mean, however, that we should avoid religious topics—to do so would make it impossible for us to understand the past—but instead we should be aware of our own prejudices and approach all religions with respect. Our job as historians is to understand people's religious ideas within their historical context and to see how religious faith manifested itself in historically observable phenomena; it is not to judge whether certain religious ideas are right or wrong, true or false.

Difficulties in being objective when studying the history of religion can stem not only from our own personal religious commitments, but also from the nature of the sources available. Very few religious sources were written simply to describe what happened but, more often, to express central doctrines or to win converts. Even those sources that do describe historical events, such as the actions of the political leaders we are examining in this chapter, were often written for the added purpose of spreading the faith. Many of these were composed long after the events occurred, so later developments colored the ways in which they were recorded. In some cases, these written records were based on extensive oral traditions, but they are now our only source for the events they describe, and we have no way to check their accuracy. They may relate events that were viewed at the time as clearly miraculous—visions in the sky, voices from heaven—but also as having actually happened. Luckily for our job as historians, we do not need to take a stand on the historicity of such events. What is important for us is that people believed that they had happened and acted accordingly.

In talking about any religious group, we often make distinctions between history, tradition, and myth, but the lines between these are never sharp and frequently contested. It is important to recognize, however, that tradition and myth are not the same; when historians use the phrase "according to tradition, . . ." they are not saying that an event is completely mythological but simply commenting on the limits of their sources. In many religions, deep divisions developed quite early not only about the religious meaning of certain events, but also about when and whether certain things happened at all. Thus, not only can our sources be obscure, they can also be contradictory. Often there is no way to resolve the contradiction, and we simply have to say "according to this tradition . . . whereas according to that tradition . . .". These divisions within religions were often more bitterly contested than differences between religions, and indeed, discords within religions continue to shape the contemporary world in profound and sometimes violent ways.

Keeping in mind these cautionary thoughts about the evaluation of all religious sources, we can now focus more specifically on the context for the sources we include here. Because we are examining the actions of certain leaders in regard to their religious communities, the evidence focuses on that aspect of their reigns. Your textbook can provide you with more general information about Ashoka and the Mauryan Empire, Constantine's reign in the Roman Empire, and the lives of Muhammad and the patriarchal caliphs.

The Mauryan emperor Ashoka was the grandson of the founder of the Mauryan Empire, Chandragupta, who had defeated one of the generals of Alexander the Great in 304 B.C.E. and expanded his holdings to include most of the Indian subcontinent. Ashoka grew up at the royal court at Pataliputra in the Ganges River Valley, where many religious traditions mingled—Brahmanism, Jainism, Buddhism—and where ideas about the role of the ruler were openly debated and discussed. The most extensive consideration of these was a treatise on government traditionally attributed to one of Chandragupta's ministers, the Brahmanical teacher Kautilya, titled *Arthashastra,* in which power and benevolence were described as the two main objectives of kingship.

At some point in his life, Ashoka accepted Buddhism, although traditions vary about exactly who converted him. They also vary about the timing of some events within Buddhism that probably occurred during or shortly before or after Ashoka's reign, such as formal splits because of disagreements about various interpretations of the Buddha's teaching. Certain aspects of the practice and prevalence of Buddhism at that time are very clear, however: we know, for example, that people often went on pilgrimages to the holy places associated with the Buddha's life, built mounds called *stupas* to house Buddhist relics, and supported communities of monks and nuns called the *sangha;* Buddhism was well established in central India, and had begun to spread north to Kashmir and south to the Deccan plateau; and a canon of sacred texts, attributed to the Buddha, had begun to appear.

Like Ashoka, the Roman emperor Constantine underwent a religious conversion some time after he became an adult, though there are discrepancies in the sources and differences of opinion among historians

Chapter 7
International
Religious
Communities
(300 B.C.E.–
800 C.E.)

about exactly when this was and how complete an acceptance and understanding of Christianity Constantine evidenced. Constantine was the son of Emperor Constantius, but his claim to the throne was challenged by a number of rivals. Though his troops elected him emperor in 306, the emperorship itself was divided at the time in a complex way, and Constantine did not become sole sovereign until 324, after he had defeated all other claimants. Much of Constantine's early reign was thus spent in warfare, and he became extremely concerned with establishing structures and institutions that would make the Roman Empire more united.

Christianity appeared to Constantine to be just such a unifying force. Christianity had originally been largely ignored by high-level Roman authorities, who regarded it as a sect within Judaism and therefore of little consequence. There were sporadic persecutions in the first century C.E., but no concerted campaign to annihilate Christianity. These persecutions may have actually helped Christianity spread, as the heroism of martyrs often impressed those who watched their public executions and who later became Christians themselves. As more non-Jews converted, Roman authorities became more concerned, particularly because Christians refused to participate in the sacrifices and ceremonies honoring the traditional Roman gods. These ceremonies were patriotic as well as religious to the Romans, for they were carried out for the good of the state and often specifically held to assure military victory. Persecution was thus

stepped up in the second and third centuries, and it became particularly vicious during the reigns of those emperors who were most concerned about the health of the empire. By this point it was too late to stop the spread of Christianity, which had a growing following among people of all classes throughout the Roman Empire and a strong bureaucratic structure based on regional officials termed bishops. There is great disagreement among historians about how much of the Roman population had become Christian by the time of Constantine, but it was certainly a sizable minority.

The history of Islam is very different from that of Buddhism and Christianity in that, from the beginning, it was both a religious and political community; Muhammad was in some ways his own Constantine. Like both Ashoka and Constantine, Muhammad experienced a religious conversion when he was an adult, but, unlike them, he was a merchant rather than a ruler. He lived in Mecca, an important trading and religious center on the Arabian peninsula, which was divided into different tribal groups and lacked the leadership of a single ruler. Muhammad's conversion involved visions of angelic beings who ordered him to preach a message of a single God and to become God's Prophet, which he began to do in his hometown of Mecca. While he slowly gathered followers there, he also provoked a great deal of resistance and in 622 migrated with his followers to Medina—this event, termed the *hegira,* marks the beginning of the Muslim calendar. At Medina,

Muhammad was much more successful, and by his death in 632 he had unified most of the Arabian peninsula into a religious/political community (termed the *umma*) of *Muslims,* a word meaning "those who comply with or submit to God's will." (The first umma was formed by the Charter of Medina in 622 and included the local Jewish community, which established a precedent for the later protection of Jews under Islam.)

Muhammad's revelations were written down by his followers during his lifetime and shortly thereafter were organized into an authoritative text, the Qur'an, regarded by Muslims as the direct words of God (Allah) to his prophet Muhammed and therefore especially revered. (These revelations were in Arabic. If Muslims use translations in other languages, they do so alongside the original Arabic.) At the same time, other sayings and accounts of Muhammad, which gave advice on matters that went beyond the Qur'an, were collected into books termed *hadith;* Muslim tradition (*Sunna*) consists of both the Qur'an and the hadith. Unfortunately for the Muslim community, neither the Qur'an nor the hadith gave clear guidance about how successors to Muhammad were to be chosen, but a group of Muhammad's closest followers elected Abu Bakr, who was a close friend of the Prophet's and a member of a small tribe affiliated with the Prophet's tribe, as *caliph,* meaning "successor." This election set a precedent for the ratification of the subsequent patriarchal caliphs, though it was unsuccessfully opposed militarily by other Arab tribes. A more serious challenge developed later among supporters of the fourth caliph, Ali. Ali claimed the caliphate because of his blood ties with Muhammad—he was the Prophet's cousin and son-in-law—and because Muhammad had designated him as *imam,* or "leader." He was assassinated shortly after becoming caliph, and his supporters began to assert that he should rightly have been the first caliph and that all subsequent caliphs were usurpers. These supporters of Ali—termed *Shi'ites*—saw Ali and subsequent imams as the divinely inspired leaders of the community, whereas the larger body of Muslims who accepted the first elections—termed *Sunnis*—regarded the caliphs as political leaders. Since Islam did not have an organized church and priesthood, the caliphs had an additional function of safeguarding and enforcing the religious law (*sharia*) with the advice of scholars (*ulama*), particularly the jurists, judges, and scholastics who were knowledgeable about the Qur'an and hadith.

Chapter 7

International

Religious

Communities

(300 B.C.E.–

800 C.E.)

THE METHOD

In reading the two central questions for this chapter, you no doubt noted that the first is largely informational and the second is comparative. This order is not accidental, for historians must first uncover information about past societies before they can begin to make comparisons. Indeed, many historians choose to devote their entire lives to the intensive study of a single culture and time period and are not especially interested in comparative questions. World history courses, including probably the one you are enrolled in, tend to provoke comparative questions, however, and some historians would argue that to a certain degree *all* history is comparative. By this they mean that we approach all other cultures from the vantage point of our own, and thus we can understand them only by comparing them to what is familiar and known. They stress that these comparisons may be implicit, but they are inescapable. Other historians, though, dispute this point and argue that the best history writing seeks to be highly objective, and as much as possible, constrains the historian's own cultural background from intruding.

Whatever they think about *implicit* comparisons, historians who make *explicit* comparisons in their work recognize that these must be derived and expressed very carefully. Not only must they think about the ways in which the events, individuals, or developments that are the subjects of their study are comparable, but they must also think about the ways in which the sources available to them are comparable. Very often the types of records left by one culture are quite different from those left by another, even regarding matters as central as political leadership. Thus, as you begin to make comparisons between the actions and ideas of the leaders who are the focus of this chapter, you will need to think about how your ideas—and the connections and comparisons you are making—are shaped by the types of sources you are using.

Most of the sources for this chapter are written; they consist primarily of pronouncements of political leaders themselves or the writings of historians or other commentators who were members of the leader's community. In no case does our evidence come from someone who was hostile to the individuals or their actions. (This is another aspect of the evidence you need to keep in mind.) Your primary method will be careful reading, and we advise you to work first on gathering information and then to go back and make your comparisons. You may find it useful to list all the actions and ideas of the leaders described in the sources, so as to summarize their roles in your own words before you begin to make comparisons.

Sources 1 through 3 all relate to King Ashoka. Source 1 is a selection of some of the so-called rock and pillar edicts, which are the best record we have of Ashoka's reign. These are inscriptions that King Ashoka ordered carved in stone on large rocks in prominent places or on tall pillars he had erected for this purpose. The edicts are found in a number of different locations throughout Ashoka's large empire, particularly along the borders. They were written in Prakrit, the language spoken at Ashoka's time, and are the oldest surviving written documents of historical importance in India. Read these edicts carefully. What convinced Ashoka that he should change the way he was ruling and acting? What does he now see as the main aim of his reign? What actions has he done to promote this aim? How does he relate to the community of Buddhist monks and nuns (the sangha, sometimes spelled Samgha)? How does he say he treats those who follow religions other than Buddhism, and how does he advise his subjects to treat people with different religious ideas?

Source 2 is a photograph of one of the Ashokan pillars, topped with a single lion. (Other pillars are topped with three lions, an emblem that is now on the state seal of India and Indian coins, or lions and the Buddhist wheel of law, an emblem reproduced on India's flag.) Each of these pillars—more than thirty have been discovered—was transported hundreds of miles from the same quarry and polished very smooth before it was inscribed. Why might Ashoka have regarded this effort as important? Why would pillars such as these be an effective way to relay the information you have just read? How would the pillars complement the visits by officials and by Ashoka himself?

The other major type of source we have for Ashoka's reign are legends, oral traditions about him that did not die out when the Mauryan Empire collapsed but spread throughout In-

dia and beyond its borders. Some of these were written down in the Pali language as part of the chronicles from the island of Sri Lanka, where Buddhist tradition holds that Ashoka's son Mahendra and daughter Samghamitra spread Buddhism. Others were written down in Sanskrit in northern India and gradually collected into a single text called the *Asokavadana*. Source 3 is from this text, relating an incident from Ashoka's life after he converted to Buddhism. When we use legends and oral traditions in historical investigations, the most important question to ask ourselves is not whether the events really happened, but why followers of an individual tell and retell them; in other words, how they worked to support their ideas. Why would the Buddhist followers of Ashoka tell this story? How does it fit with Ashoka's statements about his own ideas and reign as inscribed in the rock and pillar edicts?

Sources 4 through 6 concern the Roman emperor Constantine. Like the evidence about Ashoka, many of the records that survive from Constantine's reign are official edicts and proclamations, though these were written on papyrus and parchment rather than being inscribed on pillars. Source 4 comprises a series of edicts issued by Constantine regarding Christianity, beginning with the original edict of toleration from 311 signed by three of the then four rulers of the Roman Empire: Lactantius, Licinius, and Constantine. The remaining edicts were issued by Constantine alone and are reprinted here in chronological order. They cover a

Chapter 7

International

Religious

Communities

(300 B.C.E.–

800 C.E.)

range of actions that Constantine took either directly on behalf of the Christian church or because he was inspired by Christian ideas. Some indicate his opinion toward those following other systems of belief. Reading them will allow you to begin developing your ideas about Constantine's role.

The most important record we have of Constantine's life is a biography written shortly after his death by the historian and Christian bishop Eusebius of Caesarea (ca. 263–339?), a close adviser to Constantine. As Constantine's friend and an official in the Church, Eusebius expressed a particular point of view in his biography, but many of the events he discusses, such as Constantine's proclamations and military battles, are recorded in other sources as well. Other events are not verifiable, but, as with the legends surrounding King Ashoka, the stories about Constantine came to be considered true by later Christians. Source 5 is a series of selections from Eusebius's *Life of Constantine*. As you read these excerpts, note the actions Constantine takes in regard to the Christian church and the statements he makes about it. What convinces Constantine that he should become a Christian? How does he relate to the bishops, the Church's key officials? What does he see as most important for the Church? How do the events related here fit with the imperial edicts you read in Source 4? How might Eusebius's position as an official in the Church shape the way he reports history?

Like Ashoka, Constantine erected large monuments to his rule, most

notably the Arch of Constantine in Rome. In Source 5, you discover smaller ways in which he portrayed his religious sentiments and celebrated his reign, through coins and portraits. Source 6 shows two of these coins, one portraying Constantine with a halo and another, two soldiers with the *labarum*, the special standard that was made for the army after Constantine's vision. Why might Constantine have thought it important to issue coins with symbols such as these? Why would coins be an effective means of communicating ideas?

When we turn to the transformation of Islam from small sect to international religious community, we can no longer look at the actions of just one individual, but we must explore those of a series of rulers. Here we have four basic types of sources: the Qur'an, the hadith, histories and biographies written after the fact, and legal or other commentaries on the actions of rulers and ideas about rulership. As you read Sources 7 through 10, you need to think about how the purpose for which each was written might have shaped the discourse.

Source 7 is several verses from the Qur'an regarding the duties of believers to authorities, the rewards for believers, the treatment for those who did not accept the Prophet's words, and the attitudes Muslims were to have toward Jews and Christians. Source 8 is a selection of sayings ascribed to the Prophet from three different collections of hadith, again addressing the duties of believers toward their leaders and leaders toward the community. Because the hadith record sayings and traditions that were handed down orally for several generations, they are generally prefaced by a listing of the names of those who related them back to the early years of Islam. According to both the Qur'an and the hadith, what are the most important duties of the leaders toward the community? of the community toward leaders? What developments are to be most guarded against? How are those who are not Muslims to be treated?

Source 9 is a selection from the earliest biographer of Muhammad whose work has survived, Ibn Ishaq, who was born in Medina in 707 and died in Baghdad in 773. (The Muslim calendar uses the hegira, Muhammad's migration from Mecca to Medina in 622, as its starting date, written as A.H.; in that dating system, Ibn Ishaq's dates are A.H. 85–151.) As with Eusebius's biography of Constantine, many of the incidents recorded have been confirmed by archaeological findings and other sources, so that it is regarded as generally reliable, though, as with Eusebius, the author writes from the point of view of a committed follower and admirer. As you read Source 9, note the kinds of actions by which Muhammad spread his message. How were those who opposed him to be handled? What were the most important aspects of the Muslim community? Source 10 is from the *Book of Land-tax* by Abu Yusuf (died A.H. 182/798 C.E.), a legal scholar who wrote a lengthy book of advice for his sovereign, the caliph Harun al-Rashid. Though this evidence comes from a later period, Abu Yusuf relates a number of incidents about the earliest caliphs as part of his instructions to the present one. What actions and advice of the patriarchal caliphs Abu Bakr and Umar does he describe and praise here? What do they advise their successors?

Unlike Christianity and Buddhism, Islam avoided portraying humans or animals in its sacred art; thus the Qur'an and the hadith are never illustrated with figures, though they are often decorated with lavish designs. This convention did not extend to histories, however, and Source 11 is an illustration from one of the most famous Muslim histories, the *Jami' al-tawarikh* (World History) of Rashid al-Din, an adviser to the Muslim ruler Uljaytu (ruled 1304–1316 C.E.). This work was produced, of course, long after the early development of Islam, but its text and illustrations depict what later Muslims saw as important from their early history. Source 11 is a picture of Muhammad (the figure on the far right), addressing Ali and other Muslim leaders before the battle of Badr in the year A.H. 2, which was the first victory of Muhammad's followers against the Meccans. What aspects of Muhammad's leadership does this painting highlight?

You should now have a list of actions and ideas for each of the three individuals—and their religious communities—that are the focus of this chapter, and you have probably begun to see ways in which to compare them. As you develop your comparisons further, you may wish to turn to the Questions to Consider section for additional suggestions.

Chapter 7
International
Religious
Communities
(300 B.C.E.–
800 C.E.)

Source 1 from The Edicts of Aśoka, *ed. and trans. N. A. Nikam and Richard McKeon (Chicago: University of Chicago Press, 1959), pp. 27–29, 30, 34, 51–52, 58, 66, 67–68.*

1. Selections from Ashoka (Aśoka), Rock and Pillar Edicts

The Kaliṅga country[1] was conquered by King Priyadarśī, Beloved of the Gods,[2] in the eighth year of his reign. One hundred and fifty thousand persons were carried away captive, one hundred thousand were slain, and many times that number died.

Immediately after the Kaliṅgas had been conquered, King Priyadarśī became intensely devoted to the study of Dharma,[3] to the love of Dharma, and to the inculcation of Dharma.

The Beloved of the Gods, conqueror of the Kaliṅgas, is moved to remorse now. For he has felt profound sorrow and regret because the conquest of a people previously unconquered involves slaughter, death, and deportation.

But there is a more important reason for the King's remorse. The Brāhmaṇas and Śramaṇas [the priestly and ascetic orders] as well as the followers of other religions and the householders—who all practiced obedience to superiors, parents, and teachers, and proper courtesy and firm devotion to friends, acquaintances, companions, relatives, slaves, and servants—all suffer from the injury, slaughter, and deportation inflicted on their loved ones. Even those who escaped calamity themselves are deeply afflicted by the misfortunes suffered by those friends, acquaintances, companions, and relatives for whom they feel an undiminished affection. Thus all men share in the misfortune, and this weighs on King Priyadarśī's mind.

[Moreover, there is no country except that of the Yōnas (that is, the Greeks) where Brahmin and Buddhist ascetics do not exist] and there is no place where men are not attached to one faith or another.

Therefore, even if the number of people who were killed or who died or who were carried away in the Kaliṅga war had been only one one-hundredth or one one-thousandth of what it actually was, this would still have weighed on the King's mind.

---

1. **Kaliṅga:** the modern state of Orissa on the east coast of India.
2. **King Priyadarśī:** Ashoka's name for himself, meaning "Beloved of the Gods."
3. **Dharma:** a complex term with many shades of meaning, involving piety, morality, ethics, order, duty, mutual understanding, justice, and peace.

King Priyadarśī now thinks that even a person who wrongs him must be forgiven for wrongs that can be forgiven.

King Priyadarśī seeks to induce even the forest peoples who have come under his dominion [that is, primitive peoples in the remote sections of the conquered territory] to adopt this way of life and this ideal. He reminds them, however, that he exercises the power to punish, despite his repentance, in order to induce them to desist from their crimes and escape execution.

For King Priyadarśī desires security, self-control, impartiality, and cheerfulness for all living creatures.

King Priyadarśī considers moral conquest [that is, conquest by Dharma, *Dharma-vijaya*] the most important conquest. He has achieved this moral conquest repeatedly both here and among the peoples living beyond the borders of his kingdom. . . .

Wherever conquest is achieved by Dharma, it produces satisfaction. Satisfaction is firmly established by conquest by Dharma [since it generates no opposition of conquered and conqueror]. Even satisfaction, however, is of little importance. King Priyadarśī attaches value ultimately only to consequences of action in the other world.

This edict on Dharma has been inscribed so that my sons and great-grandsons who may come after me should not think new conquests worth achieving. If they do conquer, let them take pleasure in moderation and mild punishments. Let them consider moral conquest the only true conquest.

This is good, here and hereafter. Let their pleasure be pleasure in morality [*Dharma-rati*]. For this alone is good, here and hereafter. . . .

My highest officials, who have authority over large numbers of people, will expound and spread the precepts of Dharma. I have instructed the provincial governors, too, who are in charge of many hundred thousand people, concerning how to guide people devoted to Dharma.

King Priyadarśī says:

Having come to this conclusion, therefore, I have erected pillars proclaiming Dharma. I have appointed officers charged with the spread of Dharma, called *Dharma-mahāmātras*. I have issued proclamations on Dharma. . . .

King Priyadarśī says:

My officers charged with the spread of Dharma are occupied with various kinds of services beneficial to ascetics and householders, and they are empowered to concern themselves with all sects. I have ordered some of them to look after the affairs of the Saṃgha [the Buddhist religious orders], some to take care of the Brahmin and Ajīvika ascetics, some to work among the Nirgranthas [the Jaina monks], and some among the various other religious sects.

King Priyadarśī honors men of all faiths, members of religious orders and laymen alike, with gifts and various marks of esteem. Yet he does not value

Chapter 7

International

Religious

Communities

(300 B.C.E.–

800 C.E.)

either gifts or honors as much as growth in the qualities essential to religion in men of all faiths.

This growth may take many forms, but its root is in guarding one's speech to avoid extolling one's own faith and disparaging the faith of others improperly or, when the occasion is appropriate, immoderately.

The faiths of others all deserve to be honored for one reason or another. By honoring them, one exalts one's own faith and at the same time performs a service to the faith of others. By acting otherwise, one injures one's own faith and also does disservice to that of others. For if a man extols his own faith and disparages another because of devotion to his own and because he wants to glorify it, he seriously injures his own faith.

Therefore concord alone is commendable, for through concord men may learn and respect the conception of Dharma accepted by others.

King Priyadarśī desires men of all faiths to know each other's doctrines and to acquire sound doctrines. Those who are attached to their particular faiths should be told that King Priyadarśī does not value gifts or honors as much as growth in the qualities essential to religion in men of all faiths. . . .

Aśoka [Ashoka], Beloved of the Gods, issues the following proclamation:

For more than two and a half years, I have been a lay disciple [*upāsaka*] of the Buddha. More than a year ago, I visited the Saṁgha [the Buddhist religious orders], and since then I have been energetic in my efforts. . . .

The Saṁgha of the monks and the Saṁgha of the nuns have each been united to continue united as long as my sons and great-grandsons rule and as long as the sun and moon shine.

The monk or nun who disrupts the Saṁgha shall be required to put on white robes [instead of the customary yellow][4] and to live in non-residence (*anabasasi*). It is my desire that the Saṁgha be united and endure forever.

Everywhere in my dominions local, provincial, and state officials shall make a tour of their districts every five years to proclaim the following precepts of Dharma as well as to transact other business:

Obedience to mother and father; liberality to friends, acquaintances, relatives, priests, and ascetics; abstention from killing living creatures; and moderation in spending money and acquiring possessions are all meritorious.

4. **to put on white robes:** to leave the order of monks or nuns.

Source 2 from Borromeo/Art Resource, NY.

2. Ashokan Pillar with a Single-Lion Capital at Vaishali, India

Chapter 7

International

Religious

Communities

(300 B.C.E.–

800 C.E.)

Source 3 from John S. Strong, The Legend of King Aśoka: A Study and Translation of the *Aśokāvadāna (Princeton: Princeton University Press, 1983), pp. 234–236.*

3. From the *Asokavadana*

Not long after King Aśoka had come to have faith in the Teaching of the Buddha, he started honoring Buddhist monks, throwing himself at their feet wherever he saw them, in a crowd, or in a deserted place.

Now Aśoka had a minister named Yaśas, and although he had the utmost faith in the Blessed One,[5] he said, one day, to the king: "Your majesty, you ought not to prostrate yourself before wandering mendicants of every caste, and the Buddhist monks do come from all four castes."

To this Aśoka did not immediately respond. Sometime later, however, he told all his ministers that he needed to have the heads of various sorts of creatures, and he asked one of them to bring him the head of such and such an animal, and another to bring him the head of another animal, and so on. Finally, he ordered Yaśas to bring him the head of a human being.

Now when the ministers had gathered all these heads, Aśoka ordered them to go to the market place and sell them. Soon, all of the heads had been sold, except Yaśas's human head that no one would buy. Aśoka then told Yaśas to give his head away, but, even though it was gratis, still no one would take it.

Ashamed at his lack of success, Yaśas came back to Aśoka and said:

O king, the heads of cows, asses, sheep, deer, and birds—
    all were sold to people for a price;
but no one would take this worthless human head,
    even free of charge.

"Why is that?" Aśoka asked his minister, "why wouldn't anyone accept this human head?"

"Because it disgusted them," Yaśas replied.

"Oh?" said the king, "is it just this head that is disgusting or the heads of all human beings?"

"The heads of all humans," answered Yaśas.

"What?" said Aśoka, "is my head disgusting as well?"

Out of fear, Yaśas did not want to tell him the real fact of the matter, but the king ordered him to speak the truth, and finally he answered: "Yes."

After forcing this admission out of his minister, Aśoka then revealed to him his purpose in doing so: "You, sir, are obsessed with matters of form and superiority, and because of this attachment you seek to dissuade me from bowing down at the feet of the monks."

5. **the Blessed One:** the Buddha.

But if I acquire some merit
by bowing down a head so disgusting
that no one on earth would take it,
even free of charge,
what harm is there in that?
You, sir, look at the caste (jāti)
and not at the inherent qualities of the monks.
Haughty, deluded, and obsessed with caste,
you harm yourself and others.
When you invite someone,
or when it is time for a wedding,
then you should investigate the matter of caste,
but not at the time of Dharma.
For Dharma is a question of qualities,
and qualities do not reflect caste.
If a man of prominent family
happens to resort to vice,
the world censures him.
How then should one not honor virtue
when displayed by a man of low birth?
It is on account of men's minds
that their bodies are reviled or honored;
the minds of the Buddhist monks are pure,
therefore I honor them.

Source 4 from (a) Henry Bettenson, ed., Documents of the Christian Church *(Oxford: Oxford University Press, 1963), p. 15; (b–f) Theodosian Code, trans. and rpt. Maude Aline Huttman,* The Establishment of Christianity and the Proscription of Paganism, *Columbia University Studies in History, Economics and Public Law, no. 60 (New York: AMS Press, 1967), pp. 152, 154, 161–162, 163, 164.*

4. Constantinian Edicts

A. *EDICT OF TOLERATION,* 311

Among our other regulations to promote the lasting good of the community we have hitherto endeavoured to restore a universal conformity to the ancient institutions and public order of the Romans; and in particular it has been our aim to bring back to a right disposition the Christians who had abandoned the religion of their fathers. . . . 3. After the publication of our edict ordering the Christians to conform to the ancient institutions, many of them were brought to order through fear, while many were exposed to danger. 4. Nevertheless,

Chapter 7

International

Religious

Communities

(300 B.C.E.–

800 C.E.)

since many still persist in their opinions, and since we have observed that they now neither show due reverence to the gods nor worship their own God, we therefore, with our wonted clemency in extending pardon to all, are pleased to grant indulgence to these men, allowing Christians the right to exist again and to set up their places of worship; provided always that they do not offend against public order. 5. We will in a further instruction explain to the magistrates how they should conduct themselves in this matter. In return for this indulgence of ours it will be the duty of Christians to pray to God for our recovery, for the public weal and for their own; that the state may be preserved from danger on every side, and that they themselves may dwell safely in their homes.

B. OCT. 31, 313 (?)

The Emperor Constantine Augustus. We have learned that the clergy of the Catholic Church are so harrassed by a faction of heretics as to be burdened with nominations to office and common public business, contrary to the exemptions granted to them. Wherefore, it is ordered that if your gravity[6] should find anyone thus annoyed, another man is to be substituted for him, and from henceforth, men of the religion above mentioned are to be protected from wrongs of this kind.

C. MARCH 21, 315 (316?)

The same [Constantine] Augustus to Eumelius.[7] If any one, on account of the crimes in which he is detected, should be condemned to the arena or the mines, by no means let him be branded in the face, although both on his hands and legs the penalty of his condemnation may be marked in a single brand; while the face which is formed in the likeness of heavenly beauty shall not be dishonored.

D. MAY 15, 319

The same [Constantine] Augustus to the People.

We prohibit all soothsayers, priests of prophecy, and those who are wont to administer such rites, from entering a private house, or, under the guise of friendship, from crossing another's threshold. And if they despise this law penalties shall be meted out to them. You, who think this applies to yourselves, go to the public altars and shrines, and celebrate your customary ceremonies, for we do not forbid the full services of ancient tradition from being conducted in the day time.

6. It is unclear to whom this edict was addressed.

7. **Eumelius:** the Vicar of Africa.

E. DEC. 17, 320 (321?)

The Emperor Constantine to Maximus.[8]

If a part of our palace, or any other public building, be struck by lightning, let the customs of the old religion be observed and the haruspices[9] be consulted for the meaning of the omen, and let their words be very carefully brought together and reported to us. Permission for the practice of the custom should also be granted to others, provided that no household sacrifices are made, for these are specifically forbidden.

F. JULY 3, 321

The same [Constantine] Augustus to the People.

Every man, when dying, shall have the right to bequeath as much of his property as he desires to the holy and venerable Catholic Church. And such wills are not to be broken.

Source 5 from Eusebius, Life of Constantine the Great, *trans. Ernest Cushing Richardson, Library of Nicene and Post-Nicene Fathers, second series, vol. 1. (Grand Rapids, Mich.: Eerdmans, 1979), pp. 489, 490–491, 494, 513–514, 523, 525–526, 534, 544, 545, 546.*

5. Selections from Eusebius, *Life of Constantine*

Thus then the God of all, the Supreme Governor of the whole universe, by his own will appointed Constantine, the descendant of so renowned a parent, to be prince and sovereign: so that, while others have been raised to this distinction by the election of their fellow-men, he is the only one to whose elevation no mortal may boast of having contributed. . . .

Being convinced, however, that he [Constantine] needed some more powerful aid than his military forces could afford him, on account of the wicked and magical enchantments which were so diligently practiced by the tyrant,[10] he sought Divine assistance, deeming the possession of arms and a numerous soldiery of secondary importance, but believing the co-operating power of Deity invincible and not to be shaken. He considered, therefore, on what God he might rely for protection and assistance. . . .

Accordingly he called on him with earnest prayer and supplications that he would reveal to him who he was, and stretch forth his right hand to help him

---

8. **Maximus:** the Prefect of the City of Rome.

9. **haruspices:** a traditional Roman religious authority who interpreted the meaning of lightning and other natural events.

10. **the tyrant:** referring to two of Constantine's rivals for authority in the empire, Severus and Galerius.

Chapter 7
International
Religious
Communities
(300 B.C.E.–
800 C.E.)

in his present difficulties. And while he was thus praying with fervent entreaty, a most marvelous sign appeared to him from heaven, the account of which it might have been hard to believe had it been related by any other person. But since the victorious emperor himself long afterwards declared it to the writer of this history,[11] when he was honored with his acquaintance and society, and confirmed his statement by an oath, who could hesitate to accredit the relation, especially since the testimony of after-time has established its truth? He said that about noon, when the day was already beginning to decline, he saw with his own eyes the trophy of a cross of light in the heavens, above the sun, and bearing the inscription, CONQUER BY THIS. At this sight he himself was struck with amazement, and his whole army also, which followed him on this expedition, and witnessed the miracle.

He said, moreover, that he doubted within himself what the import of this apparition could be. And while he continued to ponder and reason on its meaning, night suddenly came on; then in his sleep the Christ of God appeared to him with the same sign which he had seen in the heavens, and commanded him to make a likeness of that sign which he had seen in the heavens, and to use it as a safeguard in all engagements with his enemies.

At dawn of day he arose, and communicated the marvel to his friends: and then, calling together the workers in gold and precious stones, he sat in the midst of them, and described to them the figure of the sign he had seen, bidding them represent it in gold and precious stones. And this representation I myself have had an opportunity of seeing.

Now it was made in the following manner. A long spear, overlaid with gold, formed the figure of the cross by means of a transverse bar laid over it. On the top of the whole was fixed a wreath of gold and precious stones; and within this, the symbol of the Saviour's name, two letters indicating the name of Christ by means of its initial characters, the letter P being intersected by X in its centre: and these letters the emperor was in the habit of wearing on his helmet at a later period. . . .[12]

Thus the pious emperor, glorying in the confession of the victorious cross, proclaimed the Son of God to the Romans with great boldness of testimony. And the inhabitants of the city, one and all, senate and people, reviving, as it were, from the pressure of a bitter and tyrannical domination, seemed to enjoy purer rays of light, and to be born again into a fresh and new life. All the nations, too, as far as the limit of the western ocean, being set free from the calamities which had heretofore beset them, and gladdened by joyous festivals, ceased not to praise him as the victorious, the pious, the common benefactor: all, indeed, with one voice and one mouth, declared that Constantine had appeared by the grace of God as a general blessing to mankind. . . .

11. that is, Eusebius.

12. This sign—a cross and the first two letters in Christ's name on the top of a long pole—was called the *labarum*.

The emperor also personally inviting the society of God's ministers, distinguished them with the highest possible respect and honor, showing them favor in deed and word as persons consecrated to the service of his God. Accordingly, they were admitted to his table, though mean in their attire and outward appearance; yet not so in his estimation, since he thought he saw not the man as seen by the vulgar eye, but the God in him. He made them also his companions in travel, believing that He whose servants they were would thus help him. Besides this, he gave from his own private resources costly benefactions to the churches of God, both enlarging and heightening the sacred edifices, and embellishing the august sanctuaries of the church with abundant offerings.

He likewise distributed money largely to those who were in need, and besides these showing himself philanthropist and benefactor even to the heathen, who had no claim on him; and even for the beggars in the forum, miserable and shiftless, he provided, not with money only, or necessary food, but also decent clothing. . . . In short, as the sun, when he rises upon the earth, liberally imparts his rays of light to all, so did Constantine, proceeding at early dawn from the imperial palace, and rising as it were with the heavenly luminary, impart the rays of his own beneficence to all who came into his presence. It was scarcely possible to be near him without receiving some benefit, nor did it ever happen that any who had expected to obtain his assistance were disappointed in their hope. . . .

> [*In an edict to the provinces,*
>   *Constantine stated:*]

"My own desire is, for the common good of the world and the advantage of all mankind, that thy people should enjoy a life of peace and undisturbed concord. Let those, therefore, who still delight in error, be made welcome to the same degree of peace and tranquillity which they have who believe. For it may be that this restoration of equal privileges to all will prevail to lead them into the straight path. Let no one molest another, but let every one do as his soul desires. Only let men of sound judgment be assured of this, that those only can live a life of holiness and purity, whom thou callest to a reliance on thy holy laws. With regard to those who will hold themselves aloof from us, let them have, if they please, their temples of lies: *we* have the glorious edifice of thy truth, which thou hast given us as our native home. We pray, however, that they too may receive the same blessing, and thus experience that heartfelt joy which unity of sentiment inspires. . . ."

> [*In 325, Constantine called the Council of*
>   *Nicaea and addressed the bishops*
>   *assembled there as follows.*]

"[I]n my judgment, intestine strife within the Church of God is far more evil and dangerous than any kind of war or conflict; and these our differences appear to me more grievous than any outward trouble. . . .

Chapter 7

International

Religious

Communities

(300 B.C.E.–

800 C.E.)

"Delay not, then, dear friends: delay not, ye ministers of God, and faithful servants of him who is our common Lord and Saviour: begin from this moment to discard the causes of that disunion which has existed among you, and remove the perplexities of controversy by embracing the principles of peace. For by such conduct you will at the same time be acting in a manner most pleasing to the supreme God, and you will confer an exceeding favor on me who am your fellow-servant. . . ."

All these things the emperor diligently performed to the praise of the saving power of Christ, and thus made it his constant aim to glorify his Saviour God. On the other hand he used every means to rebuke the superstitious errors of the heathen. Hence the entrances of their temples in the several cities were left exposed to the weather, being stripped of their doors at his command; the tiling of others was removed, and their roofs destroyed. . . .

How deeply his soul was impressed by the power of divine faith may be understood from the circumstance that he directed his likeness to be stamped on the golden coin of the empire with the eyes uplifted as in the posture of prayer to God: and this money became current throughout the Roman world. His portrait also at full length was placed over the entrance gates of the palaces in some cities, the eyes upraised to heaven, and the hands outspread as if in prayer. . . .

With regard to those who were as yet ignorant of divine truth, he provided by a second statute that they should appear on each Lord's day on an open plain near the city, and there, at a given signal, offer to God with one accord a prayer which they had previously learnt. He admonished them that their confidence should not rest in their spears, or armor, or bodily strength, but that they should acknowledge the supreme God as the giver of every good, and of victory itself. . . . The emperor himself prescribed the prayer to be used by all his troops. . . .

Hence it was not without reason that once, on the occasion of his entertaining a company of bishops, he let fall the expression, "that he himself too was a bishop," addressing them in my hearing in the following words: "You are bishops whose jurisdiction is within the Church: I also am a bishop, ordained by God to overlook whatever is external to the Church." And truly his measures corresponded with his words; for he watched over his subjects with an episcopal [as a bishop] care, and exhorted them as far as in him lay to follow a godly life.

6. Two Constantinian Coins

Chapter 7
International
Religious
Communities
(300 B.C.E.–
800 C.E.)

Source 7 from A. J. Arberry, The Koran Interpreted (Oxford: Oxford University Press, 1964).

7. Selections from the Qur'an

O you who believe! Obey God and obey the Prophet and those of you who hold authority.   (Sura 4:59)

God has promised those of you who believe and do wholesome deeds that He will surely make you successors in the land, as he made successors of those before you, and He will surely establish for them as their service (dīn) what He approves for them, and exchange for them, after their fear, security: "They shall serve Me, not associating with Me anything."   (Sura 24:55)

There is no compulsion in matters of faith. Distinct now is the way of guidance from error. He who turns away from the forces of evil and believes in God, will surely hold fast to a handle that is strong and unbreakable, for God hears all and knows everything.   (Sura 2:256)

Say (O Muslims): We believe in God and that which is revealed unto us and that which was revealed unto Abraham and Ishmael and Isaac and Jacob, and the tribes, and that which Moses and Jesus received, and that which the Prophets received from their Lord. We make no distinction between any of them, and unto Him we have surrendered.   (Sura 2:136)

Source 8 from (a) Al-Muttaqi, Kanz-al-'Ummāl, in Bernard Lewis, ed. and trans., Islam from the Prophet Muhammad to the Capture of Constantinople, vol. 1 (New York: Oxford University Press, 1987), p. 150; (b) Al-Khaṭīb al-Tibrīzī, Niches of Lamps, in John Alden Williams, ed., Themes of Islamic Civilization (Berkeley: University of California Press, 1971), pp. 65–67; (c) An-Nawawī, The Forty Traditions, in Arthur Jeffrey, ed., A Reader on Islam: Passages from Standard Arabic Writings Illustrative of the Beliefs and Practices of Muslims (Gravenhage: Mouton and Company, 1962), p. 154.

8. Selections from the Hadith

a. I charge the Caliph after me to fear God, and I commend the community of the Muslims to him, to respect the great among them and have pity on the small, to honor the learned among them, not to strike them and humiliate them, not to oppress them and drive them to unbelief, not to close his doors to them and allow the strong to devour the weak.

b. Bukhārī and Muslim, from Abū Hurayra: The Messenger of God, may God's blessing and peace be on him, said "Whoever obeys me obeys God, and whoever disobeys me disobeys God. Whoever obeys the Commander obeys me, and he who disobeys him disobeys me."

Muslim, from Umm al-Ḥuṣayn: The Messenger, may God bless him and give him peace, said "Even if a mutilated slave is made your commander, and he leads you in accord with the Book of God, hear him and obey."

Bukhārī, from Anas: The Messenger of God, the blessing of God and peace be upon him, said "Hear and obey, though an Abyssinian slave with a head like a raisin be placed over you."

Bukhārī and Muslim, from 'Umar's son: The Messenger of God—God's benediction and peace upon him—said "Hearing and obeying are incumbent on a Muslim man, so long as he is not ordered to disobey God. When he is ordered to do that, there is no hearing it and no obeying." 'Alī reported a similar tradition.

Bukhārī and Muslim, from 'Umar's son: The Messenger said—may God give him peace and blessing—"Is not each of you a shepherd, who must answer for his flock? The Imām of the people is a shepherd, and is answerable for his flock. A man is the shepherd of the people in his house, and he is answerable for his flock. A woman is shepherdess of her husband's house and children, and is answerable for them, and a slave is the shepherd of his master's wealth and is answerable for that. Thus each of you is a shepherd, and each of you is responsible for his flock."

Muslim, from 'Arfaja: I heard the Messenger of God, peace and God's blessing be upon him, say "If anyone comes to you when you are united under one man, and tries to split you or divide your Umma, then kill him."

Bayhaqī, from 'Umar's son: The Prophet, God bless him and give him peace, said "The Government (*al-Sulṭān*) is the shadow of God on the earth; all of His servants who are oppressed shall turn to it. When it is just, it shall be rewarded, and the flock must be grateful. When it is tyrannical, the burden is upon it, and the flock must be patient."

c. From Abu Najih al-Irbad ibn Sariya, with whom may God be pleased, who said: The Messenger of God, may God's blessing and peace be upon him, preached a sermon whereby our hearts were made afraid and our eyes dropped tears, so we said: "O Messenger of God, it is as though this were a farewell sermon, so give us a testamentary exhortation." He said: "My testamentary exhortation to you is that you have a pious fear of God, magnified and exalted be He; that you hearken and obey, even though it should be a slave who is appointed over you. He among you who lives long enough will see great disagreement, so take care to observe my custom and the custom of the Rightly Guided Caliphs [that is, the first four: Abu Bakr, Umar, Uthman, and Ali], holding on to them with your molar teeth. Beware of matters newly introduced, for every innovation is an error." So Abu Dawud relates it, as does al-Tirmidhi, who says, "An excellent, sound Prophetic tradition."

[181]

Chapter 7

International

Religious

Communities

(300 B.C.E.–

800 C.E.)

Source 9 from Ibn Ishaq, The Life of Muhammad, Apostle of Allah, *ed. and trans. Michael Edwards (London: The Folio Society, 1964), pp. 35, 36–37, 41, 54, 65, 74, 104, 150, 156–157, 165.*

9. Selections from Ibn Ishaq, *The Life of Muhammad, Apostle of Allah*

When Muhammad was forty years old Allah sent him as a prophet of mercy to the people of the visible and of the invisible worlds, and to all mankind. . . .

Every year the apostle of Allah spent a month praying at Hira and fed the poor who came to him; and when he returned to Mecca he walked round the Kaba[13] seven or more times, as it pleased Allah, before entering his own house. In the month of Ramadan,[14] in the year when Allah designed to bestow grace upon him, the apostle of Allah went to [Mount] Hira as usual, and his family accompanied him. In the night the angel Gabriel came with the command of Allah. The apostle of Allah later said, "He came while I was asleep, with a cloth of brocade whereon there was writing, and he said, 'Read.' I replied, 'I cannot read it.' Then he pressed the cloth on me till I thought I was dying; he released his hold and said, 'Read.' I replied, 'I cannot read it.' And he pressed me again with it, till I thought I was dying. Then he loosed his hold of me and said, 'Read.' I replied, 'I cannot read it.' Once more he pressed me and said, 'Read.' Then I asked, 'What shall I read?' And I said this because I feared he would press me again. Then he said, 'Read in the name of the Lord thy creator; who created man from a drop of blood. Read, thy Lord is the most bountiful, who taught by means of the pen, taught man what he knew not.' Accordingly I read these words, and he finished his task and departed from me. I awoke from my sleep, and felt as if words had been graven on my heart.

"Afterwards I went out, and when I was on the centre of the mountain, I heard a voice from heaven, saying, 'O Muhammad! Thou art the prophet of Allah, and I am Gabriel.' I raised my head to look at the sky, and lo! I beheld Gabriel in the shape of a man with extended wings, standing in the firmament, with his feet touching the ground. And he said again, 'O Muhammad! Thou art the apostle of Allah, and I am Gabriel.' I continued to gaze at him, neither advancing nor retreating. Then I turned my face away from him to other parts of the sky, but in whatever direction I looked I saw him in the same form. I remained thus, neither advancing nor retreating, and Khadija [Muhammad's first wife] sent messengers to search for me. They went as far as the highest part of Mecca and again returned to her, while I remained

13. **Kaba:** a house containing a black stone venerated by Arabs before Muhammad, which was retained as the most holy place in Islam.
14. **Ramadan:** ninth month of the Muslim lunar year, which came to be viewed as holy because the first of Muhammad's revelations occurred during this month.

standing on the same spot, until the angel departed from me and I returned to my family. . . ."

Soon several men and women had made their profession of Islam and it was much discussed in Mecca. Then Allah commanded his apostle to make public the revelation and to invite the people to accept it; hitherto, for the three years since his first revelation, it had been kept secret by the apostle. Allah said to him, "Publish that which thou hast been commanded, and turn away from the idolaters."

When the apostle began to spread Islam among his people as Allah had commanded him, they did not gainsay him until he began to abuse their idols; but when he had done this, they accused him of seeking power, denied his revelation, and united to injure him. The companions of the apostle of Allah went into the valleys to pray, unknown to the people; and once, whilst Sad and several companions of the apostle were at prayer, they were discovered by idolaters who heaped insults upon them, condemned their deeds, and provoked them to fight. Then Sad struck an idolater with the jawbone of a camel, and wounded him; and this was the first blood shed in Islam.

The apostle of Allah never failed to attempt the conversion of any man of note or position who came to Mecca. . . .

When Allah gave His apostle permission to wage war, the promise to fight immediately became a condition of allegiance to Islam. This had not been so at the first meeting on the hillside, when homage was paid "in the manner of women"; Allah had not then given His apostle permission to fight. He had given permission neither to wage war nor to shed blood, but only to call men to Allah, to endure insults patiently, and to pardon the ignorant. Some of the followers of the apostle had therefore been forced to flee from persecution into the countryside, some to Abyssinia, others to Medina and elsewhere.

[*Muhammad and his followers left Mecca
        for Medina.*]

The apostle of Allah remained in Medina until the following year when his mosque and his dwellings were built. He worked on them with his own hands to encourage his followers. Islam in Medina soon became so complete that only a handful of houses remained whose tenants had not made profession of Islam.

[*After a defeat of Meccan forces,
        Muhammad said:*]

" '. . . Whenever you win plunder, a fifth shall belong to Allah and His apostle, and his kindred, and orphans, and the poor, and the traveller.

" '. . . When you meet an army in battle, stand firm and remember Allah, that you may prosper; and do not quarrel, lest My cause should suffer. Be not like those who make parade of their deeds in pursuit of the approbation of

Chapter 7
International
Religious
Communities
(300 B.C.E.–
800 C.E.)

men, but act purely for the sake of Allah and for His reward in giving your religion victory; work only for this, and covet nothing else. . . . Prepare against the infidels what force you are able, that you may strike terror into your enemy and that of Allah. And whatever you shall expend for the religion of Allah, it shall be repaid unto you, and you shall not be without reward. But if they incline to peace, do you also incline to peace; and trust in Allah, for He heareth and knoweth all things. . . ."

The apostle sent out expeditions to the surrounding territory to invite the people to Allah, but not to kill. . . . The apostle of Allah specially exhorted the rich to furnish money and beasts of burden and they did so, hoping for the eternal reward; Uthman was the most liberal of them, and the apostle said, "Allah! Be pleased with Uthman; for I am pleased with him!"

When the apostle of Allah had conquered Mecca and completed the campaign of Tabuk, and when al-Taif[15] had surrendered and made profession of Islam, deputations of Arabs arrived from all directions. This, the ninth year after the Hijra [Hegira], was called the Year of Deputations. The Arabs had delayed professing Islam until they saw how the affair between the apostle and the Quraysh[16] would end, because the Quraysh were the leaders of men, the people of the Kaba and of the sacred territory, and they were acknowledged as the descendants of Ishmael, son of Abraham. Not one chief of the Arabs denied this. But when Mecca was conquered and the Quraysh submitted to Islam, the Arabs knew that they themselves were not strong enough to wage war or to show enmity to the apostle of Allah. So they entered into the religion of Allah in droves, arriving from all directions.

Source 10 from Abū Yūsuf, Kitāb al-Kharāj, *in John Alden Williams, ed.,* Themes of Islamic Civilization *(Berkeley: University of California Press, 1971), pp. 68–69, 72.*

10. From Abu Yusuf (d. A.H. 182/798 C.E.), *Book of Land-tax*

"I have heard," says Abū Yūsuf, "from Ismā'īl ibn Abī Khālid, on the authority of Zubayd ibn al-Ḥārith, that when death was drawing near to Abū Bakr, he sent for 'Umar to make him the Caliph, his successor, and people said 'Will you appoint as Caliph over us this hard, harsh man to be hard and harsh to us? What will you say to your Lord when you meet Him having appointed 'Umar over us?' He said 'Would you frighten me with my Lord? I shall tell Him "God, I have appointed over them the best of Thy people!" ' Then he sent for 'Umar and said 'I shall give you a piece of advice such that if you follow it, nothing will be dearer to you than your death when it comes, and if you do

15. **Tabuk** and **al-Taif:** cities in the northern part of Arabia.
16. **Quraysh:** Muhammad's tribe, the leading tribe in Mecca.

not follow it, nothing will be more hateful to you than the death you shall not escape. You have obligations to God at night that He will not accept from you by day, and obligations by day that He will not accept at night, and a work of supererogation is not accepted until after the performance of the obligatory works. The scales on Judgement Day will not weigh lighter for anyone than for those who sought light things, and they will not weigh heavier for anyone than for the man who sought justice in the world. . . . I have only appointed you my successor thinking of those whom I leave behind me. For I was a Companion of the Prophet, and saw one who preferred us to himself, and our people to his own family, so that we should give to them from the abundance of what is given to us. You have been my companion, and you have seen that I have only followed the path of him who was before me, and the first thing I counsel you against, 'Umar, is your self, for every self has selfish desires, and if one gives in to one of them, it demands another. Beware also of those persons among the Companions of the Messenger of God who have filled their bellies and raised their eyes. Every man of them loves himself, and all of them will be in perplexity if one of them stumbles. Take care that that one is not you. They will never cease to fear you so long as you fear God, or cease to go straight with you so long as your way is straight. That is my counsel to you, and now I wish you farewell.' "

When 'Umar was dying, he left this advice: "I advise my successor to fear God, and to respect the rights and the merits of the first emigrants to Medina; and as to the Anṣār, who lived in Medina, and in the Faith, to accept their good deeds and to be indulgent to the bad among them. As to the people of the garrison towns, they are the help of Islam, the fury of the enemy, and the bringers of wealth, so he should take only their superfluity, and by their agreement. I advise him as to the beduins that they are the source of the Arabs, and the raw stuff of Islam, and he should take only a little of their possessions, to return to the poorest among them. As to the protected peoples, let him fulfill his agreement with them and fight their enemies and not burden them beyond their endurance. . . ."

Chapter 7
International
Religious
Communities
(300 B.C.E.–
800 C.E.)

Source 11 from The Nasser D. Khalili Collection of Islamic Art. MSS 727, folio 66a.

11. Muhammad Addresses Ali and Other Leaders Before the Battle of Badr, from Rashid al-Din, *Jami'al-tawarikh*

QUESTIONS TO CONSIDER

Before you begin to make specific comparisons between the leaders and their methods of advancing their religious commitments, you should probably step back a minute and think about the different types of sources you have used. In some cases, there are quite comparable sources for two cases, but not for the third. For example, it is clear that both Ashoka and Constantine ordered the edicts included in the evidence to be inscribed or issued; we have nothing directly comparable for Muhammad. Our ability to compare the edicts of Ashoka and Constantine stops with the texts themselves, however, for though we have quite a bit of evidence about how Constantine and his successors enforced his edicts and proclamations, we have no way of knowing what impact Ashoka's edicts had on his actual reign. The language in which Ashoka's edicts were written ceased to be spoken shortly after his reign, so subsequent generations could not read them; in fact, the script in which they were written was deciphered for the first time only in 1837. Unlike the stories of Constantine told by Eusebius and others, the legends that grew up about Ashoka, including the one you read here, did so without reference to his actual edicts; people claimed the inscriptions referred to events in the legends, but they had no way of actually reading them the way Roman Christians could the laws and proclamations of Constantine.

For another example of similarity, the biographies of Eusebius and Ibn Ishaq are more like each other than the *Asokavadana*. All of these contain material that may be in the realm of legend, but we can check both Eusebius and Ibn Ishaq against other sources, something that is not possible for the *Asokavadana*. Eusebius in particular also notes his source when he is telling something his readers may have difficulty believing; in the section on Constantine's vision of the cross, for example, he stresses that Constantine himself told him about this, using "he said" rather than relating the story directly the way most of the biography is written. This same noting of sources appears even more prominently in the hadith (Source 8), where it serves to stress the authenticity of the words of Muhammad. Most of the hadith were actually written in the two centuries after Muhammad's life, when Islam had already split into Sunni and Shi'ite factions, and they are interpreted so as to argue one point of view or another. As you can see, for example, Source 8c gives a Sunni view of Muhammad's last words.

Keeping the limitations of our sources in mind, then, you can begin to compare the actions and ideas of the individuals and groups. Ashoka, Constantine, and Muhammad all had clear conversion experiences. How would you compare these and the actions that resulted directly from them? How do these experiences shape their attitudes toward military conquest as a means of expanding a religious community? What humanitarian aims

Chapter 7

International

Religious

Communities

(300 B.C.E.–

800 C.E.)

develop after the conversions, and how do they seek to achieve these?

All of these leaders had to deal with dissenters—both people who followed other religious traditions and those within their own religion who disagreed with them. How did the leaders enforce their own views? What did they advise regarding the toleration of those who disagreed? How important was unity within their religious community to these leaders? Ashoka and Constantine each had to foster a relationship with a body of clergy that already existed, the Buddhist sangha and the Christian bishops. How would you characterize their relationship with these clerics? Where did ultimate authority lay in terms of making religious policy? (For some of these questions, the sources may give contradictory information, and you may wish to turn to your textbook for further information, or else simply note the contradiction.)

The sources for each of the three groups make explicit reference to the conflict between social status and religious status or authority. How do the leaders treat individuals of modest social status but high religious or moral status? What advice do they give to their followers in this regard? The relationship between church and state is much discussed in the contemporary American political scene. What do these sources reveal about this relationship in these three religious traditions? In the minds of these leaders, should the religious community and the political community be unified, related, or separate?

Though all of these sources describe the actions of real individuals, they also convey what each tradition regarded as qualities of the ideal ruler. How would you compare the ideal ruler in these three traditions? What qualities would ideal religious communities exhibit under the leadership of such individuals? From your initial lists and comparisons, you are now ready to answer the central questions in this chapter: How did political leaders within Buddhism, Christianity, and Islam encourage the growth of their chosen religious community? What differences and similarities do you see in their actions and in what they viewed as most important in the lives of these communities?

EPILOGUE

The three religions we have explored in this chapter are three of the four largest religions found in the world today: Buddhism has around 309 million adherents, Christianity 1.8 billion, and Islam 950 million.[17] (The fourth major world religion is Hinduism with 720 million adherents, though it is more concentrated in certain geographic areas than the other three.) All three of these continue to be missionary religions; that is, they seek new converts just as they did in

17. These numbers represent 1992 statistics and come from David Chrystal, ed., *The Cambridge Factfinder* (Cambridge: Cambridge University Press, 1993). There are, of course, many ways to count allegiance to religion, and the numbers change every day, so these are estimates.

the days of Ashoka, Constantine, and Muhammad. Some of the issues we have explored in this chapter continue to be matters of concern or over the centuries have become even more complicated.

For example, each of these religions has splintered further since the periods we focused on in this chapter. Shortly after Ashoka's reign, Buddhism split into two main groups, Mahayana and Theravada (sometimes called Hinayana), and then continued to divide into a number of different sects. Christianity gradually divided into two main churches, Roman Catholicism and Eastern Orthodoxy, and the Roman Catholic Church was further split by the Protestant Reformation in the sixteenth century. New Christian denominations are created every year as groups choose to emphasize certain aspects of Christian teaching. The rift between Shi'ites and Sunnis was only the first of many within Islam, for Shi'ites themselves divided into two major groups, and other sects developed as well. Thus the unity sought by the leaders we have investigated has not been achieved, although there are movements within each of these three religions today to heal internal schisms or at least to downplay them in a desire for tolerance and understanding.

As these three religions have expanded, they have continued to confront the issue of the relationship between church and state, between the religious and political community. In some cases, the relationship is extremely intimate, in that all three are official state religions in some countries of the world. This role may have a widely differing impact, however. In some of the countries of the Middle East, for example, Islam structures almost all aspects of life, whereas in some European countries that are officially Christian, few people attend church and the church has little impact on national policies. Even in those countries where the power of the state church is extremely strong, there are still disputes about overlapping or conflicting authority and the proper role of religious leaders: should they be spiritual guides or heads of state?

On the other hand, many adherents of these religions live in countries where their religion is not the one sanctioned by the state, or where there is no official state religion, such as the United States. They, and their religious leaders, thus have to address the issues we have explored in this chapter in a different way. What should the relationship between the religious and political communities be in a country of religious pluralism? How should a person's allegiance to a country be weighed against allegiance to a religion? What are the limits of acceptable diversity within a religious community, and who has the power of exclusion? How do you handle someone who violates what is viewed as God's law in a religious tradition but has broken no state laws? Should there be a line between church and state, between the sacred and profane? Should political leaders follow the path of Ashoka, Constantine, and Muhammad and seek to expand their own religion, or should such crusades be left to those who do not hold public office?

Chapter 7
International
Religious
Communities
(300 B.C.E.–
800 C.E.)

None of these were issues when religion was closely tied to membership in a particular tribe or residence in a particular village, but as religions became international, as they came to be practiced by people over large geographic areas, the questions became pressing and problematic. Conflicts within and between religious communities are some of the most bitter, deadly, and long-lasting in the world today, and the words of Ashoka, carved in stone over two thousand years ago, still bear repeating: "The faiths of others all deserve to be honored for one reason or another. By honoring them, one exalts one's own faith and at the same time performs a service to the faith of others. By acting otherwise, one injures one's own faith and also does disservice to that of others."

CHAPTER EIGHT

REGIONAL METROPOLISES:

CONSTANTINOPLE AND TENOCHTITLÁN

(330–1521 C.E.)

THE PROBLEM

As noted in an earlier chapter, the words for civilization in most Western European languages derive from the Latin term for a city, *civitas*. The implied connection between high cultural attainment and "civic" or urban life reflects a measure of truth. First emerging in the third millennium B.C.E., in what has sometimes been termed the urban revolution, cities provided dynamic, new foci for human development. Within the next few millennia, they appeared not only across the entire breadth of Eurasia but in Africa and America as well. Originally small, largely self-contained city-states, urban communities began to change with the widening of political, religious, and economic networks during the centuries that immediately preceded the start of the common era. As imperial capitals, religious seats, or trade em-

poria, a few centers here and there began to evolve into cities on a scale much larger and far more complex in nature. Over the next thousand years, some of these like imperial Rome in the West and Changan in East Asia grew into a new kind of city that served as the hub of a huge, far-flung region. To contemporaries they were not just the biggest urban areas in their respective spheres but regional "metropolises," world-class cities that outranked all peers. Typically seats of political and religious power as well as cultural and economic magnets, they attracted polygot populations from all over a vast hinterland. Long before the advent of modern mass society, therefore, great international cities began to emerge as transregional, cosmopolitan centers.

Although imposing in their own ways, these premodern metropolises were quite different from the big cities of the twentieth century. Built before the Industrial Revolution and

[191]

Chapter 8
Regional
Metropolises:
Constantinople
and Tenochtitlán
(330–1521 C.E.)

the emergence of modern utilities and mass transit, they had to solve basic urban problems of housing, supply, sanitation, and transportation with far fewer technological means. For that very reason, of course, economics and technology played a smaller role in shaping them. Both the modern industrial city, whose concentric rings of commercial, manufacturing, and residential zones centered around a "downtown" complex of railroad depots and office buildings, and the contemporary "edge city" with its malls, airports, and theme parks strung out along arterial highways typically evolved in haphazard response to the changing technologies and material needs of mass, democratic societies. Older cities, though certainly affected by physical considerations, tended to be shaped more by ideals than material concerns. And the patterns and rhythms of life within them conveyed a very different urban experience from that of the modern West. To comprehend the nature of any premodern metropolis, therefore, we need to free ourselves from current conceptions of what constitutes a city.

Unfortunately, neither historians nor others who study cities have agreed on a simple, generic definition, and efforts to list a comprehensive set of urban characteristics have generally met with much criticism. For in addition to such commonly accepted features as the presence of a large population, a ruling elite or class, diversified manufacturing, and long-distance trade, regionally unique traits like the possession of writing or metallurgy complicate the issue.

Lewis Mumford in his classic study *The City in History* thus cautions: "No single definition will apply to all its manifestations and no single description will cover all its transformations."[1] In truth, a certain amount of consensus does exist. All scholars, for example, agree that urban life entails a high concentration of people living together in some sort of interdependent community. And most regard a population of about five thousand as the minimum necessary for a true city. Furthermore, experts generally concur that cities are primarily nonagricultural communities with formal institutions that provide diverse services to surrounding areas as well as to their own inhabitants. But beyond these few essentials, cities have varied widely in size, role, and character, making it difficult to generalize about their historical identity. For that reason, an understanding of any urban type has to be sought first and foremost through an analysis of actual examples.

This chapter accordingly asks you to consider two of the world's greatest cities in late traditional times, roughly speaking, from about the twelfth through the fifteenth centuries. The two presented here, Constantinople and Tenochtitlán, do not represent especially unique examples for this era, which coincides with the end of the Middle Ages in Europe. Other contemporary metropolises such as Baghdad or the Chinese city of Hangzhou would serve equally well as case studies. The choice of Constan-

1. Lewis Mumford, *The City in History: Its Origins, Its Transformations, Its Prospects* (New York: Harcourt Brace Jovanovich, 1961), p. 3.

tinople and Tenochtitlán, however, highlights the global nature of the phenomena, contrasting as it does two cities, one in the Mediterranean and the other in Mesoamerica, that were quite literally worlds apart. Moreover, because Western Europeans visited and recorded their impressions of both sites during this era, this choice invites implicit comparisons with their homelands where truly great urban centers had yet to develop.

Your task in this chapter is to determine the nature of these two early metropolises. Through a review of the materials on Constantinople and Tenochtitlán, that appear as Evidence later in this chapter, you should not only discover what these two metropolises were like at their height but learn something about the nature of big, premodern cities in general. To do so, you will have to decide what the dominant features of each city were and how these gave them a distinct identity. Then, by comparing these elements, you should be able to consider whether or not they shared enough in common to represent a generic type. In short, the problem here involves determining the nature of these cities and asking what they represent.

BACKGROUND

Although differing in many respects, Constantinople and Tenochtitlán both achieved regional preeminence primarily as imperial capitals. First and foremost seats of government, they represented conscious attempts by rulers to legitimize political authority. For this reason, both were built in imitation of older and more renowned centers of power whose grandeur and might their founders hoped to regain. Yet neither remained merely a political seat. Each in its own way became a major religious site and a hub of interregional trade as well as the dominant center of high culture in its sphere. Nonetheless, their fortunes remained closely tied to those of the empires that they represented, and when these fell, both cities quickly lost their original grandeur.

Of the two, Constantinople was by far the oldest, but its rise to fame as a Roman capital came late in its history. The city dates back to 658 B.C.E., when Greek colonists from Megara first settled it. Named Byzantium in honor of their leader Byzas, it remained no more than a provincial port throughout most of antiquity. Its only noteworthy feature was its location: it stood at the tip of a promontory jutting out into the narrow strait, known as the Bosphorus, that separates Europe from Asia. This strait connects the Black Sea to the north with the Sea of Marmara to the south and through it—and the even narrower channel of the Hellespont—to the Aegean entrance of the Mediterranean. By imperial times, Roman expansion into Greece and Asia Minor made this waterway the most important artery in the rich, eastern half of the empire. With the decline of Rome and its western provinces in

Chapter 8
Regional
Metropolises:
Constantinople
and Tenochtitlán
(330–1521 C.E.)

the fourth century C.E., this eastern portion of the empire gained ever greater importance as a reservoir of wealth and manpower. And Byzantium, perched upon an easily defended headland dominating the most crucial waterway in the East, assumed new strategic value. It was apparently this strategic consideration that led Emperor Constantine to select the city as a replacement for Rome in 324 when he sought a better base from which to revive the empire.

Though Rome itself had ceased to be the actual imperial residence for some time before this change, it continued to hold great symbolic importance. In selecting Byzantium, therefore, Constantine apparently made much of its similarity with the older capital, particularly the fact that it, like Rome, stood among hills. To enhance the similarity, he refurbished the city in typical Roman style. But Constantinople, or "Constantine's city," as the site came to be called after its formal consecration in 330, was a seaport rather than an inland center. Built on a triangular peninsula, it faced water on two sides: the Sea of Marmara on the south and a deep inlet off the Bosphorus on the north. This inlet, called the Golden Horn because of its crescent-like shape, provided the city with a well-protected deep-water harbor that made it one of the best ports in the Mediterranean world. Taking full advantage of the maritime character of the site, its original Megaran founders had concentrated most of their public buildings in Greek fashion atop a tall hill, named the Acropolis, that overlooked the water at the

very tip of the peninsula. The sea and seafarers thus dominated the city.

Byzantium differed from Rome in another respect as well. Imperial Rome rose to fame without walls, only adding them in 268 when the growing threat of barbarian invasion from across the Alps led Emperor Aurelius to see to the city's defenses. But the unsettled conditions of his time led Constantine to wall off Byzantium's landward side immediately, giving the city a well defined western boundary. Later, Emperor Theodosius built an even more massive rampart farther to the west, considerably enlarging the city, and subsequent rulers raised sea walls along both the Golden Horn and the Marmaran shore. These defenses, which gave Constantinople a reputation of impregnability, attracted attention throughout the West and made the city a frequently copied prototype for the walled cities of medieval times.

Despite its extensive fortification, however, Constantinople ultimately covered four times the area of Rome. The heart of the city remained near the tip of the peninsula, where Constantine refurbished existing buildings and added what came to be called simply the Great Palace. As the first Christian emperor and one who actively patronized his faith, Constantine also built a number of churches throughout the city. Later emperors continued his interest in public construction. Emperor Theodosius not only built new land walls to the west of those erected under Constantine to enlarge the city but also added many internal monuments and improvements. Even more lavish, however, was Emperor Justinian, who launched an extensive building program to renovate the city as part of his effort to revitalize the Roman state. Along with many secular works, he ordered the construction of St. Sophia, a colossal church designed to be the greatest and most impressive building in all Christendom. During Justinian's reign from 527–565, in fact, the city probably reached the peak of its development with a population somewhere around 500,000 to 600,000—far in excess of that of contemporary Rome, which had shrunk rapidly in size as well as stature.

By the time of Justinian the city assumed the basic layout that it was to retain for the better part of the next millennium. Public life centered around a complex of buildings that stood just southwest of the Acropolis, the original heart of the city, near the tip of the peninsula. These included not only the Great Palace and the church of St. Sophia, the chief seats respectively of imperial political and religious life, but a great stadium-like race course called the Hippodrome and the Baths of Zeuxippus, both of which offered important public entertainments. Between them passed the Mese, or "Midway," the city's principal street. This grand avenue ran westward from the foot of St. Sophia to the Forum of Theodosius, where it forked into branches that continued out to the two most important entry points in the landward walls—the Golden Gate and the Gate of Charisos—which opened to the main imperial highways linking the city to the rest of the empire. Along

its approximately two-mile course stood additional forums, colonnaded squares in which markets and other public affairs could be conducted with some shelter from the weather. The largest and most imposing of these, the Forum of Theodosius, also served as the terminus of the raised aqueduct, built by order of Emperor Valens, which kept the many fountains and cisterns of the city filled with an adequate supply of fresh water. Most private homes and shops lined the secondary streets that branched off the Mese to thread their way up and down the six hills across which the city spread.

The decline of imperial might and wealth following Justinian's reign curtailed further building, and subsequent rulers added little to the city other than an occasional small church or monument. Moreover, by the eighth century, dwindling imperial fortunes together with a series of earthquakes and plagues appear to have severely reduced the population to perhaps a third or less of its peak figure. Thus it was a much smaller city that survived to become the regional metropolis of the Western world during Europe's Middle Ages. It was also a more complex city, combining its original Roman heritage with strong Greek and Christian influences. In its layout and most prominent secular buildings, of course, Constantinople continued to reflect the urban ideals of ancient Rome. But because of the Hellenistic culture of its populace, who spoke mainly Greek, the city's distinctly eastern character soon overpowered its Latin legacy. This feature was especially marked in religious

[195]

Chapter 8
Regional
Metropolises:
Constantinople
and Tenochtitlán
(330–1521 C.E.)

affairs, for the city served as the seat of the Orthodox Christian faith whose churches conformed to the Greek or Eastern rites rather than those of Rome. Moreover, as an important trade as well as political and religious center throughout the Middle Ages, the city continued to attract people from all over the Mediterranean and Asia Minor. Its many foreign quarters, filled with Italians, Jews, Armenians, and Slavs, gave it a cosmopolitan flavor that was enriched by a constant influx of still more exotic traders and diplomats coming from as far away as Britain and Persia.

Relative to Constantinople, Tenochtitlán was a young city. Founded by a people known as the Aztecs in the fourteenth century, the city quickly grew from a small local center into the largest city in the Americas as they expanded their control over Mesoamerica. The Aztecs, a Nahuatl-speaking group who called themselves the Mexica or Tenocha, came late into this area from an original homeland located somewhere in the arid lands farther to the northwest. According to their legends, they had dwelt there in a city called Azatlán, the "Place of the Herons," built on a paradisiacal island located in the midst of a desert lake. At the beginning of the twelfth century, however, they and seven neighboring tribes left their homeland at the order of their chief god, Huitzilopochtli, on a long migration southward. By the century's end they reached the shores of a new lake, Lake Texcoco, high up in the Valley of Mexico, where for nearly a century, they served indigenous tribes as mercenaries. In 1325,

however, the Aztecs retreated into the marshes of Lake Texcoco to found a new city of their own at a site where, in fulfillment of a prophecy attributed to their god Huitzilopochtli, they found an eagle perched on a cactus growing out of a stone.

The city they erected in the marshes took its name, Tenochtitlán—the "Place of the Prickly Pear Cactus"—from this prophecy. And the image of an eagle on a cactus provided not only a glyph or written emblem for the city but, combined with a sheaf of spears, served as the imperial symbol of the Aztecs. Like the founders of Constantinople, the Aztec builders of Tenochtitlán developed their city in imitation of an older ideal. But two different models influenced its design. One was the legendary paradise, Azatlán, in imitation of which they founded their new city on an island off the southwestern shore of Lake Texcoco. But in actual layout, Tenochtitlán followed another more historic model, an impressive ruin lying less than fifty miles away in the northeastern part of the Valley of Mexico.

All that remained of a great city dating back to the middle of the first millennium of the common era, this deserted ruin exercised a tremendous influence over all the peoples of Mesoamerica. The Aztecs, who knew nothing of its builders' identity, called it simply Teotihuacán, or the "City of the Gods," on the assumption that only divine beings could have built so grand a place. Despite extensive archaeological work in recent decades, we know little more about its builders than the Aztecs did. This first great metropolis of the Americas, however, clearly attests to a long prior tradition of urban development in the area. At its height around the year 500 C.E., Teotihuacán may have been home to as many as 200,000 people, making it one of the world's largest cities at the time. Even more impressive than its immense pyramids, its great residential quarters and workshops, or its vast market compound, is its careful layout around an expansive avenue of monumental buildings leading to the city's titanic Pyramid of the Sun. In spite of the grandeur of their city, Teotihuacán's inhabitants began to drift away sometime after 750 for reasons still unknown to us, eventually leaving it an empty ruin. Even in abandonment, the old site continued to serve as an urban model for subsequent Central American people. None, however, succeeded as well as the Aztecs in recapturing its grandeur.

In order to duplicate the monumental scale of Teotihuacán, the Aztecs had to expand their original island site through extensive landfills and hydraulic projects, allowing them to enlarge its shoreline and connect it with an adjacent island that held a separate community named Tlaltelolco. As part of this endeavor, they also found a solution to the damaging alkalinity of the landlocked Lake Texcoco: they built a huge dike across the southwest corner to isolate streams bringing in fresh water from the brackish main body of the lake lying east and north of the city. Within this fresh water zone, they reclaimed many acres of marshland around the city's edge for agricul-

tural use by building up *chinampas,* floating fields of heaped-up mud and vegetation anchored in place with stakes and willow trees. In addition, they built great causeways to the north, south, and west to link the island complex to the mainland. These connected the city to trade routes that fanned out across the Valley of Mexico, making it the hub of a mammoth network of commerce that spread across the whole of Central America.

Because the northern community of Tlaltelolco developed independently until conquered and annexed by the expanding Aztecs in the 1470s, the island complex retained two distinct populations, each focused upon its own *teocalli,* or ceremonial center. That of Tenochtitlán proper occupied the geographic center, but the more northerly *teocalli* of Tlaltelolco outshone it in magnificence. Both featured enormous enclosures containing temples and priestly quarters around which clustered ancillary markets, administrative courts, and palaces. Beyond these great centers spread a maze of streets and canals along which stood many smaller markets, workshops, and residential sections. Made primarily of stucco-covered adobe, most of the buildings in these latter sections were low, one- or two-storied structures that adjoined open courtyards. Those in Tenochtitlán were organized into four wards dispersed around the central temple enclosure.

By its zenith at the end of the fifteenth century, this prodigious urban complex probably held 200,000 to 300,000 people, a population greater

Chapter 8

Regional

Metropolises:

Constantinople

and Tenochtitlán

(330–1521 C.E.)

than that of any contemporary European city, including Constantinople. But this figure fails to include the population of the half dozen or so satellite communities that developed on the shore of the lake, particularly where the causeways began. The larger metropolitan area of Tenochtitlán, therefore, may well have contained a population twice or more in size, making it one of the world's greatest urban areas at the time. Many of these people were not Aztecs but older inhabitants of the region whose city-states had been subjected to Aztec rule. They and other ethnic

groups who migrated into the metropolitan area from more distant vassal states or came as traveling merchants infused it with a very diverse population. A constant flow into the city of tribute missions and organized merchant groups from as far away as the deserts of the north and Yucatan to the south added even more to its cosmopolitanism. Many of these immigrant groups and visitors tended to settle in separate neighborhoods and markets where they perpetuated their own customs and languages, adding great cultural variety to the city's life.

THE METHOD

The physical remains of old cities, whether ancient or more recent, provide the best information about their main features. Ideally, then, we should turn to archaeology, the science that studies the material culture of the past, for evidence about the nature of these early metropolises. But because modern Mexico City and Istanbul overlay old Tenochtitlán and Constantinople, archaeologists have not been able to do the extensive work required to uncover them. Although occasionally new construction, particularly in Mexico City, has allowed them to excavate a few important sites, for the most part they have not been able to do much fieldwork. So historical archaeology, or the investigation of material sites built in historical times, provides only limited evidence for us to use in understanding these particular cities.

As a result, the bulk of our information must come from documents. You will find two sets in the Evidence section that follows, one for Constantinople and one for Tenochtitlán. Sources 1 and 2 present eyewitness accounts of Constantinople left behind by two medieval European travelers, Benjamin of Tudela, a Spanish rabbi who visited the city in the course of a long trip across the Mediterranean in the years 1160–1173, and Robert of Clari, a French soldier who took part in the sack of the city in 1203 by Western Europeans bound on the Fourth Crusade. You can identify many of the sites they describe in Source 3, a medieval illustrated map of Constantinople. Source 4 provides an illustration of the most celebrated of these, the great church of St. Sophia. Two Byzantine accounts complete this picture of medieval Constantinople: Source 5, an account from the *Historia* of the chronicler George Acropolites, describes an imperial procession through the city in celebration of its recovery from invaders in 1261 by Emperor Michael VIII; and Source 6, an imperial Chrysobull (or decree) of 1082, sheds light on economic matters in the city.

Similar materials reflect life in Tenochtitlán at its height. Source 7 comes from a letter written by the Spanish conqueror of the city, Hernan Cortés, to King Charles V of Spain, and Source 8 presents the recollections of one of his lieutenants, Bernal Días del Castillo, as recorded in his history *The Discovery and Conquest of Mexico*. A parallel visual record appears in Source 9, a Spanish map of the city made at the time of its conquest in the sixteenth century. Source 10 shows a line drawing of the excavated site of the Great Temple area, and Source 11, an Aztec drawing from the so-called Florentine Codex, depicts the Great Temple that formed the city's central feature. This Codex, an illustrated manuscript now in Madrid, preserves Aztec accounts of traditional life as transcribed into both Nahuatl and Spanish by Bernardino de Sahagún soon after the conquest. Source 12 consists of excerpts from several such accounts of city sights from this invaluable testament.

Interpreting the sources for Tenochtitlán presents special problems. Unlike the Byzantines, the Aztecs had no writing system of their own, and so the oldest written descriptions of their capital date from the time of its downfall and come from the hands of the Europeans who destroyed it. Despite their obvious appreciation of many aspects of Tenochtitlán, such observers hardly viewed the city with

dispassionate eyes, and their remarks need to be considered cautiously. The inhabitants of Constantinople, of course, did write, and they left us considerable records of their own. But here, too, we must be wary of problems. Many of the surviving accounts come from outsiders who either passed through the city themselves or obtained their information second-hand from other visitors. And outsiders necessarily view places from an unusual perspective.

Before historians can use such testimony, then, they have to determine its degree of credibility. Obvious cultural and religious biases leading to overexaggerations and false observations are often easy to spot. Those who openly glorify their own cultural or religious superiority, for example, may well play down the impressiveness of what they have seen elsewhere. Other factors, however, may cause more subtle distortions. Invaders often inflate the size and splendor of conquered sites to enhance their reputation at home or to awe rivals. Be aware, too, that outsiders generally have interests and purposes quite different from those of the inhabitants, and they may frequent only certain quarters to the exclusion of others. For example, a religious pilgrim might remain unaware of the activities of a market or craft quarter, whereas a merchant hurrying to sell his wares could be completely oblivious to major religious sites. So as you analyze the materials that follow, try to discern not only who wrote each account but for whom and why. The answers to these questions should tell you which

Chapter 8

Regional

Metropolises:

Constantinople

and Tenochtitlán

(330–1521 C.E.)

source may be more believable for a particular aspect of city life. By then crosschecking and integrating pieces from different accounts, you should be able to obtain a reasonably clear and accurate picture of what these cities were like.

Begin this attempt by trying to determine what physical features stood out most in each of these cities. Did certain districts or complexes catch the eye of visitors more than others? What constituted the most imposing public monuments and civic symbols? Were there special places for work, residence, and entertainment? How did people move about within the city, and where did the principle lines of access take them? Once you have a list of these features, locate each of them on the maps included and give some thought to the general pattern that emerges. Ask yourself how the parts interrelated and what elements seemed most to shape the overall layout of the city. Do any clear centers of city life seem to stand out from others? Can you tell what sorts of activities dominated city life?

Once you have gained a general sense of the layout and chief structures of each city, ask yourself what such features indicate about the course of events in Constantinople and Tenochtitlán. Try to determine from the physical elements those chief concerns or activities around which public life revolved. Did certain of them predominate? Were there, for example, defensive works? What would such features indicate about urban life and the relationship between the cities and their surrounding country-

side? What, if anything, seemed to provide the locus for communal life? Were there large open spaces or public buildings where crowds could gather? What would they have done there? What provisions existed for mass movement and supply of resources like food? Similarly, try to determine what most defined civic identity through a consideration of the nature of public spaces and monuments. Did certain complexes command more notice than others? What did they house or commemorate? Who would have participated in or benefited from them?

On the basis of this analysis, ask yourself what such elements suggest about the function and nature of these early metropolises. Both were obviously imperial capitals, but were they merely political centers? To what extent did they also function as important focal points for economic, religious, or cultural life? It might help to compare them with more recent cities. Think for a moment how cities are laid out today and what features dominate contemporary urban landscapes? Note how airports, freeways, corporate headquarters, malls, and theme parks reflect the pattern and rhythm of the contemporary urban life with its emphasis on commercial activities and preoccupation with *mass* mobility, consumerism, and entertainment. What do the features of Constantinople and Tenochtitlán reveal about the nature of earlier urban life? Whose interests did they most seem to serve? How might you define or characterize such cities?

Source 1 from Manuel Komroff, ed., Contemporaries of Marco Polo *(New York: Liveright, 1928), pp. 264–267.*

1. From Benjamin of Tudela, *Travels of Rabbi Benjamin of Tudela, 1160–1173*

The circumference of the city of Constantinople is eighteen miles; one-half of the city being bounded by the continent, the other by the sea, two arms of which meet here; the one a branch or outlet of the Russian, the other of the Spanish sea. Great stir and bustle prevails at Constantinople in consequence of the conflux of many merchants, who resort thither, both by land and by sea, from all parts of the world for purposes of trade, including merchants from Babylon and from Mesopotamia, from Media and Persia, from Egypt and Palestine, as well as from Russia, Hungary, Patzinakia, Budia, Lombardy and Spain. In this respect the city is equalled only by Bagdad, the metropolis of the Mahometans [Muhammadans].

At Constantinople is the place of worship called St. Sophia, and the metropolitan seat of the Pope of the Greeks, who are at variance with the Pope of Rome. It contains as many altars as there are days of the year, and possesses innumerable riches, which are augmented every year by the contributions of the two islands and of the adjacent towns and villages. All the other places of worship in the whole world do not equal St. Sophia in riches. It is ornamented with pillars of gold and silver, and with innumerable lamps of the same precious materials.

The Hippodrome is a public place near the wall of the palace, set aside for the king's sports. Every year the birthday of Jesus the Nazarene is celebrated there with public rejoicings. On these occasions you may see there representations of all the nations who inhabit the different parts of the world, with surprising feats of jugglery. Lions, bears, leopards, and wild asses, as well as birds, which have been trained to fight each other, are also exhibited. All this sport, the equal of which is nowhere to be met with, is carried on in the presence of the king and the queen.

King Manuel has built a large palace for his residence on the sea-shore, near the palace built by his predecessors; and to this edifice is given the name of Blachernes [Blachernae]. The pillars and walls are covered with pure gold, and all the wars of the ancients, as well as his own wars, are represented in pictures. The throne in this palace is of gold, and ornamented with precious stones; a golden crown hangs over it, suspended on a chain of the same

[201]

Chapter 8

Regional

Metropolises:

Constantinople

and Tenochtitlán

(330–1521 C.E.)

material, the length of which exactly admits the emperor to sit under it. This crown is ornamented with precious stones of inestimable value. Such is the lustre of these diamonds, that, even without any other light, they illumine the room in which they are kept. Other objects of curiosity are met with here which it would be impossible to describe adequately.

The tribute, which is brought to Constantinople every year from all parts of Greece, consisting of silks, and purple cloths, and gold, fills many towers. These riches and buildings are equalled nowhere in the world. They say that the tribute of the city alone amounts every day to twenty thousand florins, arising from rents of hostelries and bazaars, and from the duties paid by merchants who arrive by sea and by land. The Greeks who inhabit the country are extremely rich, and possess great wealth in gold and precious stones. They dress in garments of silk, ornamented with gold and other valuable materials. They ride upon horses, and in their appearance they are like princes. The country is rich, producing all sorts of delicacies, as well as abundance of bread, meat, and wine. They are well skilled in the Greek sciences, and live comfortably, "every man under his vine and his fig tree." The Greeks hire soldiers of all nations, whom they call barbarians, for the purpose of carrying on their wars with the sultan of the Thogarmim, who are called Turks. They have no martial spirit themselves, and, like women, are unfit for warlike enterprises. . . .

No Jews dwell in the city with them; they are obliged to reside beyond the one arm of the sea, where they are shut in by the channel of Sophia on one side, and they can reach the city by water only, when they want to visit it for purposes of trade. The number of Jews at Constantinople amounts to two thousand Rabbanites and five hundred Caraites, who live on one spot, but divided by a wall. The principals of the Rabbanites, who are learned in the law, are the rabbi Abtalion, Obadiah, Aaron Khuspo, Joseph Sargeno and Eliakim the elder. Many of them are manufacturers of silk cloth, many others are merchants, some being extremely rich; but no Jew is allowed to ride upon a horse, except Solomon Hamitsri, who is the king's physician, and by whose influence the Jews enjoy many advantages even in their state of oppression, which is very severely felt by them; and the hatred against them is increased by the practise of the tanners, who pour out their filthy water in the streets and even before the very doors of the Jews, who, being thus defiled, become objects of contempt to the Greeks.

Their yoke is severely felt by the Jews, both good and bad; for they are exposed to be beaten in the streets, and must submit to all sorts of bad treatment. Still the Jews are rich, good, benevolent, and religious men, who bear the misfortunes of their exile with humility. The quarter inhabited by the Jews is called Pera.

Source 2 from Robert of Clari, The Conquest of Constantinople, *trans. Edgar Holmes Mc-Neal (New York: W. W. Norton, 1969), pp. 101, 102–103, 105, 107, 108–110, 111–112.*

2. From Robert of Clari, *Conquest of Constantinople,* 1203

Not since the world was made, was there ever seen or won so great a treasure or so noble or so rich, not in the time of Alexander nor in the time of Charlemagne nor before nor after. Nor do I think, myself, that in the forty richest cities of the world there had been so much wealth as was found in Constantinople. For the Greeks say that two thirds of the wealth of this world is in Constantinople and the other third scattered throughout the world. . . .

When the city was captured and the pilgrims were quartered, as I have told you, and the palaces were taken over, then they found in the palaces riches more than a great deal. And the palace of Boukoleon was very rich and was made in such a way as I shall tell you. Within this palace, which was held by the marquis, there were fully five hundred halls, all connected with one another and all made with gold mosaic. And in it there were fully thirty chapels, great and small, and there was one of them which was called the Holy Chapel, which was so rich and noble that there was not a hinge nor a band nor any other part such as is usually made of iron that was not all of silver, and there was no column that was not of jasper or porphyry or some other rich precious stone. . . .

[And there was another palace in the city, called the palace of Blachernae.] And there were fully twenty chapels there and at least two hundred chambers, or three hundred, all connected with one another and all made of gold mosaic. And this palace was so rich and so noble that no one could describe it to you or recount its great nobility and richness. In this palace of Blachernae there was found a very great treasure, for one found there the rich crowns which had belonged to former emperors and the rich ornaments of gold and the rich cloth of silk and gold and the rich imperial robes and the rich precious stones and so many other riches that no one could number the great treasure of gold and silver that was found in the palaces and in many other places in the city. . . .

Then the pilgrims regarded the great size of the city, and the palaces and fine abbeys and churches and the great wonders which were in the city, and they marveled at it greatly. And they marveled greatly at the church of Saint Sophia and at the riches which were in it.

Now I will tell you about the church of Saint Sophia, how it was made. Saint Sophia in Greek means Sainte Trinité ["Holy Trinity"] in French [*sic*].[2] The

---

2. Robert of Clari apparently knew no Greek and so misunderstood the meaning of the church's name. *Saint Sophia* means "Holy Wisdom," not "Holy Trinity."

Chapter 8
Regional
Metropolises:
Constantinople
and Tenochtitlán
(330–1521 C.E.)

church of Saint Sophia was entirely round, and within the church there were domes, round all about, which were borne by great and very rich columns, and there was no column which was not of jasper or porphyry or some other precious stone, nor was there one of these columns that did not work cures. . . .

Elsewhere in the city there is another gate which is called the Golden Gate. On this gate there were two elephants made of copper which were so large that it was a fair marvel. This gate was never opened except when an emperor was returning from battle after conquering territory. And when an emperor returned from battle after conquering territory, then the clergy of the city would come out in procession to meet him, and the gate would be opened, and they would bring out a chariot of gold, which was made like a cart with four wheels, such as we call a *curre*.

Now in another part of the city there was another marvel. There was an open place near the palace of Boukoleon which was called the Games of the Emperor. This place was a good bowshot and a half long and nearly a bowshot wide. Around this place there were fully thirty rows of seats or forty, on which the Greeks used to mount to watch the games, and above these rows there was a loge, very dainty and very noble, where the emperor and the empress sat when the games were held, and the other high men and ladies. And if there were two sides playing at the same time, the emperor and the empress would wager with each other that one side would play better than the other, and so would all the others who watched the games.

. . . Now about the rest of the Greeks, high and low, rich and poor, about the size of the city, about the palaces and the other marvels that are there, we shall leave off telling you. For no man on earth, however long he might have lived in the city, could number them or recount them to you. And if anyone should recount to you the hundredth part of the richness and the beauty and the nobility that was found in the abbeys and in the churches and in the palaces and in the city, it would seem like a lie and you would not believe it.

Source 3 from the British Library.

3. Illustrated Map of Constantinople, 13th century

Chapter 8
Regional
Metropolises:
Constantinople
and Tenochtitlán
(330–1521 C.E.)

Source 4 from Bildarchiv Foto Marburg/Art Resource, NY.

4. Interior, Saint Sophia

Source 5 from George Acropolites, Historia, *ed. A. Heisenberg, in Deno John Geanakoplos,* Byzantium *(Chicago: University of Chicago Press, 1984), pp. 374–375.*

5. George Acropolites, "The Byzantine Recovery of Constantinople: Thanksgiving and Celebration," 1261

The emperor [Michael VIII Palaeologus] reached Constantinople on the fourteenth day of August, but he did not wish to enter the city the same day, so he pitched his tents in the monastery of Cosmidion. . . . And after spending the night there and arising, he made his entrance as follows: since the Patriarch Arsenios was not present . . . it was at once necessary that one of the prelates pronounce the prayers. George, metropolitan of Cyzicus . . . whom they call Kleidas, fulfilled this task. Getting up on one of the towers of the Golden Gate and having with him also the icon of the *Theotokos,* the image named after the monastery of the *Hodegetria,* he recited prayers for all to hear. Then the emperor, putting aside his mantle, fell to his knees on the ground, and with him all those behind fell to their knees. And after the first prayer was over, the deacon motioned them to rise, and all standing chanted *Kyrie eleison* [Lord have mercy] one hundred times.

When this was over, another prayer was recited by the prelate. And then the same thing happened as after the first. And this was done until the completion of all the prayers. When the religious part of the ceremony had been performed, the emperor entered the Golden Gate in a way which honored God more than the emperor, for he marched on foot with the icon of the Mother of God preceding him. And he went up to the monastery of Studius, and after leaving there the icon of the most immaculate Mother of God, he mounted his horse and went to the Church of the Wisdom of God [St. Sophia]. There he worshiped Our Lord Chirst and rendered proper thanks to him. Then he arrived at the Great Palace and the Byzantine population was filled with great and immense joy and exultation. For there was no one who could not dance or exult with joy, being scarcely able to believe this event because of its unexpectedness and the enormous outpouring of jubilation. Since it was necessary that the patriarch also be in Constantinople, . . . after a few days the emperor entered the holy building, the temple of Great Wisdom, in order that he might hand over the *cathedra* [the patriarch's throne] to the prelate. And finally there assembled with the emperor all the notables of the archons and the entire multitude. Then the emperor, taking the arm of the patriarch, said, "Take your throne now, O lord, and enjoy it, that of which you were so long deprived."

Chapter 8

Regional

Metropolises:

Constantinople

and Tenochtitlán

(330–1521 C.E.)

Source 6 from G. Tafel and G. Thomas, eds., Urkunden zur Älteren Handelsund Staats-geschichte der Republik Venedig, *in Deno John Geanakoplos,* Byzantium *(Chicago: University of Chicago Press, 1984), pp. 286–287.*

6. Chrysobull Detailing Extraordinary Privileges for the Venetians, 1082

No one is ignorant of those things which have been done by the faithful Venetians, how after they had gathered together different types of ships, they came to Epidamnus (which we call Dyrrachium) and how they provided for our assistance numerous seaborne fighting men, how their fleet conquered by force the wicked expedition [of the Normans], and how they lost some of their own men. We also know how even now they continue to be our allies, and about those things which have been done by their rowers [*thalattokopi*], men who work on the sea. Even if we should not mention this, everyone knows it perfectly well.

Wherefore, in recompense for their services of this kind, Our Majesty decrees through this present chrysobull, that the Venetians annually receive a gift of twenty pounds [of gold], so that they might distribute this among their own churches in whatever manner they see fit. . . . In addition, those workshops situated in the quarter of Perama [on the Golden Horn across from Pera], together with their upper chambers, which have an entrance and exit throughout, which extend from the Ebraica [gate] up to the Vigla [gate], both inhabited or uninhabited, and in which Venetians and Greeks stay—[all of] these we grant to them as factories, as well as three docks [*scalae*] which end in this aforementioned area. We also grant to St. Akyndinos the property, that is, a mill, lying alongside this church, which belongs to the house of Peter and which has an income of twenty bezants [Byzantine gold coins]. Similarly, we give the church of the Holy Apostle Andrew in Dyrrachium, together with all the imperial payments except the one which is set aside there to be given to the [harbor] barges.

It is also granted to the Venetians that they may conduct business in every type of merchandise in all parts of the empire, that is around great Laodicea, Antioch, Mamistra, Adana, Tarsus, Attalia, Strobilos, Chios, Ephesus, Phocea, Dyrrachium, Valona, Corfu, Bonditza, Methone, Coron, Nauplia, Corinth, Thebes, Athens, Negropont, Demetrias, Thessalonika, Chrysopolis, Peritho-rion, Abydos, Redestos, Adrianople, Apros, Heraclea, Selymbria, and the megalopolis itself [Constantinople], and indeed in all other places which are under the authority of our pious clemency, without their paying anything at all for any favor of commerce or for any other condition on behalf of their business—[payments] which are made to the fisc [*demosion*] such as the *xylokalamos, limenatikos, poriatikos, kaniskios, hexafolleos, archontikios* [i.e. charges for mooring ships, disembarking, and unloading cargo, and taxes on imports, exports, purchases, and sales], and exemption from all other taxes which have to be paid to engage in commerce. For in all places of business Our Majesty has given them the permission that they be free of such exactions. And the Venetians are removed [from the authority of] the *eparchos parathalassitos* [sic] himself, the *heleoparochos*, the *genikos*, the *chartularii*, the *hypologoi*, and of all officials of this sort. Let no one who carries out imperial or other duties presume to be contemptuous of the provisions which have been specified here. For permission has been granted to the Venetians to deal in whatever types of goods and merchandise anyone may mention, and they have the ability to make any purchase and remain free from all exactions [*dationes*].

Source 7 from Hernan Cortés: Letters from Mexico, *ed. and trans. A. R. Pagden (New York: Grossman, 1971), pp. 83–84, 102–106, 107–108, 109.*

7. Letter of Hernan Cortés to Charles V, King of Spain

This great city of Temixtitan [Tenochtitlán] is built on the salt lake, and no matter by what road you travel there are two leagues from the main body of the city to the mainland. There are four artificial causeways leading to it, and each is as wide as two cavalry lances. The city itself is as big as Seville or Córdoba. The main streets are very wide and very straight; some of these are on the land, but the rest and all the smaller ones are half on land, half canals where they paddle their canoes. All the streets have openings in places so that the water may pass from one canal to another. Over all these openings, and some of them are very wide, there are bridges made of long and wide beams joined together very firmly and so well made that on some of them ten horsemen may ride abreast. . . .

This city has many squares where trading is done and markets are held continuously. There is also one square twice as big as that of Salamanca, with arcades all around, where more than sixty thousand people come each day to buy and sell, and where every kind of merchandise produced in these lands is found; provisions as well as ornaments of gold and silver, lead, brass, copper, tin, stones, shells, bones, and feathers. . . .

Finally, besides those things which I have already mentioned, they sell in the market everything else to be found in this land, but they are so many and so varied that because of their great number and because I cannot remember many of them nor do I know what they are called I shall not mention them. Each kind of merchandise is sold in its own street without any mixture whatever; they are very particular in this. Everything is sold by number and size, and until now I have seen nothing sold by weight. There is in this great square

Chapter 8

Regional

Metropolises:

Constantinople

and Tenochtitlán

(330–1521 C.E.)

a very large building like a courthouse, where ten or twelve persons sit as judges. They preside over all that happens in the markets, and sentence criminals. There are in this square other persons who walk among the people to see what they are selling and the measures they are using; and they have been seen to break some that were false. . . .

There are, in all districts of this great city, many temples or houses for their idols. . . .

Amongst these temples there is one, the principal one, whose great size and magnificence no human tongue could describe, for it is so large that within the precincts, which are surrounded by a very high wall, a town of some five hundred inhabitants could easily be built. All round inside this wall there are very elegant quarters with very large rooms and corridors where their priests live. There are as many as forty towers, all of which are so high that in the case of the largest there are fifty steps leading up to the main part of it; and the most important of these towers is higher than that of the cathedral of Seville. . . .

There are three rooms within this great temple for the principal idols, which are of remarkable size and stature and decorated with many designs and sculptures, both in stone and in wood. Within these rooms are other chapels, and the doors to them are very small. Inside there is no light whatsoever; there only some of the priests may enter, for inside are the sculptured figures of the idols, although, as I have said, there are also many outside.

There are in the city many large and beautiful houses, and the reason for this is that all the chiefs of the land, who are Mutezuma's [Montezuma's] vassals, have houses in the city and live there for part of the year; and in addition there are many rich citizens who likewise have very good houses. All these houses have very large and very good rooms and also very pleasant gardens of various sorts of flowers both on the upper and lower floors.

Along one of the causeways to this great city run two aqueducts made of mortar. Each one is two paces wide and some six feet deep, and along one of them a stream of very good fresh water, as wide as a man's body, flows into the heart of the city and from this they all drink. The other, which is empty, is used when they wish to clean the first channel. Where the aqueducts cross the bridges, the water passes along some channels which are as wide as an ox; and so they serve the whole city.

Canoes paddle through all the streets selling the water; they take it from the aqueduct by placing the canoes beneath the bridges where those channels are, and on top there are men who fill the canoes and are paid for their work. At all the gateways to the city and at the places where these canoes are unloaded, which is where the greater part of the provisions enter the city, there are guards in huts who receive a *certum quid* of all that enters. I have not yet discovered whether this goes to the chief or to the city, but I think to the chief, because in other markets in other parts I have seen this tax paid to the ruler of the place. Every day, in all the markets and public places there are many workmen and craftsmen of every sort, waiting to be employed by the day. The people of this city are dressed with more elegance and are more courtly in their bearing than those of the other cities and provinces, and because Mutezuma and all those chieftains, his vassals, are always coming to the city, the people have more manners and politeness in all matters. Yet so as not to tire Your Highness with the description of the things of this city (although I would not complete it so briefly), I will say only that these people live almost like those in Spain, and in as much harmony and order as there, and considering that they are barbarous and so far from the knowledge of God and cut off from all civilized nations, it is truly remarkable to see what they have achieved in all things.

Source 8 from Bernal Díaz del Castillo, The Discovery and Conquest of Mexico, *trans. A. P. Maudsley (New York: Farras, Straus and Cudahy, 1956), pp. 191–192, 215–219.*

8. From Bernal Díaz del Castillo, *The Discovery and Conquest of Mexico*

Our Captain and all of those who had horses went to Tlaltelolco on horseback, and nearly all of us soldiers were fully equipped, and many Caciques whom Montezuma had sent for that purpose went in our company. When we arrived at the great market place, called Tlaltelolco, we were astounded at the number of people and the quantity of merchandise that it contained, and at the good order and control that was maintained, for we had never seen such a thing before. . . . In this way one could see every sort of merchandise that is to be found in the whole of New Spain. . . .

When we arrived near the Great Cue and before we had ascended a single step of it, the Great Montezuma sent down from above, where he was making his sacrifices, six priests and two chieftains to accompany our Captain. On ascending the steps, which are one hundred and fourteen in number, they attempted to take him by the arms so as to help him to ascend (thinking that he would get tired) as they were accustomed to assist their lord Montezuma, but Cortés would not allow them to come near him. When we got to the top of the great Cue, on a small plaza which has been made on the top where there was a space like a platform with some large stones placed on it, on which they put the poor Indians for sacrifice, there was a bulky image like a dragon and other evil figures and much blood shed that very day.

So we stood looking about us, for that huge and cursed temple stood so high that from it one could see over everything very well, and we saw the three causeways which led into Mexico, that is the causeway of Iztapalapa by which we had entered four days before, and that of Tacuba, and that of

[211]

Chapter 8

Regional

Metropolises:

Constantinople

and Tenochtitlán

(330–1521 C.E.)

Tepeaquilla, and we saw the fresh water that comes from Chapultepec which supplies the city, and we saw the bridges on the three causeways which were built at certain distances apart through which the water of the lake flowed in and out from one side to the other, and we beheld on that great lake a great multitude of canoes, some coming with supplies of food and others returning loaded with cargoes of merchandise; and we saw that from every house of that great city and of all the other cities that were built in the water it was impossible to pass from house to house, except by drawbridges which were made of wood or in canoes; and we saw in those cities Cues and oratories like towers and fortresses and all gleaming white, and it was a wonderful thing to behold; then the houses with flat roofs, and on the causeways other small towers and oratories which were like fortresses.

After having examined and considered all that we had seen we turned to look at the great market place and the crowds of people that were in it, some buying and others selling, so that the murmur and hum of their voices and words that they used could be heard more than a league off. Some of the soldiers among us who had been in many parts of the world, in Constantinople, and all over Italy, and in Rome, said that so large a market place and so full of people, and so well regulated and arranged, they had never beheld before.

Then our Cortés said to Montezuma: "Your Highness is indeed a very great prince and worthy of even greater things. We are rejoiced to see your cities, and as we are here in your temple, what I now beg as a favour is that you will show us your gods and Teules." Montezuma replied that he must first speak with his high priests, and when he had spoken to them he said that we might enter into a small tower and apartment, a sort of hall, where there were two altars, with very richly carved boardings on the top of the roof. On each altar were two figures, like giants with very tall bodies and very fat, and the first which stood on the right hand they said was the figure of Huichilobos their god of War. . . . Then we saw on the other side of the left hand there stood the other great image the same height as Huichilobos, and it had a face like a bear and eyes that shone, made of their mirrors which they call *Tezcat,* and the body plastered with precious stones like that of Huichilobos, for they say that the two are brothers; and this Tezcatepuca was the god of Hell and had charge of the souls of the Mexicans, and his body was girt with figures like little devils with snakes' tails. The walls were so clotted with blood and the soil so bathed with it that in the slaughter houses of Spain there is not such another stench.

Source 9 from the Newberry Library.

9. Spanish Illustrated Map of Tenochtitlán, Printed in Nuremberg, 1524

Chapter 8
Regional
Metropolises:
Constantinople
and Tenochtitlán
(330–1521 C.E.)

Source 10 from the Museo del Templo Mayor. Photographer: Saturnino Vallejo y German Zuniga.

10. The Excavated Site of the Great Temple Enclosure

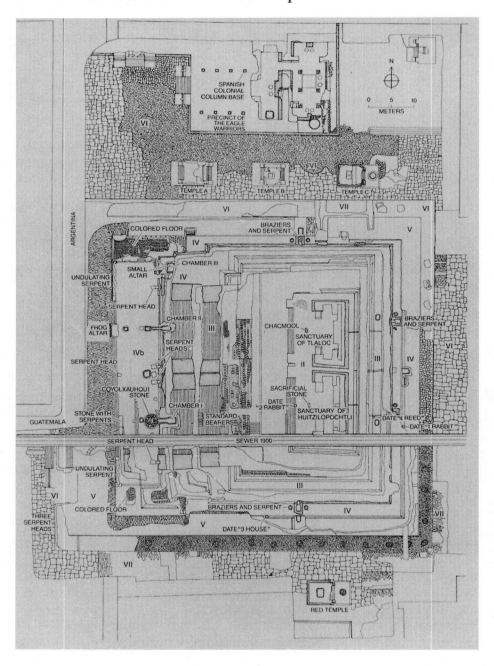

Source 11 from Bernardino de Sahagún, Historia de las Cosas de Nueva España, *trans. Arthur J. O. Anderson and Charles E. Dibble (Santa Fe, N.M.: The School of American Research and the University of Utah, 1954). Photograph: Courtesy, Patrimonio Nacional, Biblioteca Real.*

11. The Great Temple Enclosure at Tenochtitlán, from the Florentine Codex

Chapter 8

Regional

Metropolises:

Constantinople

and Tenochtitlán

(330–1521 C.E.)

Source 12 from Bernardino de Sahagún, Historia de las Cosas de Nueva España, *trans. Arthur J. O. Anderson and Charles E. Dibble (Santa Fe, N.M.: The School of American Research and the University of Utah, 1954), Part XII, pp. 269, 270–271, Part IX, pp. 29, 58.*

12. From Bernardino de Sahagún, The Florentine Codex

TEOCALLI

It means house of the god. In idolatrous times it was named *teocalli.* It is high, just an artificial mountain with levels, with steps. Some have one hundred steps, etc. And on its summit there stood two small houses, or just one; there the image of the demon, the devil, was guarded. This *teocalli* has levels, a landing, a stairway, a junction; it has a house, a house standing; it has a parapet, a column; it has columns.

It has a portal, corners, an entrance, a covering to the entrance, a stone column, a column, a door bar, a façade, a frontispiece, a wooden enclosure. It is roofed with thin slabs, with planks; it is uncovered; it is protected, with a parapet, with conduits. It is high, very high, very good, surpassingly good. It is a place to show, a place to exhibit.

TECPANCALLI

It means the house of the ruler, or the government house, where the ruler is, where he lives, or where the rulers or the townsmen, the householders, assemble. It is a good place, a fine place, a palace; a place of honor, a place of dignity. There is honor, a state of honor.

It is a fearful place, a place of fear, of glory. There is glory, there are glories, things are made glorious. There is bragging, there is boasting; there are haughtiness, presumption, pride, arrogance. There is self-praise, there is a state of gaudiness. There is much gaudiness, there is much arrogance—a state of arrogance. It is a place where one is intoxicated, flattered, perverted. There is a condition of knowledge; there is knowledge. It is a center of knowledge, of wisdom.

The ruler, when he beheld and knew that the common folk and vassals were very fretful, then commanded that the ball game be played, in order to animate the people and divert them. He commanded the majordomos to take out the rubber ball, and the girdles, and the leather hip guards, and the leather gloves with which the ruler's ball players were dressed and arrayed. And things were arranged on the ball court; there was sprinkling, there was sanding, there was sweeping.

On the two sides, on either hand, it was limited by walls, very well made, in that the walls and floor were smoothed. And there, in the very center of the ball court, was a line, drawn upon the ground. And on the walls were two stone, ball court rings. He who played caused [the ball] to enter there; he caused it to go in. Then he won all the costly goods, and he won everything from all who watched there in the ball court. His equipment was the rubber ball, the leather gloves, girdles, and leather hip guards.

QUESTIONS TO CONSIDER

As you go over the sources in search of clues that will help you determine the nature of these early metropolises, look for features that reappear in more than one account. Benjamin of Tudela and Robert Clari, the authors of Sources 1 and 2, had different reasons for visiting Constantinople, and their personal interests may have affected what they saw and remembered of the city. Yet both call attention to three of the city's dominant structures: St. Sophia, the Boukoleon palace, and the Hippodrome. Symbolic of the city's mixed Christian, Roman, and Greek heritage, these buildings all stood near the base of the original Acropolis. They formed the Capitolium, a central complex where the great thoroughfare known as the Mese, the city's main artery, began its course out to the landward walls. Together with public baths and the nearby Forum of Constantine, they defined the heart of the city as well as the administrative center of the imperial government. All three provided dramatic arenas for public spectacles. But note how, according to both sources, all three, including the stadium, housed religious as well as imperial functions. What explains the close connection between sports, religion, and politics in the life of this city? Would this same combination be likely in a twentieth-century city?

You can easily locate these and other major sites in Source 3, an illustrated medieval map of Constantinople. The map clearly shows one of the city's most often remarked features—its great encircling walls. What do such fortifications suggest about the city's relationship to the surrounding countryside and its regional position? Built by a series of early emperors, these walls were primarily intended to protect the administrative machinery of the empire. Most of the major government buildings, in fact, clustered together near the Capitolium. If you look at the apex of the triangular peninsula that juts out into the water on the map, you can see this area. Can you identify any of the buildings depicted?

The domed structure is the church of St. Sophia, or "Holy Wisdom." Why does it appear so large? St. Sophia was the biggest building then known in the Christian world, and, as Source 4 shows, it did enclose a vast space under its dome. But its size here is probably symbolic of its eminent role as the seat of the patriarch or head of the Greek Orthodox Church and the sacred light it was said to radiate throughout the Byzantine Empire. Like the entire complex of which it formed the hub, the church served an important civic function,

[217]

Chapter 8

Regional

Metropolises:

Constantinople

and Tenochtitlán

(330–1521 C.E.)

too. It provided a staging area for great public processions that proceeded down the Mese to the Golden Gate, symbolically the most important entry into the city. Something of their appearance can be glimpsed in Source 5, which describes the return of Emperor Michael VIII Palaeologus into the city following its recovery from the Crusaders. Note how St. Sophia plays a prominent role in the celebrations. Of course, as the drawing of the city shows, and Robert of Clari's account confirms, many smaller churches, abbeys, and imperial monuments dotted the rest of the cityscape. What do they tell about this metropolis?

Perhaps less obvious in the general accounts of Constantinople is its role as a major seaport and center of economic activity. The medieval map clearly reveals the city's maritime character showing many *porta*, or sea gates, giving direct access to the waterfront. Think for a moment how the encircling sea would have eased problems of sanitation, transportation, and supply in a premodern city of this size. Constantinople's proximity to important sea routes also promoted a great deal of trade and industry. Both Rabbi Benjamin and Robert of Clari hint at this aspect of the city's life. Notice how both dwell on the fabulous material wealth of the city, the one finding it comparable only to Baghdad, the center of the Muslim world, and the other rating it without peer. Much of this wealth derived from what the rabbi called "the conflux of many merchants" who came "from all parts of the world," giving the city a very cosmopolitan and mercantile character. Whom does

he specifically mention as inhabitants or visitors? By the eleventh century, Italians dominated most of the commerce in the eastern Mediterranean and Black Seas. What role did they play in the life of Constantinople?

Source 6, a Chrysobull, or imperial edict, authorizing Venetian trade rights, indicates not only the extent of their privileges but affords a brief glimpse into the complex economic life of the city. Note its mention of specialized workshops, factories, mills, docks, and barges as well as its list of various taxes levied on different port activities and commercial transactions. Clearly commerce and manufacturing flourished in Constantinople during Europe's Middle Ages. Observe, too, the high concentration of Venetians in a section of the city along the fashionable port side of the Golden Horn called Perama—just opposite the separate walled community of Pera, which, according to Rabbi Benjamin, served as the Jewish quarter and a center of silk manufacturing. Apparently the splendid harbor of the Golden Horn had drawn most of the economic activity and commercial wealth of the city to its shores by this time. The map hints at this trend in its depiction of many multistoried houses in these quarters, presumably the residences of rich merchants. The allure of this essentially mercantile quarter seems to have attracted members of the political elite, too. Can you find the Blanchernae Palace overlooking the water of the Golden Horn near the end of the land wall? What might this indicate about the impact of the sea and commerce on the character of the city?

[218]

Water influenced the layout of Tenochtitlán even more than Constantinople, for it was an island city, surrounded on all sides by water. Its watery setting, of course, was an inland lake, as the city stood on a high plateau far from the sea. The Spanish conquistadors Hernan Cortés and Bernal Díaz made much of this setting, as you can see from Sources 7 and 8. Note that both remark on the lake's contribution to the city's defense as well as to its transportation system. Because of Lake Texcoco—and the strength of Aztec forces—the city needed no walls. Instead of ramparts, therefore, the most impressive external features of the city were the great causeways that linked it with the lakeshore. As Cortés writes, two of these doubled as aqueducts, bringing an ample supply of fresh water into the city from landward sources. These causeways appear clearly in Source 9, an early Spanish map of the city. Notice their great extent as well as the many outlying communities that clustered around their junction with the shore. This drawing also shows the great wickerwork dike built east of the city to hold back brackish water and the many channels weaving in and out of the *chinampas* (floating fields) on its perimeter. What impression do you gain from these documents about the likely role waterways played in the city's life? Would they have facilitated trade over a vast region? Or would they merely have made a widely dispersed urban area possible in the premodern period?

Of the various causeways, the most impressive seems to have been the one that entered from the south, along which Cortés and his party first entered the city. As he relates, this causeway, which began in the satellite city of Ixtapalapa and spanned Lake Xochimilco before continuing across Lake Texcoco proper, led directly to the enclosure of the Great Temple that formed the center of Tenochtitlán. Within the walls of this temple, built high on a pyramid of stone, stood sanctuaries dedicated to the Aztecs' patron god Huitzilpochtli and the rain god Tlaloc. All around it, Cortés says, spread towers and courts inhabited by priests. A large plaza, which served as the main market, occupied the area in front of this enclosure, and various imperial and noble residences flanked it on either side. Like the Capitolium of Constantinople, this entire complex, known as the Great Teocalli, provided the main focus of public life. The drawing of the excavated site shown in Source 10 gives some idea of its original layout. It was named after the large temple, or *teocalli*, that loomed over it, but, as you can see, it contained many other components. How do these compare with those of the Capitolium in Constantinople?

The nature of the activities that occurred around the Great Temple complex can be inferred from Díaz's detailed description of the similar, though somewhat larger, *teocalli* of Tlatelolco, the neighboring city that became virtually one with the Aztec capital after its conquest. Note Díaz's open astonishment at the number of people and the amount of goods in the arcaded marketplace associated with this compound, as well as his keen interest in the wealth seen there. Like Constantinople, Tenochtitlán served as a regional economic

Chapter 8

Regional

Metropolises:

Constantinople

and Tenochtitlán

(330–1521 C.E.)

center whose merchants, according to Díaz, traded in "every sort of merchandise that is to be found in the whole of New Spain," that is, all of Mesoamerica. His description of the marketplace at Tlateloco matches Cortés's portrayal of a great square in the city "twice as big as that of Salamanca" where "more than sixty thousand people come each day to buy and sell." They both note the orderliness of the trading as well as the wide variety of produce on display. To what do they attribute this order?

Díaz shows equal astonishment over the vast court of the temple itself and the Great Cue (pyramid) that stood in its center. From the summit, the highest point in the city, he could look out beyond the immediate precincts of the capital to survey the entire metropolitan area spread out across the shores of the surrounding lakes. His comparisons of Tenochtitlán's size with that of Europe's great cities of the time, including Constantinople, merit special notice. One of Cortés's letters to Charles V echoes Díaz's praise of Tenochtitlán, claiming that even "in Spain there is nothing to compare" with the main palace adjacent to the Tenochtitlán *teocalli* in which the Aztec ruler Montezuma lived. But both accounts evince disgust over the ceremonies conducted in its temple enclosures, for Europeans found the human sacrifice practiced by the Aztecs as part of their religion upsetting. What does Díaz reveal about his feelings on this issue? Clearly he regards Europeans as culturally superior in this respect, though they, too, engaged in mass killing under other circumstances and did

not refrain from eventually slaughtering large numbers of Aztecs.

Source 11, an Aztec drawing of the Great Temple enclosure at Tenochtitlán, illustrates the kind of sacrificial ceremonies that so repulsed the Spaniards. At the top center appears the Great Temple itself with sacrificial blood streaming down the steps from its two sanctuaries. Like many other Mesoamerican peoples, the Aztecs considered blood to be a source of vitality that supported the cycle of life. They thus sacrificed people in order to replenish the vitality of the gods whom they believed returned it to humanity in full measure through the fecundity of life. Although only a few victims were killed in ordinary rituals, as many as eighty thousand prisoners were sacrificed here on the altar stones in victory celebrations following the conquest of rival states. On these latter occasions, the Aztecs invited vassal chieftains and allied rulers to witness the gory spectacle, suggesting that such rites had important political as well as religious functions. What might these have been? How may such activities have shaped the way in which neighboring peoples understood the nature or significance of the city?

As you can see from a comparison with the excavated site, the drawing of the Great Temple provides a faithful picture of this ceremonial heart of the city where its people sought daily renewal through sacrifice. Note, in this context, Díaz's account of the emperor personally assisting the priests in such rites as part of a state religion. In Tenochtitlán, like Constantinople, palace and temple stood together, creating an almost inseparable focus for public life. As Source 12 indicates, both the *teocalli,* or "house of god," and the *tecpancalli,* or "house of the ruler," were designed to awe people with the power and grandeur of their residents. The description of the ball games played in the courts adjacent to the Great Temple complex shows a similar purpose in the imperial patronage of sports. Compare the alliance of religious and athletic events here with those of the Hippodrome at Constantinople. To what extent did public life in both cities focus on a display of ruling powers, whether human or divine? What does this fusion of sacred and secular suggest about their nature as cities?

EPILOGUE

Because of their grandeur and wealth in late traditional times, both Constantinople and Tenochtitlán attracted the attention of covetous outsiders who eventually brought them to grief. The Spanish conquest and sack of Tenochtitlán in 1521 are, of course, generally well known. For all of his earlier admiration of the city, after seizing control of it, Cortés set about its complete destruction. He had already torn down the great dike during his attack on the city, destroying its immediate agricultural environs; and after occupying it, he ordered all the principal buildings razed, the waterways filled in with the rubble, and most of its former inhabitants relocated, claiming the need to purge it of its barbaric religious cults. A Nahuatl lament for the dying city preserves some of the anguish this destruction wrought: "Let me not be angry that the grandeur of Mexico is to be destroyed./ The smoking stars gather together against it; the one who cares for flowers is about to be destroyed."[3] Using the labor of allied tribes whom he brought to the area, Cortés built a new, Spanish-style colonial settlement renamed Mexico City upon the ruins of the old Aztec capital. Ironically, the builders of the new city erected the Metropolitan Cathedral over part of the old *teocalli* enclosure on a site adjacent to their colonial headquarters (where the present National Palace stands), thus perpetuating in a new form the close conjunction of temple and palace.

Constantinople's plight was neither as dramatic nor complete, but Constantine's city, too, suffered from invasion. The first of these came in 1203 when "Latin" participants of the Fourth Crusade, diverted from their original purpose by the lure of Constantinople's wealth and what they deemed its heretical Greek church, sacked and occupied the city. Remarking that "they revealed their race to be lovers of gold," a Byzantine chronicler complained that "these Westerners spared neither the living nor the dead" when they looted the city and showed "complete indiffer-

3. This lament is translated by Daniel G. Brinton in his *Ancient Nahuatl Poetry* (New York: AMS Press, Inc., 1969), p. 123; this version is a reprint of an older edition printed in Philadelphia in 1890.

Chapter 8
Regional
Metropolises:
Constantinople
and Tenochtitlán
(330–1521 C.E.)

ence and impiety" in stripping St. Sophia and other churches of all valuables.[4] Though dominated by Venetians, who coveted Constantinople's economic superiority, most of these so-called Latin conquerors were Franks, who, after thoroughly looting its moveable wealth, attempted to control the city for the next few decades. But a great fire that broke out during their occupation had devastated nearly half the city; and under their subsequent colonial rule, Constantinople not only failed to rebuild but slid into a rapid economic decline.

Thus, though restored to Greek control under Michael VIII Palaeologus in 1261, the city never regained its former wealth or stature. Its trade and territories passed gradually into the hands of others, and by the early fifteenth century it was reduced to a shadow of its original glory with wide empty spaces within its walls given over to orchards and fields of grain or filled with crumbling ruins. As a result of their declining fortunes, the Byzantines could not stem the tide of Turkish-speaking Muslim people moving in from the east. In 1453 one of these, known as the Ottoman Turks, seized the city and ended Byzantine rule for good. Unlike the earlier Latin conquerors, however, they successfully rebuilt the city under the name Istanbul to serve as the capital of an expansionary, new

Islamic empire that straddled the Bosphorus and spread westward into Europe as well as southeastward into Palestine and Africa. Symbolically, they transformed St. Sophia into a mosque and built a new imperial residence, known as the Topkapi Sarayi, nearby on the old Acropolis, reaffirming afresh the traditional importance of temple and palace in the city's identity.

The role that Western Europeans played in the decline of both of these metropolises merits some thought. Many of the sources imply that religious beliefs underlay their violent behavior. And their almost obsessive interest in gold and other material wealth is also well documented. As various of the above accounts demonstrate, Venetians, Franks, and later Spaniards, too, found these cities far richer than anything they knew. Their often naive amazement over the wealth and size of such metropolises points out the relative "underdevelopment" of urban centers in their homelands during this era. Because of this relative backwardness, Westerners later tended to equate the emergence of great urban centers with modern economic development. An appreciation of the scope of premodern metropolises like Constantinople, Tenochtitlán, Baghdad, Hangzhow, and Osaka, however, calls this view into question. Their impressive scale, in fact, suggests that efforts to understand world history using Western European patterns of development as a standard may be misleading.

4. These remarks by Nicetas Chomates appear in an excerpt from his *Historia* translated in Deno John Geanakoplos, *Byzantium* (Chicago: University of Chicago Press, 1984), p. 371.

CHAPTER NINE

TWO FACES OF "HOLY WAR":

CHRISTIAN AND MUSLIM "JIHADS"

(1095–1270s)

In about the year 634, the Muslim caliph Umar (the second successor to Islam's founder and prophet Muhammad ibn Abdullah) initiated a series of *jihads*[1] against non-Muslims, holy wars that took the so-called pillars (or principles) of Islam out of the Arabian peninsula and throughout the Middle East, across North Africa, into Sicily and Spain, and as far east as India and westernmost China. Similarly, on November 27, 1095, in a field in Clermont, France, the Roman Catholic pope Urban II called on Western Christians to undertake a *crusade*,[2] or holy war, to capture

Jerusalem from the Muslims. Thus for over six hundred years, both Islam and Christianity, two religious faiths with a great deal in common, were willing to resort to religious warfare to extend their doctrines and territories.

And yet, in spite of the fact that Muslims had been in Italy and Spain for over three hundred years before Pope Urban's 1095 call for a crusade, neither side seems to have been particularly curious about the other, and virtually no accounts exist containing Christians' perceptions of Muslims nor Muslims' of Christians. Indeed, the papacy labeled Christians who dealt with Muslims as traitors and warned that such treason meant loss of all their property. For their part, Muslims thought Christians were primitive and had nothing to teach them (Usamah ibn Muniqidh called Christians "animals"). Muslims who converted to Christianity were put to death.

1. **jihad:** literally "struggle" in Arabic, although it is more often loosely translated as "holy war."
2. **crusade:** the word is derived from the French word *croix* ("cross" in English), hence also a "holy war."

Chapter 9
Two Faces of
"Holy War":
Christian and
Muslim "Jihads"
(1095–1270s)

Beginning at about the time of Urban's proclamation and the arrival of the first Christian army in Palestine in 1098, the number of written accounts by one side about the other increased dramatically. Appearing when they did during the period Europeans refer to as the Crusades, there is little doubt that these accounts created perceptions and stereotypes in the minds of Christians who had never met Muslims, and vice versa. Moreover, it is clear that these accounts helped to formulate ideas by one camp of how the other should be treated.

Your tasks in this chapter are twofold. First, by examining the accounts written by Christians and by Muslims, determine the impressions that each side created of the other. Second, reach some conclusions about how those perceptions and stereotypes (whether accurate or inaccu-

rate) might have influenced the ways Christians and Muslims chose to deal with one another.

Before you begin, we must issue a note of caution. From the evidence provided by Christians, you will *not* be able to determine what Muslims were *really* like, but only what Christians perceived (or wanted their readers to perceive) Muslims were like. This is equally true of the Muslim accounts. Indeed, it is quite possible that some of the writers had never even met the people about whom they were writing. Even so, what you *do* learn will prove extremely important, for perceptions, impressions, and stereotypes are often just as powerful as facts in prompting individuals to action. To paraphrase historian Claude Van Tyne, what people *think* is true may be more important to them than what is *really* true.

BACKGROUND

The 500s and early 600s was a period of great change in the Arab world. Increased trade had brought a new level of prosperity, but that prosperity in turn had produced tribal and class divisions. Old values of tribal unity and sharing wealth were giving way to new values of individual and family accumulation. At the same time, Arabs began to feel a strong sense of religious inferiority. Neighboring Jews and Christians (with whom Arab merchants traded) boasted that their respective faiths were superior to other religions because they were built on divine revelations, something Arabs had not re-

ceived. Hence one could say that the Arabian peninsula was in economic, social, political, and intellectual crisis.

The appearance of Muhammad ibn Abdullah (ca. 570–632) ultimately solved each of these crises. Orphaned at an early age and raised by an uncle, Muhammad became a merchant, traveling in mercantile caravans as far as Palestine where he surely became familiar with both Judaism and Christianity. Marriage to a wealthy widow freed him from the need to work long hours to make a living, and the extremely pious merchant spent a good deal of time in meditation and prayer.

Around the year 610, Muhammad began to experience what he said were divine revelations from God (*Allah* in

Arabic) and God's messengers (he claimed his first vision was of the angel Gabriel). Gathering around him a small group of followers, he began to preach what he insisted was not a new religious faith but a reform of Arabs' traditional faith. Initially, Muhammad's message was a simple one: there was but one God (Allah), the same God, he said, who was worshiped by Jews and Christians; humans must prepare themselves for a last judgment; it was the duty of each believer to care for the poor and oppressed and to work to create a just society based on God's will and divine revelations. One can see how Muhammad and his teachings filled several needs in Arabic society. He advocated Arab unity over class and tribal divisions, care for the poor in a region of growing prosperity but unequal distribution of wealth, and Islam's parity with other religions because of the revelations Muhammad experienced.[3]

By the time of Muhammad's death in 632, most people living in the Arabian peninsula had become Muslims. Muhammad's successor Abu Bakr (called a *caliph*, or "successor to the Prophet") ordered that all of Muhammad's revelations be collected and printed in one book, the Qur'an (Koran) which was published in 651. Muslims accepted the teachings of both Jews and Christians (the most significant exception being the Christian assertion of Jesus' deity)[4] and claimed

that Muhammad was the last and ultimate prophet in a long line that included Abraham, Moses, and Jesus.

The death of Abu Bakr in 634 brought Umar to the caliphate. Under Umar, Islam launched a series of jihads to carry the faith to non-Arabs in North Africa, the Middle East, India, China, and Europe. In addition to the religious imperative, there also were economic reasons for these wars of expansion, especially the extension of trade routes under Arab control and the reaping of tribute paid by vanquished peoples. Jews and Christians living in conquered lands were allowed to practice their faiths, but economically and politically, they were definitely second-class citizens. Christians were allowed to make pilgrimages to Jerusalem, a holy city that they now shared with Jews and Muslims.[5]

Beneath the surface, however, Islam was never as unified as Muslims claimed. In 656 the third caliph, Uthman, was murdered and a division soon arose among Muslims as to who would succeed him. These two divisions, the Sunnis and the Shi'ites, also differed over whether caliphs, like the Prophet, were divinely inspired.[6] In

3. *Islam*, in Arabic, means "submission (to God)," and a *Muslim* is "one who submits."

4. Muslims called Jews and Christians People of the Book (the Tanakh to Jews and the Old and New Testaments of the Bible to Christians).

5. Muslims believed that Muhammad ascended to heaven from the Dome of the Rock, located in Jerusalem on the very site of the Temple where Jesus taught, destroyed by Roman armies in the first century. In 691, Caliph Abd al-Malik built a pavilion on the rock. Both Christians and Muslims believed the rock possessed curative powers, and pilgrims chipped off fragments to take them home.

6. The name *Sunni* was derived from the Arabic word *Sunna*, a collection of the Prophet's sayings and instructions for conduct in certain situations. *Shi'ite* is Arabic for "supporter" or "partisan."

Chapter 9

Two Faces of

"Holy War":

Christian and

Muslim "Jihads"

(1095–1270s)

time, the split became permanent. Also, sometime between 1071 and 1085 the Seljuk Turks, recently converted to Islam, swept into Palestine and captured Jerusalem from the Arabs. Thus by the time Christians from Western Europe began their own "holy war" in 1097 (known by Europeans as the First Crusade), the Muslim world was badly fragmented and extremely vulnerable to outside intrusions.

At the same time that the Muslim world was becoming increasingly divided, Western Europe was showing signs of increased energy. After centuries of comparatively modest population increases, suddenly population grew more rapidly, creating a surplus agricultural population and a resulting desire for more land. For example, it has been estimated that between about 950 and 1347 (the year the Black Death first appeared in Europe) the population of Europe increased threefold—some areas, like Saxony, gained tenfold. At the same time, trade with the eastern Mediterranean grew significantly, which fed the desires, especially in the commercial cities of Italy, for more trade connections with the Middle East. Finally, the social order produced a class of knightly warriors who were anxious to extend their power through combat.

Politically Europe was even more fragmented than the Muslim world. Kings, for the most part weak, were unable to enforce peace within their domains. In an effort to keep the lords of Europe away from each other's throats as well as to enhance the power of the papacy, popes in the eleventh century attempted to promote the Peace of God movement among Christians. European nobles, the movement proclaimed, would not engage in warfare against one another.

The Peace of God movement shows that the power of the popes was increasing and that religious enthusiasm was on the rise in Europe. Itinerant preachers whipped up crowds into fevers of religious excitement in which visions and miracles of healing were reported. In about the year 1000, an old Christian myth was revived and spread throughout much of Europe. Before the second coming of Christ and the resulting end of the world, the story went, an emperor from the West would be crowned in Jerusalem and would battle the Antichrist in that holy city. The circulation of this myth was especially rampant during the widespread famine of 1033.

Hence a number of factors were pushing Christian Europe toward its own version of a jihad. Population growth spurred a hunger for land and, in turn, a drive for new lands to be brought under Europeans' control gained momentum. The knightly warriors could maintain the Peace of God among Christians while at the same time uniting to battle "pagans" elsewhere. Crusades could also increase the power of the papacy and, finally, would direct the religious enthusiasm toward a productive end. Therefore, when Pope Urban II in 1095 issued his call for a crusade, many Christians took up the cry "God wills it!" "You should be especially aroused," Urban challenged his listeners at Clermont, "by the knowledge that . . . the holy places are shamelessly misused and sacrilegiously defiled with their filth." The first armies set off in August 1097[7]; they captured Jerusalem on July 15, 1099.

As noted earlier, Muslim incursions into North Africa, the eastern Mediterrranean, Sicily, Italy, Spain, and southern France did not mean that they learned a great deal about Christian Europe, or that European Christians learned a great deal about them. Instead, what is striking is the apparent utter lack of curiosity that each side displayed toward the other. Beginning about the time of the First Crusade, however, the number of written accounts by both Christians and Muslims increased dramatically. Your tasks are to determine what those perceptions were *and* how they helped to shape opinion on how the other side was to be treated.

THE METHOD

The Evidence section of this chapter contains three Muslim accounts of European crusaders and three European Christian accounts of Muslims. Usamah ibn-Munqidh (1095–1188) was born in Syria, educated by private tutors, was a merchant and government administrator, and knew Europeans quite well. Source 1 is his account of the "curious" crusaders. For his part, Ibn al-Athir (1160–1233) was one of three brothers, all of whom became noted Arabic scholars. He traveled extensively to collect material for his historical writing, and in Source 2, he glories in the 1187 retaking of Jerusalem. Imad ad-Din (1125–1201) was a scholar who was best known as a secretary to the sultan Saladin. Source 3 is an excerpt from his *History of the Fall of Jerusalem*.

As to the Christian sources, *The Song of Roland* (Source 4), written in approximately 1100 by an anonymous author, purports to be a historical account of the Battle of Roncesvalles in 778 in which Charlemagne's rear guard (commanded by Count Roland) was massacred. The actual attack, however, was made by Basques, but the poet substituted Muslims as the villains in his song, perhaps an understandable replacement since *The Song of Roland* was composed during the First Crusade. The second Christian selection (Source 5) is by Peter Tudebode, a priest who journeyed on the First Crusade. One or possibly two of his brothers were killed in battle during the siege of Antioch. Some controversy continues to surround Peter Tudebode's account because many scholars believe that some of it was plagiarized from earlier writers. Finally, Source 6 is by William of Tyre, probably the most widely read account by a Christian of the Crusades. William was born around 1130 in or near Jerusalem to European parents. He was extremely well-educated both in Palestine and Europe and had

7. A ragtag army of peasants led by the itinerant holy man Peter the Hermit began its march earlier, slaughtered Jews on its way across Europe, and was wiped out before reaching Palestine. It has been estimated that one-fourth of all "crusaders" (more often they referred to themselves as pilgrims) died on their way to the Holy Land.

Chapter 9

Two Faces of
"Holy War":
Christian and
Muslim "Jihads"
(1095–1270s)

command of six languages, including Arabic and Persian. He was ordained a Roman Catholic priest, returned to what Christians referred to as the Holy Land, and was made Archbishop of Tyre, a position he held from 1175 to approximately 1185. By the time Saladin conquered Jerusalem in 1187, William had disappeared from view and probably had died.

At first glance, all of these sources present some potential problems. To begin with, we cannot be certain that any of the authors were eyewitnesses to the events they describe. (The anonymous author of *The Song of Roland* almost surely wasn't, and some events William of Tyre wrote about took place before he was born.) To be sure, as secretary to Saladin, Imad ad-Din was in an excellent position to witness the events he recounted. But that is not proof that he actually *did* see them, and we cannot be sure how much he embellished what he saw or heard.

And yet, in this chapter, these are not the obstacles that they might be elsewhere. This is because, as noted above, we are seeking the *perceptions* that each side had of the other and the images and stereotypes that were deliberately created for a myriad of purposes (one pilgrim on the First Crusade, the Fulcher of Charters, described people "so tall that they can mount elephants as easily as horses").[8] Each author is attempting to create an impression in the minds of readers. To that end, he may accurately report events, or he may liberally exaggerate, interpret, or simply invent (as the author of *The Song of Roland* did when he substituted Muslims for Basques).

As you finish each selection, think of some adjectives that readers of the account might have used to describe "the enemy." Keep a running list of these adjectives as you proceed through the evidence. Be willing also to read between the lines. Sometimes a particular author, in genuinely trying to describe or explain a specific incident, may have nevertheless created a perception in the minds of his readers, intentionally or unintentionally. Be alert for such instances.

Keep the central questions of the chapter in mind: In the written accounts by Muslims and Christians, what impressions did each side create of the other? How might those perceptions or stereotypes have influenced the way each side chose to deal with and treat each other, both during and after the period Europeans refer to as the Crusades?

8. See Fulcher of Charters, *A History of the Expedition to Jerusalem, 1095–1127*, trans. Frances Rita Ryan (Knoxville: University of Tennessee Press, 1969), p. 287.

THE EVIDENCE

MUSLIMS ON CHRISTIANS

Source 1 from Usamah ibn-Munqidh, An Arab-Syrian Gentleman and Warrior in the Period of the Crusades, *trans. Philip K. Hitti (New York: Columbia University Press, 1929; reprint, Princeton: Princeton University Press, 1987), pp. 161–169.*

1. Usamah ibn-Munqidh
Describes the Franks

Their lack of sense.—Mysterious are the works of the Creator, the author of all things! When one comes to recount cases regarding the Franks,[9] he cannot but glorify Allah (exalted is he!) and sanctify him, for he sees them as animals possessing the virtues of courage and fighting, but nothing else; just as animals have only the virtues of strength and carrying loads. I shall now give some instances of their doings and their curious mentality.

In the army of King Fulk, son of Fulk, was a Frankish reverend knight who had just arrived from their land in order to make the holy pilgrimage and then return home. He was of my intimate fellowship and kept such constant company with me that he began to call me "my brother." Between us were mutual bonds of amity and friendship. When he resolved to return by sea to his homeland, he said to me:

> My brother, I am leaving for my country and I want thee to send with me thy son (my son, who was then fourteen years old, was at that time in my company) to our country, where he can see the knights and learn wisdom and chivalry. When he returns, he will be like a wise man.

Thus there fell upon my ears words which would never come out of the head of a sensible man; for even if my son were to be taken captive, his captivity could not bring him a worse misfortune than carrying him into the lands of the Franks. However, I said to the man:

> By thy life, this has exactly been my idea. But the only thing that prevented me from carrying it out was the fact that his grandmother, my mother, is so fond of him and did not this time let him come out with me until she exacted an oath from me to the effect that I would return him to her.

---

9. Most Muslims called all the crusaders "Franks" even though they knew full well that they were not all French.

Chapter 9

Two Faces of

"Holy War":

Christian and

Muslim "Jihads"

(1095–1270s)

Thereupon he asked, "Is thy mother still alive?" "Yes," I replied. "Well," said he, "disobey her not." . . .

Their curious medication.—A case illustrating their curious medicine is the following:

The lord of al-Munayṭirah wrote to my uncle asking him to dispatch a physician to treat certain sick persons among his people. My uncle sent him a Christian physician named Thābit. Thābit was absent but ten days when he returned. So we said to him, "How quickly hast thou healed thy patients!" He said:

They brought before me a knight in whose leg an abcess had grown; and a woman afflicted with imbecility. To the knight I applied a small poultice until the abscess opened and became well; and the woman I put on diet and made her humor wet. Then a Frankish physician came to them and said, "This man knows nothing about treating them." He then said to the knight, "Which wouldst thou prefer, living with one leg or dying with two?" The latter replied, "Living with one leg." The physician said, "Bring me a strong knight and a sharp ax." A knight came with the ax. And I was standing by. Then the physician laid the leg of the patient on a block of wood and bade the knight strike his leg with the ax and chop it off at one blow. Accordingly he struck it—while I was looking on—one blow, but the leg was not severed. He dealt another blow, upon which the marrow of the leg flowed out and the patient died on the spot. He then examined the woman and said, "This is a woman in whose head there is a devil which has possessed her. Shave off her hair." Accordingly they shaved it off and the woman began once more to eat their ordinary diet—garlic and mustard. Her imbecility took a turn for the worse. The physician then said, "The devil has penetrated through her head." He therefore took a razor, made a deep cruciform incision on it, peeled off the skin at the middle of the incision until the bone of the skull was exposed and rubbed it with salt. The woman also expired instantly. Thereupon I asked them whether my services were needed any longer, and when they replied in the negative I returned home, having learned of their medicine what I knew not before. . . .

Another wants to show to a Moslem God as a child.—I saw one of the Franks come to al-Amīr Mu'īn-al-Dīn (may Allah's mercy rest upon his soul!) when he was in the Dome of the Rock and say to him, "Dost thou want to see God as a child?" Mu'īn-al-Dīn said, "Yes." The Frank walked ahead of us until he showed us the picture of Mary with Christ (may peace be upon him!) as an infant in her lap. He then said, "This is God as a child." But Allah is exalted far above what the infidels say about him!

Franks lack jealousy in sex affairs.—The Franks are void of all zeal and jealously. One of them may be walking along with his wife. He meets another man who takes the wife by the hand and steps aside to converse with her while the husband is standing on one side waiting for his wife to conclude the conversation. If she lingers too long for him, he leaves her alone with the conversant and goes away.

Here is an illustration which I myself witnessed:

When I used to visit Nāblus, I always took lodging with a man named Mu'izz, whose home was a lodging house for the Moslems. The house had windows which opened to the road, and there stood opposite to it on the other side of the road a house belonging to a Frank who sold wine for the merchants. He would take some wine in a bottle and go around announcing it by shouting, "So and so, the merchant, has just opened a cask full of this wine. He who wants to buy some of it will find it in such and such a place." The Frank's pay for the announcement made would be the wine in that bottle. One day this Frank went home and found a man with his wife in the same bed. He asked him, "What could have made thee enter into my wife's room?" The man replied, "I was tired, so I went in to rest." "But how," asked he, "didst thou get into my bed?" The other replied, "I found a bed that was spread, so I slept in it." "But," said he, "my wife was sleeping together with thee!" The other replied, "Well, the bed is hers. How could I therefore have prevented her from using her own bed?" "By the truth of my religion," said the husband, "if thou shouldst do it again, thou and I would have a quarrel." Such was for the Frank the entire expression of his disapproval and the limit of his jealousy. . . .

Ordeal by water.—I once went in the company of al-Amīr Mu'īn-al-Dīn (may Allah's mercy rest upon his soul!) to Jerusalem. We stopped at Nāblus. There a blind man, a Moslem, who was still young and was well dressed, presented himself before al-Amīr carrying fruits for him and asked permission to be admitted into his service in Damascus. The amīr consented. I inquired about this man and was informed that his mother had been married to a Frank whom she had killed. Her son used to practice ruses against the Frankish pilgrims and cooperate with his mother in assassinating them. They finally brought charges against him and tried his case according to the Frankish way of procedure.

They installed a huge cask and filled it with water. Across it they set a board of wood. They then bound the arms of the man charged with the act, tied a rope around his shoulders and dropped him into the cask, their idea being that in case he was innocent, he would sink in the water and they would then lift him up with the rope so that he might not die in the water; and in case he was guilty, he would not sink in the water. This man did his best to sink when they dropped him into the water, but he could not do it. So he had to submit to their sentence against him—may Allah's curse be upon them! They pierced his eyeballs with red-hot awls. . . .

Chapter 9

Two Faces of

"Holy War":

Christian and

Muslim "Jihads"

(1095–1270s)

Source 2 from Francesco Gabrieli, Arab Historians of the Crusades *(Berkeley: University of California Press, 1969), pp. 141–142, 144.*

2. Ibn al-Athir, The Capture of Jerusalem, 1187

When the Franks saw how violently the Muslims were attacking, how continuous and effective was the fire from the ballistas and how busily the sappers were breaching the walls, meeting no resistance, they grew desperate, and their leaders assembled to take counsel. They decided to ask for safe-conduct out of the city and to hand Jerusalem over to Saladin.[10] They sent a deputation of their lords and nobles to ask for terms, but when they spoke of it to Saladin he refused to grant their request. "We shall deal with you," he said, "just as you dealt with the population of Jerusalem when you took it in 492/1099, with murder and enslavement and other such savageries!" The messengers returned empty-handed. Then Baliān ibn Barzān asked for safe-conduct for himself so that he might appear before Saladin to discuss developments. Consent was given, and he presented himself and once again began asking for a general amnesty in return for surrender. The Sultan still refused his requests and entreaties to show mercy. Finally, despairing of this approach, Baliān said: "Know, O Sultan, that there are very many of us in this city, God alone knows how many. At the moment we are fighting half-heartedly in the hope of saving our lives, hoping to be spared by you as you have spared others; this is because of our horror of death and our love of life. But if we see that death is inevitable, then by God we shall kill our children and our wives, burn our possessions, so as not to leave you with a *dinar* or a *drachma* or a single man or woman to enslave. When this is done, we shall pull down the Sanctuary of the Rock and the Masjid al-Aqsa and the other sacred places, slaughtering the Muslim prisoners we hold—5,000 of them—and killing every horse and animal we possess. Then we shall come out to fight you like men fighting for their lives, when each man, before he falls dead, kills his equals; we shall die with honour, or win a noble victory!" Then Saladin took counsel with his advisers, all of whom were in favour of his granting the assurances requested by the Franks, without forcing them to take extreme measures whose outcome could not be foreseen. "Let us consider them as being already our prisoners," they said, "and allow them to ransom themselves on terms agreed between us." The Sultan agreed to give the Franks assurances of safety on the understanding that each man, rich and poor alike, should pay ten *dinar*, children of both sexes two *dinar* and women five *dinar*. All who paid this sum within forty days should go free, and those who had not paid at the end of the time should

10. **Saladin:** Muslim sultan Salah ad-Din, whose real name was Yusuf ibn-Ayyub. *Salah-ad-Din* means "Rectifier of the Faith," a name Yusuf took up when he began his jihad against Christians.

be enslaved. Baliān ibn Barzān offered 30,000 *dinar* as ransom for the poor, which was accepted, and the city surrendered on Friday 27 rajab/2 October 1187, a memorable day on which the Muslim flags were hoisted over the walls of Jerusalem. . . .

The Grand Patriarch of the Franks left the city with the treasures from the Dome of the Rock, the Masjid al-Aqsa, the Church of the Resurrection and others, God alone knows the amount of the treasure; he also took an equal quantity of money. Saladin made no difficulties, and when he was advised to sequestrate the whole lot for Islām, replied that he would not go back on his word. He took only the ten *dinar* from him, and let him go, heavily escorted, to Tyre.

At the top of the cupola of the Dome of the Rock there was a great gilded cross. When the Muslims entered the city on the Friday, some of them climbed to the top of the cupola to take down the cross. When they reached the top a great cry went up from the city and from outside the walls, the Muslims crying the *Allāh akbar* in their joy, the Franks groaning in consternation and grief. So loud and piercing was the cry that the earth shook. . . .

Source 3 from Francesco Gabrieli, Arab Historians of the Crusades *(Berkeley: University of California Press, 1969), pp. 136–137, 148–149, 163, 170–171, 204, 207.*

3. From Imad ad-Din, *History of the Fall of Jerusalem*

At the same time as the King was taken the "True Cross"[11] was also captured, and the idolaters who were trying to defend it were routed. It was this cross, brought into position and raised on high, to which all Christians prostrated themselves and bowed their heads. Indeed, they maintain that it is made of the wood of the cross on which, they say, he whom they adore was hung, and so they venerate it and prostrate themselves before it. They had housed it in a casing of gold, adorned with pearls and gems, and kept it ready for the festival of the Passion, for the observance of their yearly ceremony. When the priests exposed it to view and the heads (of the bearers) bore it along all would run and cast themselves down around it, and no one was allowed to lag behind or hang back without forfeiting his liberty. Its capture was for them more important than the loss of the King and was the gravest blow that they sustained in that battle. The cross was a prize without equal, for it was the supreme object of their faith. To venerate it was their prescribed duty, for it

11. The religious excitement in Europe led to the "discovery" of numerous relics both before and during the Crusades. Some of these relics were portions of the "True Cross" of Christ's crucifixion (see above), the Holy Lance (that pierced Jesus's side), and the Crown of Thorns. Thus, the loss of what was believed to have been the cross to Saladin was a devastating blow to the crusaders.

[233]

Chapter 9

Two Faces of

"Holy War":

Christian and

Muslim "Jihads"

(1095–1270s)

was their God, before whom they would bow their foreheads to the ground, and to which their mouths sang hymns. They fainted at its appearance, they raised their eyes to contemplate it, they were consumed with passion when it was exhibited and boasted of nothing else when they had seen it. They went into ecstasies at its reappearance, they offered up their lives for it and sought comfort from it, so much so that they had copies made of it which they worshipped, before which they prostrated themselves in their houses and on which they called when they gave evidence. So when the Great Cross was taken great was the calamity that befell them, and the strength drained from their loins. Great was the number of the defeated, exalted the feelings of the victorious army. It seemed as if, once they knew of the capture of the Cross, none of them would survive that day of ill-omen. They perished in death or imprisonment, and were overcome by force and violence.

Here[12] are pictures of the Apostles conversing, Popes with their histories, monks in their cells, priests in their councils, the Magi with their ropes,[13] priests and their imaginings; here the effigies of the Madonna and the Lord, of the Temple and the Birthplace, of the Table and the fishes, and what is described and sculpted of the Disciples and the Master, of the cradle and the Infant speaking. Here are the effigies of the ox and the ass, of Paradise and Hell, the clappers and the divine laws. Here, they say, the Messiah was crucified, the sacrificial victim slain, divinity made incarnate, humanity deified. Here the dual nature was united, the cross was raised, light was extinguished and darkness covered the land. Here the nature was united with the person, the existent mingled with the non-existent, the adored Being was baptized and the Virgin gave birth to her Son.

They continued to attach errors like this to the object of their cult, wandering with false beliefs far from the true forms of faith, and said: "We shall die in defence of our Lord's sepulchre, and we shall die in fear of its slipping from our hands; we shall fight and struggle for it: how could we not fight, not contend and join battle, how could we leave this for them to take, and permit them to take from us what we took from them?" They made far-reaching and elaborate preparations, stretching out endlessly to infinity. They mounted deadly weapons on the walls, and veiled the face of light with the sombre curtain of walls. They sent out their demons, their wolves ran hither and thither, their impetuous tyrants raged; their swords were unsheathed, the fabric of their downfall displayed, their blazing firebrands lit. . . .

When Jerusalem was purified of the filth of the hellish Franks and had stripped off her vile garments to put on the robe of honour, the Christians, after paying their tax, refused to leave, and asked to be allowed to stay on in safety, and gave prodigious service and worked for us with all their might,

12. **Here:** refers to the Church of the Holy Sepulchre, a church that Christians believed enclosed the sites of Jesus' crucifixion and the tomb from which, they claim, he was resurrected.

13. **Magi . . . ropes:** refers to the Qur'an XX, 69, which describes Egyptian Magi casting down ropes before Moses and making them appear to be serpents.

carrying out every task with discipline and cheerfulness. They paid "the tax for protection permitted to them, humbly." They stood ready to accept whatever might be inflicted on them, and their affliction grew as they stood waiting for it. Thus they became in effect tribute-payers, reliant upon (Muslim) protection; they were used and employed in menial tasks and in their position they accepted these tasks as if they were gifts.

The Franks had cut pieces from the Rock,[14] some of which they had carried to Constantinople and Sicily and sold, they said, for their weight in gold, making it a source of income. When the Rock reappeared to sight the marks of these cuts were seen and men were incensed to see how it had been mutilated. Now it is on view with the wounds it suffered, preserving its honour for ever, safe for Islam, within its protection and its fence. This was all done after the Sultan left and after an ordered pattern of life had been established. . . .

There arrived by ship three hundred lovely Frankish women, full of youth and beauty, assembled from beyond the sea and offering themselves for sin. They were expatriates come to help expatriates, ready to cheer the fallen and sustained in turn to give support and assistance, and they glowed with ardour for carnal intercourse. They were all licentious harlots, proud and scornful, who took and gave, foul-fleshed and sinful, singers and coquettes, appearing proudly in public, ardent and inflamed, tinted and painted, desirable and appetizing, exquisite and graceful, who ripped open and patched up, lacerated and mended, erred and ogled, urged and seduced, consoled and solicited, seductive and languid, desired and desiring, amused and amusing, versatile and cunning, like tipsy adolescents, making love and selling themselves for gold, bold and ardent, loving and passionate, pink-faced and unblushing, black-eyed and bullying, callipygian[15] and graceful, with nasal voices and fleshy thighs, blue-eyed and grey-eyed, broken-down little fools. . . .

Among the Franks there were indeed women who rode into battle with cuirasses [armor breastplates] and helmets, dressed in men's clothes; who rode out into the thick of the fray and acted like brave men although they were but tender women, maintaining that all this was an act of piety, thinking to gain heavenly rewards by it, and making it their way of life. Praise be to him who led them into such error and out of the paths of wisdom! On the day of battle more than one woman rode out with them like a knight and showed (masculine) endurance in spite of the weakness (of her sex); clothed only in a coat of mail they were not recognized as women until they had been stripped of their arms. Some of them were discovered and sold as slaves; and everywhere was full of old women. These were sometimes a support and sometimes a source of weakness. They exhorted and incited men to summon their

14. See note 5.
15. **callipygian:** having shapely buttocks.

Chapter 9
Two Faces of
"Holy War":
Christian and
Muslim "Jihads"
(1095–1270s)

pride, saying that the Cross imposed on them the obligation to resist to the bitter end, and that the combatants would win eternal life only by sacrificing their lives, and that their God's sepulchre was in enemy hands. Observe how men and women led them into error; the latter in their religious zeal tired of feminine delicacy, and to save themselves from the terror of dismay (on the day of Judgment) became the close companions of perplexity, and having succumbed to the lust for vengeance, became hardened, and stupid and foolish because of the harm they had suffered. . . .

EUROPEANS ON MUSLIMS

Source 4 from The Song of Roland *(anon.), trans. Frederick Goldin (New York: W. W. Norton, 1978), pp. 51–52, 76, 88, 106–107, 120, 125, 162.*

4. From *The Song of Roland*

1.

Charles the King, our Emperor, the Great,
has been in Spain for seven full years,
has conquered the high land down to the sea.
There is no castle that stands against him now,
no wall, no citadel left to break down—
except Saragossa, high on a mountain.
King Marsilion holds it, who does not love God,
who serves Mahumet [Muhammad] and prays to Apollin.
He cannot save himself: his ruin will find him there.

2.

King Marsilion was in Saragossa.
He has gone forth into a grove, beneath its shade,
and he lies down on a block of blue marble,
twenty thousand men, and more, all around him.
He calls aloud to his dukes and his counts:
"Listen, my lords, to the troubles we have.
The Emperor Charles of the sweet land of France
has come into this country to destroy us.
I have no army able to give him battle,
I do not have the force to break his force.
Now act like my wise men: give me counsel,
save me, save me from death, save me from shame!"

No pagan there has one word to say to him
except Blancandrin, of the castle of Valfunde.

3.

One of the wisest pagans was Blancandrin,
brave and loyal, a great mounted warrior,
a useful man, the man to aid his lord;
said to the King: "Do not give way to panic.
Do this: send Charles, that wild, terrible man,
tokens of loyal service and great friendship:
you will give him bears and lions and dogs,
seven hundred camels, a thousand molted hawks,
four hundred mules weighed down with gold and silver,
and fifty carts, to cart it all away:
he'll have good wages for his men who fight for pay.
Say he's made war long enough in this land:
let him go home, to France, to Aix, at last—
come Michaelmas you will follow him there,
say you will take their faith, become a Christian,
and be his man with honor, with all you have.
If he wants hostages, why, you'll send them,
ten, or twenty, to give him security.
Let us send him the sons our wives have borne.
I'll send my son with all the others named to die.
It is better that they should lose their heads
than that we, Lord, should lose our dignity
and our honors—and be turned into beggars!"

4.

Said Blancandrin: "By this right hand of mine
and by this beard that flutters on my chest,
you will soon see the French army disband,
the Franks will go to their own land, to France.
When each of them is in his dearest home,
King Charles will be in Aix, in his chapel.
At Michaelmas he will hold a great feast—
that day will come, and then our time runs out,
he'll hear no news, he'll get no word from us.
This King is wild, the heart in him is cruel:
he'll take the heads of the hostages we gave.
It is better, Lord, that they lose their heads
than that we lose our bright, our beautiful Spain—

Chapter 9

Two Faces of
"Holy War":

Christian and

Muslim "Jihads"

(1095–1270s)

and nothing more for us but misery and pain!"
The pagans say: "It may be as he says."

[*Thus the Muslim king Marsilion devises a
plot to trick Charlemagne (Charles the
Great) into leaving Spain. The wicked
Ganelon, jealous of Roland (Charlemagne's
nephew), convinces Charlemagne to give
the command of the rear guard to his rival
and then betrays the rear guard to
Marsilion.*]

68.

King Charles the Great cannot keep from weeping.
A hundred thousand Franks feel pity for him;
and for Roland, an amazing fear.
Ganelon the criminal has betrayed him;
got gifts for it from the pagan king,
gold and silver, cloths of silk, gold brocade,
mules and horses and camels and lions.
Marsilion sends for the barons of Spain,
counts and viscounts and dukes and almaçurs,
and the emirs, and the sons of great lords:
four hundred thousand assembled in three days.
In Saragossa he has them beat the drums,
they raise Mahumet upon the highest tower:
no pagan now who does not worship him
and adore him. Then they ride, racing each other,
search through the land, the valleys, the mountains;
and then they saw the banners of the French.
The rear-guard of the Twelve Companions
will not fail now, they'll give the pagans battle.

[*The Muslim trap is sprung and the battle
is described, sometimes in gruesome
detail.*]

95.

A king is there whose name is Corsablis,
a Berber, come from that far country.
He spoke these words to all his Saracens [Syrian Muslims]:
"Now here's one battle we'll have no trouble with,
look at that little troop of Frenchmen there,

a few odd men—they're not worth noticing!
King Charles won't save a single one of them.
Their day has come, they must all die today."
And Archbishop Turpin heard every word:
no man on earth he wants so much to hate!
digs with spurs of fine gold into his horse,
comes on to strike with all his awful might;
smashed through his shield, burst the rings of his hauberk,[16]
sent his great lance into the body's center,
drove it in deep, he made the dead man shake,
knocked him down, dead, lance straight out, on the road;
looks to the ground and sees the swine stretched out;
there is something, he says, he must tell him:
"You pagan! You nobody! You told lies there:
King Charles my lord is our safeguard forever!
Our men of France have no heart for running.
As for your companions—we'll nail them to the ground;
and then you must all die the second death.[17]
At them, you French! No man forget what he is!
Thanks be to God, now the first blow is ours";
and shouts Munjoie! Munjoie! to hold the field.

96.

And Gerin strikes Malprimis of Brigal,
who finds his good shield now not worth one cent;
shatters the precious boss of pure crystal,
knocks the whole half of it down to the ground;
bursts through the hauberk's rings into the flesh,
buries his good lance deep in his body;
the pagan falls, all his sinews one mass,
down to the ground. Satan takes away his soul.

97.

And Gerer, his companion, strikes the Amurafle,
rips through his shield, the rings of his hauberk,
sends his good lance tearing through his entrails,
drives it in well, it passes through his body,
knocks him down, dead, lance straight out, on the ground.
Said Oliver: "We're fighting like good men."

16. **hauberk:** a long tunic of chain mail.
17. **second death:** the death of the soul, or eternal damnation.

[239]

Chapter 9

Two Faces of

"Holy War":

Christian and

Muslim "Jihads"

(1095–1270s)

[*Gradually the Muslims' superior numbers
make themselves felt. Rather than sound
his horn for help, however, Roland vows
that he will die in battle as a noble knight.*]

141.

Roland returned to his place on the field,
strikes—a brave man keeping faith—with Durendal,
struck through Faldrun de Pui, cut him to pieces,
and twenty-four of the men they valued most;
no man will ever want his vengeance more!
As when the deer turns tail before the dogs,
so the pagans flee before Roland the Count.
Said the Archbishop: "You! Roland! What a fighter!
Now that's what every knight must have in him
who carries arms and rides on a fine horse:
he must be strong, a savage, when he's in battle;
for otherwise, what's he worth? Not four cents!
Let that four-cent man be a monk in some minster,
and he can pray all day long for our sins."
Roland replies: "Attack, do not spare them!"
And with that word the Franks began again.
There was a heavy loss of Christian men.

142.

When a man knows there'll be no prisoners,
what will that man not do to defend himself!
And so the Franks fight with the fury of lions.
Now Marsilion, the image of a baron,
mounted on that war horse he calls Gaignun,
digs in his spurs, comes to strike Bevon,
who was the lord of Beaune and of Dijon;
smashes his shield, rips apart his hauberk,
knocks him down, dead, no need to wound him more.
And then he killed Yvorie and Yvon,
and more: he killed Gerard of Rousillon.
Roland the Count is not far away now,
said to the pagan: "The Lord God's curse on you!
You kill my companions, how you wrong me!
You'll feel the pain of it before we part,
you will learn my sword's name by heart today";
comes on to strike—the image of a baron.

He has cut off Marsilion's right fist;
now takes the head of Jurfaleu the blond—
the head of Jurfaleu! Marsilion's son.
The pagans cry: "Help, Mahumet! Help us!
Vengeance, our gods, on Charles! the man who set
these criminals on us in our own land,
they will not quit the field, they'll stand and die!"
And one said to the other: "Let *us* run then."
And with that word, some hundred thousand flee.
Now try to call them back: they won't return.

143.

What does it matter? If Marsilion has fled,
his uncle has remained: the Algalife,
who holds Carthage, Alfrere, and Garmalie,
and Ethiopia: a land accursed;
holds [its] immense black race under his power,
the huge noses, the enormous ears on them;
and they number more than fifty thousand.
These are the men who come riding in fury,
and now they shout that pagan battle cry.
And Roland said: "Here comes our martrydom;
I see it now: we have not long to live.
But let the world call any man a traitor
        who does not make them pay before he dies!
My lords, attack! Use those bright shining swords!
Fight a good fight for your deaths and your lives,
let no shame touch sweet France because of us!
When Charles my lord comes to this battlefield
and sees how well we punished these Saracens,
finds fifteen of their dead for one of ours,
I'll tell you what he will do: he will bless us."

144.

When Roland sees that unbelieving race,
those hordes and hordes blacker than blackest ink—
no shred of white on them except their teeth—
then said the Count: "I see it clearly now,
we die today: it is there before us.
Men of France, strike! I will start it once more."
Said Oliver: "God curse the slowest man."
And with that word, the French strike into battle.

Chapter 9

Two Faces of
"Holy War":
Christian and
Muslim "Jihads"
(1095–1270s)

176.

Count Roland lay stretched out beneath a pine;
he turned his face toward the land of Spain,
began to remember many things now:
how many lands, brave man, he had conquered;
and he remembered: sweet France, the men of his line,
remembered Charles, his lord, who fostered him:
cannot keep, remembering, from weeping, sighing;
but would not be unmindful of himself:
he confesses his sins, prays God for mercy:
"Loyal Father, you who never failed us,
who resurrected Saint Lazarus from the dead,
and saved your servant Daniel from the lions:
now save the soul of me from every peril
for the sins I committed while I still lived."
Then he held out his right glove to his Lord:
Saint Gabriel took the glove from his hand.
He held his head bowed down upon his arm,
he is gone, his two hands joined, to his end.
Then God sent him his angel Cherubin
and Saint Michael, angel of the sea's Peril;
and with these two there came Saint Gabriel:
they bear Count Roland's soul to Paradise.

[*Charlemagne returns to the scene of battle*
to find Roland and all the rear guard dead.
He then sets out to avenge Roland by
defeating the Muslims and then executing
the traitor Gravelon.]

187.

King Marsilion flees to Saragossa,
dismounts in shadow beneath an olive tree,
gives up his sword, his helmet, his hauberk,
lies down in shame, on the green grass, outraged:
he has lost his right hand, cleanly cut off,
faints from the loss of blood and chokes with pain.
And before him stands his wife Bramimunde,
who weeps and wails, the fury of her lament!
and thirty thousand men, and more, with her,
cursing King Charles and the sweet land of France.
They rush into a crypt to Apollin
and rail at him, disfigure him to vileness:

[242]

"Eh! you bad god, the shame you have done us!
Why did you let our king be beaten to dishonor?
You give bad wages to men who serve you well."
They tear away his scepter and his crown,
lay hands on him atop a lofty column
and throw him to the ground beneath their feet,
and beat him with big sticks, smash him to pieces;
and tear from Tervagant his great carbuncle,
and throw the god Mahum into a ditch,
and pigs and dogs bite him and befoul him.

289.

Bavarians and Alemans returned,
and Poitevins, and Bretons, and Normans,
and all agreed, the Franks before the others,
Ganelon must die, and in amazing pain.
Four war horses are led out and brought forward;
then they attach his two feet, his two hands.
These battle horses are swift and spirited,
four sergeants come and drive them on ahead
toward a river in the midst of a field.
Ganelon is brought to terrible perdition,
all his mighty sinews are pulled to pieces,
and the limbs of his body burst apart;
on the green grass flows that bright and famous blood.
Ganelon died a traitor's and recreant's death.
Now when one man betrays another,
    it is not right that he should live to boast of it.

Source 5 from Peter Tudebode, Historia de Hierosolymitano Itinere *(History of the Jerusalem Journey), trans. John Hugh Hill and Laurita L. Hill (Philadelphia: American Philosophical Society, 1974), pp. 54–55, 58–59, 115.*

5. From Peter Tudebode, *History of the Jerusalem Journey*

The Turkish attack was so overwhelming that our men took to their heels over the nearest mountain or the most convenient path; and those who were swift of foot survived, but the laggards met death for the name of Christ. More than one thousand knights or footmen martyred on that day rose joyfully to heaven and, bearing the stole of customary white-robed martyrdom, glorified

Chapter 9

Two Faces of

"Holy War":

Christian and

Muslim "Jihads"

(1095–1270s)

and praised our triune God in whom they happily triumphed; and they said in unison: "Our God! Why did you not protect our blood which was shed today for your name?"

Following a different road, Bohemond with a few knights gave his horse free rein and sped to the assembled group of beset crusaders. Burning with anger over the death of our men, we invoked the name of Jesus Christ and, being assured of the crusade to the Holy Sepulchre, moved as a united front against our foes and joined in battle with one heart and mind. The Turks, enemies of God and us, stood around stunned and paralyzed with fear because they thought that they could overwhelm and slaughter us as they had done the troops of Raymond and Bohemond.

But Omnipotent God permitted no such thing. Knights of the true God, protected on all sides by the sign of the Cross, rushed pell-mell and courageously struck the Turks. In the ensuing rout the besieged scurried to safety by way of the narrow bridge to Antioch. The survivors, who could not push their way through the jam of people and horses, were snuffed out in everlasting death, and their miserable souls returned to the devil and his legions. We knocked them in the head and drove them into the river with our deadly lances so that the waters of the swift Orontes seemed to flow crimson with Turkish blood. If by chance one of them crawled up the bridge posts or struggled to swim to land, he was wounded. All along the river banks we stood pushing and drowning the pagans in the pull of the rapid stream.

The din of battle coupled with the screams of Christians and Turks rang out to the elements, and the rain of missiles and arrows darkened the sky and obscured the daylight. Strident voices within and without Antioch added to the noise. Christian women of Antioch came to loopholes on the battlements, and in their accustomed way secretly applauded as they watched the miserable plight of the Turks. Armenians, Syrians, and Greeks, willingly or unwillingly, by daily orders of the tyrannical Turkish leaders, sped arrows against us. Twelve Turkish emirs in line of duty met death in soul and body as well as fifteen hundred of their most experienced and brave soldiers who were also the core of Antioch's defense.

The survivors in Antioch did not have the *esprit de corps* to shout and gibber by day and night as had been their custom. Only night broke off the skirmishing of crusaders and their opponents and so ended the fighting, the hurling of javelins, the thrusting of spears, and the shooting of arrows. So by the strength of God and the Holy Sepulchre the Turks no longer possessed their former spirit, either in words or deeds. As a result of this day, we refitted ourselves very well in horses and other necessities. . . .

On another day the Turks led to the top of an Antiochian wall a noble knight, Rainald Porchet, whom they had imprisoned in a foul dungeon. They then told him that he should inquire from the Christian pilgrims how much they would pay for his ransom before he lost his head. From the heights of the wall Rainald addressed the leaders: "My lords, it matters not if I die, and I

[244]

pray you, my brothers, that you pay no ransom for me. But be certain in the faith of Christ and the Holy Sepulchre that God is with you and shall be forever. You have slain all the leaders and the bravest men of Antioch; namely, twelve emirs and fifteen thousand noblemen, and no one remains to give battle with you or to defend the city."

The Turks asked what Rainald had said. The interpreter replied: "Nothing good concerning you was said."

The emir, Yaghi Siyan, immediately ordered him to descend from the wall and spoke to him through an interpreter: "Rainald, do you wish to enjoy life honorably with us?"

Rainald replied: "How can I live honorably with you without sinning?"

The emir answered: "Deny your God, whom you worship and believe, and accept Mohammed and our other gods. If you do so we shall give to you all that you desire such as gold, horses, mules, and many other worldly goods which you wish, as well as wives and inheritances; and we shall enrich you with great lands."

Rainald replied to the emir: "Give me time for consideration"; and the emir gladly agreed. Rainald with clasped hands knelt in prayer to the east; humbly he asked God that He come to his aid and transport with dignity his soul to the bosom of Abraham.

When the emir saw Rainald in prayer, he called his interpreter and said to him: "What was Rainald's answer?"

The interpreter then said: "He completely denies your god. He also refuses your worldly goods and your gods."

After hearing this report, the emir was extremely irritated and ordered the immediate beheading of Rainald, and so the Turks with great pleasure chopped off his head. Swiftly the angels, joyfully singing the Psalms of David, bore his soul and lifted it before the sight of God for Whose love he had undergone martyrdom.

Then the emir, in a towering rage because he could not make Rainald turn apostate, at once ordered all the pilgrims in Antioch to be brought before him with their hands bound behind their backs. When they had come before him, he ordered them stripped stark naked, and as they stood in the nude he commanded that they be bound with ropes in a circle. He then had chaff, firewood, and hay piled around them, and finally as enemies of God he ordered them put to the torch.

The Christians, those knights of Christ, shrieked and screamed so that their voices resounded in heaven to God for whose love their flesh and bones were cremated; and so they all entered martyrdom on this day wearing in heaven their white stoles before the Lord, for Whom they had so loyally suffered in the reign of our Lord Jesus Christ, to Whom is the honor and glory now and throughout eternity. Amen. . . .

When our lords saw these atrocities, they were greatly angered and held a council in which the bishops and priests recommended that the crusaders

Chapter 9

Two Faces of
"Holy War":

Christian and

Muslim "Jihads"

(1095–1270s)

hold a procession around the city. So the bishops and priests, barefooted, clad in sacred vestments, and bearing crosses in their hands, came from the church of the Blessed Mary, which is on Mount Zion, to the church of Saint Stephen, the Protomartyr, singing and praying that the Lord Jesus Christ deliver his holy city and the Holy Sepulchre from the pagan people and place it in Christian hands for His holy service. The clerks, so clad, along with the armed knights and their retainers, marched side by side.

The sight of this caused the Saracens to parade likewise on the walls of Jerusalem, bearing insignia of Mohammed on a standard and pennon. The Christians came to the church of Saint Stephen and there took their stations as is customary in our processions. In the meantime the Saracens stood on the walls, screamed, blared out with horns, and performed all kinds of acts of mockery. To add insult to injury they made from wood a cross similar to the one on which, pouring forth His blood, the most merciful Christ redeemed the world. Afterward they inflicted great sorrow upon the Christians when, in the sight of all, they beat upon the cross with sticks and shattered it against the walls, shouting loudly, *Frango agip salip*," which means "Franks, is this a good cross?"

Source 6 from William of Tyre, A History of Deeds Done Beyond the Sea, *2 vols., trans. Emily Atwater Babcock and A. C. Krey (New York: Columbia University Press, 1943), vol. 1, pp. 60, 68–69, 306–307; vol. 2, p. 323.*

6. From William of Tyre, *A History of Deeds Done Beyond the Sea*

In the time of the Roman Emperor Heraclius, according to ancient histories and Oriental tradition, the pernicious doctrines of Muhammad had gained a firm foothold in the Orient. This first-born son of Satan falsely declared that he was a prophet sent from God and thereby led astray the lands of the East, especially Arabia. The poisonous seed which he sowed so permeated the provinces that his successors employed sword and violence, instead of preaching and exhortation, to compel the people, however reluctant, to embrace the erroneous tenets of the prophet. . . .

There was a certain infidel living in the city, a treacherous and wicked man, who persecuted our people with insatiable hatred. This man was determined to devise some scheme that would bring about their destruction. One day, he stealthily threw the carcass of a dog into the temple court, a place which the custodians—and indeed the whole city as well—were most careful to keep scrupulously clean. Worshippers who came to the temple to pray the next morning found the mouldering body of the unclean animal. Almost frantic, they at once roused the whole city with their cries. The populace quickly ran to the temple, and all agreed that without question the Christians were responsible for the act. Need more be said? Death was decreed for all Christians, since it was judged that by death alone could they atone for such an act of sacrilege. The faithful, in full assurance of their innocence, prepared to suffer death for Christ's sake. As the executioners, with swords unsheathed, were about to carry out their orders, however, a young man, filled with the spirit, came forward and offered himself as the sacrifice. "It would be most disastrous, O brethren," he said, "that the entire church should die in this way. Far better were it that one man should give his life for the people, that the whole Christian race may not perish. Promise me that annually you will reverently honor my memory and that the respect and honor due to my family shall be maintained forever. On these terms, at the command of God, I will deliver you from this massacre." The Christians heard his words with great joy and readily granted what he asked. They promised that, on the day of palm branches, in perpetual memory of him, those of his lineage should bear into the city, in solemn procession, the olive which signifies our Lord Jesus Christ.

The young man then gave himself up to the chief men of Jerusalem and declared that he was the criminal. In this way he established the innocence of the other Christians, for, when the judges heard his story, they absolved the rest and put him to the sword. Thus he laid down his life for the brethren and, with pious resignation, met death, that most blessed sleep, confident that he had acquired grace in the sight of the Lord. . . .

There was a certain noble of the Turkish race named Balas living in that part of the country, who had formerly been the lord of Seruj. At that time, he had been allied by treaty with the count, and before the Latins arrived in such numbers the two had been on very friendly terms. This man perceived that Baldwin's affection toward him had become less. Led either by his own feelings of resentment, or possibly by the request of the citizens, he went to the count and begged as a favor that he would come personally to receive the one fortress which still remained in his [Balas's] possession. He declared that Baldwin's favor would be all-sufficient for him and would be esteemed as a valuable heritage. He said also that he intended to bring his wife and children, with all he possessed, to Edessa and pretended to stand in great fear of his fellow countrymen, because he had become so friendly with the Christians. To carry out this wish, the count was persuaded to set a day to visit the place. At the time appointed, he set out with two hundred knights and marched to the fortress, whither Balas had preceded him. The latter, however, had secretly strengthened the defenses of the castle by introducing a hundred valiant knights, splendidly armed. This force was concealed inside in such a way that not a man was visible.

Chapter 9

Two Faces of

"Holy War":

Christian and

Muslim "Jihads"

(1095–1270s)

When Baldwin arrived before the castle, Balas begged that he would take only a few of his staff with him into the fortress. He gave as an excuse for this request the risk of danger to his property if the entire force were introduced. His persuasive words almost induced the count to accede to his wishes in every respect. Fortunately, however, some of the wise noblemen in attendance on Baldwin had a certain foreboding of treachery. Almost by force they held the count back against his protest and prevented his entering the castle. They rightly distrusted the evil designs of the rascal and judged it safer that the trial be first made by others. The count acquiesced in this prudent counsel. He ordered twelve of his bravest men, well armed, to enter the place. Meanwhile, he himself with the rest of his band remained quietly outside near by until he should see with his own eyes the result of the experiment. No sooner had the gallant band entered than they fell victims to the perfidious treachery of the wicked Balas. For the hundred Turks mentioned above at once emerged from their hiding places, armed to the teeth. They seized the betrayed knights and, in spite of their efforts to resist, threw them into chains. This result distressed the count greatly. Anxious about the fate of his loyal men whom he had lost by so dastardly a trick, he drew nearer to the castle and earnestly admonished Balas to remember the oath of fidelity which he had taken. On the strength of this fealty, he urged him to return the prisoners so treacherously seized and to receive instead a large sum of money as ransom. Balas absolutely refused to consider this proposition, however, unless Seruj were returned to him. The count perceived that he could do nothing more, for the castle was situated on a steep precipice and was impregnable both because of its strength and because of the skill with which it was built. . . .

The reason for the title caliph is as follows: Muhammad, their prophet, or rather their destroyer, who was the first to draw the peoples of the East to this kind of superstition, had as his immediate successor one of his disciples named Abu-Bakr. The latter was succeeded in the kingdom by Omar, son of Khattab, who was likewise followed by Uthman, and he by Ali, son of Abu-Talib. All these prophets were called caliphs, as were also all who followed them later, because they succeeded their famous master and were his heirs. But the fifth in the succession from Muhammad, namely Ali, was more warlike than his predecessors and had far greater experience in military matters than his contemporaries. He was, moreover, a cousin of Muhammad himself. He considered it unfitting that he should be called the successor of his cousin and not rather a great prophet himself, much greater, in fact, than Muhammad. The fact that in his own estimation and that of many others he was greater did not satisfy him; he desired that this be generally acknowledged. Accordingly, he reviled Muhammad and spread among the people a story to the effect that the Angel Gabriel, the propounder of the law, had actually been sent to him from on high but by mistake had conferred the supreme honor on Muhammad. For this fault, he said, the angel had been severely blamed by the

Lord. Although these claims seemed false to many from whose traditions they differed greatly, yet others believed them, and so a schism developed among that people which has lasted even to the present. Some maintain that Muhammad is the greater and, in fact, the greatest of all prophets, and these are called in their own tongue, Sunnites; others declare that Ali alone is the prophet of God, and they are called Shiites.

QUESTIONS TO CONSIDER

Begin with the three Muslim accounts of Christians. Usamah's account (Source 1) is extremely valuable not only because he was well acquainted with Christians but also because he offers his readers numerous examples to support his main view of his European Christian foes. Examine and analyze each of Usamah's illustrations. What point is he trying to make by relating the story of the Frank who wanted to take Usamah's son back to Europe to make him a "wise man"? How does this story shed light on Usamah's perception of the Franks? Similarly, Usamah describes in some detail two medical "case studies," comparing the European remedies to the Muslim treatment. What does he intend his readers to think after reading about those two patients? Would readers get the same impressions from his account of the Christians' "ordeal by water"? What are those impressions likely to have been? In his "God as a child" story, Usamah is remarkably restrained (see later accounts by Muslims and Christians of each other's faith). What point is communicated?

Because the subject reappears in Imad ad-Din's account, the subject of male-female relations deserves to be examined a bit more closely. In the "lack of jealousy" story, Usamah offers a very curious tale of a Frank who returns home to find his wife in bed with another man. What impression of European Christians do you think Usamah intends to give? What would his readers' reactions have been?

Ibn al-Athir's account (Source 2) is primarily concerned with Saladin's conquest of Jerusalem in 1187, and his portraits of European crusaders seem extremely vague. From reading the two accounts (the first of Franks suing for surrender terms and the second of Franks leaving the city), what impressions would readers get of the European crusaders? What adjectives best describe their behavior?

It matters little that Imad ad-Din's view (Source 3) of Christianity contains a number of errors and misperceptions—each side was remarkably ignorant of the other's faith. What is important is the perception of Christian beliefs that he attempts to convey. What impressions would Imad's readers have gathered from his story of the devotion of the European crusaders to the "True Cross"? How is the Church of the Holy Sepulchre depicted by Imad? How does he describe the treatment of Muslim holy sites by Christians? What stereotypes of European crusaders would that

Chapter 9

Two Faces of

"Holy War":

Christian and

Muslim "Jihads"

(1095–1270s)

likely have put in the minds of Imad's readers? Finally, Imad portrays two groups of Frankish women. What do the descriptions tell readers about European women—and men?

Finally, reexamine each of the Muslim accounts. Do you notice any threads that are common to all three sources?

As explained earlier, *The Song of Roland* is a poetic recounting of the Battle of Roncesvalles (778) between the rear guard of Charlemagne's army and Basque attackers. Roncesvalles was a historical event, but when the song was composed around 1100, Muslims were substituted for the Basques. The Muslims trick Charlemagne into returning to France, intending to massacre the rear guard of his army. How would you characterize the poet's view of Muslim tactics? Like Imad ad-Din, *Roland's* composer suffers from major misperceptions about Islam (see verse 68). How would those misperceptions affect the impressions of readers? Note especially that slain Muslims are denied an afterlife except with Satan (verses 95–96); in contrast, God immediately dispatches three angels to the battlefield to "bear Count Roland's soul to Paradise" (verse 176). What impressions about eternal destiny does the composer imply? This impression would only be strengthened by the account (verse 187) of the Muslims rejecting their gods.

Verses 143 and 144 contain a physical description of the Moors, who have also been inserted into the story. What seems to have struck the composer the most about their physical appearance? Moreover, the composer calls them "that unbelieving race" (verse 144), linking physical and religious differences together. What stereotypes would have been created in the minds of readers?

The Roman Catholic priest Peter Tudebode also wrote of Christian souls transported immediately to heaven (the martyrdom of Rainald Porchet) and the "everlasting death" of the Turks. According to Peter Tudebode, how does the Turkish emir react to the faithfulness of Rainald? What perceptions was Peter Tudebode trying to communicate to his readers in that account? in his account of Muslims' mockery of crosses?

William of Tyre was the Christian chronicler most familiar with Palestine and its Muslim population. Yet the first paragraph makes it clear that, to William, Muhammad is the "first-born son of Satan," a false prophet whose successors were converted to Islam by force. Interestingly, the "dog carcass" story and the "Balas trap" story both sketch the same stereotype of Muslims. What is that stereotype?

Now repeat for the Christian writers the process that you followed for the Muslim writers; that is, look for any common themes or stereotypes that all the accounts share.

As you examined and analyzed the Muslim and the European accounts, you doubtless noticed that some of the perceptions held by Muslims and European Christians about each other were remarkably similar. What similarities did you identify? How do you account for them?

Finally, without being too explicit, all of the accounts advocate ways in which the other side should be treated. How do the perceptions (and misperceptions) lead directly to those conclusions? What attitudes and behaviors do you think might have been recommended? To answer these questions, you will have to exercise some historical imagination. Put yourself in the position of an intelligent but uniformed person who is reading these accounts soon after they were written. How do the implicit stereotypes affect your view of how the targeted group should be treated? Explain.

EPILOGUE

The perceptions that Muslims and European Christians had of one another made it almost inevitable that the wars known in the West as the Crusades would be carried on with extreme ferocity. As some of the evidence above suggests, civilians and combatants often were slaughtered indiscriminately, as Christians were exhorted to "slay for God's love," and both Muslim and Christian warriors were promised immediate admission to heaven if they died while fighting in a holy war (jihad).[18] Although no accurate estimates of losses are available (some historians insist the Crusades cost the West between 4 and 5 *million* people out of a total population of around 50 million, a figure most historians believe is too high), it can be said that fewer than one-half of the pilgrims who set out on a crusade ever returned. Muslim losses, although not that high, were also frightful.

Gradually the crusading spirit declined in the West, partly because of the meager results they achieved and partly because Europe had turned to other concerns. The Black Death struck Europe in 1347, killing over five times the number felled in the Crusades. England lost between a quarter and a half of its total population to the plague, and the number of deaths were just as appalling in other parts of Europe and Asia (the plague had struck China in 1331, and a more serious outbreak occurred in 1353). In addition, the Hundred Years War (1337–1453) kept Europe in an almost perpetual state of upheaval, diverting its attention from any future crusades. In the Muslim world, political disunity and the Mongol threat turned Muslim attention away from Europeans. Too, the so-called crusader states (four European-ruled principalities on the eastern shores of the Mediterranean) all had succumbed again to Muslim control.

One would expect that the long period of contact between the Muslim and Christian worlds would have produced a great deal of cross-fertilization of culture, ideas, goods, and

18. St. Bernard wrote that "a Christian glories in the death of a pagan because Christ is glorified; the liberality of the King [God] is revealed in the death of the Christian, because he is led out to his reward." Quoted in Norman Daniel, *Islam and the West: The Making of an Image,* rev. ed. (Oxford: Oneworld Publishing, 1993), p. 136.

Chapter 9
Two Faces of
"Holy War":
Christian and
Muslim "Jihads"
(1095–1270s)

knowledge. Indeed, this was the case, although more of these kinds of exchanges took place in Spain and Italy than in the Middle East. From the Arabs, the West acquired a great deal of knowledge of medicine, astronomy, chemistry, physics, and mathematics.[19] Paper, invented in China, was adopted by the Arabs and transmitted to Europe. Arabs had preserved a great deal of Greek philosophy (much of which had been lost in the West), and it was by way of the Arabs that Europe "rediscovered" Aristotle. Arabic courtly literature (adab) was translated and became the bases of some European literature (including Shakespeare's *Taming of the Shrew*). Trade between the two worlds was intensified.

Not surprisingly, Muslims borrowed almost nothing from the West. The Islamic world simply didn't

19. In medicine, the Arab *al-Qanun* (The Canon) became *the* medical textbook in the West. In physics the Arabs gave the West the pendulum; in astronomy a more accurate method of predicting an eclipse; in mathematics the field of algebra (practically an Arab creation), the zero, and the decimal point. Before Europeans borrowed paper from the Arabs, they wrote on papyrus or parchment.

think it had much to learn from the West. Muslims did adopt some European clothing and liked some European food, but these were minor compared to what Muslims exported to Europeans.

Yet, although the spirit of holy warfare declined in both the Muslim and Christian worlds, the perceptions and misperceptions that each side created of the other remained strong for centuries, and one can find their unhealthy residues even today in the struggles between the West and Iran and (later) Iraq, in the Arab-Israeli conflicts, and in the reemergence of Islamic fundamentalism. Behind the struggles over oil and geopolitics lie images, perceptions, and stereotypes that are centuries old and durable even today.

Writing at the time of the Crusades, Friar Felix Fabari wrote of Muslims, "The easterners are men of a different kind to us, they have other passions, other ways of thinking, other ideas . . . they are influenced by other stars. . . ." Such observations of fundamental differences go a long way toward explaining—and worse, justifying—a jihad.

CHAPTER TEN

ROMANCES AND BEHAVIOR

IN ARISTOCRATIC JAPAN AND ITALY

(1000–1350)

Until the twentieth century, "history" for the most part meant the story of rulers and armies, the rise and fall of kings and empires. Thus events in the private lives of men and women are rarely mentioned in the chronicles that form the basis of much of our knowledge of premodern societies (unless they affected political developments). People's emotions and desires were viewed as even less appropriate subjects for historical record.

This does not mean, however, that earlier cultures discounted the role of emotions or were not interested in how emotions shaped human action. They simply did not explore feelings in histories or biographies, but in fiction. Writers created characters whose desires led them to great heights and depths, and readers avidly followed their emotional adventures. Some-times writers borrowed characters from oral traditions or myths, telling familiar stories in new ways or making up fresh situations. At other times they invented characters whose stories then became part of oral tradition as those who could read told or read the stories to those who could not. In time these fictional romances became an important part of the literary heritage of many cultures.

Romances may be fiction, but, like all types of writing, they grow out of a specific cultural and historical background; every culture has a limited repertoire of assumptions and concepts that shape even fictional characters. Authors create characters as individuals with certain physical and emotional qualities, and then place them in settings and make them act in ways that will be believable to the reader. If romances thus reflect their own culture, they also help to shape it, as readers often learn what is expected of a woman or man

Chapter 10

Romances and

Behavior in

Aristocratic

Japan and Italy

(1000–1350)

faced with a certain dilemma by reading how these fictional characters responded. Romances do not teach directly like sermons or collected sayings of wise elders, but they usually give a clear idea of what is desirable and undesirable behavior. For later readers, like us, they also can provide details about aspects of life in the past that official histories never mention, such as styles of clothing or ideals of appearance.

Romances or other types of fiction therefore offer insights into earlier cultures that cannot be gained from official or academic histories alone. Your task in this chapter will be to use two romances from sharply divergent cultures—Murasaki Shikibu's *The Tale of Genji* from tenth-century Japan and Giovanni Boccaccio's *The Elegy of Lady Fiammetta* from fourteenth-century Italy—to explore aspects of private life and the relations between men and women. How do romances both portray and shape conventional standards of male and female behavior? What special problems arise in using fiction as a historical source?

BACKGROUND

The two romances in this chapter come from cultures that are widely separated chronologically and geographically, and yet they share certain characteristics. Both Murasaki's Japan and Boccaccio's Italy were aristocratic cultures in which a person's social level and family of birth largely determined his or her opportunities in life, but in which there was at least some social mobility. Both were urban cultures, for Murasaki the capital city of Heian Kyo (later Kyoto) and for Boccaccio the northern Italian city of Florence, both large cities by premodern standards, with populations of about 100,000. Both cities were the centers of a cultural flowering at the time these works were written, enjoying literature and art supported by the city's wealthiest and most powerful families (in Florence this cultural revival is termed the Renaissance).

There were also similarities between the two cultures in some aspects of language and learning. In both places, a learned language was normally used for history, philosophy, and other types of serious literature—Chinese in the case of Japan and Latin in the case of Italy—but an increasing number of works were being produced in the vernacular—Japanese and Italian. Women were excluded from most institutionalized learning in both cultures, so they were less likely to know the learned language; vernacular literature thus differed from learned literature in that it was aimed at an audience of both men and women. One's learning was to be worn lightly in both places, with men and to some degree upperclass women expected to be familiar with the established literary tradition and quote easily from it, but not to be pedantic.

In both cultures families had a great deal to say about who their sons and daughters married, for marriage among the upper classes was regarded as an opportunity to increase family wealth and prestige. Affection between spouses, though nice, was hardly an adequate basis for marriage. In both Heian Kyo and Florence, upper-class women spent most of their lives indoors, somewhat secluded from public life, and did not hold official positions of power; they could inherit and own property but generally had to have a man look after their legal affairs as they did not appear in court on their own behalf. In both cultures men were regarded as superior to women, an attitude that derived from religious beliefs. In Heian Japan, Buddhism taught that a woman could not be reborn into a higher category without first being born as a man; in Renaissance Florence, Christianity taught that women were responsible for bringing sin into the world. Both cultures accepted a sexual double standard, with extramarital affairs regarded as completely normal for men and openly discussed.

In other ways Heian Japan and Renaissance Italy differed dramatically. In Japan, Buddhism mixed easily with other religions and traditional ideas, so that people's individual belief systems were a blend with many sources, what we usually term *syncretism*. Astrology, omens, and notions about lucky and unlucky days and directions often influenced their actions. Buddhism taught that all worldly things are transitory and people should strive to control their passions, to the point of eliminating desire; after death, a person's soul migrated into another body, which could be higher or lower in status depending on his or her actions in the present life. The most proper attitude was one of *aware*, a gentle melancholy toward the world's passing things. Because of the quickness with which they fade, flowers captured the essence of these ideas, and both men and women used flowers and perfume to express their thoughts.

Though most men had only one wife, among the aristocracy polygamy was quite common. A man's first wife, chosen carefully by the two families to enhance their economic and political power, was generally the most important. Great attention was paid to a family's status at court, for the Heian aristocracy was divided into many ranks, with the highest receiving great privileges in terms of tax exemptions and household staffs provided by the government. Distinctions in rank were maintained by imperial edicts and law codes that stipulated, for example, where families of each rank could live, what kind of carriages they could travel in, and what they could wear. The marriage procedure included certain rituals that bestowed a religious blessing and assured that the community recognized the two persons as a couple; secondary wives were also often joined to their husband with a similar ritual, giving them the same legal status as the first wife. If a man was especially wealthy or important, he might also have official concubines who joined his household in a ceremony only slightly less elaborate than those for his wives. All of these women might live in the same household, although aristocratic houses

Chapter 10
Romances and
Behavior in
Aristocratic
Japan and Italy
(1000–1350)

were large and spread-out, with each wife and concubine inhabiting (and rarely leaving) her own quarters. Men also pursued frequent short- or long-term love affairs with women who did not live in their households, and as long as these women were not married, they were not stigmatized for such affairs and could later make perfectly honorable marriages. Wives, concubines, and even siblings or half-siblings often lived in the same house for years without seeing one another. Women were usually secluded behind screens or shades from all men except their closest family members, so that only their sleeves or shadows could be seen, although these shades were made of thin materials and voices in the next room could be heard easily. The shades were rolled up only on the hottest days, with houses thus quite dark and gloomy.

Because of this physical separation of men and women, contact between them often began with letter writing. People fell in love through writing, placing great importance not only on the content of letters, but the words chosen, the way these were drawn, and the color combinations of inks and papers. Men tended to write in Chinese characters, whereas women wrote in *kana*, a phonetic script of Japanese as it was spoken. Their letters and literary works often contained Chinese poetry, however, for familiarity with classical Chinese poetry was essential for well-bred aristocrats of both sexes. Artistic sensitivity to painting and music was also expected, as was at least some skill in painting or playing a musical instrument.

In Renaissance Florence, Christianity was the religion of most of the population, although educated individuals were certainly familiar with the myths and stories about the classical Greek and Roman gods and goddesses. One of the distinctive features of Renaissance culture was an emphasis on classical studies and a conscious return to classical ideas and forms, a movement termed *humanism*. In the same way that Japanese aristocrats quoted Chinese poems, well-educated Italians referred to classical mythology to enrich and broaden their letters and other writings. People did not believe in this mythology in a religious sense, however, for unlike Buddhism, which accommodated other beliefs and encouraged syncretism, Christianity required its followers to repudiate other religions. Like Buddhism, Christianity encouraged believers to concentrate on the life to come, although this was not a life within another body as in Buddhism, but a life after death in either heaven or hell. Christianity did not regard passion or strong emotions as evil in themselves but felt these should be channeled into religious purposes. In fact, love and longing for God were often expressed in Christian literature in highly emotional terms that would have seemed very strange to people living in Heian Japan.

Men in Renaissance Florence could have only one wife at a time, though because of high death rates many people married more than once during their lives, and many households contained combinations of full siblings, half-siblings, and step-siblings.

By this time Christianity rejected concubinage, so that although wealthy men often had mistresses, this relationship had no legal standing. A man might set his mistress up in an independent household and support her financially, but he would not move her into the household with his wife. Upper-class women were not out in public working the way lower-class women were, or conducting business the way upper-class men were, but they were not as secluded as the women in Heian Japan. Wealthy families often ate festive meals together in full view of all their neighbors, and women attended religious ceremonies and public celebrations regularly. Thus there were more chances for men and women to see each other, and though letter-writing was important, it was not as essential for making romantic contacts as it was in Japan.

When we turn from the social and literary background of these two works to the authors themselves, the differences are more striking than the similarities. Murasaki Shikibu (978–ca. 1030) was the daughter of an ambitious government official and gained an education in classical Chinese literature and history by sitting in on the lessons her father provided for her brother. At about age twenty she married a much older man who died soon afterward, leaving Murasaki with a daughter. For a while she lived in seclusion and probably began work on *The Tale of Genji* during this time. In about 1005 her father secured a position for her as a lady-in-waiting to the empress, and Murasaki was welcomed into the imperial court.

During this time she worked on a diary as well as *Genji* and was joined in her literary pursuits by a number of other women. The most famous of these was Sei Shonagon, the author of *The Pillow Book*, a collection of stories and descriptions of upper-class Heian life; Murasaki's daughter also became a well-known author.

The Tale of Genji is extremely long and complex, over twice as long as *War and Peace* and containing over 430 characters. Virtually every facet of it has provoked intense argument since it was written. We do not know exactly what order Murasaki wrote it in, because to some degree each chapter stands alone and often circulated independently. *Genji* appeared long before the invention of the printing press, so those who wished to have the book for themselves had to copy it or pay someone to do so. It quickly became a classic, and one contemporary commentator has estimated that there have been more than ten thousand books about *Genji* since the original was written. Its reputation and complexity led later Japanese critics to doubt whether it could really have been written by a woman, although Murasaki's authorship is not questioned at all today. (This often happened with great literary works written by women throughout the world, and Japan is unusual in that almost all its literary classics were written by women. This was the result of the fact that men regarded Chinese as the apropriate language for their writings, a feeling so strong that when men did write in Japanese, they pretended that their works were written

Chapter 10

Romances and

Behavior in

Aristocratic

Japan and Italy

(1000–1350)

by women. The opposite pattern is found throughout most of the rest of the world: women used male pen names to make it more likely that their works would be taken seriously.)

Giovanni Boccaccio (1313–1375) was the illegitimate son of a northern Italian merchant and an unknown mother. His father provided him with a good education, hoping that he would become a lawyer. Instead, Boccaccio became a writer, first gaining a reputation at the court of Naples in southern Italy, and then in Florence, where he became friends with the most famous poet and humanist of his time, Petrarch (1304–1374). Under Petrarch's influence, Boccaccio became a scholar of Greek and continued to write both Latin and Italian works. He never married, though he did father five children. Shortly after his move to Florence, sometime between 1343 and 1345, Boccaccio wrote *The Elegy of Lady Fiammetta,* which apparently became quite popular because over seventy manuscript copies survive from around Europe. He also wrote satires, poetry, biographies, mythological treatises, geographical dictionaries, and commentaries on the works of other writers.

Several years after writing *Fiammetta,* Boccaccio wrote his greatest work, the *Decameron,* a collection of one hundred stories about men and women of all social classes who exhibit both good and bad human qualities—anger, despair, deceit, tenderness, jealousy. The *Decameron* is usually regarded as the first significant prose work in Italian, and it served as the model for many later works in Italian and other vernacular European languages. In contrast to the situation in Japan, writing in the vernacular in Europe did not become the province of female authors, for men wrote the major works in both Latin and the newly developing literary languages of Italian, French, English, and German. Both Petrarch and Boccaccio doubted the importance of their Italian works late in life, preferring their more serious Latin volumes, but it was the Italian ones that were to have the greatest influence. Female authors in Europe did write works modeled on Petrarch's sonnets and Boccaccio's *Decameron,* but no female-authored title in Europe would attain the status of *The Tale of Genji.*

THE METHOD

All types of sources from the past must be used very carefully, for even those that appear simply to relate historical facts, such as events during the reign of a monarch, or the births and deaths of family members, were written for a specific purpose and with a specific audience in mind. This is even more the case when we use fiction, for the authors are not attempting to tell a true story, but to tell a story that will interest readers and that supports a certain theme or thesis. Unless letters or other documents from authors tell us directly what points they are attempting to make, we must also be tentative in concluding the intent of the author in a literary piece; it might have been quite different from what we infer, particularly for works as old as *The Tale of Genji* or *The Elegy of Lady Fiammetta*.

Literary conventions also shape fictional works. All authors, even the most innovative, work within certain literary forms. For instance, they decide whether their work will be poetry or prose, whether it will be first-person narrative or third-person, whether they as an author will speak in the narrative or not. They choose which language to write in and adjust their vocabulary to suit the audience. They decide whether to base their characters on real individuals and whether to use actual historical events as the setting for the plot. Because they are also influenced by their own reading, they often model their work on earlier works, incorporating familiar themes and motifs. Other authors intentionally break with tradition, adding unexpected plot twists and unconventional characters, but their stories are effective precisely because both they as authors and we as readers realize they are doing this. Thus even stories that violate the customary plot lines or characterizations expect readers to be familiar with certain conventions. (You can see this most easily in satire. A dialogue, for example, between the Lone Ranger and Tonto in which the Lone Ranger begins with "How! Me Lone Ranger, him Tonto" is recognizable as satire only if you know that these are normally Tonto's lines.)

Because of the literary nature of your sources in this chapter, and be-cause you will only be reading excerpts from these works, it might be helpful for you to know the plot of each work before you begin. *The Tale of Genji* is the story of Genji, the son of the emperor and his favorite concubine, a woman whom the emperor loves so much that all the rest of the court is jealous. This jealousy and ill-will are so strong that they lead to the death of Genji's mother while he is still a small child. Though Genji grows up at court, becoming a handsome and talented young man, he is officially relegated to the status of a commoner and can never hope to become emperor himself. (His name, in fact, is actually that of the nonroyal clan to which he is assigned, the Genji.) He is married off to a princess slightly older than himself, Princess Aoi, a member of the most powerful clan, the Fujiwaras. He becomes good friends with her brother, To-no-Chujo, and they both have many love affairs. In one of these, To-no-Chujo has a daughter by a woman with whom he has lost contact; Genji later finds the woman and has a brief affair with her, during which she dies while lying next to Genji because of the jealous spirit of another of Genji's lovers. Guilt drives Genji to find her daughter, Tamakazura, and he presents her at court as if she were his own daughter. Genji himself secretly fathers a son by the woman who has taken his mother's place as the emperor's favorite concubine and has a number of other children. Later he falls in love with Tamakazura, but she rejects him; he then reveals her true parentage to both her and her father, and she assumes a position at court. Genji also

Chapter 10

Romances and

Behavior in

Aristocratic

Japan and Italy

(1000–1350)

takes in the abandoned daughter of another prince, Lady Murasaki, whom he weds after his first wife dies; Murasaki is often thought of as the romantic heroine of the story, as she becomes Genji's favorite. (The author of *The Tale of Genji* also gets her name from this character. We do not know what her real name was, as women in Heian Japan were usually simply referred to by their father's or brother's titles. "Shikibu" is in fact a title once held by the author's father, and the nickname "Murasaki" may have been given to her by a witty courtier who had read part of *Genji*.) Genji builds a large house for his many women and their children, and the plot becomes more complex as their various stories are told. Genji dies shortly after Murasaki does, and the final third of the book relates stories about his younger brother and other characters.

The plot of *The Elegy of Lady Fiammetta* is much less complicated because the work is much shorter. The unnamed female narrator, like Genji well brought up and physically attractive, marries and is quite content in her life until she falls in love with a stranger. The two see each other as often as they can, and her lover gives them each a nickname, Panfilo ("loves all") and Fiammetta ("little flame"), so that they can talk about their feelings in the presence of others. On the pretext of going to visit his dying father, Panfilo leaves, promising to return on a specific date. He does not return, and Fiammetta learns that he has fallen in love with, and married, another woman. The rest of the book recounts Fiammetta's emotions and

actions as she compares her situation with that of other abandoned women.

Murasaki Shikibu did not set her story in the distant past, but in the near past in a milieu familiar to her readers. Although she was not explicit in providing historical details, she does refer to past emperors and events, and most commentators believe her story to have been set sometime between 900 and 925, or about a century before she wrote *Genji*. Though Genji and the other characters in the book are not actual historical people, they correspond loosely to real figures, and when the emperor ruling during her lifetime heard *Genji* being read aloud, he commented: "She [Murasaki Shikibu] must have read the *Chronicles of Japan* . . . she seems very learned." The clan of Lady Aoi and her brother To-no-Chujo, the Fujiwaras, had no rivals by Murasaki's time, and some commentators have seen in the book a critique of the power that they held (though Murasaki herself was a member of a lesser branch of the Fujiwaras.)

The "historical" Fiammetta has also been a concern of scholars and readers since Boccaccio's day, particularly because she is a character not only in this work but in many of his other poems and prose works as well. In some of Boccaccio's poems and prefaces, he describes her as his inspiration, leading literary scholars to speculate about just who she was. Maria d'Aquino, an illegitimate daughter of Robert of Naples, was proposed as a possibility, with the love affair reconstructed from Boccaccio's literary works. Unfortunately there is no historical evidence of Maria d'Aquino's existence, and even the literary record yields conflicting evidence about the details of their love affair, particularly if *The Elegy of Lady Fiammetta* is read as a description of reality. Recent scholars have given up the search for the historical Fiammetta and instead examine what roles she plays in Boccaccio's fiction and speculate about why he chose to use her as a device in so many of his works. Dante and Petrarch, two other central figures in the Italian Renaissance, also wrote many works in which they claimed to be inspired by female characters—Beatrice in the case of Dante and Laura in the case of Petrarch—so that such speculations involve not only Boccaccio but Italian Renaissance literature in general.

Now that you know something of the background and plot of these two works, you can begin reading the excerpts carefully. Our focus in this chapter is the fictitious portrayal of male and female behavior, and the social opinions of the authors that emerge from this portrayal. As you read, you may wish to make a few notes: How are the characters themselves described, physically and emotionally? What actions by the characters are presented in a positive light? Which are presented negatively? What actions are narrated in a matter-of-fact manner, with little comment from the authors? What basic ideas about what is important in life emerge from the authors' portrayals of their characters' actions? Who do the authors surmise should be or will be reading their works? Why do they think people should read them? Assuming the audiences are as expected, what messages about acceptable male and female behavior might they receive? Are the messages clear, or are there alternative ways to interpret what happens to the characters?

As you read, keep in mind our second question as well: What special problems arise in using fiction as a historical source? This question encourages us to think about the limits to our assumptions. Might we be safer in using fiction solely as a source for historical details—like styles of dress or tastes in architecture—rather than as a source for ideas about acceptable human behavior? Can we ever really know how earlier readers would have interpreted these works? Fictional characters are often interesting because they are extraordinary, or at least have extraordinary experiences. Are they thus models for normal behavior, or countermodels whose experiences are meant to contrast with the normal? In other words, are we (or any readers) supposed to be like them, or be glad we're not?

Chapter 10

Romances and

Behavior in

Aristocratic

Japan and Italy

(1000–1350)

Source 1 from Murasaki Shikibu, The Tale of Genji, *trans. Edward Seidensticker (New York: Alfred Knopf, 1976), pp. 20–22, 32–35, 40–46, 436–439.*

THE EVIDENCE

1. From Murasaki Shikibu,
The Tale of Genji

[*Genji has married Lady Aoi and has had a
number of love affairs; because of his good
looks and many talents, he comes to be
called "shining."*]

"The shining Genji": it was almost too grand a name. Yet he did not escape criticism for numerous little adventures. It seemed indeed that his indiscretions might give him a name for frivolity, and he did what he could to hide them. But his most secret affairs (such is the malicious work of the gossips) became common talk. If, on the other hand, he were to go through life concerned only for his name and avoid all these interesting and amusing little affairs, then he would be laughed to shame. . . .

It had been raining all day. There were fewer courtiers than usual in the royal presence. Back in his own palace quarters, also unusually quiet, Genji pulled a lamp near and sought to while away the time with his books. He had Tō no Chūjō with him. Numerous pieces of colored paper, obviously letters, lay on a shelf. Tō no Chūjō made not attempt to hide his curiosity.

"Well," said Genji, "there are some I might let you see. But there are some I think it better not to."

"You miss the point. The ones I want to see are precisely the ones you want to hide. The ordinary ones—I'm not much of a hand at the game, you know, but even I am up to the ordinary give and take. But the ones from ladies who think you are not doing right by them, who sit alone through an evening and wait for you to come—those are the ones I want to see."

It was not likely that really delicate letters would be left scattered on a shelf, and it may be assumed that the papers treated so carelessly were the less important ones.

"You do have a variety of them," said Tō no Chūjō, reading the correspondence through piece by piece. This will be from her, and this will be from *her*, he would say. Sometimes he guessed correctly and sometimes he was far afield, to Genji's great amusement. Genji was brief with his replies and let out no secrets.

"It is I who should be asking to see *your* collection. No doubt it is huge. When I have seen it I shall be happy to throw my files open to you."

"I fear there is nothing that would interest you." Tō no Chūjō was in a contemplative mood. "It is with women as it is with everything else: the flawless ones are very few indeed. This is a sad fact which I have learned over the years. All manner of women seem presentable enough at first. Little notes, replies to this and that, they all suggest sensibility and cultivation. But when you begin sorting out the really superior ones you find that there are not many who have to be on your list. Each has her little tricks and she makes the most of them, getting in her slights at rivals, so broad sometimes that you almost have to blush. Hidden away by loving parents who build brilliant futures for them, they let word get out of this little talent and that little accomplishment and you are all in a stir. They are young and pretty and amiable and carefree, and in their boredom they begin to pick up a little from their elders, and in the natural course of things they begin to concentrate on one particular hobby and make something of it. A woman tells you all about it and hides the weak points and brings out the strong ones as if they were everything, and you can't very well call her a liar. So you begin keeping company, and it is always the same. The fact is not up to the advance notices."

Tō no Chūjō sighed, a sigh clearly based on experience. Some of what he had said, though not all, accorded with Genji's own experience. "And have you come upon any," said Genji, smiling, "who would seem to have nothing at all to recommend them?"

"Who would be fool enough to notice such a woman? And in any case, I should imagine that women with no merits are as rare as women with no faults. If a woman is of good family and well taken care of, then the things she is less than proud of are hidden and she gets by well enough. When you come to the middle ranks, each woman has her own little inclinations and there are thousands of ways to separate one from another. And when you come to the lowest—well, who really pays much attention?"

They talked on, of the varieties of women. . . .

At this point two young courtiers, a guards officer and a functionary in the ministry of rites, appeared on the scene, to attend the emperor in his retreat. Both were devotees of the way of love and both were good talkers. . . .

"Let me tell you a story about a foolish woman I once knew," said Tō no Chūjō. "I was seeing her in secret, and I did not think that the affair was likely to last very long. But she was very beautiful, and as time passed I came to think that I must go on seeing her, if only infrequently. I sensed that she had come to depend on me. I expected signs of jealousy. There were none. She did not seem to feel the resentment a man expects from a woman he visits so seldom. She waited quietly, morning and night. My affection grew, and I let it be known that she did indeed have a man she could depend on. There was something very appealing about her (she was an orphan), letting me know that I was all she had.

"She seemed content. Untroubled, I stayed away for rather a long time. Then—I heard of it only later—my wife found a roundabout way to be objec-

Chapter 10

Romances and

Behavior in

Aristocratic

Japan and Italy

(1000–1350)

tionable. I did not know that I had become a cause of pain. I had not forgotten, but I let a long time pass without writing. The woman was desperately lonely and worried for the child she had borne. One day she sent me a letter attached to a wild carnation." His voice trembled.

"And what did it say?" Genji urged him on.

"Nothing very remarkable. I do remember her poem, though:

" 'The fence of the mountain rustic may fall to the ground.
Rest gently, O dew, upon the wild carnation.'

"I went to see her again. The talk was open and easy, as always, but she seemed pensive as she looked out at the dewy garden from the neglected house. She seemed to be weeping, joining her laments to the songs of the autumn insects. It could have been a scene from an old romance. I whispered a verse:

" 'No bloom in this wild array would I wish to slight.
But dearest of all to me is the wild carnation.'

"Her carnation had been the child. I made it clear that my own was the lady herself, the wild carnation no dust falls upon.

"She answered:

" 'Dew wets the sleeve that brushes the wild carnation.
The tempest rages. Now comes autumn too.'

"She spoke quietly all the same, and she did not seem really angry. She did shed a tear from time to time, but she seemed ashamed of herself, and anxious to avoid difficult moments. I went away feeling much relieved. It was clear that she did not want to show any sign of anger at my neglect. And so once more I stayed away for rather a long time.

"And when I looked in on her again she had disappeared.

"If she is still living, it must be in very unhappy circumstances. She need not have suffered so if she had asserted herself a little more in the days when we were together. She need not have put up with my absences, and I would have seen to her needs over the years. The child was a very pretty little girl. I was fond of her, and I have not been able to find any trace of her. . . .

The guards officer took up again. "In women as in men, there is no one worse than the one who tries to display her scanty knowledge in full. It is among the least endearing of accomplishments for a woman to have delved into the Three Histories and the Five Classics; and who, on the other hand, can go through life without absorbing something of public affairs and private? A reasonably alert woman does not need to be a scholar to see and hear a great many things. The very worst are the ones who scribble off Chinese characters at such a rate that they fill a good half of letters where they are most out of place, letters to other women. 'What a bore,' you say. 'If only she had mastered a few of the feminine things.' She cannot of course intend it to be so, but the words read aloud seem muscular and unyielding, and in the end hopelessly mannered. I fear that even our highest of the high are too often guilty of the fault."

[*Genji goes to visit his wife at her house at Sanjo but cannot spend the night there because he has broken a directional taboo on his journey. He decides to spend the night at the household of the governor of Kii, who has just had a new garden with ponds and brooks built near his house.*]

Having heard that his host's stepmother, who would be in residence, was a high-spirited lady, he listened for signs of her presence. There were signs of someone's presence immediately to the west. He heard a swishing of silk and young voices that were not at all displeasing. Young ladies seemed to be giggling self-consciously and trying to contain themselves. The shutters were raised, it seemed, but upon a word from the governor they were lowered. There was a faint light over the sliding doors. Genji went for a look, but could find no opening large enough to see through. Listening for a time, he concluded that the women had gathered in the main room, next to his. . . .

Genji found a cool place out near the veranda and lay down. His men were quiet. Several young boys were present, all very sprucely dressed, sons of the host and of his father, the governor of Iyo. There was one particularly attractive lad of perhaps twelve or thirteen. Asking who were the sons of whom, Genji learned that the boy was the younger brother of the host's stepmother, son of a guards officer no longer living. His father had had great hopes for the boy and had died while he was still very young. He had come to this house upon his sister's marriage to the governor of Iyo. He seemed to have some aptitude for the classics, said the host, and was of a quiet, pleasant disposition; but he was young and without backing, and his prospects at court were not good.

"A pity. The sister, then, is your stepmother?"

"Yes."

"A very young stepmother. My father had thought of inviting her to court. He was asking just the other day what might have happened to her. Life," he added with a solemnity rather beyond his years, "is uncertain."

"It happened almost by accident. Yes, you are right: it is a very uncertain world, and it always has been, particularly for women. They are like bits of driftwood." . . .

Chapter 10

Romances and

Behavior in

Aristocratic

Japan and Italy

(1000–1350)

The wine was having its effect, and his men were falling asleep on the veranda.

Genji lay wide awake, not pleased at the prospect of sleeping alone. He sensed that there was someone in the room to the north. It would be the lady of whom they had spoken. Holding his breath, he went to the door and listened.

"Where are you?" The pleasantly husky voice was that of the boy who had caught his eye.

"Over here." It would be the sister. The two voices, very sleepy, resembled each other. "And where is our guest? I had thought he might be somewhere near, but he seems to have gone away."

"He's in the east room." The boy's voice was low. "I saw him. He is every bit as handsome as everyone says."

"If it were daylight I might have a look at him myself." The sister yawned, and seemed to draw the bedclothes over her face.

Genji was a little annoyed. She might have questioned her brother more energetically.

"I'll sleep out toward the veranda. But we should have more light." The boy turned up the lamp. The lady apparently lay at a diagonal remove from Genji. "And where is Chūjō?[1] I don't like being left alone."

"She went to have a bath. She said she'd be right back." He spoke from out near the veranda.

All was quiet again. Genji slipped the latch open and tried the doors. They had not been bolted. A curtain had been set up just inside, and in the dim light he could make out Chinese chests and other furniture scattered in some disorder. He made his way through to her side. She lay by herself, a slight little figure. Though vaguely annoyed at being disturbed, she evidently took him for the woman Chūjō until he pulled back the covers.

"I heard you summoning a captain," he said, "and I thought my prayers over the months had been answered."[2]

She gave a little gasp. It was muffled by the bedclothes and no one else heard.

"You are perfectly correct if you think me unable to control myself. But I wish you to know that I have been thinking of you for a very long time. And the fact that I have finally found my opportunity and am taking advantage of it should show that my feelings are by no means shallow."

His manner was so gently persuasive that devils and demons could not have gainsaid him. The lady would have liked to announce to the world that a strange man had invaded her boudoir.

"I think you have mistaken me for someone else," she said, outraged, though the remark was under her breath.

1. **Chūjō:** one of her ladies-in-waiting.
2. Chūjō means "captain," the rank that Genji holds.

The little figure, pathetically fragile and as if on the point of expiring from the shock, seemed to him very beautiful.

"I am driven by thoughts so powerful that a mistake is completely out of the question. It is cruel of you to pretend otherwise. I promise you that I will do nothing unseemly. I must ask you to listen to a little of what is on my mind."

She was so small that he lifted her easily. As he passed through the doors to his own room, he came upon the Chūjō who had been summoned earlier. He called out in surprise. Surprised in turn, Chūjō peered into the darkness. The perfume that came from his robes like a cloud of smoke told her who he was. She stood in confusion, unable to speak. Had he been a more ordinary intruder she might have ripped her mistress away by main force. But she would not have wished to raise an alarm all through the house.

She followed after, but Genji was quite unmoved by her pleas.

"Come for her in the morning," he said, sliding the doors closed.

The lady was bathed in perspiration and quite beside herself at the thought of what Chūjō, and the others too, would be thinking. Genji had to feel sorry for her. Yet the sweet words poured forth, the whole gamut of pretty devices for making a woman surrender. . . .

. . . She was weeping. He had his hands full but would not for the world have missed the experience.

"Why must you so dislike me?" he asked with a sigh, unable to stop the weeping. "Don't you know that the unexpected encounters are the ones we were fated for? Really, my dear, you do seem to know altogether too little of the world."

"If I had met you before I came to this,"[3] she replied, and he had to admit the truth of it, "then I might have consoled myself with the thought—it might have been no more than self-deception, of course—that you would someday come to think fondly of me. But this is hopeless, worse than I can tell you. Well, it has happened. Say no to those who ask if you have seen me."

One may imagine that he found many kind promises with which to comfort her.

The first cock was crowing and Genji's men were awake.

"Did you sleep well? I certainly did."

"Let's get the carriage ready."

Some of the women were heard asking whether people who were avoiding taboos were expected to leave again in the middle of the night.

Genji was very unhappy. He feared he could not find an excuse for another meeting. He did not see how he could visit her, and he did not see how they could write. Chūjō came out, also very unhappy. He let the lady go and then took her back again.

---

3. That is, before she was married.

Chapter 10
Romances and
Behavior in
Aristocratic
Japan and Italy
(1000–1350)

"How shall I write to you? Your feelings and my own—they are not shallow, and we may expect deep memories. Has anything ever been so strange?" He was in tears, which made him yet handsomer. The cocks were now crowing insistently. He was feeling somewhat harried as he composed his farewell verse:

"Why must they startle with their dawn alarums
When hours are yet required to thaw the ice?"

The lady was ashamed of herself that she had caught the eye of a man so far above her. His kind words had little effect. She was thinking of her husband, whom for the most part she considered a clown and a dolt. She trembled to think that a dream might have told him of the night's happenings.

This was the verse with which she replied:

"Day has broken without an end to my tears.
To my cries of sorrow are added the calls of the cocks." . . .

[Genji attempts to use the woman's young
    brother as a go-between, sending
        messages to her through him.]

He treated the boy like a son, making him a constant companion, giving him clothes from his own wardrobe, taking him to court. He continued to write to the lady. She feared that with so inexperienced a messenger the secret might leak out and add suspicions of promiscuity to her other worries. These were very grand messages, but something more in keeping with her station seemed called for. Her answers were stiff and formal when she answered at all. She could not forget his extraordinary good looks and elegance, so dimly seen that night. But she belonged to another, and nothing was to be gained by trying to interest him. His longing was undiminished. He could not forget how touchingly fragile and confused she had seemed. . . .

[Much later in the novel, To-no-Chujo's
daughter Tamakazura, Genji's second wife
  Murasaki, and one of Genji's concubines,
the Akashi lady, spend their time at Genji's
    house at Rokujo in cultural pursuits.]

The rains of early summer continued without a break, even gloomier than in most years. The ladies at Rokujo amused themselves with illustrated romances. The Akashi lady, a talented painter, sent pictures to her daughter.

Tamakazura was the most avid reader of all. She quite lost herself in pictures and stories and would spend whole days with them. Several of her young women were well informed in literary matters. She came upon all sorts of interesting and shocking incidents (she could not be sure whether they were true or not), but she found little that resembled her own unfortunate career. There was *The Tale of Sumiyoshi,* popular in its day, of course, and still well thought of. She compared the plight of the heroine, within a hairbreadth of being taken by the chief accountant, with her own escape from the Higo person.[4]

Genji could not help noticing the clutter of pictures and manuscripts. "What a nuisance this all is," he said one day. "Women seem to have been born to be cheerfully deceived. They know perfectly well that in all these old stories there is scarcely a shred of truth, and yet they are captured and made sport of by the whole range of trivialities and go on scribbling them down, quite unaware that in these warm rains their hair is all dank and knotted."

He smiled. "What would we do if there were not these old romances to relieve our boredom? But amid all the fabrication I must admit that I do find real emotions and plausible chains of events. We can be quite aware of the frivolity and the idleness and still be moved. We have to feel a little sorry for a charming princess in the depths of gloom. Sometimes a series of absurd and grotesque incidents which we know to be quite improbable holds our interest, and afterwards we must blush that it was so. Yet even then we can see what it was that held us. Sometimes I stand and listen to the stories they read to my daughter, and I think to myself that there certainly are good talkers in the world. I think that these yarns must come from people much practiced in lying. But perhaps that is not the whole of the story?"

She pushed away her inkstone. "I can see that that would be the view of someone much given to lying himself. For my part, I am convinced of their truthfulness."

He laughed. "I have been rude and unfair to your romances, haven't I. They have set down and preserved happenings from the age of the gods to our own. *The Chronicles of Japan* and the rest are a mere fragment of the whole truth. It is your romances that fill in the details.

"We are not told of things that happened to specific people exactly as they happened; but the beginning is when there are good things and bad things, things that happen in this life which one never tires of seeing and hearing about, things which one cannot bear not to tell of and must pass on for all generations. If the storyteller wishes to speak well, then he chooses the good things; and if he wishes to hold the reader's attention he chooses bad things, extraordinarily bad things. Good things and bad things alike, they are things of this world and no other.

"Writers in other countries approach the matter differently. Old stories in our own are different from new. There are differences in the degree of seriousness. But to dismiss them as lies is itself to depart from the truth. Even in

4. **Higo:** an obnoxious rural suitor of Tamakazura.

Chapter 10

Romances and

Behavior in

Aristocratic

Japan and Italy

(1000–1350)

the writ which the Buddha drew from his noble heart are parables, devices for pointing obliquely at the truth. To the ignorant they may seem to operate at cross purposes. The Greater Vehicle is full of them, but the general burden is always the same. The difference between enlightenment and confusion is of about the same order as the difference between the good and the bad in a romance. If one takes the generous view, then nothing is empty and useless."

He now seemed bent on establishing the uses of fiction.

"But tell me: is there in any of your old stories a proper, upright fool like myself?" He came closer. "I doubt that even among the most unworldly of your heroines there is one who manages to be as distant and unnoticing as you are. Suppose the two of us set down our story and give the world a really interesting one."

"I think it very likely that the world will take notice of our curious story even if we do not go to the trouble." She hid her face in her sleeves.

"Our curious story? Yes, incomparably curious, I should think." Smiling and playful, he pressed nearer.

"Beside myself, I search through all the books,
And come upon no daughter so unfilial.

"You are breaking one of the commandments."

He stroked her hair as he spoke, but she refused to look up. Presently, however, she managed a reply:

"So too it is with me. I too have searched,
And found no cases quite so unparental."

Somewhat chastened, he pursued the matter no further. Yet one worried. What was to become of her?

Murasaki too had become addicted to romances. Her excuse was that Genji's little daughter insisted on being read to.

"Just see what a fine one this is," she said, showing Genji an illustration for *The Tale of Kumano*. The young girl in tranquil and confident slumber made her think of her own younger self. "How precocious even very little children seem to have been. I suppose I might have set myself up as a specimen of the slow, plodding variety. I would have won that competition easily."

Genji might have been the hero of some rather more eccentric stories.

"You must not read love stories to her. I doubt that clandestine affairs would arouse her unduly, but we would not want her to think them commonplace."

What would Tamakazura have made of the difference between his remarks to her and these remarks to Murasaki?

"I would not of course offer the wanton ones as a model," replied Murasaki, "but I would have doubts too about the other sort. Lady Atemiya in *The Tale of the Hollow Tree,* for instance. She is always very brisk and efficient and in control of things, and she never makes mistakes; but there is something unwomanly about her cool manner and clipped speech."

"I should imagine that it is in real life as in fiction. We are all human and we all have our ways. It is not easy to be unerringly right. Proper, well-educated parents go to great trouble over a daughter's education and tell themselves that they have done well if something quiet and demure emerges. It seems a pity when defects come to light one after another and people start asking what her good parents can possibly have been up to. Yet the rewards are very great when a girl's manner and behavior seem just right for her station. Even then empty praise is not satisfying. One knows that the girl is not perfect and looks at her more critically than before. I would not wish my own daughter to be praised by people who have no standards."

He was genuinely concerned that she acquit herself well in the tests that lay before her.

Source 2 from Giovanni Boccaccio, The Elegy of Lady Fiammetta, *ed. and trans. Mariangela Causa-Steindler and Thomas Mauch (Chicago and London: University of Chicago Press, 1990), pp. 1, 3–4, 7–8, 25–26, 113–115, 116, 119, 124–125, 127, 156, 157, 159.*

2. From Giovanni Boccaccio, *The Elegy of Lady Fiammetta*

> *Here begins the book called* THE ELEGY OF LADY FIAMMETTA, *sent by her to women in love.*

PROLOGUE

Unhappy people customarily take greater pleasure in lamenting their lot when they see or hear that someone else feels compassion for them. Therefore, since I am more eager to complain than any other woman, to make certain that the cause of my grief will not grow weaker through habit but stronger, I wish to recount my story to you, noble ladies, and if possible to awaken pity in you, in whose hearts love perhaps dwells more happily than in mine. And I do not care if my speech does not reach the ears of men; in fact if I could, I would entirely keep it away from them, for the harshness of one of them is still so alive in me that I imagine the others to be like him, and I would expect jeering laughter from them rather than compassionate tears. I pray that

Chapter 10

Romances and

Behavior in

Aristocratic

Japan and Italy

(1000–1350)

you alone, in whom I recognize my own open-mindedness and inclination for misfortunes, may be my readers; and as you read, you will find neither Greek myths embellished with many lies, nor Trojan battles befouled with much blood, but stories of love stirred by innumerable desires; in them, there will appear before your eyes the wretched tears, the impetuous sighs, the doleful voices, and the stormy thoughts that have troubled me with constant torment and have taken away from me appetite, sleep, joyful memories, and treasured beauty all at once. . . .

At that season when the newly clad earth displays her beauty more than at any other time of the year, I came into the world born of noble parents and welcomed by a benign and generous Fortune. Cursed be the day I was born, more detestable to me than any other! How much luckier it would have been if I had not been born of if I had been led from that wretched birth to my tomb, or if I had not lived longer than the teeth sown by Cadmus and if Lachesis had cut her threads as soon as she had spun them.[5] Innumerable woes, now the sad reason for my writing, would have found a conclusion at a tender age. But what is the use of lamenting this now? I am here all the same, and it has pleased and still pleases God that I should be here.

As has been said, I was welcomed into the world's most sublime pleasures, and I grew up in them; from infancy to delightful childhood I was raised by a revered teacher from whom I learned all the manners suitable to a young noblewoman. And as my body grew with the passing of time, my charms, which were the specific cause of my troubles, multiplied. Alas, what pride I took in them, although I was still young, and how I improved on them with care and artful means upon hearing them praised by many people!

But once I had passed from childhood to a more mature age, trained by nature stirring within me, I learned of the desires lovely young women can arouse in young men, and I became aware that my beauty in particular, an unwelcome gift to anyone who wishes to live virtuously, set afire young men my own age as well as other noblemen. By various means which I then hardly understood, they tried countless times to kindle in me the same fire which was burning in them, and which in the future would not only warm me but would consume me more than any other woman. I was also insistently urged by many of them to enter into marriage; but when among those many, one suitable to my station in every respect obtained me, the pestering throng of suitors lost nearly all hope and stopped pursuing me with their behavior. Therefore, duly satisfied with such a husband, I lived in bliss until the raging passion later took hold of my young mind with a fire I had never felt before. Alas, there was never anything which might please me or any other woman

---

5. **Cadmus:** a Greek hero who, after his companions were killed by a dragon, took the dragon's teeth and sowed them; the teeth turned into soldiers who immediately killed one another. **Lachesis:** one of the three Fates, goddesses who measure out and cut the threads of each person's life, thus controlling destiny.

that was not quickly granted to my satisfaction. I was my young husband's sole good and only joy, and I loved him just as he loved me. Oh, how much happier than any other woman I could call myself, had such love lasted in me forever!

While I was living contentedly, and as I was being continually entertained, Fortune, who is quick to overturn human affairs, became envious of the very gifts she had bestowed and wished to retract her favors, but not knowing where to place her venom, with subtle guile she made misfortune find its way through my very own eyes. . . .

> [*She describes going out for holiday celebrations and how her beauty impressed both men and women.*]

While I went on in this way, seldom looking at others but much admired by many and believing that my beauty captivated other people, it happened that someone else's beauty unfortunately captured me. And as I was already close to that fateful moment which was to be the cause of certain death or of a life more wretched than any other, I was moved by an unknown spirit, and with my eyes raised in due solemnity, I gazed piercingly through the crowd of surrounding youths, and apart from everyone else, alone and leaning against a marble column, exactly opposite me, I saw a young man; moved by an inevitable fate, I did something I had never done before with anyone else: I began to take mental stock of him and his manner. I must say that according to my judgment, which was still free from the influence of love, he was very handsome and very pleasing in his gestures, and he was dressed most nobly; his soft curly beard still barely shadowed his cheeks as a clear sign of his youth, and he stared at me, no less adoring than cautious, across the crowd of men. To be sure, I had the strength to refrain from looking at him for long, but neither the estimation of the other things just mentioned, nor any other incident could dissuade me from thinking about him, even if I made an effort. Since his image was already imprinted upon my mind, I observed it within myself with a certain quiet delight as if I were adducing new reasons to confirm the judgment I had made of him.

But during these intermittent looks, since I was not protecting myself from love's snares, at one point I stared into his eyes much more intently than usual, and in them I seemed to read words that said, "O woman, our blessedness lies in you alone!" I would certainly lie if I said that these words displeased me; on the contrary, they pleased me so much that they drew from my breast a soft sigh, accompanied by these words: "And mine in you." But I became conscious of myself and deprived him of them. To what avail? What had not been said, the heart understood by itself, and it kept within itself that which might have allowed me to remain free, if it had been said.

[273]

Chapter 10

Romances and

Behavior in

Aristocratic

Japan and Italy

(1000–1350)

So from that moment on I granted more power of judgment to my foolish eyes and indulged them with more of what they had come to desire; and certainly if the gods, who draw all things to their predetermined end, had not deprived me of understanding, I could have remained my own woman, but I put off to the very end all consideration and followed my appetite, and I immediately became susceptible to being caught; for not unlike fire which leaps from one spot to another, a most subtle ray of light left the young man's eyes and hit my own, and it did not rest there satisfied, but by some mysterious route it suddenly reached my heart and penetrated it. Terrified at this sudden visitation, my heart drew all its vital powers to itself, leaving me all pale and chilled. But I did not remain this way for long before the opposite happened; and not only did I feel my heart grow warm again, but as my energies returned to their proper places, they brought with them such a heat that it drove away my pallor and made me very red and as hot as fire; and as I looked at the one from whom this came, I sighed. From that moment on, I could not have any other thought than to please him. . . .

[*She is able to see her beloved regularly, and they talk about their feelings in the presence of others by using the names Panfilo and Fiammetta for each other.*]

His desire and my own made each day drag on one after the other, tense with expectation, and each of us bore this with bitterness because one would show it to the other by speaking cryptically, and the other would appear extremely disdainful, just as you ladies do, who may be looking for the strength to do what you would like to do most and which you know women who are loved usually do. Thus, somewhat mistrustful of me in this matter, and more lucky than wise in what happened to him and with more impudence than talent, he found a convenient time and place and obtained from me that which I wanted just as much as he did, although I feigned the contrary. Surely, if this were the reason for my loving him, I would confess to feeling a sorrow unlike any other every time this came back into my mind; but (and may God be my witness in this) this incident was and is the least important reason for the love I carry for him; however, I don't deny that I cherished it then, as I do now.

And what woman would be so unwise as not to want something she adores close by rather than far away? And the greater the love, would she not wish it all the closer? I say then, that after such an event, which in the past I had imagined but had never experienced, and under these circumstances, fate and our wits helped us to solace ourselves at length and with immense pleasure not once but many times, although it seems to me now that the time then flew by faster than any wind. But while we were living those happy moments, as Love, whom I can offer as my only witness, can truly tell, he was never allowed to come to me without fear, since he came to me only in secret. Oh how he adored my chamber and how cheerfully it always welcomed him! I have seen him revere it more than any temple. Oh how many tender kisses and amorous embraces, and how many nights were spent talking more than if it were daytime, and how many pleasures, dear to each lover, we had there during those joyful hours! . . .

[*Panfilo then leaves, promising to return on a certain date. He does not; instead he marries someone else. Fiammetta sinks into despair and confides in the old woman who had been her childhood nurse.*]

"Even in the most sizzling corner of hell, with its most terrible tortures for those who are damned, there is no punishment like mine. Tityus[6] is cited as an example of excruciating pain by ancient authors who say that vultures continually peck at his ever-renewing liver, and I certainly do not consider this a meagre punishment, but it is nothing in comparison with mine, because while the vultures peck at his liver, a thousand fears, stronger than any bird's beak, continually tear my heart apart. Similarly, they say that Tantalus[7] is dying of hunger and thirst while surrounded by waters and fruit, but placed in the middle of worldly pleasures, affectionately hungry for my lover and unable to have him, I certainly suffer as much as he does, or more, since the proximity of the waves and the nearby fruit give him some hope that sometime he will be able to satisfy himself fully, but I now completely despair of anything in which I had hoped to find my consolation, and since I love more than ever the one who by his own free will is kept in someone else's power, I have been deprived of all hope. . . .

. . . Death would therefore not be grievous to me, but a relief from grief. So let my dear husband come and take revenge for himself and at the same time free me from suffering; let his knife slit open my miserable bosom and let him take out my aching soul, my love, and my sorrow all at the same time with much blood; may he tear apart my heart, the holder of these things, as the principal deceiver and as the one who shelters his enemies, just as the perpetrated inequity deserves."

When my old nurse saw that I had ceased speaking and was deep in tears, she began talking softly to me:

"My dear girl, what are you saying? Your words are useless and your intentions terrible. I am very old and have seen many things in this world, and I

6. **Tityus:** a handsome giant who attempted to seduce Zeus's wife Hera; she punished him by condemning him to Hades, where vultures feed on his liver.
7. **Tantalus:** a son of Zeus punished for a crime against the gods by being placed in a pool of water that receded every time he bent to drink, and near a fruit tree with branches that sprung away every time he reached to pick fruit.

Chapter 10

Romances and

Behavior in

Aristocratic

Japan and Italy

(1000–1350)

have certainly been familiar with the love affairs of many ladies, and even though I am not to be counted among you, I have nevertheless been well acquainted with the poisonous love which weighs just as heavily on humble people as on more powerful ones, and more so at times, since the poor have fewer ways open to satisfy their desire than do those people who with their riches find them in their leisure; besides, I have never felt (or heard it said) that which you speak of as being so painful to you and nearly impossible, is as hard as you indicate. And even if such grief were extremely great, you should not let it consume you, as you are doing, to the point that you seek death, which you are asking for more out of anger than reason. . . . He is also not the first to do such a thing, nor are you the first to whom this has happened. Jason abandoned Hypsipyle in Lemnos to return to Medea in Thessaly; Paris left Oenone in the forest of Ida and went back to Helen in Troy; and Theseus left Ariadne in Crete to join Phaedra in Athens;[8] but neither Hypsipyle nor Oenone nor Ariadne killed themselves, rather, by putting aside their futile thoughts, they forgot their false lovers. . . .

Not once but many times my wise nurse spoke to me in this fashion, believing that she could chase my sufferings away and restrict my worries to those about dying, but few or none of her words touched my preoccupied mind fruitfully; most of them were lost to the four winds; each day my disease invaded my aching soul more and more, and so I lay on my sumptuous bed with my face down and hidden by my arms, turning over in my mind a variety of grand things. . . .

[*Fiammetta decides to commit suicide.*]

. . . I started out towards the stairs leading to the highest part of my lodgings; and having already broken out of my bedchamber and crying loudly, I looked wildly around all of the house and said in a weak, broken voice:

"O home that was so hostile to me when I was happy, stand eternal and let my lover know of my fall if he returns; and you, my dear husband, comfort yourself and look right away for a wiser Fiammetta. Dear sisters, relatives, any other women companions and friends, faithful maidservants, live on in the good graces of the gods."

With these words I was angrily pushing myself along a disgraceful course, but my old nurse, like someone aroused from sleep by a frenzy, left her spinning, amazed at seeing this, suddenly lifted her very heavy limbs and began screaming and following me as fast as she could. With a voice I found hard to believe, she said:

---

8. **Hypsipyle:** the daughter of the king of Lemnos, who bore Jason two sons before he left her for Medea. **Oenone:** a young Trojan shepherdess whom Paris married and deserted; she refused to heal him when he received his fatal wounds but later felt remorse and threw herself on his funeral pyre. **Ariadne:** the daughter of the king of Crete, who fell in love with Theseus and helped him escape from the Labryinth; he later abandoned her on the island of Naxos.

"My girl, where are you running? What madness is driving you? Is this the result of my words in which you said you had taken comfort? Where are you going? Wait for me!"

Then, even more loudly she screamed:

"Maids, come and stop this insane woman and calm her madness."

Her shouting served no purpose, and her laborious running even less: I seemed to have grown wings, and I was running towards my death faster than any wind. But unexpected circumstances, contrary to good as well as to evil intentions, saved my life, because while my very long garments could have been a hindrance to my purpose for their length, they did not impede my running, but somehow, as I was hurrying, they tangled themselves around a sharp piece of wood and halted my impetuous flight, and no matter how hard I pulled, not a piece of them came free. Because of this my heavy nurse reached me as I was trying to untangle them; red in the face and screaming, I remember saying to her:

"You wretched old woman, if you care for your life, go away. You think you are helping me, but you are harming me; let me die now while I am disposed toward it with the greatest will, because he who stops from dying the one who wishes to die does not do anything else but kill him; you are killing me, in the belief that you are saving me from death, and like an enemy you try to prolong my suffering."

My tongue was shouting, my heart was ablaze with ire, and my frantic hands, intending to untangle, were entangling myself, and no sooner did I think of the alternative of disrobing than my screeching nurse reached me and hindered me as much as she could; but once I became free, all of her strength would have been inadequate, if at her screams the young maids had not rushed in from everywhere and held me fast.

[*Her nurse tells her that it is cowardly and
dishonorable to commit suicide, and she
becomes calmer.*]

There is no anger that burns so fiercely that it does not become very cold with the passing of time. I saw myself for several days in the state I am depicting and clearly recognized the truth in my wise nurse's words, and I bitterly regretted my past folly. But even though my madness consumed itself in time and vanished, my love did not change at all because of it; on the contrary, I was left with the melancholy I used to feel at other such incidents, and I could hardly bear the idea that I had been abandoned for another woman.

[*Throughout the rest of the book,
Fiammetta continues to compare her
situation with that of abandoned women
from antiquity and mythology, and argues*

Chapter 10

Romances and

Behavior in

Aristocratic

Japan and Italy

(1000–1350)

that her pain is even greater. In the final
chapter, Fiammetta speaks directly to
her book.]

O dear little book of mine, snatched from the near burial of your lady, here it is that your end has come more quickly than that of our misfortunes, as is my wish; therefore, just as you have been written by my own hand and in many places damaged by my tears, present yourself to women in love; if, as I strongly hope, pity guides you, and if the rules of Love have not changed since we became miserable, those women will gladly receive you. . . .

If by chance you should fall into the hands of a woman who manages the affairs of the heart so well as to laugh at our sorrows and reprove us for being insane, bear the mocking with humility; it is the least of our troubles; remind her that Fortune is fickle and can very quickly make you and me joyous, and her like us, in which case we would return her laughter, mockery for mockery.

And if you find another who cannot keep her eyes dry as she reads but is sad and full of compassion for our misfortunes and multiplies your blotches with her tears, gather them within you along with my own, and consider them holy. . . .

Live then. No one can deprive you of this, and remain an eternal example to happy and unhappy people of your lady's anguish.

QUESTIONS TO CONSIDER

The first scene from *The Tale of Genji* included in the evidence is a discussion between Genji, his friend and brother-in-law To-no-Chujo, and several courtiers about women. Reread the first paragraph; what is it that Genji feels he would be "laughed to shame" about? What does To-no-Chujo's attitude about Genji's many letters from women reveal about expectations for men's behavior? (Remember that Genji is the husband of his sister.) What does his discussion about women in theory, and the story he then tells about one of his affairs, reveal about expectations for female behavior? for male? What role does social class play in these expecta-

tions? (When To-no-Chujo speaks of "rank," he is talking about levels of social status *within* the aristocracy. Common people almost never appear in *The Tale of Genji* or other literature from Heian Japan.) What role does poetry play in the interchanges between women and men? What do the comments of the guards officer reveal about attitudes toward learned women? Why do you think Murasaki Shikibu included this, considering that she was highly learned herself?

The next scene occurs later in the same chapter; Genji spends the night at the household of the governor of Kii after spending the day with his wife. How do Genji's actions fit with the expectations for male behavior that you have already discovered?

How do the lady's fit with those for female behavior? Why do you think Murasaki does not disclose her name? What is the reaction of her lady-in-waiting, Chujo, to the events? What does the episode say about marriage among the aristocracy in Heian Japan?

The final scene in Source 1 occurs much later in the book, when Genji comes upon Tamakazura and other women reading romance novels. Who does he expect will read romances? What purpose do they serve, in his opinion? How does this compare with the type of storytelling he and his friends engage in, as we have just seen? How does his attitude toward the purpose of novels differ when he is talking to Tamakazura, To-no-Chujo's daughter to whom he was attracted, and to Murasaki about their own daughter? What does he see as the relation between novels and real life?

Turn now to the selections from *The Elegy of Lady Fiammetta.* To whom does Fiammetta address her book, both at the beginning and the end? What does her discussion of her appearance and upbringing reveal about expectations for women in Renaissance Italy? How does she describe her marriage and her husband? her first glimpse of her beloved? her first feelings of true love? What does the choice of names her beloved uses reveal (or foreshadow) about subsequent events in the story? What role do classical mythological figures play in Fiammetta's account? What is her nurse's response to her tragedy? What does the nurse have to say about the role of social class in love affairs?

By now, you have probably noticed some similarities—and some distinct differences—between the two works themselves and the attitudes toward male and female behavior and the relations between men and women they convey. How would you compare the attraction of Fiammetta toward her beloved and of Genji toward the unnamed lady, his host's stepmother? How is love itself described in the two works? What is the connection between sexual relations and shame or honor in the two? How is it different for men versus women? How would you compare the reactions of Chujo, the unnamed lady's lady-in-waiting, and Fiammetta's nurse? What role does fate, or Fortune, play in the two works? How do the ideals for male and female beauty differ in the two?

In both of these selections, an author of one sex is describing the feelings and opinions of members of the other—Murasaki creates the conversations of men about women in the first excerpt, and Boccaccio's entire elegy is spoken through the voice of Fiammetta. How might this have shaped the way they told their stories? Other than in Heian Japan, most of the literature that has been preserved from all periods before the twentieth century was written by men. Because of this, we often must rely on male-authored texts to learn about women's attitudes or lives. How would you use *Genji*, which is actually written by a woman, differently from *Fiammetta,* which is only written in a female voice, to draw conclusions about women's ideas or expectations for female behavior?

Chapter 10

Romances and

Behavior in

Aristocratic

Japan and Italy

(1000–1350)

Now that you have read the selections, you can develop answers to the two central questions for this chapter. How do romances both portray and shape conventional standards of male and female behavior? What special problems arise in using fiction as a historical source?

By two centuries after *The Tale of Genji* was written, scholars in Japan were trying to produce a complete, authoritative version from the many manuscript and partial copies that existed, and the work was considered required reading for anyone who wanted to be considered learned. Thus *Genji* became a classic, in the same way that Homer's *Iliad* and Virgil's *Aeneid* did in Europe. Like these works, *Genji* was revered not only as great literature, but as a historical source, a description of the way things had actually been in Genji's time. Like many classics, it was also viewed as a commentary on the way things were *supposed* to be, and thus it was used by scholars as a way to criticize what they perceived as a cultural decline in their own day. Even people who had not read it became familiar with many scenes and characters because these were discussed in other literary works or depicted in art, in the same way that people who have not read the *Iliad* know about the Trojan War it chronicles. In fact, some scholars would say that *Genji* served one of the functions of the Bible in the West—not, of course, as a source of religious teaching and inspiration, but as a common point of cultural reference with people alluding to it all the time and assuming everyone was familiar with the stories it contained.

The Elegy of Lady Fiammetta did not achieve this status as a classic, although Boccaccio's *Decameron* did, its stories becoming the basis for artistic and literary works and Boccaccio attaining status as an author whose name was familiar even to people who had not read his works. *Fiammetta* thus does not create a literary tradition, but it fits into one that is common in Western literature, the tradition of the abandoned woman. As you have read, Fiammetta and her nurse compare her situation to that of many women from classical history and mythology who have likewise been loved and left behind. Male authors only rarely write in a female voice in the West, but when they do, it is often to tell a story of feeling abandoned, either by a lover or by God, as romantic and religious feelings are often linked in Western literature in a way they are not in Japan.

The popularity of romances did not end in Murasaki's or Boccaccio's time, of course, but continues to our own, with even grocery store shelves flaunting their alluring covers and the air waves filled with musical versions. Like *Genji* and *Fiammetta*, contemporary romances both portray and shape standards of male and female behavior. Can you identify ways in which your own ideas of conventional behavior have been shaped by romance novels? What would you see as contemporary romantic conventions; in other words, how do you expect people in these stories and songs to act? If you were a historian working hundreds of years from now, with popular romances and country music lyrics as your only source for late-twentieth-century culture, what impressions would you get of male and female behavior? of the relations between men and women? What other types of sources might you look to for information, sources that don't exist for our study of tenth-century Japan or fourteenth-century Italy?

CHAPTER ELEVEN

MEDICINE AND REPRODUCTION

IN THE MIDDLE AGES (1000–1500)

Along with ideas about how the world began, every human culture has also developed theories regarding what we now term "reproduction," that is, the process by which humans and other animals give rise to offspring. These have varied widely throughout history, and human reproduction in particular has often been linked to religious beliefs. In some religions, gods reproduce themselves in ways that are similar to human reproduction, thus giving reproduction divine sanction; in others, this divine sanction comes from the words or actions of a god or gods regarding reproduction; in still others, reproduction is regarded as evil or negative, established by malevolent deities or demons as a way to distract humans from their true spiritual pursuits.

The three Western monotheistic religious traditions—Judaism, Christianity, and Islam—all regard reproduction as established by the creator God at the beginning of time. In the words of Hebrew Scripture, also part of the Christian Old Testament, God says to the first humans, "Be fruitful and multiply." Jewish and Muslim tradition take these words to be divine commandments for all and frown on celibacy for either men or women. Christianity developed a more ambivalent attitude, praising individuals who chose a life of chastity but also cherishing children as a positive good; individuals and groups within Christianity who see sexuality and reproduction as unmitigated evils have been generally viewed as heretics—that is, as deviating from correct belief.

Reproduction is not only a religious issue, however; from very early times, it has also been a matter of medical concern. Though all aspects of health and disease were historically viewed as influenced by divine will and action, human intervention was generally acceptable. (There were invariably some who opposed this view, as there continue to be today in groups such as the Christian Scientists.) This intervention might take the form of prayers and intercessions, but it also included treatments that were not primarily religious. Some of the earliest records from ancient Egypt, for example, indicate that doctors identified and treated such diseases as diabetes, bronchitis, hemorrhoids, and skin cancer. The Chinese pharmacology currently undergoing a resurgence has roots in a tradition that is thousands of years old. In ancient Greece, philosophers such as Aristotle (384–322 B.C.E.) and physicians such as Hippocrates (ca. 460–370 B.C.E.) were interested not simply in clinical practice, but also in developing medical theories about the way in which the body—and the mind—operates.

For many of these ancient practitioners and theorists, reproduction was an essential part of medical knowledge and practice; Aristotle, for example, wrote an entire treatise on it: *The Generation of Animals.* His ideas, and those of other ancient authorities, became the basis for theories of reproduction and treatment of reproductive difficulties—as well as most other ailments—for nearly two thousand years in the Near East, North Africa, and Europe. Later scholars within Judaism, Christianity, and Islam built on the ancient Greeks, creating a body of medical literature that was translated into many languages and spread over a vast area. Your task in this chapter is to use some of that literature to answer these questions: What central ideas regarding reproduction were shared by Jewish, Christian, and Islamic medical writers in the Middle Ages? How were these translated into practical advice for patients and medical practitioners?

BACKGROUND

Though in many respects their cultures differed widely, in terms of medical understanding and practice the Muslims, Jews, and Christians who lived in the Near East, North Africa, and Europe during the medieval period shared a common tradition. This tradition they inherited primarily from the ancient Greeks, most notably Hippocrates and Galen (ca. 130–200 C.E.). Galen is credited with over five hundred works, mostly on medical topics, based on earlier medical knowledge and supported by his own observation and experimentation. His interests were so wide-ranging and his findings so influential that his work was considered the medical canon for centuries—until the seventeenth century or later in Europe and until the nineteenth through much of the Arabic world. Like the writings of Aristotle on other scientific subjects, the word of Galen was considered nearly as authoritative as the Hebrew and Christian Scriptures and the Muslim Qur'an.

Galen's ideas and writings were copied and taught within the Roman Empire (he lived for much of his life in Rome, though he continued to write in Greek) and, after the collapse of the western Roman Empire, within the eastern Roman, or Byzantine Empire, particularly at Alexandria, Athens, and Edessa. During the fifth and sixth centuries, the Byzantine emperors ordered many medical schools to close, and the physicians and scientists moved farther eastward, first to Jundishapur in Persia. Here they came into contact with Indian and Persian medicine and combined these with Greek teachings into a single system. Once the Muslims conquered this area, many physicians moved to Baghdad, the capital of this part of the Islamic world, where they were welcomed at the caliph's court. Most of these physicians retained their allegiance to Christianity and Judaism, but also learned the native tongue and began to translate medical texts into Arabic.

During the early centuries of the Abbasid caliphate, which began in 749, Baghdad continued to be an important center of medical treatment and research. Rhazes (Arabic al-Razi, 860–932) was the director-in-chief of the main hospital in Baghdad and became the most important clinical physician in Islam. He was the first to identify—based on clinical observation—the distinction between measles and smallpox, and his treatise on these diseases was translated into many languages and published throughout the western world; it circulated in Europe as late as the eighteenth century. His longer medical works, *The Book of al-Mansur* and *Continens*, were studied closely in the Islamic world and Europe until the seventeenth century and remain esteemed works within traditional Islamic medicine.

While Rhazes was celebrated for his accurate observations, the most influential Islamic medical writer was Avicenna (Arabic Ibn Sina, 980–1037), who was also a philosopher and interpreter of Aristotle. Avicenna was dubbed "Prince of Physicians" throughout both Europe and the Islamic world, and his major work, the *Canon of Medicine*, integrated medical traditions from a number of different cultures. Written originally in Arabic, this volume was later translated into Latin and other languages, and in its Latin version became one of the books most often printed in Europe after the development of the printing press in the fifteenth century. In the *Canon* Avicenna discusses the general principles of health and disease, the diseases of particular organs and those like fever that affect the whole body, and simple and compound drugs. He also pays attention to the philosophical principles of medicine, and to what we would term the psychological aspects of illness, for many of his cases involve psychosomatic ailments. Ideas about reproduction and the treatment of reproductive ailments are found throughout the work. The *Canon* of Avicenna became the most important book for all students of medicine within Islam, and its Latin version was indispensable for medical students in Europe until the seventeenth century.

At the time that physicians in the Islamic world were translating Greek works and developing their own theories of health and disease, medical treatment in Europe was largely in the hands of local healers. With the collapse of the Roman Empire in the West, the ability to read Greek declined and schools that taught medicine disappeared, so learned medicine lagged far behind that in Islam. Before the eleventh century, only two or three of Galen's works were available in Latin, whereas over one hundred were available in Arabic. This gap began to close in the tenth and eleventh centuries, when a few cities in Europe gradually developed first informal and then formal centers of medical training. The most prominent of these was at Salerno in southern Italy, where male and female medical practitioners received training through apprenticeship followed by instruction in an organized medical school. Individuals associated with Salerno, such as the convert from Islam and later Benedictine monk Constantine the African (f. 1065–1085), began to translate medical works out of Arabic. These translations included writings by Galen and Hippocrates, which had originally been written in Greek, and those by Rhazes, Avicenna, and other Islamic physicians originally written in Arabic. Constantine often did not translate whole works, choosing instead to combine the ideas of many authors—and his own—on particular subjects; reproduction is a key issue in his treatises *On Coitus* and *On Human Nature*. Gradually copies of all of Constantine's works spread throughout Europe, and, blended with those of other translators and commentators, formed the program of study under medical faculties that were beginning to be organized within the newly develop-ing universities in such cities as Paris and Bologna. Along with works by Galen, Hippocrates, and Constantine himself, students of medicine also turned to a treatise on gynecology by another ancient Greek physician, Soranus of Ephesus (fl. ca. 100–120), which had been translated into Latin by a North African scholar known as Muscio in the sixth century.

This shared Galenic/Islamic tradition was one in which medical ideas were very closely linked to philosophy and to ideas about the natural world in general. Prime among these was the notion of the four bodily *humors*, four fluids—blood, phlegm, black bile, and yellow bile—contained in the body that influenced bodily health. Each individual was thought to have a characteristic temperament, or *complexion*, determined by his or her particular balance of the four humors, in the same way that we might describe a person today as having a "positive outlook" or a "Type-A" personality. These four humors corresponded to four qualities—hot, cold, wet, and dry—and to the four basic elements in the Aristotelian universe—earth, air, fire, and water. The organs were viewed primarily as channels for the humors, rather than as having only one specific function. Disease was understood to be an imbalance of bodily humors, which could be diagnosed by taking a patient's pulse or examining his or her urine. Treatment was thus an attempt to bring the humors back into balance, which might be accomplished through diet or drugs—usually mixtures of therapeutic herbal or mineral substances—or through a direct attempt to rebalance the humors through emetics, purgatives, or bloodletting. These therapies were somewhat gender-distinctive because the bodily humors were also gender-related: women were regarded as tending toward the cold and wet, men toward the hot and dry. The exact balance of humors was different for each individual, however, with the healthy body capable of maintaining this on its own. Thus treatment, whether diet, drugs, or bloodletting, was aimed at eradicating any obstacles to this natural balancing, rather than at altering the balance itself.

Blood was viewed as in some ways the dominant humor. According to Avicenna, phlegm was "imperfectly matured blood" that could be transformed into blood if heat were applied correctly. In his opinion, blood also carried phlegm, black bile, and yellow bile throughout the body, and it was these substances ·that were partially responsible for the different textures of body parts—the hardness of bones and the softness of the brain, for example. Though some commentators thought the source of semen was the brain, as both were soft and whitish, most saw semen—and milk—as transformed blood, gradually "cooked" until it was whitish. The agent in all of these transformations was heat, which was also a critical factor in many issues concerning reproduction. The sex of an infant, for example, was determined largely by the amount of heat present during intercourse and gestation: males resulted when there was the proper amount of heat, which caused their

sexual organs to be pushed outside the body, and females when there was too little heat, which caused their sexual organs to remain internal. Men's greater heat continued throughout their lives, causing them to burn up their hair and go bald and to develop broader shoulders and bigger brains (because heat rises and causes matter to expand).

Though medical theorists agreed about a great deal, irreconcilable conflicts divided certain schools of thought. In the area of reproduction, the sharpest disagreement was between the ideas of Aristotle and those of Galen and his followers regarding the role of the mother and father in conception. Aristotle held that the mother provided the matter out of which an infant was formed, and the father, though he did not provide any material part of the embryo, supplied the "active principle," the force that brought this inert matter to life; women were "passive" in reproduction, and their menstrual fluid was a deficient form of semen. Galen and his followers held that both the male and female produced seed, so that both contributed both materially and actively to the generation of the child. (The word *generation* was generally used in the ancient and medieval world to describe the process that we label *reproduction*.) Each sex produced both strong and weak seed, with strong seed the source of males and weak seed, of females; the sex of a child depended on the balance of these two and the amount of heat present during generation.

Despite disagreements, the ideas of this body of medical literature spread throughout Europe, North Africa, and the Near East, and familiarity with this literature became the mark of a professional physician. In the Islamic world medical teaching was carried out largely in hospitals, and in Europe at the new universities, where medicine, along with law and theology, became one of the standard disciplines of advanced study. The influence of this Galenic/Islamic tradition did not stop with those who could read learned languages, however, for beginning in the fourteenth century in Europe, translations and compilations appeared in the vernacular languages. These Dutch, English, German, Irish, Italian, and French medical texts often included information on reproduction taken straight from Avicenna or Constantine the African mixed in with ideas and treatments from more local medical traditions. (Translation is less of an issue in the Islamic world; because the Qur'an was revealed to Muhammad in Arabic, study of that language was even more central to all learning than study of Latin was in Europe.) Once the printing press was developed in the mid-fifteenth century, these vernacular medical works and the Latin translations were very frequently reprinted. Medical works in Arabic, such as Avicenna's *Canon*, were also printed beginning in the sixteenth century. It is difficult to gauge how often the treatments they recommend were actually applied, but the ideas they contain were shared by most of the population, from the highly learned to the illiterate.

THE METHOD

One of the greatest dangers in exploring the history of science or medicine is viewing people who lived in earlier centuries as foolish or ignorant. How, we ask, could they have held such idiotic ideas? Couldn't they see what was in front of them? Many of the earliest historians of science, and even more the earliest historians of medicine who were often retired physicians, themselves gave in to this intellectual arrogance, for they viewed the story of science and medicine in a linear fashion, as constant advance from the unenlightened past to the brilliant present. Increasingly, however, historians of science point out that in every era, including our own, scientific knowledge is shaped by people's preexisting ideas; these ideas allow even the most "objective" scientists to see things only in certain ways. (This can perhaps best be seen in contemporary subatomic physics, in which attempts are now being made to trace the paths of types of particles whose existence was not known about until very recently, or in the discussions among astrophysicists and astronomers about the presence of "dark matter." Now that dark matter, or the neutrino, is a concept, scientists begin to see it and try to trace its effects.)

Thus it is important, as you examine the sources for this chapter, not to view them solely from the vantage point of medicine in the 1990s. Rather, try first simply to understand the view

[287]

of the body and reproductive processes they contain. The sources are arranged roughly in chronological order, and they contain information on a variety of topics, for reproduction was linked to a number of other medical issues, such as general health, gynecology, obstetrics, and embryology, and to nonmedical issues such as ethics, religion, and astrology. Many of the medical works from which these sources come are extremely long, and some are still available in their entirety only in Latin or Arabic. As you read them, it might be best to make a list of the key ideas and topics that emerge. These might include such topics as basic anatomy and physiology, sexual intercourse, conception, gender differences, fetal development, difficulties in conception and birth, and the relations between general health and reproduction. Not every author covers every topic, but through this list you can begin to discern key ideas. At the same time, you will find it useful to keep a list of proposed remedies for ailments. This tool will help you answer the second main question and also give you further clues to the general medieval understanding of the reproductive process.

Source 1 includes selections from the *Canon* of Avicenna, written in Arabic at the beginning of the eleventh century and translated into Latin by Gerard of Cremona, translator of many medical and scientific works, during the second half of the twelfth century. How does Avicenna compare the male and female reproductive organs? What happens at the moment of conception? How is the embryo formed in the uterus?

Source 2 is a short treatise about impotence, written by Constantine the African in the late eleventh century as part of his longer work *Pantechne.* It was frequently copied in later medical works, usually without naming him as the author, a very common practice. What sort of spells does Constantine view as interfering with intercourse? What remedies does he propose?

Source 3 is an excerpt from the treatise *The Diseases of Women*, attributed to Trota or Trotula of Salerno, a woman medical practitioner active in that city in the eleventh century. Trotula is a very mysterious figure whose work and even existence have been the source of great debate for centuries. By the twelfth century, several treatises were circulating in Europe under her name—this being one of them—and for the next several centuries they were the most widely circulated medical works on gynecological issues and were translated out of Latin into French, Irish, German, English, Flemish, and Catalan. By the sixteenth century, however, some medical authorities denied that works showing such familiarity with learned medicine could have been written by a woman. (Because women were excluded from the medical schools attached to universities in Europe, they could not receive theoretical training; their healing activities, along with those of men who had not been university trained, were often prohibited beginning in the thirteenth century as university-bred physicians sought to gain a monopoly on medical practice.) This debate was only finally laid to rest about a decade ago, when it was demonstrated that most of the works attributed to her, including the one excerpted here, were not written by her, but that she had, in fact, authored a different medical work, the *Practica secundam Trotam*, and thus was a real person. Most of the medical writers and practitioners of the Middle Ages, however, regarded Trotula as an important authority and cited her along with male authors when they were attempting to demonstrate the validity of a particular idea. It may seem ironic that they did this at the same time they were prohibiting women from studying or practicing medicine, but Trotula was thought to have written in the period before Salerno became an official medical school, and was simply regarded as transcending the normal rules applying to women. How does Trotula characterize the differences between men and women? Does she adopt an Aristotelian or Galenic view about the role of the two sexes in reproduction? Why do women menstruate? Is menstruation harmful or beneficial? What are some of the causes for failure to conceive? What remedies are recommended? What does the author suggest to encourage the birth of a boy? Why do you think there is no corresponding advice to encourage the birth of a girl? How does a fetus develop, and what can be done to discourage miscarriage?

Source 4 contains excerpts from two works of Moses Maimonides (1135–1204), a Jewish rabbi, philosopher, and physician. Maimonides was born in Cordoba, Spain, but emigrated to Egypt and became the chief physician at the court of the sultan Saladin in Cairo. He was reputed to have been invited to become the physician for Richard the Lionhearted in England, but never left Egypt. He wrote numerous religious and philosophical works, including a massive commentary on the Torah, and at least ten medical works. His religious works were penned in Hebrew, and his medical works in Arabic, with many of these later translated into Hebrew, Latin, and other European languages. The selections included here are from two works, *Ethical Conduct* and *Regimen of Health*. What does Maimonides see as important to general health? How does this relate to his views about sexual intercourse?

Source 5 is another work with a spurious attribution—*On the Secrets of Women,* written in Latin in the late thirteenth or early fourteenth century by the pseudo–Albertus Magnus. The *real* Albertus Magnus was a prominent thirteenth-century theologian, philosopher, and scientist, and this work was most likely written by one of his followers, though we cannot be sure exactly which one. The fact that it was quickly attributed to the real Albertus Magnus—even though the text refers to him as a person different from the author—gave it weighty authority, and it became the most popular book of this type in the later Middle Ages. There are over eighty manuscript copies known today, and it was printed over fifty times in the period 1450–1500 and over seventy times in the sixteenth century. Read this evidence carefully. How does the author present the differences of opinion regarding the male and female role in conception? How does he describe the process of conception itself? What is the role and cause of menstruation? According to the author, how does the fetus receive nourishment and air? What general attitudes about sexual difference emerge from this text?

The works we have looked at so far, though they combine academic and popular medicine and were often eventually translated, were directed specifically to a learned—and therefore male—audience. Source 6 is somewhat different, an excerpt from one of the earliest printed midwives' manuals in Europe, the *Rosegarden for Midwives and Pregnant Women* written in German by Eucharius Rösslin, a pharmacist and physician in Frankfurt, and printed for the first time in Strasbourg in 1513. The *Rosegarden* was translated—often under a different title—into Latin, French, Czech, Polish, Spanish, Dutch, and English, with over one hundred known printed versions, and by the later sixteenth century was mentioned in city midwifery ordinances as recommended reading. Rösslin draws on a huge range of Greek and Arabic authorities, most prominently the Muscio translations of Soranus of Ephesus; these, rather than any hands-on experience, form the basis of his advice, though he also includes remedies grounded in popular traditions. The *Rosegarden* includes sections on diet and conduct for pregnant women, specific instructions for midwives during normal and difficult births, and instructions for the care of newborns. It also deals with rather grim topics, such as how to deliver a child

that has died in the uterus. The portion included here covers the period just before and during a birth. As you read this, note Rösslin's advice to the mother and to the midwife. How does this fit with the more general ideas about health and bodily processes you have read so far? What is the midwife's role in a normal birth procedure?

Medical ideas were transmitted largely through words in the Middle Ages, but elaborate copies of treatises were occasionally illustrated, and after the development of the printing press, woodcuts and engravings became an important feature of medical works, particularly those designed at least in part for a popular audience. Sources 7 through 10 are four medical illustrations: Source 7, a manuscript illumination of Constantine the African doing a uroscopy for women and men; Source 8, a thirteenth-century manuscript illumination of a birth; Source 9, a caesarean section in a fourteenth-century manuscript of the Arabic writer al-Biruni's *Chronology of Ancient Nations*; and Source 10, a sixteenth-century engraving of a birth scene that was frequently used to illustrate pseudo–Albertus Magnus's *On the Secrets of Women*. How do these illustrations reinforce or refute the ideas presented in the written texts? How do they depict medical personnel? How do the attendants at the two births differ from those at the caesarian section? Do these figures attempt to portray actual medical procedures or to illustrate medical principles?

Source 1 from Avicenna, Canon, *tr. Gerard of Cremona, translated and reprinted in Danielle Jacquart and Claude Thomasset,* Sexuality and Medicine in the Middle Ages, *tr. Matthew Adamson (Cambridge, Polity Press, 1988), pp. 36, 55, 63, 77.*

1. From Avicenna, *The Canon of Medicine,* 11th century

I say that the instrument of reproduction in the woman is the womb (*matrix*) and that it was created similar to the instrument of reproduction in the man, that is to say the penis and what goes with it. However, one of these instruments is complete and stretches outwards, whereas the other is smaller and held on the inside, to some extent constituting the opposite of the male instrument. The covering of the womb is like the scrotum, the cervix [= vagina] like the penis. There are two testicles in women as in men, but in men they are larger, turned outwards and tend to be spherical in shape; in women they are small, of a rather flattened roundness, and they are located on the inside, in the vulva. . . .

The sublime God created the testicles to be, as you know, the principal members which engender sperm from the moisture that is brought to them in the veins; this moisture is like the residue of the food that has reached the fourth stage in the whole body.[1] It is a better-digested and subtler blood. . . .

As soon as the two seeds have been mixed, the ebullition[2] of which we have spoken takes place and the swollen part and the first membrane are created; then all the sperm is suspended from the horn-shaped protuberances,[3] and it there finds its nourishment as long as it is still sperm, until it starts to draw its nourishment from the menstrual blood and from the cavities [the openings of the veins] to which the membrane which has been formed is attached. According to Galen, this membrane is like a protective coating left behind by the sperm of the female when it flows towards the place where the male's sperm also flows, and if it does not join with the sperm of the male at the very moment it is shed, it nonetheless mixes with it during intercourse. . . .

After that, the blood which is voided by the woman at the time of menses is used for nourishment. Part is transformed in accordance with its similarity to the spermatic substance: it forms the parts of the body that have come from

1. Food was thought to be digested in stages within the body.
2. **ebullition:** the process of bubbling up.
3. The uterus was thought to have "horns," or growths sticking out on each side, which were shown in anatomical illustrations into the seventeenth century; these horns were thought to contain blood vessels.

[291]

the sperm, and it increases the sperm by nourishing it. Another part does not act as nourishment but, through coagulation, is used to fill the empty spaces of the principal parts of the body, and makes flesh and fat. A last part consists of superfluous matter and is no good for either of the above-mentioned purposes: it stays put until childbirth, when nature expels it as being superfluous.

Source 2 from Henry E. Sigerist, Essays in Biology *(Berkeley: University of California Press, pp. 541–546. Reprinted in Edward Grant,* A Source Book in Medieval Science *(Cambridge: Harvard University Press, 1974), pp. 768–769.*

2. Constantine the African's Treatise on Impotence, 11th century

A short treatise about the people who, impeded by spells, are unable to have intercourse with their wives.

There are people who, impeded by diabolical spells, are unable to have intercourse with their wives. We do not want to deprive our book of their applause, for the remedy, if I am not wrong, is most sacred.

Now, if this should happen to somebody, he must set his hope in the Lord and He will be merciful. Since, however, there are many kinds of spells, it is necessary that we discuss them. Some spells are made of animated substances such as the testicles of a cock. If they are put under the bed with blood of the cock, they bring it about that the people lying on the bed cannot have intercourse. Some are made of letters written with the blood of a bat. Some are made of inanimate substances, for instance if a nut or an acorn is divided in two, and one half is put on one side, the other on the other side, of the road along which the bride and bridegroom must proceed.

There are others also which are made from beans which are not softened with hot water nor cooked on the fire. This spell is very bad if four such beans are placed on the roof or on the road or over or under the door.

There are others also which are of metal, such as those that are of iron or lead, for instance, the iron ones made of the needle with which the dead men or women have been sewn. And because these spells are devilish and are particularly in women, they are sometimes cured by divine, sometimes by human measures.

If therefore bridegroom and bride are disturbed by the above-mentioned spells, it is better to talk about them than to keep silent, for if the victims are not succored they are separated and thus disgraced, and doing this evil they seem to sin not only against their relatives but also against the Holy Ghost.

If we wish to extirpate the spell properly, we must look out: if the above-mentioned spell is under the bed, it must be removed. But if the author of this spell removes it in daytime and puts it back at night, or vice versa, then bridegroom and bride must acquire another house and lie down there.

If the spell is made of letters, which is recognized by the fact that bridegroom and bride do not love each other, one must search above and under the threshold of the door, and if something is found it must be taken to the bishop or priest. If not, one must do what is indicated below.

If a nut or an acorn are the cause of this spell, the woman shall take a nut or an acorn and divide it in two. And with one half the man shall proceed on one side of the road and deposit it there; the woman, however, shall put the other half on the other side of the road. Thereupon bridegroom and bride shall take both parts of the nut without having removed the shell. And then the nut shall thus be made whole again and shall be kept for seven days. Having done this they shall have intercourse.

If, however, it happens on account of beans, it can be cured with divine rather than human means. If it is on account of the needles for the dead, the spells must be sought either in the pillow or in the mattress. If they are not found, the victims shall lie together in another house.

Bile of a male dog purifies the house and brings it about that no evil remedy be brought to the house.

Sprinkle the walls of the house with dog's blood, and it will be liberated from every spell. . . .

If, however, on account of impending sins, the above-mentioned measures did not help at all, they shall go to a priest or the bishop. And if the bishop has permitted it and no remedy is found, after having confessed to the bishop or an ordained priest they shall take Holy Communion on the day of the Holy Resurrection or Ascension in Whitsuntide. Having received the Body and Blood of the Lord, bridegroom and bride shall give each other the kiss of peace.

And after they have received the benediction of the bishop or priest, the bishop or priest shall give this verse of the prophet written on paper: The voice of the Lord is upon the waters: the great Lord is upon many waters [Psalms 28:3]. Thereafter they shall go home and shall abstain from intercourse for three days and three nights. Then they shall perform it, and thus all diabolical power is destroyed.

The little treatise on spells has come to an end. Thanks be to God. Amen.

Source 3 from Trotula of Salerno, The Diseases of Women, *translated by Elizabeth Mason-Hohl, M.D. (Los Angeles: Ward Ritchie Press, 1940), pp. 1–3, 16–25. Reprinted in Edward Grant,* A Source Book in Medieval Science *(Cambridge: Harvard University Press, 1974), pp. 761–763, 764–766.*

3. From Pseudo–Trotula of Salerno, *The Diseases of Women*, 12th century

PROLOGUE

Since God, the author of the universe, in the first establishment of the world, distinguished the individual natures of things each according to its own kind, He differentiated the human race above the other creatures by means of extra-ordinary dignity. To it, beyond the condition of other animals, He gave free-dom of reason and of intellect. Moreover, desiring its generation to subsist perpetually, He created it male and female in different sexes that by means of their fertile propagation future offspring may never cease to come forth. Blending their embraces with a pleasing mixture, He made the nature of the male hot and dry and that of the female cold and wet so that the excess of each other's embrace might be restrained by the mutual opposition of contrary qualities. The man's constitution being hot and dry might assuage the woman's coldness and wetness and on the contrary her nature being cold and wet might soothe his hot and dry embrace. Likewise that the male having the stronger quality might pour seed into the woman as into a field and the woman endowed with a weaker quality, subject as it were to the function of the man, might naturally take unto her bosom the poured out seed. Since then women are by nature weaker than men it is reasonable that sicknesses more often abound in them especially around the organs involved in the work of nature. Since these organs happen to be in a retired location, women on ac-count of modesty and the fragility and delicacy of the state of these parts dare not reveal the difficulties of their sicknesses to a male doctor. Wherefore I, pitying their misfortunes and at the instigation of a certain matron, began to study carefully the sicknesses which most frequently trouble the female sex. Since in women not so much heat abounds that it suffices to use up the mois-tures which daily collect in them, their weaknesses cannot endure so much ex-ertion as to be able to put forth that moisture to the outside air as in the case of men. Nature herself, on account of this deficiency of heat, has assigned for them a certain specific purgation namely the menses, commonly called flow-ers. For just as trees do not produce fruit without flowers so women without menses are deprived of the function of conception. This purgation occurs in women just as 'pollutio'[4] occurs in men. . . . If such purgations have been of

---

4. **pollutio:** nocturnal emissions, or "wet dreams."

normal time and regularity, Nature sufficiently unloads women of superfluous moisture. If the menstruation has taken place too copiously various sicknesses arise from it. . . . Diarrhoea occurs too on account of excessive coldness in the womb, either because the veins are very slender as in thin women since in this case thick and excessive fluids do not have free channels through which they can break forth, or because the liquids are thick and viscous and because of clotting their egress is hindered. . . . Sometimes the periods fail because of excessive grief or anger or excitement or fear. If they have ceased for a long time there is a suspicion of serious future illness. Often the urine is changed into a red color or into a color like the washings from fresh meat; sometimes the woman's appearance is changed into a gray or leaden color, or into the color of grass. . . .

CHAPTER 11
ON THE HINDRANCES TO CONCEPTION AND
OF THE THINGS WHICH MAKE FOR IMPREGNATION

Certain women are useless for conceiving either because they are too thin and lean or because they are too fat. In these latter the flesh folded around the opening of the womb binds it and does not permit the seed of the man to enter it. Some have a womb so soft and slippery that the seed having been received cannot be retained in it. Sometimes this happens through a defect of the male who has seed so thin that when it is poured into the vagina it slips out because of its own liquidness. Some men also have testicles cold and dry; these men rarely or never beget, because their seed is useless for procreation. It is evident therefore that conception is hindered as often by a defect of the man as of the woman. If it is by a defect of the woman it happens either from excessive warmth or from excessive moistures of the womb. Sometimes on account of its natural softness the womb cannot retain the seed injected into it, and often because of its excessive moisture it suffocates the seed. Often because of its excessive heat the womb burns the seed up and she cannot conceive. . . .

If conception be hindered because of a defect of the male it would be from a lack of force impelling the sperm, a defect of the organ, or a defect of heat. If it be from a defect of heat, the sign is that he is not eager for copulation. Hence he ought to anoint his loins with arrogon or take seed of colewort and euphorbia and reduce them to a fine powder. Then mix them with the oils of fleabane[5] and of weasel and with this anoint his loins. If it happens through a defect of the spirit the sign will be that he has desire but the penis is not erected. We aid him with an ointment that generates spirit. If it happens through a defect of the sperm the sign is that when he copulates he emits either none or too little seed. We aid him with things that increase sperm such as orris, domestic parsnips, and the like.

---

5. **arrogon, colewort, euphorbia** and **fleabane:** all plants.

If the woman or the man be sterile you will ascertain it by this method: take two jars and into each put bran. Into one of them put the urine of the man and into the other put the urine of the woman and let the jars be left for nine or ten days. If the barrenness be from a defect of the woman you will find many worms and the bran foul in her jar. On the other hand you will have similar evidence from the other urine if the barrenness be through a defect of the man. But if you have observed such signs in neither urine neither will be the cause of the barrenness and it is possible to help them to conceive by the use of medicines. If they wish to have a male child let the man take the womb and vulva of a hare and have it dried and pulverized; blend it with wine and let him drink it. Let the woman do the same with the testicles of the hare and let her be with her husband at the end of her menstrual period and she will conceive a male. . . .

CHAPTER 12
ON THE FORMATION OF THE SEED WHEN CONCEIVED

In the first month occurs a small clot of blood. In the second occurs the formation of the blood and of the body; in the third the nails and hair are produced. In the fourth motion and therefore women are nauseated. In the fifth the foetus receives the likeness of father or mother. In the sixth, the binding together of the sinews. In the seventh, the bones and sinews are strengthened; in the eighth nature helps and the child puts on flesh. In the ninth, it proceeds from darkness into light.

CHAPTER 13
ON THE POSITION OF THE FOETUS IN THE MOTHER'S WOMB

Galen gives the report that the foetus is fastened in the womb just as the fruit is on the tree, which when it comes forth from the blossom is very tender and falls from any occasion whatsoever. When it has become full grown, riper, and established, it clings to the tree and will not fall on slight occasion. When it has become completely ripe it will fall of itself and not any other occasion. Thus when a child is first produced from a conceived seed the ligaments by which it is fastened to the womb are tender and unfirm and therefore it is easily let fall by abortion. On account of a cough, diarrhoea, dysentery, excessive activity or anger, or loss of blood, a woman can lose her foetus. But when a soul or life has been infused into the child[6] it clings a little more firmly and does not slip quickly. When the child has ripened it is quickly let out by the office of nature. Hippocrates says that if a woman requires bleeding or purgation, you should not do these things before the fourth month. In the fifth or sixth months she can be bled or purged cautiously, if there be necessity, with a mild . . . decoction according as the strength of the patient shall be able to tol-

6. Many ancient and medieval authors thought that a child received its soul about the time the mother first felt movement. That point in a pregnancy is still termed *quickening*, which originally meant "coming to life."

erate. Beyond and before this time an evacuation will be dangerous. When the time for parturition has arrived the child moves more violently and struggles toward the exit. Nature in its own time causes the vulva to be opened, the foetus finds its own exit and thus it is expelled by the force of nature from its own resting place, the afterbirth.

CHAPTER 14
ON SIGNS OF PREGNANCY

For knowing whether a woman is carrying a male or female child take water from a spring and let the woman draw out two or three drops of blood or of milk from the right breast. Let them be poured into the water and if they seek the bottom she is bearing a male; if they float on top she is bearing a female. Hippocrates said that the woman who is bearing a male is well colored and has the right breast larger; if she is pale she is bearing a female and has the left breast larger.

Source 4 from Jacob Minkin, The Teachings of Maimonides *(Northvale, N.J.: Jason Aronson, 1987), pp. 384, 386–387; and "Moses Maimonides' Two Treatises on the Regimen of Health," trans. Ariel Bar-sela, Hebbel E. Hoff, and Elias Faris,* Transactions of the American Philosophical Society, *n.s. 54,4 (1964):29.*

4. From Moses Maimonides, *Ethical Conduct* and *The Regimen of Health*, ca. 1190s

ETHICAL CONDUCT

At every period of life, it should be one's care to secure free action of the bowels, approximating to a relaxed condition. It is a leading principle in medicine that if there is constipation or if the bowels move with difficulty, grave disorders result. How is a slight costive[7] condition to be remedied? If the patient is a youth, he should eat, every morning, salty foods well cooked and seasoned with olive oil, fish brine and salt, without bread. Or he should drink the liquid of boiled spinach or St. John's bread, mixed with olive oil, fish brine and salt. An old man should drink, in the morning, honey diluted with warm water, and wait about four hours before taking his breakfast. This regimen should be observed for one day, or, if necessary, for three or four successive days till the bowels move freely.

   Honey and wine are bad for young children, but good for the aged, particularly in the winter. The quantity taken in the summer should be two-thirds of that consumed in the winter.

---

7. **costive:** constipated.

Another great principle of hygiene, physicians say, is as follows: As long as a person takes active exercise, works hard, does not overeat and keeps his bowels open, he will be free from disease and will increase in vigor, even though the food he eats is coarse. . . .

Whosoever indulges in sexual dissipation becomes prematurely aged; his strength fails; his eyes become dim; a foul odor proceeds from his mouth and armpits; the hair of his head, eye-brows and eye-lashes drop out; the hair of his beard, armpits and legs grow abnormally; his teeth fall out; and besides these, he becomes subject to numerous other diseases. Medical authorities have stated that for each one who dies of other maladies, a thousand are the victims of sexual excess. A man should, therefore, be careful in this regard if he wishes to lead a happy life. He should only cohabit when he finds himself in good health and vigor, experiences involuntary erections which persist after he has diverted his mind to other things, is conscious of a heaviness from the loins downwards as if the spermatic cords were being drawn and his flesh is hot. Such a condition calls for cohabitation which then is conducive to health. One should not cohabit when sated with food, nor when one is hungry, but only after a meal has been digested. Before and after coition, attention should be paid to the excretory functions.

THE REGIMEN OF HEALTH

The behavior of all men regarding coitus is known. And that is, that there is not one who uses it for the sake of the regimen of health, or for the sake of procreation, but merely for pleasure; thus they lust until fatigued, at all times, and at every opportunity. It is already manifest among those who know, that coitus is detrimental to all men except some few whose temperament is such that a little of it does no harm. But men differ only in the degree of harm; among them are those whom it harms greatly, and among them are those whom it harms but little. Its harm to the young that are of moist temperament is little. Its harm to the old, the convalescent, and those of dry temperament is very great. Among the convalescents we have already seen some who copulated and died that very day, or suffered syncope[8] and recurrence of fever, and died after a few days. On the whole, it is a pernicious matter for the sick and the convalescent, and very detrimental to the old and to all of dry temperament. It is improper for anyone to copulate before the food in the stomach is digested, or when hungry, or when thirsty, or in a state of inebriety, or after leaving the bath, or following exercise or before it, or for a day before blood-letting and for a day thereafter. Whoever desires the continuance of health, should drive his thoughts from coitus all he can.

8. **syncope:** fainting.

[298]

Source 5 from Helen Rodnite Lemay, Women's Secrets: A Translation of Pseudo–Albertus Magnus' *De Secretis Mulierum* with Commentaries *(Albany: State University of New York Press, 1992), pp. 63–64, 65, 69, 84, 85–86, 107, 109, 117.*

5. Pseudo–Albertus Magnus, *On the Secrets of Women,* late 13th or early 14th century

Now that we have finished our introductory remarks, designed to prepare the reader's mind toward this subject matter, let us turn to the matter of the book, and first let us examine the generation of the embryo. Note therefore that every human being who is naturally conceived is generated from the seed of the father and the menses of the mother, according to all philosophers and medical authorities. And I say "medical authorities" because Aristotle did not believe that the father's seed was part of the substance of the fetus, but rather that the fetus proceeded from the menses alone, and afterwards he states that the seed exudes like vapor from the menses. The doctors,[9] on the other hand, believe that the fetus is made up of male and female seed together.

Having set forth both opinions, we must now see how that seed is received in woman. When a woman is having sexual intercourse with a man she releases her menses at the same time that the man releases sperm, and both seeds enter the *vulva* (vagina) simultaneously and are mixed together, and then the woman conceives. Conception is said to take place, therefore, when the two seeds are received in the womb in a place that nature has chosen. And after these seeds are received, the womb closes up like a purse on every side, so that nothing can fall out of it. After this happens, the woman no longer menstruates. . . .

The menses in woman, just like the sperm in man, is nothing other than superfluous food which has not been transformed into the substance of the body. In woman it is called "menses" because it flows at least once every month when the woman reaches the proper age, that is, 12, 13, or, most frequently, 14. This flow takes place every month in order to purge the body. In some women it begins at the new moon, in some afterwards, and thus all women do not have their pain at the same time. Some have more suffering, some less; some have a shorter flow than others, and this is all determined by the requirement and the complexion of the individual woman.

The third question is why menses, which are superfluous food, flow in women, and sperm does not flow in men, for this is also superfluous food. To this I reply that woman is cold and humid by nature, whereas man is hot and dry. Now humid things naturally flow, as we see in the fourth book of the

---

9. **doctors:** that is, Galen and his followers.

Meteorology,[10] and this is especially true of that humid substance which is in women, for it is watery. In men, on the other hand, the humid substance resembles air, and, further, man has natural heat, and this heat acts upon the humid. Since nature never does anything in vain, as is noted in the first book *On Heaven and Earth*,[10] and because the heat in women is weaker than that in men, and all their food cannot be converted into flesh, nature takes the best course. She provides for what is necessary, and leaves the excess in the place where the menses are kept. Enough has been said on this subject, for to go into more detail would be to give more than the subject demands. . . .

Now that we have examined the preceding questions, let us turn to the formation of the fetus in the womb. The first matter received in the womb has the nature of milk for the first six days, for the natural heat in the male sperm and in the womb causes it to become white as milk. Then that matter is changed to the nature or color of blood that is thickened, as if it were well cooked, and this lasts nine days. During the next twelve days the members of the fetus begin to be formed.

We note here that according to the philosopher[11] each living thing is composed from the four elements, such that terrestrial matter is used for the composition of bones and watery matter for the watery parts of the body, and thus with the others. During the following eighteen days the face is formed by nature, and the body is disposed according to three dimensions, namely length, width, and depth. After this, nature begins to strengthen the fetus until its exit. . . .

Certain women have more pain in childbirth than others, because sometimes the fetus presents its hand and sometimes its feet, and these are dangerous situations. . . . Therefore it is necessary that the women who assist in childbed be skillful, and expert in their work. I have heard from many women that when the fetus presents the head during birth, then the operation goes well, and the other members follow easily. . . .

If a woman dies from an illness before giving birth, the infant in the uterus can live for some time if he can get air. Thus doctors say that the mouth of the woman should be held open with a certain instrument so that air can enter, and if the body is then opened the child will live. In this manner, the first person to be called "Caesar" was born. *Caesar* means "cut" (*caesus*) from his mother's womb.[12]

10. *Meteorology* and *On Heaven and Earth* are two treatises attributed to Aristotle.

11. **the philosopher:** that is, Aristotle.

12. Throughout the Middle Ages, both European and Arabic writers repeated the legend that Julius Caesar had been cut from his mother's womb. Though this story originated in a linguistic search for the roots of Caesar's name (hence the comment about "cut"), it came to be regarded as fact and this procedure became known as "caesarean section." During the Middle Ages, it was generally performed only on women who were dead, in order to extract the infant and—in Christian areas—baptize it.

When a child is born he immediately begins to cry. According to philosophers, this is because the baby finds birth painful because of the narrow openings, and also because of the cold air that he feels when he leaves the womb. If a child is male he naturally has a coarser voice than a female. Women say that a male cries "Ah! Ah! Ah!" because "A" makes a coarser sound than "E," and the opposite seems to be true of girls, for they have a thinner voice and cry "Ay! Ay!"[13]. . .

In connection with this subject the most curious question of all arises: how does the baby lying in the womb receive food, since the womb is closed up everywhere? The child is enclosed in the womb by a natural power which is hidden in the complexion of the fetus. The first thing that develops is a certain vein or nerve which perforates the womb and proceeds from the womb up to the breasts. When the fetus is in the uterus of the mother her breasts are hardened, because the womb closes and the menstrual substance flows to the breast. Then this substance is cooked to a white heat, and it is called the flower of woman; because it is white like milk it is also called the milk of woman. After being cooked in this way, it is sent through the vein to the womb, and there the fetus is nourished with its proper and natural food. This vein is the umbilical cord which is cut off by the midwives at birth, and thus we see newborn babies with their cord tied with a piece of iron. This is to prevent anything from leaving the baby's body from this vein, which is called the umbilicus, and which is suspended in the mother's womb with the amniotic sac. . . .

Note that according to Avicenna if the semen falls in the left side of the womb a female is generated, and if it falls in the right side the child will be a male. If it should land in the middle, however, a hermaphrodite, participating in both the nature of male as well as female, is conceived. The hermaphrodite is given the masculine species, for the male is the worthier, although he really has both natures.

13. The differences between the cries of male and female infants were explained by some medieval philosophers as resulting from their identification with Adam and Eve. Boys' initial cry was "Oh, A(dam)" and girls', "Oh, E(ve)"; both were wailing because of the burden of Original Sin, which Western Christianity after Augustine generally taught was passed down through sexual intercourse.

Source 6 from Caroline Gisela March-Long, "Early Modern German Obstetrical Manuals: Das Frawenbüchlein (c. 1495) and Der Rosengarten (1513)," M.A. thesis, Duke University, 1993, pp. 125, 127–129.

6. From Eucharius Rösslin, *Rosegarden for Midwives and Pregnant Women,* 1513

When the pregnant woman nears delivery, she should drink mature wine mixed with water. She should also have a regimen of food and drink, a regimen a month before birth which makes one moist but not too fat, and one should avoid what makes one dry, constipated, weighs down, presses or constricts. When the woman is even nearer to delivery, when she still has twelve or fourteen days and feels some pain and pressure, she should sit in a bath up to her navel every day, sometimes more often, but not too long (so that she doesn't get weak). She should move around with easy work and movements, walking and standing more than she did before. Such things help the fetus come into position.

Another regimen for the time of delivery which the woman should need if she feels pressure, pain and some moistness begins to show and flow out of the vagina. This regimen takes place in two ways. The first is that one brings on a quick descent and delivery. The other way to lessen complications, labour pains, and pain is for her to sit down for an hour and then stand up and climb up and down the stairs shouting loudly. The woman should force out and hold her breath (breathe heavily) so that she puts pressure on her intestines and bears down. ITEM: The woman should also drink those medicines that are written about afterwards for they force the child downward into delivery position. When she feels the uterus dilate and plenty of fluid flow to her genitals (i.e., water breaks), she should lie on her back, but not completely lying down or standing. It should be a middle position between lying and standing. She should tilt her head more towards the back than the front. In southern German and in Italian/French areas, the midwives have special chairs for delivery. They are not high, but hollowed out with an opening in the inside. The chair should be prepared so that the woman can lean on her back. One should fill and cover the back of the same chair with cloth and when it is time, the midwife should lift the cloth and turn them first to the right and then to the left side. The midwife should sit in front of her and pay careful attention to the child's movement in the womb. The midwife should guide and control her arms and legs with her hands which are coated with white-lily or almond oil or the like. And with her hands in the same way, the midwife should also gently grasp the mother, as she well knows. The midwife should also instruct, guide, and teach the mother, and strengthen her with food and drink. She should urge the woman on to work with soft, kind words so that she begins to breathe deeply. One should dry her stomach off gently above the navel and hips. The midwife should comfort the woman by predicting a successful birth of a baby boy. And if the woman is fat, she should not sit, rather lie on her body and lay her forehead on the ground and pull her knees up underneath so that the womb has pressure applied to it. Afterwards, she should anoint her internally with white-lily oil and, if necessary, the midwife should open the woman's cervix with her hands and afterwards, the woman will deliver quickly.

Source 7 from Loren MacKinney, Medical Illustrations in Medieval Manuscripts *(Berkeley: University of California Press, 1965), fig. 8. Original manuscript in Bodleian Library, Oxford, MS Rawl C. 328, folio 3.*

7. Constantine the African Performs Uroscopy, 15th-century Manuscript

Source 8 from the Osterreichische Nationalbibliothek.

8. Birth Scene, 13th-century Manuscript

9. Caesarean Section, 14th-century Arabic Manuscript

Source 10 from Albertus Magnus, Daraus man alle Heimlichkeit des weiblichen Geschlechts erkennen kann *(reprint Frankfurt, 1977), p. 7.*

10. Birth Scene from Pseudo–Albertus Magnus, *On the Secrets of Women,* 16th-century Illustration

If you have been making lists of the ideas and treatments presented, you have probably assembled what appears to be a great amount of disparate material. Now it is time for you to pull this material together. Turn first to the issue of basic anatomy. What does the womb look like, according to Avicenna? How do pseudo-Trotula and pseudo–Albertus Magnus describe the connections between the womb and the brain? the womb and the breasts? How does pseudo–Albertus Magnus describe the ability of the fetus to breathe?

Now look at issues of physiology. Constantine the African and pseudo-Trotula both discuss impediments to sexual intercourse or conception. How do these fit with humoral theory? What else besides the humors can influence bodily functioning? Maimonides goes on at great length about the dangers of too much sexual intercourse for men; does this idea appear to come from humoral theory or from some other source? Several of the authors, including Trotula, Maimonides, and Rösslin, discuss the dangers of diarrhea and constipation. Why do you think medieval authors saw these problems as so serious? Does this concern with digestive processes seem to come from humoral theory or from clinical and practical experience? Medical theory taught that inspecting the urine was a key way to diagnose illness. Based on the information in Source 3 about hindrances to conception, what might

Constantine the African be looking for in the woman's urine he is examining in Source 7?

Avicenna, pseudo-Trotula, and pseudo–Albertus Magnus all describe anatomical and physiological differences between men and women. To what do they ascribe these differences? Do they see the reproductive organs in women and men as anatomically similar or completely distinct? How do the authors relate the process of menstruation to sexual difference? Why is there no similar process in men? How do they value anatomical and physiological differences (in other words, which is superior—male or female)? In the Middle Ages, the right/left dichotomy was a very strong intellectual concept, with right being seen as good and left as bad. (This is reflected in the word *sinister* which comes from the Latin word for "left.") How does this dichotomy relate to that of male/female in matters of reproduction?

Now look at issues of fetal development, beginning with conception. Are Avicenna and pseudo–Albertus Magnus primarily Aristotelian or Galenist in their interpretations? What physiological changes do they describe happening in the uterus at the moment of conception? Several of the authors use words taken from food processing such as *coagulation* or *thickening* to describe the first part of fetal development. How does this fit with humoral theory and ideas about the role of heat? What are the significant milestones in fetal development?

Rösslin and the illustrations in Sources 8 through 10 all depict birth procedures. How would you compare Rösslin's advice to midwives with the births shown in Sources 8 and 10? What might the flasks on the table in the foreground of Source 10 contain? How would you compare these scenes with that of the caesarean section shown in Source 9? Given pseudo-Albertus's discussion of letting a fetus breathe in the womb before doing a caesarean, would you expect the delivery shown in Source 9 to save the life of the infant? In the background of Source 10, what might the men pointing to heavenly bodies indicate about astrological beliefs regarding birth? (A section of *On the Secrets of Women* not reprinted here also discusses the influence of the planets on fetal development.)

Now consider issues of medical treatment and advice. How would you compare the advice given by Constantine the African on neutralizing spells to the conception hints of pseudo-Trotula? How do these fit with Rösslin's suggestions for easing delivery? What might account for the differences between these authors? What range of treatment and action was available to medieval people concerned about their health? According to the authors represented here, what is the connection between general health and reproduction for either men or women? How would you summarize their primary advice

for those who want to have a long life and many children?

You have probably recognized that not all medical ideas and treatments arise from strict humoral theory, but also from other sources, such as local familiarity with the therapeutic properties of various plants and mixtures, learned ideas about the influence of the heavenly bodies, popular notions of black and white magic, general ideas about gender hierarchy, and—most important in the Middle Ages—religious belief in God as the ultimate source of healing and well-being. We may often view these ideas as contradictory and try to draw a sharp line between science and superstition. As you have noticed, that line was not sharp for medieval medical writers, nor was the line between magic and religion. As you answer the central questions for this chapter, ask yourself also how the variety of sources of medical "wisdom" might have benefited medieval people. Why might both physicians and patients have preferred a range of theories and treatments?

You are now ready to answer the questions for this chapter: What central ideas regarding reproduction were shared by Jewish, Christian, and Islamic medical writers in the Middle Ages? How were these translated into practical advice for patients and medical practitioners?

EPILOGUE

Ideas about reproduction changed very slowly in Europe and the Islamic world. During the seventeenth century, many university-trained physicians in Europe began to give up humoral theory for other systems of anatomy and physiology based largely on experiments and observation. In 1628, William Harvey discovered the circulation of the blood. (The circulation of blood through the lungs had been discovered in the thirteenth century by the Islamic physician Ibn-an-Nafis, although it was not widely recognized until the Spanish physician Michael Servetus's treatise on the subject in the sixteenth century.) The increasing use of human dissection slowly produced enough evidence to lead people to doubt Galen on a variety of anatomical and physiological issues.

However, observation alone was not enough to change ideas, and in fact it occasionally led to what appear to be even more bizarre notions than those held in the Middle Ages. During the seventeenth and eighteenth centuries, the debate between the Galenist and Aristotelian views of conception continued, but now both sides were armed with microscopes. Those who supported a basically Aristotelian position—that the active principle came from the man—claimed to have observed tiny men in human spermatazoa, complete with arms, heads, and legs. William Harvey thought that sperm was so powerful it could act at a distance like a magnet. He backed up this idea not by quoting ancient authorities as his medieval predecessors had, but by experimentation; he dissected large numbers of does just after sexual intercourse and, seeing no sperm in their uteruses, determined that sperm did not need to touch the egg to fertilize it. Those who supported a more active role for the ovum also claimed that humans were preformed in it, but they were somewhat hampered by the fact that the egg was not definitively identified until 1827, a remarkably late date considering its size relative to that of spermatazoa, which the Dutch scientist Anton von Leeuwenhoek identified correctly in the 1670s.

Misconceptions continued in the nineteenth and twentieth centuries. Until the 1840s most authorities believed that females—both human and other mammals—ovulated only with intercourse or orgasm, despite anatomical evidence to the contrary. That the female experience could be so different from the male was a notion very hard to give up, though by this point medical writers no longer believed, as Avicenna had, that the "womb is like the scrotum and the vagina like the penis." In the 1870s the removal of healthy ovaries became a popular treatment for women judged to be psychologically abnormal, though the physicians who performed the procedure were less clear about the exact link between the brain and reproductive organs than Trotula had been seven centuries earlier. These high-minded misconceptions were accompanied by popular ones, many of which still exist. You probably know people who swear they can tell the sex of a fetus by some aspect of the mother's body, and recently a state senator commented that he knew a woman's allegations of rape were false because she subsequently became pregnant, which was impossible if she had suffered "true" rape.

Except in cases such as those of the state senator, we don't yet know which of our contemporary ideas about reproduction will appear as far-fetched seven hundred years from now as those in this chapter do to us. What we do know is that today's ideas are just as connected to realms beyond medicine as were those of the Middle Ages. The kinds of issues that concerned medieval medical writers on reproduction— What can a couple do who cannot conceive? What is the source of differences between men and women? When does life begin? and more—are still with us, and not simply in medical textbooks.

CHAPTER TWELVE

TRANS-ASIAN CONTACTS:

THE BASIS OF A WORLD SYSTEM

(1200–1450)

In recent years interest has been growing in a global approach to history—that is, a focus on the connections between states and regions rather than on their isolated development. This methodology reflects current awareness that a new level of world integration began to emerge in the early modern era, roughly speaking, during the years from 1500 to 1750. In that period, increasing contacts—initially economic and demographic but eventually political and even cultural—began drawing once separate peoples and cultures together in previously unimagined ways. Not only did African, Asian, and European peoples heighten their contacts with one another in this era; they became involved with whole "new worlds" in the Americas and Oceania. As connections multiplied, what people in one part of the globe did began to affect all others as never before. Ultimately people everywhere found themselves living in a so-called global village, a single, worldwide community. This kind of community is often called a "world system."

Actually, a world system need not span the globe. As used in this phrase, the word *world* means only a separate or self-contained region. The parts of such a region, though closely connected and interdependent enough to make up a unified system, simply have to remain isolated from those of other regions to form a "world" of their own. In earlier stages of history, in fact, several such systems may have existed simultaneously in different parts of the globe. A world system, then, does not necessarily entail everyone everywhere.

The modern world system, of course, did cover the whole earth.

Developed initially through the efforts of Western Europeans to link other regions to their homeland in maritime networks of commerce and colonization, it centered on the North Atlantic Ocean. But in its heyday, the system spread far beyond its Atlantic hub to include the entire globe. Given the important role Western Europeans played in creating this global network, generations of historians looked to the rise of Europe as the key dynamic in modern history. But recent scholarship has begun to suggest that in drawing the world together Europeans may, in fact, have depended on the existence of a still older system in whose development they played only a modest role.

Although not as extensive as the modern world system, which became fully global in scope, this earlier one brought the peoples and cultures of the Old World into contact with one another. Based on long-distance trans-Asian connections that flourished from the tenth through the fifteenth century, it centered around Central Asia and the Indian Ocean rather than Europe and the North Atlantic. Europeans, who were then in the midst of their medieval period, remained largely marginal to it. Yet, as Columbus's voyages in search of the "Indies" attest, the lure of its enormous wealth played an important part in stimulating the later European expansion that proved so instrumental in the formation of the truly global modern system. Better understanding of this earlier system, then, may lead us not only to push back the time frame of global integration but also to rethink the origins of the modern world and especially the role non-European peoples may have played in its inception.

The problems you face here, therefore, are to determine (1) how extensive this system was and (2) whether or not it can legitimately be considered a significant stage in world integration. To do so, you will first have to sift through the various pieces of evidence to identify specific interactions, both institutional and informal, that linked peoples together in an interdependent system. Keep the following five questions in mind as you consider each such connection. What enterprises drew people together? Who took part in them? Where did they meet? Where did they come from? And how did they get there? On the basis of your answers to these questions, you should be able to estimate how far the system extended and what it entailed. Then decide for yourself if it truly formed a significant "world system."

BACKGROUND

Long-distance contact across Asia stretches far back through history. Ultimately most travel and communication shifted toward the sea and maritime routes across the Indian Ocean. But in early days, dating back to the first millennium of the common era, contact occurred through overland routes that wound across the arid

Chapter 12

Trans-Asian

Contacts:

The Basis of a

World System

(1200–1450)

interior of Central Asia. One overland route in particular stood out. Often called the Silk Road because of the large amount of silk that flowed westward across it from China, it provided the main link between eastern and western Eurasia throughout antiquity and most of the period known in Europe as the Middle Ages.

For millennia, great mule and camel trains, known as caravans, plodded slowly across this inland route, stimulating the rise of rich commercial cities along its course. But because the pack animals could carry only limited loads, early trade was restricted to small lots of lightweight goods. For this reason, merchants in the trade preferred to deal in expensive luxury goods like silks, carpets, porcelain, and metalware that had a high ratio of value to weight. To pay the high cost of such goods and of outfitting caravans, merchants generally banded together into companies so that they could pool funds and bargain collectively. Usually these companies hired professional caravaneers to oversee the pack trains. And since in antiquity Persian and other Iranian-speaking peoples made up the majority of the population along the trade route, they provided most of its professional carriers. Persian, in fact, served as the original trade language, some of whose words— like the word *caravan* (from old Persian *kārwān*)—continue in use even today.

The eastern terminus of the Silk Road lay in the markets of China's inland cities. From China, it threaded northwestward through the Tarim Basin and around the sandy wastes

of the Taklamakan Desert to the high passes of the snow-covered Pamir Mountains or the more northerly Tienshan range. From there it descended into the Caspian region where it forked into two legs. One ran west through the Caucasus Mountains to termini along the Black Sea; the other turned south to Persia, branching again, westward toward the Mediterranean and eastward to India. Because of the rugged and arid nature of most of the terrain this route traversed, adjoining areas lacked large populations, and long stretches of desolate land separated settled sites. These conditions fostered a tradition of political separatism in which small city-states and autonomous kingdoms prevailed, and people remained local in their allegiances. But the constant flow of travelers through the area kept inhabitants up-to-date on happenings elsewhere. They thus became purveyors of new fashions and ideas as well as goods, and they passed major religions like Buddhism and Islam from one civilization to another.

The spread of Islam across the inland route, which followed the Arab conquest of Persia in the mid-600s, drew the peoples of Inner Asia closer together, offsetting in part their diversity. In the next few centuries, Islamicized cities along the inland route prospered as never before, benefiting from the growing volume of trade occasioned by development at both extremes of Asia. In the east, the Tang dynasty (618–907), based in Changan in north China, created a vast empire stretching from the Pacific to the Pamirs that stimulated economic growth throughout East Asia. Similar growth also occurred in western Asia under the Abbasid dynasty (750–1258), based in Baghdad, which built an equally immense Muslim state extending from the eastern Mediterranean to the Iranian plateau. The demand for new goods generated in these two giants dramatically increased the commerce and traffic flowing between them.

Profits derived from this trade made the cities along the caravan route among the wealthiest and most sophisticated in the world. People from adjoining areas thus flocked to them, including waves of Turkic-speaking migrants, who were drifting westward off the steppes or grasslands of East Asia. Conversion to Islam helped these Turkic migrants to blend into existing Iranian communities, but they remained a distinct population that began to outnumber the original inhabitants and to alter local traditions. Turkic rulers, known as *khans*, even began to succeed in building large regional states called *khanates*. But it was still another incoming group, the Mongols, who first unified the area under a single government.

The Mongols first penetrated the area when Chingis Khan reached the fringes of the trade route after defeating the Xixia state southwest of the Mongolian steppes and invading its western neighbor, Karakhitai, in the early 1200s. In the decades that followed, Mongol khans conquered westward to Baghdad, destroying the last Abbasid caliph there in 1258. By then, however, the Mongol empire had split into four parts. The lands along the old Silk Road formed the core of one of these, known as the Khanate of Jagadai. Richest of the four, Jagadai's resources encouraged its rulers to break with the supreme khanate further to the east and so outlive its collapse in the mid-1300s. Jagadai became the base of a new Central Asia empire under the Turko-Mongolian Khan Timur that lasted until his death in 1405. Under Mongol control, trade and travel expanded to new levels. Military traffic, of course, increased tremendously since the Mongols dispatched great armies back and forth across Central Asia. But diplomatic contacts increased, too, as neighboring peoples sought to negotiate with and placate the khans. Mongol rulers also welcomed foreign merchants into their lands, hoping to sell them *ortaqs*, or trade monopolies, and to recruit them as administrators. Marco Polo, for example, was recruited in just this way along with many other "colored eyes," as the Western émigrés were known.

By the Mongol era, however, much trans-Asian traffic had already begun shifting southward onto the Indian Ocean. Although the causes remain unclear, this trend was probably the result of explosive economic growth that began in eastern and western Asia during the Tang and Abbasid periods. In both regions the development of commercial economies, based upon affluent, urban markets with rising populations, spawned a rising demand for bulky commodities and foodstuffs. The volume of these new goods probably exceeded what overland caravans could handle. Because ships could carry greater cargoes of goods at lower cost, they posed a

Chapter 12

Trans-Asian

Contacts:

The Basis of a

World System

(1200–1450)

logical alternative—once navigational improvements made sailing across the open ocean relatively safe. Eventually, as maritime travel proved its reliability, more and more of the luxury trade, too, shifted south to the sea, drawing other forms of traffic along with it. Thus began a long, slow decline in the wealth and importance of Central Asia and its great cities.

Although travel by sea ultimately became easier than by land, seafaring also posed its problems. For one thing, travel across the Indian Ocean depended on the right winds. Powerful air fronts known as monsoons control the weather across the Indian Ocean and in the adjacent equatorial regions of Africa and the South Pacific. These fronts result from permanent high-pressure areas created at the equator by the evaporation of tropical waters. The warm, humid masses of air they produce flow northward all year, but during part of the year the build-up of temporary high-pressure zones over the mountains of Africa, western Asia, and northern India creates a counterflow of air that pushes them back south. This annual ebb and flow of air gives the Indian Ocean a two-season climate. A dry spell lasting from October to April annually alternates with an onslaught of heavy rains from April to October. The reversal of prevailing breezes that accompanies this seasonal shift creates two distinct sailing seasons.

For half of the year from April through September the southwest monsoon winds blow toward India and up along the Indochina coast, making travel from west to east or south to north relatively easy. But then, when the northeast monsoon sweeps down off the land beginning in October, the winds veer sharply about and blow toward the southwest for the next six months. During this period, travel east or north becomes difficult, but ships sailing on a southern or western heading have favorable winds. Because older sailing vessels took more than six months to cross the area, this seasonal shift of winds forced them to lay over for several months in ports they could reach conveniently during periods of favorable breezes. Ships from Arabia and Persia reached these points along the western coast of India, whereas those coming down from Indonesia and East Asia found safe harbor along the tip of the Malay peninsula or on the nearby island of Java. These havens became great emporia in their own right, for they became centers of intermediate trade as well as places for reoutfitting during the lay-over season.

The need to break voyages at these sites produced a natural division of maritime traffic in Asia into three zones: one in the South Pacific, one in the western Indian Ocean, and one lying in between, in the eastern Indian Ocean. Two outlying areas—the Mediterranean and coastal northeastern Asia—fed additional traffic into the system from opposite ends of the Old World. The lack of direct sea links between the Mediterranean and the Indian Ocean, however, forced overland transshipment of all goods and people between them, creating a sharp break between the central zones and this western extension. Originally dominated by Byzantine Greeks, in the eleventh and twelfth centuries, trade at this end came under the control of Italians from Venice and Genoa. No such break marked the eastern extension. Traffic there flowed directly into the ports of southeastern China whose merchant communities dominated most of the trade throughout the whole eastern region.

Iranian-speaking peoples, who conducted much of the overland trade, initially pioneered long-distance sea travel as well. Operating from home ports along the Persian Gulf, they developed many of the early sailing routes across the Indian Ocean. But Arabs living along the Gulf and the Red Sea soon joined them, venturing even farther to Indonesia and south China where they not only traded in season but planted resident communities. Chinese sources, in fact, indicate that by the ninth century as many as 100,000 Arabs dwelt in Canton, the chief southern port of the Tang empire. Further expansion of trade, particularly in the tenth and eleventh centuries, apparently created more traffic than these pioneers could handle. Besides, as Turkic migrations and the Mongol conquest disrupted key markets in the Muslim world, waning profits at home made it hard for Persians and Arabs to retain commercial mastery throughout the entire trade area. Indigenous people, of course, had always participated in trade with them, conducting the secondary wholesale and com-

modity markets that supplied them with goods. As Muslim dominance faltered, locals merely expanded into the long-distance trade.

In time, Indians, Indonesians, and Chinese thus entered the long-distance trade too, giving Asian maritime traffic a very cosmopolitan character. Because most of the newcomers limited their operations to one of the natural subregions of the system, cultural differences reinforced natural divisions. Despite much sharing of technologies and commercial practices, groups in each zone developed their own ways of operating. Even shipbuilding varied markedly from one locale to another, and as the three principal sailing vessels of the area—Arabian *dhows*, Malay *praus*, and Chinese *junks*—demonstrate, each tradition was unique.

A tradition of political as well as cultural diversity persisted across this vast maritime region, and no single state ever united it. Impressive empires did occasionally emerge on its margins such as the Abbasid caliphate in western Asia, the sultanate of Delhi in India, and various Chinese states established both before and after the Mongol conquest. But none of them ever came close to dominating the maritime area as the Mongols did the inland trade region. Far from hindering the movement of goods and people throughout the area, lack of political unity may have promoted it.

As the huge Ming Chinese fleets that circumnavigated the entire area in the early fifteenth century prove, some of the larger Asian empires certainly had the potential to control the

Chapter 12

Trans-Asian

Contacts:

The Basis of a

World System

(1200–1450)

sea lanes. From 1407 to 1433 Ming fleets, numbering in the hundreds of ships, made a total of seven voyages into the Indian Ocean in an extraordinary display of might. But neither the Ming empire nor any other Asian power sought to emulate the Mongol example on land by actually trying to conquer and control the entire maritime area. A few like the Mamluk sultanate of Egypt, which emerged in the thirteenth century, did attempt to police portions of the region. And occasionally a local potentate would impose taxes on local traffic and trade. True maritime trade empires based on the conquest of ports and control of sea lanes, however, came only later when the Portuguese arrived and introduced new monopolistic tactics to the area in the sixteenth century. Until then, small city-states and local kingdoms prevailed throughout the region, fostering a tradition of open ports and free trade.

Such political fragmentation promoted large-scale piracy. But it also encouraged a flexible system of trade in which many small merchants ex-changed a wide variety of goods throughout many markets. In this preindustrial age regional specialization had not yet become pronounced. Goods could often be obtained from many sources, and when they became scarce in one place, they were usually available elsewhere. So, too, if certain ports became inaccessible, others equally good could generally be found. This flexibility cushioned the trade from local disruptions, but it made business decisions much harder to make. Merchants and ship masters had to anticipate volatile market and port conditions months in advance, a task further complicated by the long lay-overs. They not only had to make shrewd guesses about what to take where on their outbound run, but how to find suitable goods for their return voyage. These conditions stimulated a great deal of experimentation. For that reason, people, goods, and ideas circulated widely throughout the system, making it an important channel for cross-cultural contact and trade.

THE METHOD

To evaluate the nature of these trans-Asian contacts, we would ideally like to have detailed statistics about trade and travel throughout the area. Unfortunately the kinds of documents that would provide such information—like caravansary registries, port records, ship manifests, or merchant contracts—have not yet come to light. Given the climate in much of the area over which these contacts occurred, they probably never will, since most such materials would long ago have rotted away even if they had been put aside in some safe place. In their absence, we can never build any detailed, statistical models of the system nor reconstruct all of its elements with precision. So we have to content ourselves with far more impression-istic—and imprecise—evidence.

Such evidence includes mainly the letters, diaries, and travel accounts of people who journeyed through the system, brief references in histories and surveys, and a few artifacts and illustrations. Even materials of this sort are rare for the period from the ninth through the twelfth centuries. So most of the sources here date from the thirteenth century or later. The map that appears as Source 1, though not an old document, depicts the area in which the system emerged at about that time. It recreates the "humanscape" of the thirteenth century, showing what then stood out as the most important regions and cities of the Old World. Use it to locate places mentioned in the text and to trace the course of journeys and contacts described in the other sources. It provides a concrete framework to use in visualizing the system as a whole.

The other materials given here document the nature of the system, beginning with its overland portions. Source 2 comes from the *Book of Description of Countries*, written by a fourteenth-century Italian businessman, Francis Balducci Pegolotti, who worked for a major Florentine firm, the house of Bardi. Intended as a practical survey of commerce of the day, it tells what a western merchant entering the overland trade with Asia from the Black Sea would find. A somewhat earlier travel account from the mid-thirteenth century appears as Source 3; written by a European monk named William of Rubruck, it records his journey on a diplomatic mission to the Mongols for a French king across terrain described by Pegolotti. Source 4 shows the kind of ox-cart both mention as the usual vehicle for overland travel. Balancing

these Western accounts are entries from a travel diary kept by a thirteenth-century Chinese, Li Zhichang, who journeyed over the eastern half of the area from China to Chingis Khan's camp in Samarkand (Source 5).

The rest of the materials focus on the maritime parts of the system. Source 6 is a letter sent back to Europe in 1292 by a Franciscan monk from Italy, John of Monte Corvino, who passed through India on his way to the Mongol court as a papal envoy. John's letter gives a thorough overview of trade and traffic in the western part of the Indian Ocean at this time. The kind of ship he mentions is illustrated in Source 7: the Arab dhow. East Africa, of course, formed part of this sphere, and Source 8, taken from the *Travels of Marco Polo*, details what the famous Venetian traveler discovered there on his return to Europe at the end of the thirteenth century. Source 9, from a work by the fourteenth-century Muslim traveler, Ibn Batuta, provides a glimpse of the eastern half of the maritime region. Shipping there depended on the Chinese junk, depicted in Source 10. And the final piece of evidence, Source 11 from the official Chinese history of the Ming dynasty, the *Ming Shi,* shows Zheng He's use of such new seapower on his spectacular voyages across the entire region from 1402–1433.

The relative abundance of travelers' accounts from different parts of the area during the thirteenth century suggests that the scope and frequency of contacts was increasing dramatically at this time. Most writers took pains to supply useful advice to those countrymen back home

[319]

Chapter 12

Trans-Asian

Contacts:

The Basis of a

World System

(1200–1450)

whom they seemed to assume would follow in their footsteps. Like tourists today, they devoted attention to practical aspects of travel and to local attractions likely to interest future visitors. They also carefully recorded whatever specific information about their immediate business might prove helpful to successors. Those with mercantile interests, for instance, listed new foods, fabrics, and other goods of potential trade value, whereas diplomatic emissaries noted local politics and alliances. Such accounts give us a rough picture of the broader system.

The wonder of discovery that fills so many of these accounts, however, warns us that cross-cultural contacts were still at an early stage. Descriptions of novelties and far-fetched tales compete with practical observations. And expressions of bewilderment, disbelief, and even disgust often punctuate the narratives. These features point out that the writers on whom we rely for information on the system were often outside observers who, out of ignorance, may have misunderstood what they saw. Strong religious and cultural beliefs, moreover, often colored their reactions—and may on occasion have affected their observations as well.

So we must treat this material critically to factor out the false and improbable. Historians often deal with this problem by checking one source against another. Details that appear in several accounts are more likely to be reliable than those found only once. When such cross-checking is impossible, historians look for clues that a given writer may have had deeper knowledge of a certain place by virtue of long residence there or other special circumstances. Distinguishing between different kinds of information also helps. What a visiting trader reports about goods and their availability in a port, for instance, can probably be accepted more readily than his remarks about local religious customs or diplomatic initiatives.

With this advice in mind, look over the material that follows for information on the nature of the system. As you will soon discover, commercial relations played a substantial role, so you need to pay special attention to trade within the region. Try to determine not only what was traded but who traded it where and with whom. Begin by trying to work out the physical networks of commerce. What were the principal trade routes and what areas did they connect? Where did goods enter the system and to whom did they eventually pass? Who conducted the trade to such points and how did goods get exchanged at intermediary emporia or lay-overs? What does the overall pattern of trade suggest about the extent and nature of relations between different areas and peoples? How far did goods circulate? Were certain areas economically move developed—more "advanced"—than others, or were all roughly equal?

Look for other kinds of activities occurring within the system, too. Political and religious concerns motivated many of the contacts noted in these sources. What or who inspired them? Empires and religious spheres seem to have been expanding into new territories during this period. Where did they meet? And what did their confrontations indicate about the larger political and religious dynamics of Eurasia? Do you see indications of material or technological borrowing? What attracted notice, and by whom? Do you find hints that some regions seemed technologically more advanced than others and thus served as a source of innovation to others? Finally, do you see signs of cultural exchange, whether of concrete items like foodstuffs and artistic creations or of abstract ideas and beliefs?

Once you have listed different kinds of contacts, consider how they fit together as a whole. Think about the relative frequency and importance of certain activities over others. Did any dominate? Were the same peoples involved in different interactions? Did political and other noneconomic contacts occur over the same routes and in the same centers that served as channels of trade? Did certain areas stand out, perhaps indicating that they were key points of contact? What do these features suggest about the nature of the system? Is there evidence of a common pattern in the flow of goods, people, and ideas from one area to another? What does this reveal about the early stages of global integration? Finally, note how all such questions require you to think in terms of a much larger entity than a single cultural area. The idea of such a system forces us to think about how the focus of historical study affects what we see.

1. **Thirteenth-Century Asia**

PACIFIC OCEAN

KHINGAN MTS

Japan Sea

Khanbaligh (Cambalic)

Yellow Sea

Karakorum

Huang He (Yellow)

Huang

Chang Jiang (Yangtze)

Chuanzhou (Zaitun)

Changan

MONGOLIA

CHINA

DESERT OF GOBI

TARIM BASIN

Salween R.

Sea of China

INDONESIA

MALAYA

JAVA

PAMIR

Patna

Bay of Bengal

CEYLON

INDIA

Delhi

Malabar

INDIAN OCEAN

Samarkand

TURKESTAN

Indus R.

Aral Sea

Urgani

PERSIA

Hormuz

Arabian Sea

Caspian Sea

CAUCASUS

Baghdad

ARABIA

Aden

Mogadishu

ETHIOPIA

Zanzibar

MADAGASCAR

Don R.

Tana

Crimea

Soldaia

Black Sea

Kiev

Constantinople

CYPRUS

Alexandria

Red Sea

Nile R.

EGYPT

1,000 mi.

1,000 km

500

500

0

0

Source 2 from Henry Yule, Cathay and the Way Thither, vol. 3 (London: The Hakluyt Society, 1914), pp. 143–155.

2. From Francis Balducci Pegolotti, *Book of Description of Countries*, ca. 1320s

CHAPTER I.
INFORMATION REGARDING THE JOURNEY TO CATHAY, FOR SUCH AS WILL GO BY TANA AND COME BACK WITH GOODS.

In the first place, from Tana [Taman] to Gintarchan may be twenty-five days with an ox-waggon, and from ten to twelve days with a horse-waggon. On the road you will find plenty of *Moccols,* that is to say, of *gens d'armes.* And from Gittarchan to Sara may be a day by river, and from Sara to Saracanco, also by river, eight days. You can do this either by land or by water; but by water you will be at less charge for your merchandize.

From Saracanco to Organci may be twenty days' journey in camel-waggon. It will be well for anyone travelling with merchandize to go to Organci, for in that city there is a ready sale for goods. From Organci to Oltrarre is thirty-five to forty days in camel-waggons. But if when you leave Saracanco you go direct to Oltrarre, it is a journey of fifty days only, and if you have no merchandize it will be better to go this way than to go by Organci.

From Oltrarre to Armalec is forty-five days' journey with pack-asses, and every day you find Moccols. And from Armalec to Camexu is seventy days with asses, and from Camexu until you come to a river called_____is forty-five days on horseback; and then you can go down the river to Cassai, and there you can dispose of the *sommi* of silver that you have with you, for that is a most active place of business. After getting to Cassai you carry on with the money which you get for the *sommi* of silver which you sell there; and this money is made of paper, and is called *balishi.* And four pieces of this money are worth one *sommo* of silver in the province of Cathay. And from Cassai to Gamalec [Cambalec], which is the capital city of the country of Cathay, is thirty days' journey.

CHAPTER II.
THINGS NEEDFUL FOR MERCHANTS WHO DESIRE TO MAKE THE JOURNEY TO CATHAY ABOVE DESCRIBED.

In the first place, you must let your beard grow long and not shave. And at Tana you should furnish yourself with a dragoman [interpreter]. And you must not try to save money in the matter of dragomen by taking a bad one instead of a good one. For the additional wages of the good one will not cost you so much as you will save by having him. And besides the dragoman it

Chapter 12

Trans-Asian

Contacts:

The Basis of a

World System

(1200–1450)

will be well to take at least two good men servants, who are acquainted with the Cumanian tongue. And if the merchant likes to take a woman with him from Tana, he can do so; if he does not like to take one there is no obligation, only if he does take one he will be kept much more comfortably than if he does not take one. Howbeit, if he do take one, it will be well that she be acquainted with the Cumanian tongue as well as the men.

And from Tana travelling to Gittarchan you should take with you twenty-five days' provisions, that is to say, flour and salt fish, for as to meat you will find enough of it at all the places along the road. And so also at all the chief stations noted in going from one country to another in the route, according to the number of days set down above, you should furnish yourself with flour and salt fish; other things you will find in sufficiency, and especially meat.

The road you travel from Tana to Cathay is perfectly safe, whether by day or by night, according to what the merchants say who have used it. Only if the merchant, in going or coming, should die upon the road, everything belonging to him will become the perquisite of the lord of the country in which he dies, and the officers of the lord will take possession of all. And in like manner if he die in Cathay. But if his brother be with him, or an intimate friend and comrade calling himself his brother, then to such an one they will surrender the property of the deceased, and so it will be rescued.

And there is another danger: this is when the lord of the country dies, and before the new lord who is to have the lordship is proclaimed; during such intervals there have sometimes been irregularities practised on the Franks, and other foreigners. (They call *Franks* all the Christians of these parts from Romania westward.) And neither will the roads be safe to travel until the other lord be proclaimed who is to reign in room of him who is deceased.

Cathay is a province which contained a multitude of cities and towns. Among others there is one in particular, that is to say the capital city, to which is great resort of merchants, and in which there is a vast amount of trade; and this city is called Cambalec. And the said city hath a circuit of one hundred miles, and is all full of people and houses and of dwellers in the said city.

You may calculate that a merchant with a dragoman, and with two men servants, and with goods to the value of twenty-five thousand golden florins, should spend on his way to Cathay from sixty to eighty *sommi* of silver, and not more if he manage well; and for all the road back again from Cathay to Tana, including the expenses of living and the pay of servants, and all other charges, the cost will be about five *sommi* per head of pack animals, or something less. And you may reckon the *sommo* to be worth five golden florins. You may reckon also that each ox-waggon will require one ox, and will carry ten cantars Genoese weight; and the camel-waggon will require three camels, and will carry thirty cantars Genoese weight; and the horse-waggon will require one horse, and will commonly carry six and half cantars of silk, at 250 Genoese pounds to the cantar. And a bale of silk may be reckoned at between 110 and 115 Genoese pounds.

You may reckon also that from Tana to Sara the road is less safe than on any other part of the journey; and yet even when this part of the road is at its worst, if you are some sixty men in the company you will go as safely as if you were in your own house.

Anyone from Genoa or from Venice, wishing to go to the places above-named, and to make the journey to Cathay, should carry linens with him, and if he visit Organci he will dispose of these well. In Organci he should purchase *sommi* of silver, and with these he should proceed without making any further investment, unless it be some bales of the very finest stuffs which go in small bulk, and cost no more for carriage than coarser stuffs would do.

Merchants who travel this road can ride on horseback or on asses, or mounted in any way that they list to be mounted.

Whatever silver the merchants may carry with them as far as Cathay the lord of Cathay will take from them and put into his treasury. And to merchants who thus bring silver they give that paper money of theirs in exchange. This is of yellow paper, stamped with the seal of the lord aforesaid. And this money is called *balishi;* and with this money you can readily buy silk and all other merchandize that you have a desire to buy. And all the people of the country are bound to receive it. And yet you shall not pay a higher price for your goods because your money is of paper. And of the said paper money there are three kinds, one being worth more than another, according to the value which has been established for each by that lord.

And you may reckon that you can buy for one *sommo* of silver nineteen or twenty pounds of Cathay silk, when reduced to Genoese weight, and that the *sommo* should weigh eight and a half ounces of Genoa, and should be of the alloy of eleven ounces and seventeen deniers to the pound.

You may reckon also that in Cathay you should get three or three and a half pieces of damasked silk for a *sommo;* and from three and a half to five pieces of *nacchetti* of silk and gold, likewise for a *sommo* of silver.

Source 3 from Christopher Dawson, The Mongol Mission *(London: Sheed & Ward, 1955), reprinted as* Mission to Asia *(New York: Harper Torchbooks, 1966), pp. 91–92, 114–115.*

3. From *The Journey of William of Rubruck,* 1253

Be it known therefore to your holy Majesty that in the year of Our Lord one thousand two hundred and fifty-three on the seventh of May we entered the Sea of Pontus [Black Sea] which is commonly called the Greater Sea. It is one thousand four hundred miles in length, as I learned from merchants, and is divided into two parts, for about the middle of it there are two points of land, one in the north and the other in the south.

Chapter 12

Trans-Asian

Contacts:

The Basis of a

World System

(1200–1450)

. . . In the middle of the south side, as it were at the apex, there is a city called Soldaia [Sudak], which looks towards Sinopolis, and all the merchants coming from Turkey and wishing to go to northern lands make their way thither, and similarly those coming from Russia and northern territories who wish to cross to Turkey. The latter bring squirrel and ermine and other valuable furs, while the former carry materials of cotton or bombax, silk stuffs and sweet-smelling spices. To the east of this province is a city called Matrica [Taman]; here the river Tanais [Don] empties itself into the Sea of Pontus through an opening twelve miles wide.

Before this river reaches the Sea of Pontus it forms a kind of sea [Sea of Azov] towards the north, which is seven hundred miles in breadth and length and nowhere reaches a depth of more than six paces; consequently large vessels do not enter it, but merchants from Constantinople going to the aforesaid city of Matrica send their barks as far as the river Tanais in order to buy dried fish, namely sturgeon and barbot and other fish in enormous quantities.

And so we reached Soldaia on May 21st. Certain merchants from Constantinople had arrived before us and had announced that envoys were coming thither from the Holy Land who wished to visit Sartach. Now I had preached publicly on Palm Sunday in St. Sophia's that I was not an envoy either of you or anybody else, but that I was going among these unbelievers in accordance with our Rule. Then when we landed the said merchants warned me to mind my words, for they had given out that I was an envoy, and if I were to deny that I was such, then I would not be allowed to proceed.

Thereupon I spoke in the following manner to the prefects of the city or rather to their deputies, for the prefects had gone to Baatu in the winter bearing their tribute and had not yet returned. "We heard it told of your lord Sartach in the Holy Land that he was a Christian and the Christians rejoiced exceedingly over this fact, especially the most Christian lord, the King of the French, who is on a pilgrimage there and is fighting against the Saracens in order to wrest the Holy Places from their hands: for this reason I desire to go to Sartach and bring to him a letter of my lord the King, in which he admonishes him concerning the good estate of the whole of Christendom." They received us with joy and lodged us in the episcopal church. The Bishop of that church had been to Sartach and he told me many good things about him which I, for my part, was not to discover later.

They then gave us the choice as to whether we would like carts with oxen, or pack horses, to carry our belongings. The merchants from Constantinople advised us to accept the carts and even to buy covered carts for ourselves like the ones the Ruthenians use for carrying their furs, and into these to put such of our things as I did not wish to unpack every day; for if I took the horses, I should have to unload them at every stopping place and pack them on to other horses; moreover I would be able to ride at a more gentle pace with the oxen. I followed their advice, but it was bad advice for I was on the road for two months before I reached Sartach: a journey I could have completed in one month if I had gone with horses.

On the advice of the merchants I had brought with me from Constantinople fruit, muscatel wine and choice biscuits to present to the chief men of the city so that I might be granted permission to travel about, since they look with no favourable eye upon anyone coming to them empty-handed. On failing to find the prefects of the city there, I placed all these things in a cart, as I was told that Sartach would be delighted with them, if only I could get them as far as him.

So we set off on our journey about June 1st with our own four covered carts and with two others I had received from them in which was carried bedding for sleeping on at night. They gave us five horses to ride on, for we were five in number, myself, my companion Friar Bartholomew of Cremona, Gosset the bearer of this letter, Abdullah the interpreter, and a boy, Nicholas, whom I had bought at Constantinople out of the alms you gave me. They also gave us two men who drove the carts and looked after the oxen and horses.

And so we travelled with great hardship from place to place, until, a few days before the feast of St. Mary Magdalene [July 22nd, 1253], we reached the great river Tanais which separates Asia from Europe, as the river of Egypt separates Asia from Africa.

So we walked for three days without coming across a soul, and just when we as well as the oxen were tired out and we did not know where we could find the Tartars, suddenly two horses came running up to us; we caught them with great joy and our guide and the interpreter mounted them, so that they could look and see in what direction we could find some people. When at last on the fourth day we came across some men we rejoiced like shipwrecked mariners on reaching port.

Chapter 12
Trans-Asian
Contacts:
The Basis of a
World System
(1200–1450)

4. Tang Chinese Ox-Cart

Source 5 from Arthur Waley, The Travels of an Alchemist *(London: Routledge and Sons, 1923), pp. 79, 82–83, 85–86, 92–93, 113.*

5. From Li Zhichang, *The Travels of Chang Chun*, 1221

On the 27th day of the eighth month (September 15th) we reached the foot of the Yin Shan. Here some Uighurs came out to meet us, and presently we reached a small town. The ruler of the place brought us grape-wine, choice fruits, large cakes, huge onions, and strips of Persian linen, a foot for each person.

Looking south towards the Yin Shan we saw three sharp peaks standing out against the sky. The Master made a poem about them and presented it to the student Li Po-hsiang (this student is a phrenologist). After passing through two other towns we reached Chambalig. The ruler is an Uighur and an old friend of Chinkai. He brought with him all his family and a number of Hui-ho priests, who came a long way out to meet us. Upon our arrival we were entertained upon a terrace and the Uighur ruler's wife gave us grape-wine, and also put in front of us water-melons that weighed as much as a measure each, and sweet melons as large as (porcelain) pillows. Their scent and taste is quite different from what we are used to in China; but the garden-vegetables are the same as ours. A priest came and waited upon the Master. By means of an interpreter he asked this priest what scriptures he read. He replied that since he had received the tonsure and submitted to the rules of the order, he had worshipped the Buddha and followed no other teaching; which was natural enough, for the dominions of the T'ang dynasty extended to this place. But west of this one finds no Buddhist priests, the Hui-ho people only worshipping the western quarter.

One more stage brought us to the town of Almalig, which we reached on the 27th day of the ninth month. We were met by the Moslem ruler of the place and the Mongol darugachi (governor) with their retinues. They gave us lodging in a fruit-garden to the west. The natives call fruit *a-li-ma*, and it is from the abundance of its fruits that the town derives its name. It is here that they make the stuff called "tu-lu-ma" which gave rise to the popular story about a material made from "sheep's wool planted in the ground." We now procured seven pieces of it to make into winter clothes. In appearance and texture it is like Chinese willow-down—very fine, soft and clean. Out of it they make thread, ropes, cloth and wadding.

The farmers irrigate their fields with canals; but the only method employed by the people of these parts for drawing water is to dip a pitcher and carry it on the head. Our Chinese buckets delighted them.

On the eighteenth day of the eleventh month (December 3rd, 1221) after crossing a great river, we reached the northern outskirts of the mighty city of

Chapter 12

Trans-Asian

Contacts:

The Basis of a

World System

(1200–1450)

Samarkand. The Civil Governor his Highness I-la, together with the Mongol and local authorities, came to meet us outside the town. They brought wine and set up a great number of tents. Here we brought our wagons to a stop.

After a time we entered the city by the north-east gate. The town is built along canals. As no rain falls during the summer and autumn, two rivers have been diverted so as to run along every street, thus giving a supply of water to all the inhabitants. Before the defeat of the Khwārizm Shah there was a fixed population here of more than 100,000 households; but now there is only about a quarter this number, of whom a very large proportion are native Hui-ho. But these people are quite unable to manage their fields and orchards for themselves, and are obliged to call in Chinese, Kitai and Tanguts. The administration of the town is also conducted by people of very various nationality. Chinese craftsmen are found everywhere. The Master's words were translated into Mongo by A-hai. The Emperor was delighted with his doctrine and on the nineteenth, when there was a bright night, sent for him again. On this occasion too he was much pleased by what he heard, and sent for the Master to his tent once more on the twenty-third (October 29th). He was here treated with the same regard as before and the Emperor listened to him with evident satisfaction. He ordered that the Master's words should be recorded, and especially that they should be written down in Chinese characters, that they might be preserved from oblivion. To those present he said: "You have heard the holy Immortal discourse three times upon the art of nurturing the vital spirit. His words have sunk deeply into my heart. I rely upon you not to repeat what you have heard." During the remainder of the Imperial Progress to the east, the Master constantly discoursed to the Emperor concerning the mysteries of Tao.

Source 6 from Henry Yule, Cathay and the Way Thither, *vol. 3 (London: The Hakluyt Society, 1914), pp. 58–67.*

6. John of Monte Corvino, Letter from India, ca. 1292

To you Friar Bartholomew of Santo Concordio, your brother in all things, Menentillus of Spoleto, wisheth health and wisdom in Christ!

And because I wot of the great curiosity that you have in regard to all science, and that, much as you do know, you would fain know everything and especially things that are new to you; and in truth that you are one whose desire is to have knowledge and information of all kinds; therefore transcribe I for you certain matters just as they have been written from India by a certain Minorite Friar (the travelling companion of Brother Nicolas of Pistoia, who died in Upper India), when on his way to the court of the Lord of all India.

The bringer of the letter I have seen and spoken with, and it was in his arms that the said Brother Nicholas did die. The letter was to the effect following:

"*Concerning the state of things as to the country itself in Upper India.* The condition of the country of India aforesaid is this. The land is well enough peopled; and there be great cities therein, but the houses are wretched, being built of sandy mud, and usually thatched with leaves of trees. Hills there are few; rivers in some places are many, in others few. Springs there are few or none; wells in plenty; and the reason is this, that water is generally to be found at the depth of two or three paces, or even less. This well water is indeed not very good to drink, for it is somewhat soft and loosens the bowels; so they generally have tanks or excavations like ponds, in which they collect the rain water, and this they drink. They keep few beasts. Horses there are none, except it be in possession of the king and great barons. Flies there be few, and fleas none at all. And they have trees which produce fruit continually, so that on them you find fruit in every stage up to perfect ripeness at one time. In like manner they sow and reap at almost all seasons, and this because it is always warm and never cold. Aromatic spices are to be had good cheap, some more so and some less so, according to what spices they be. They have trees that produce sugar, and others that produce honey, and others that produce a liquor that has a smack of wine. And this the natives of those countries use for drink. And those three things are to be had at very small cost. And the pepper plant is here also. It is slender and knotty like a vine; and indeed 'tis altogether very like a vine, excepting that it is more slender, and bears transplanting.

"Ginger is a reed-like plant, and, like a cane-root, it can be dug and transplanted. But their canes here are more like trees, being sometimes a cubit in girth and more, with slender prickly branches round about, and small leaves.

"The Brazil tree is a slender lofty and thorny tree, all red as it were, with leaves like fern. The Indian nuts are as big as melons, and in colour green like gourds. Their leaves and branches are like those of the date tree.

"The cinnamon tree is of a medium bulk, not very high, and in trunk, bark, and foliage, is like the laurel; indeed, altogether it resembleth the laurel greatly in appearance. Great store of it is carried forth of the island which is hard by Maabar.

"The state of things as regards the inhabitants of India is as follows:—The men of this region are idolaters, without moral law, or letters, or books. They have indeed an alphabet which they use to keep their accounts, and to write prayers or charms for their idols; albeit they have no paper, but write upon leaves of trees like unto palm leaves. They have no conscience of sin whatever. They have idol-houses in which they worship at almost all hours of the day; for they never join together in worship at any fixed hour, but each goes to worship when it pleases himself. And so they worship their idols in any part of these temples, either by day or by night. They frequently set forth their fasts and feasts, but they have no fixed recurring day to keep, either weekly or

Chapter 12

Trans-Asian

Contacts:

The Basis of a

World System

(1200–1450)

monthly. Their marriages take place only at one time of the year; and when the husband dies the wife cannot marry again. The sin of the flesh they count not to be sin, nor are they ashamed to say so.

"In the regions by the sea are many Saracens, and they have great influence but there are few of them in the interior. There are a very few Christians, and Jews, and they are of little weight. The people persecute much the Christians, and all who bear the Christian name.

"But India is a region of great extent, and it hath many realms and many languages. And the men thereof are civil and friendly enough, but of few words, and remind me somewhat of our peasants. They are not, strictly speaking, black, but of an olive colour, and exceedingly well formed both women and men. They go barefoot and naked, except that they wear a cloth round the loins, and boys and girls up to eight years of age wear nothing whatever, but go naked as they came from their mother's womb. They shave not the beard; many times a day they wash; bread and wine they have none. Of the fruits that we make use of they have few or none; but for their daily food they use rice and a little milk; and they eat grossly like pigs, to wit, with the whole hand or fist, and without a spoon.

"The state of things in regard to the Sea of India is this. The sea aboundeth greatly with fish; and in some parts of it they fish for pearls and precious stones. The havens are few and bad; and you must know that the sea here is the Middle Sea or Ocean. Traversing it towards the south there is no continent found but islands alone, but in that sea the islands are many, more than 12,000 in number. And many of these are inhabited, and many are not.

"You can sail (upon that sea) between these islands and Ormes and (from Ormes) to those parts which are called [Minibar] is a distance of 2,000 miles in a direction between south and south-east; then 300 miles between east and south-east from Minibar to Maabar, which (latter however) you enter steering to the north; and from Menabar [Maabar?] you sail another 300 miles between north-east and north to Siu Simmoncota. The rest I have not seen, and therefore I say nothing of it.

"The shores of the said sea in some places run out in shoals for 100 miles or more, so that ships are in danger of grounding. And they cannot make the voyage but once a year, for from the beginning of April till the end of October the winds are westerly, so that no one can sail towards the west; and again 'tis just the contrary from the month of October till March. From the middle of May till the end of October the wind blows so hard that ships which by that time have not reached the ports whither they are bound, run a desperate risk, and if they escape it is great luck. And thus in the past year there perished more than sixty ships; and this year seven ships in places in our own immediate neighbourhood, whilst of what has happened elsewhere we have no intelligence. Their ships in these parts are mighty frail and uncouth, with no iron in them, and no caulking. They are sewn like clothes with twine. And so if the twine breaks anywhere there is a breach indeed! Once every year therefore

[332]

there is a mending of this, more or less, if they propose to go to sea. And they have a frail and flimsy rudder like the top of a table, of a cubit in width, in the middle of the stern; and when they have to tack, it is done with a vast deal of trouble; and if it is blowing in any way hard, they cannot tack at all. They have but one sail and one mast, and the sails are either of matting or of some miserable cloth. The ropes are of husk.

"Moreover their mariners are few and far from good. Hence they run a multitude of risks, insomuch that they are wont to say, when any ship achieves her voyage safely and soundly, that 'tis by God's guidance, and man's skill hath little availed.

"This letter was written in Maabar, a city of the province of Sitia in Upper India, on the 22nd day of December in the year of our Lord MCCX (CII or CIII)."

Chapter 12

Trans-Asian

Contacts:

The Basis of a

World System

(1200–1450)

Source 7 from the Bibliothèque nationale de France.

7. Illustration of Arab Dhow, 13th century

Source 8 from Travels of Marco Polo, *trans. Manuel Komroff (New York: Liveright Publishing Corp., 1953), pp. 312–315.*

8. From *Travels of Marco Polo*, ca. 1290s

OF THE GREAT ISLAND OF MADAGASCAR

Leaving the island of Soccotera, and steering a course between south and south-west for a thousand miles, you arrive at the great island of Madagascar, which is one of the largest and most fertile in the world. In circuit it is three thousand miles.

The inhabitants are Saracens, or followers of the law of Mahomet [Muhammad]. They have four sheikhs, which in our language may be expressed by "elders," who divide the government amongst them. The people subsist by trade and manufacture, and sell a vast number of elephants' teeth, as those animals abound in the country, as they do also in that of Zenzibar, from whence the exportation is equally great.

The island is visited by many ships from various parts of the world, bringing assortments of goods consisting of brocades and silks of various patterns, which are sold to the merchants of the island, or bartered for goods in return. They make large profits.

Ships do not visit other numerous islands lying further south; this and the island of Zenzibar alone being frequented. This is because of the sea current that runs with such force towards the south that it renders their return impossible. The vessels that sail from the coast of Malabar for this island, perform the voyage in twenty or twenty-five days, but in their returning voyage are obliged to struggle for three months; so strong is the current of water, which constantly runs to the southward.

OF THE ISLAND OF ZENZIBAR

Beyond the island of Madagascar lies that of Zenzibar, which is reported to be in circuit two thousand miles. The inhabitants worship idols, have their own peculiar language, and do not pay tribute to any foreign power. They are large in stature, but their height is not proportioned to the bulk of their bodies. Were it otherwise, they would appear gigantic.

They are, however, strongly made, and one of them is capable of carrying what would be a load for four of our people. At the same time, he would require as much food as five. They are black, and go naked, covering only the private parts of the body with a cloth. Their hair is so crisp, that even when dipped in water it can with difficulty be drawn out. They have large mouths, their noses turn up towards the forehead, their ears are long, and their eyes so large and frightful, that they have the aspect of demons. The women are

Chapter 12

Trans-Asian

Contacts:

The Basis of a

World System

(1200–1450)

equally ill-favoured, having wide mouths, thick noses, and large eyes. Their hands, and also their heads, are large and out of proportion.

Many trading ships visit the place, which barter the goods they bring for elephants' teeth and ambergris [perfume ingredient found in whale intestines], of which much is found on the coasts of the island, in consequence of the sea abounding with whales.

Source 9 from Travels of Ibn Batuta, *ed. and trans. Samuel Lee (New York: Burt Franklin, n.d.), pp. 169–170, 172–173.*

9. From *Travels of Ibn Batuta,*
ca. 1353

The first town we entered in the country of Malabar was that of Abi Sardar which is small, and is situated on a large estuary of the sea. We next came to the city of Kākanwar, which is large, and also upon an estuary of the sea. It abounds in the sugar-cane. The Sultan is an infidel. He sent his son as a pledge to our vessel, and we landed accordingly, and were honourably received. He also sent presents to the ship, as marks of respect to the Emperor of India. It is a custom with them, that every vessel which passes by one of their ports shall enter it, and give a present to its Sultan; in this case they let it pass, but otherwise they make war upon it with their vessels, they then board it out of contempt, and impose a double fine upon the cargo, just in proportion to the advantage they usually gain from merchants entering their country.

We next arrived at the city of Manjarūn, which is situated upon a large estuary of the sea, called the *"estuary of the wolf,"* and which is the greatest estuary in the country of Malabar. In this place are some of the greatest merchants of Persia and Yemen. Ginger and black pepper are here in great abundance. The king of this place is the greatest of the kings of Malabar, and in it are about four thousand Mohammedan merchants. The king made us land, and sent us a present.

We next came to the town of Hīlī, which is large and situated upon an estuary of the sea. As far as this place come the ships of China, but they do not go beyond it; nor do they enter any harbour, except that of this place, of Kālikūt, and of Kawlam.

The city of Hīlī is much revered both by the Mohammedans and infidels, on account of a mosque, the source of light and of blessings, which is found in it. To this seafaring persons make and pay their vows, whence its treasury is derived, which is placed under the control of the principal Moslem. The mosque maintains a preacher, and has within it several students, as well as readers of the Korān, and persons who teach writing.

We next came to Kālikūt, one of the great ports of the district of Malabar, and in which merchants from all parts are found. The king of this place is an infidel, who shaves his chin just as the Haidarī Fakeers of Room do. When we approached this place, the people came out to meet us, and with a large concourse brought us into the port. The greatest part of the Mohammedan merchants of this place are so wealthy, that one of them can purchase the whole freightage of such vessels as put in here; and fit out others like them. Here we waited three months for the season to set sail for China: for there is only one season in the year in which the sea of China is navigable. Nor then is the voyage undertaken, except in vessels of the three descriptions following: the greatest is called a junk, the middling sized a zaw, the least a kakam. The sails of these vessels are made of cane-reeds, woven together like a mat; which, when they put into port, they leave standing in the wind. In some of these vessels there will be employed a thousand men, six hundred of these sailors, and four hundred soldiers. Each of the larger ships is followed by three others, a middle-sized, a third, and a fourth sized. These vessels are no where made except in the city of El Zaitūn in China, or in Sīn Kīlān, which is Sin El Sin. They row in these ships with large oars, which may be compared to great masts, over some of which five and twenty men will be stationed, who work standing. The commander of each vessel is a great Emir. In the large ships too they sow garden herbs and ginger, which they cultivate in cisterns (made for that purpose), and placed on the sides of them. In these also are houses constructed of wood, in which the higher officers reside with their wives; but these they do not hire out to the merchants. Every vessel, therefore, is like an independent city. Of such ships as these, Chinese individuals will sometimes have large numbers: and, generally, the Chinese are the richest people in the world.

Chapter 12

Trans-Asian

Contacts:

The Basis of a

World System

(1200–1450)

Source 10 from John E. Vollmer et al., Silk Roads, China Ships *(Toronto: Royal Ontario Museum), p. 100. Illustration: Jim Loates/Visutronx.*

10. Artist's Rendition of a Chinese Junk, ca. 12th or 13th century

Source 11 from Ming Shi, *trans. Dun J. Li, in* The Civilization of China *(New York: Scribner's, 1975), pp. 279–281.*

11. From Zhang Ting-yu et al., *Zheng He's Voyages*, 1402–1483

Cheng Ho [Zheng He], a native of Yunnan, was popularly known as San-pao the Grand Eunuch. At one time he served as a staff member in the feudatory of King Ch'eng; later he was promoted to the position of grand eunuch in recognition of his contribution to King Ch'eng's successful revolt against Emperor Ming Hui-ti [r. 1399–1402]. After his accession to the throne, Emperor Yung-lo, the former King Ch'eng, suspected that his defeated predecessor Hui-ti might have escaped from Nanking and be residing somewhere in the South Seas and wanted very much to know his whereabouts. Besides, he wished to glorify Chinese arms in the remote regions and show off the wealth and power of the Central Kingdom. It was this combination of motives that promoted him to launch Cheng Ho's voyages.

In the sixth month of the third year of Yung-lo [1405] Cheng Ho and his deputy Wang Ching-hung, as ordered by the emperor, proceeded with their journey to the Western Ocean. Well furnished with treasure and accompanied by more than 27,800 officers and men, they sailed in sixty-two giant ships, each of which measured forty-four *chang* [ca. 517 feet] in length and eighteen *chang* [ca. 212 feet] in width. The ships left the Liuchia River [near modern Shanghai] for the sea and then sailed southward to Fukien wherefrom they proceeded with sails full-blown to Champa. From Champa the Chinese envoys visited one country after another. They read the imperial decree that demanded the submission of the kingdoms they visited and rewarded generously those rulers who agreed to submit. As for those who chose not to obey, force was used to assure their compliance.

In the ninth month of the fifth year of Yung-lo [1407] Cheng Ho returned to the capital and presented to the emperor tribute-bearing envoys from the kingdoms he had visited. The emperor was greatly pleased and granted titles and financial rewards to all of those who had been presented to him. Cheng Ho also brought back many prisoners of war, including the captured king of Palembang.

Palembang was formally known as Sanfuch'i whose ruler, a Chinese named Ch'en Tsu-yi, had been active as a pirate in the South Seas before he was captured by Cheng Ho. When Cheng Ho demanded his surrender, he said he would, but in secret he was planning to launch an attack upon Cheng Ho's ships. Once the perfidy was recognized, Cheng Ho attacked and won a decisive victory. Ch'en Tsu-yi was captured alive and later brought to Peking. He was executed shortly afterward.

In the ninth month of the sixth year of Yung-lo [1408] Cheng Ho sailed again for Ceylon. Upon his arrival, the king of Ceylon, a man named Alagakkonara, invited him to visit his city with fine promises. Once inside the city, Cheng Ho was presented with a demand for gold and silk; moreover, Alagakkonara had already ordered an attack on the Chinese ships. Taking advantage of the fact that practically all the Ceylonese troops had been out of the city for this attack, Cheng Ho personally led two thousand soldiers to attack the city itself. The surprise worked, and Alagakkonara and his family, together with many high-ranking officials, were captured alive. The Ceylonese troops hurried back to rescue their king, only to be routed by the Chinese. In the sixth month of the ninth year of Yung-lo [1411] the captured Ceylonese, including their king, were presented to the Chinese emperor for a determination of their fate. The emperor decided to forgive them and ordered them to be returned to Ceylon. By then all of Indochina had been pacified and brought under Chinese jurisdiction. Frightened by Chinese might, more and more kingdoms sent envoys to China to pay their tribute.

Cheng Ho served three emperors with distinction and conducted seven voyages altogether. Among the more than thirty kingdoms he had visited

Chapter 12

Trans-Asian

Contacts:

The Basis of a

World System

(1200–1450)

were the following: Champa, Java, Camboja, Palembang, Siam, Calicut, Malacca, Borneo, Sumatra, Aru, Cochin, Quilon, Chola, Cail, Jurfattan, Koyampadi, Ceylon, Lambri, Pahang, Kelantan, Hormus, Brawa, Maldives, Sunda, Mogedoxu, Malinde, Sana, Zufar, Juba, Bengal, Mecca, Lide, and Battak.[1] The amount of treasure he brought to China from these kingdoms was of course enormous, but the expense to China herself was even more staggering. Beginning in the Hsüan-teh period [1426–35] these kingdoms, occasionally, still sent tribute missions to China, but they could not be compared with the tribute missions of the Yung-lo period [1403–24] that were not only more sumptuous but also more frequent. By then Cheng Ho had become too old to undertake any strenuous task. Long after his death, however, his achievement was still so highly regarded that Chinese generals and admirals, whenever serving abroad, kept mentioning it as a way to impress foreigners. Even laymen spoke of the Seven Voyages of the Grand Eunuch as a most outstanding event of the Ming dynasty.

QUESTIONS TO CONSIDER

Filled with so many details, many of which seem obscure, this material can be overwhelming. But remember you are trying to discern the overall structure and nature of interregional contacts, not every detail. To that end, first familiarize yourself with Source 1, the historical map of the area. Then, as you look at each source, ask how it speaks to the basic questions posed at the start of this chapter: How extensive was this trans-Asian system? And does it constitute a significant step in world integration?

Source 2 gives a broad view of the overland silk route in the early four-teenth century. Its author, Francis Balducci Pegolotti, did not travel the Silk Road himself but, drawing on information from other European travelers, hoped to encourage his firm to enter the Asian trade, which other Italian merchants had found very lucrative. Notice how he views the enterprise from the perspective of a Mediterranean trader. From where did Pegolotti assume an Italian merchant party would begin? By what general route and using what conveyance would they travel? To whom might they turn for aid on the way besides the "moccols," or Mongols? What sort of capitalization and currency would such a party require? What trade goods does Pegolotti recommend securing? Finally, what can

1. Champa is part of modern Vietnam. Java, Palembang, Borneo, Sumatra, Aru, Lambri, Sunda, Lide, and Battak form part of modern Indonesia. Camboja is modern Cambodia; Siam is modern Thailand. Calicut, Cochin, Quilon, Chola, Cail, Jurfattan, Koyampadi, Maldives, and Bengal are located on the coast of modern India. Malacca, Pahanq, and Kelantan are located in the Malay Peninsula. Hormus is located at the head of the Persian Gulf; Sana, Zufar, and Mecca are located on the Arabian Peninsula. Brawa, Mogedoxu, Malinde, and Juba are located on the eastern coast of Africa.

you infer from his account about the ease and extent of overland trade?

Source 3 gives another European view of travel across Inner Asia. Its author, William of Rubruck, though a Fleming from one of Europe's most commercially advanced areas, was not interested in trade. He was a Christian monk whom Louis IX of France secretly sent to Asia in 1253 to negotiate an alliance with the Mongols. Louis was directing a crusade against the Muslim Mamluks of Egypt and hoped to secure aid from the Mongols, who were already assailing the Caspian frontiers of the Muslim world. William's immediate goal was to sound out a local Mongol ruler called Sartak or Sartach, who governed the Crimean area for Batu, head of the western khanate of Kypchak. But ultimately he crossed the whole of Asia to meet Mongka Khan at his Mongolian capital, Karakorum. On his arrival he found he was not the only European emissary there. The pope, too, had sent people to seek an alliance with Mongka Khan against Muslims. How would you characterize this kind of interregional contact? But look from whom William sought advice on his way. Like the merchants who helped him, he used the Pontus or Black Sea as his gateway to Asia. Mongol fighting with the Abbasid caliphate had already shifted the western end of trade northward from Persia and the eastern Mediterranean to this locale, allowing Greek, Armenian, and Italian traders in the area to take advantage of the situation. In this context, note William's comments about goods flowing into the area from Russia and Turkey.

Constantinople was the chief Western emporium for the Asian trade, but William outfitted his party for overland travel at Soldaia, a city on the southern shore of the Crimean Peninsula. His first goal, Matrica or Taman on the northeastern coast of the Black Sea at the mouth of the Tanais (Don) River, was the true embarkation point to the East. An Italian colony outside the city of Azak (modern Azov), it served as a key transshipment at the western end of the Silk Road during the Mongol era. Check what Pergolotti, who called it Tana, says about Taman. How long, judging from William's date entries, did it take to reach this point from Constantinople? Beyond lay open steppe or grassland, running past Batu's headquarters on the Etilia (Volga) River all the way to Mongolia. William offers a clear picture of his traveling party: six ox-carts for goods, five riding horses, two companions, a slave boy, and Abdullah (his dragoman, or Turkic interpreter and guide), plus two caravaneers. Compare this party with Pergolotti's ideal merchant group. What does the size of such parties suggest about security along the way? Both sources indicate that ox- or camel-carts provided the usual conveyance for goods across Inner Asia. Look at Source 4, which illustrates such a vehicle. How much cargo do you think six such carts could hold? What kinds of goods would most likely be shipped this way over long distances?

Conditions at the eastern end of Inner Asia can be glimpsed in Source 5, a travel diary kept by a Chinese named Li Zhichang. Li accompanied

[341]

Chapter 12

Trans-Asian

Contacts:

The Basis of a

World System

(1200–1450)

a famous religious master on a trip in 1221 to meet Chingis Khan, the founder of the Mongol Empire, who had summoned him to an audience to find out more about the Chinese doctrine of Taoism. When their party arrived in Mongolia, however, they discovered that the khan had already left Karakorum to begin his Inner Asian conquests. So, equipped with carts, a cavalry escort, and the Mongol guide Chinkai, they set out along a northern leg of the old Silk Road for Transoxiana above modern Afghanistan, where they caught up with Chingis Khan near the city of Samarkand.

Li's party, of course, traveled on a religious mission. Unlike William of Rubruck, who a generation later tried without success to interest Mongka Khan in his beliefs, Li's master not only wins a hearing but inspires his host to record his teachings. Look for other indications of the religious contacts in the sources that follow. Pay particular attention to references to Islam. The Mongols showed little interest in this religion, but as you can see here, it prevailed all along the Silk Road from the Black Sea to China. By the thirteenth century, in fact, most residents across this region were Turkic-speaking Muslims like the Uighurs who hosted Li's party en route.

Li points out, however, that other peoples were moving among them. Who were they, and what did they contribute to the area? The large scale movements of people in the Mongol era apparently accelerated the sharing of products and technology across Eurasia. In this context, think

about Li's keen interest in what to him were the exotic foods and products of the far west. Notice his remarks about grape wine, "Persian" linen, and cotton, a fiber still so rare in China that he termed it "sheep's wool planted in the ground." Li's attention to new plants and foodstuffs has parallels in other sources. What does it imply about contemporary contacts? His comment about the local Turkic farmers' delight in Chinese buckets also suggests something about the way technology, too, may have been spreading. Do you find similar evidence elsewhere?

Li's destination, Samarkand, was once the greatest mercantile center and crossroads in all Inner Asia. But note what Li says about its condition at the time of his visit. Dislocations late in the thirteenth century led to further decline in the overland trade, shifting commerce and travel southward to sea routes across the Indian Ocean. Source 6 suggests how this shift affected the western side of this maritime sphere. Because a rebellion by the Mongol ruler of Jagadai closed travel across Inner Asia, John had to make his way east by the sea route. It took him years to reach his destination, Cambalec or Khanbaligh, the new "city of the Khan," built by Kubilai Khan during the 1260s to replace Karakorum. In another letter sent back to Europe from Khanbaligh in 1305, John recommends the land route to China over the sea lanes. It takes only five or six months to cross, he says, and is "safer and more secure." By contrast he finds the sea passage "long and perilous since it involves two sea voyages, the first of which is about the distance of Acre [in Palestine] from the province of Provence, but the second is like the distance between Acre and England, and it may happen that the journey is scarcely completed in two years."[2]

Source 6, John's earlier letter, tells what he found during the first stage of his trip from the Middle East to India. It gives a general survey of Upper India—the area along the western shore of India from the Indus down to the rich commercial cities of the Malabar coast. Southward lay Lower India, then considered a different realm. As John indicates, travelers reached these lands by sailing across the "Sea of India" from Ormes (Hormuz) on the Persian Gulf. Pay special attention to what he says about the sailing seasons that prevailed along this leg and the risks incurred by those who ignored them. What other hazards besides off-season gales does he mention as a danger to mariners in this area? Despite such risks, many ships must have been sailing this route judging from John's claim of no less than sixty perishing during the year of his stay. Most were probably small Arab dhows like the one shown as Source 7. Notice which of these caught John's eye. As he remarks, such ships sailed to western India for cargoes of aromatics, fruits, spices, and pears. How much of such cargo do you think these dhows could safely carry?

2. These remarks appear in a "Second Letter of John of Monte Corvino" translated in Raymond Dawson, *Mission to Asia* (New York: Harper Torchbooks, 1965), p. 226.

These exotic goods attracted traders to the Malabar coast not only from Hormuz and western Asia, but from China and Africa, too. Relations between this area and the East African coast, which lay due west, were so common, that the region around the Horn of Africa near modern Ethiopia was called Middle India. Fed by goods from several large empires in the interior as well as Aden on the Red Sea, coastal East Africa formed an important adjunct to the India trade. In Source 8 Marco Polo cites its commercial significance, and particularly that of Madagascar and Zanzibar (Zenzibar, in the selection), on his return to Europe along the water route in 1293 or 1294. Notice what goods the area supplied—and absorbed. Where do you suppose the "silks" bartered here were obtained? Marco Polo's comments on Zanzibar's black inhabitants shows that the world of the Indian Ocean included people of many types. His depictions, of course, betray obvious racial bias. Do such feelings infect any of the other sources? How often do the source writers take care to distinguish racial traits? Do these seem as important to them as ethnic or religious differences?

Religion certainly caught the eye of some. Note which religions figure in these accounts. By the thirteenth century, Islam had spread throughout the entire trade area, and Muslim communities could be found in almost every port from Mogadishu on the African coast to Zaitun in China. John of Corvino observes the "many Saracens," or Arabs, who lived along

[343]

Chapter 12

Trans-Asian

Contacts:

The Basis of a

World System

(1200–1450)

the Malabar coast in India. They were probably traders and their descendants who settled there permanently to work as brokers for the seasonal influx of Arab and Persian merchants. Though he declares that they had "great influence," he remains strangely silent about why. He nowhere explains, for example, that "the Lord of all India" was a Turkic Muslim whose sultanate of Delhi ruled the northern part of the subcontinent under the nominal authority of the Abbasid caliphate.

By contrast, the fourteenth-century Arab traveler from North Africa, Ibn Batuta, left a detailed picture of Islam's impact across the Indian Ocean. As he notes in Source 9, an account written near the end of his career, Muslims lived all along its coasts. Notice not only what he says about resident Muslims—their homelands, numbers, and occupations—but what he records about their efforts to spread their beliefs. For all that he extols the wealth of Muslim merchants from Yemen and Persia, Ibn Batuta deems the Chinese "the richest people in the world." During the thirteenth and fourteenth centuries, they served as principal carriers in the eastern half of the trade between India and the Pacific. In a passage not given here, Ibn Batuta praises Zaitun or Chuanzhou, China's chief emporium on the eastern end of the trade, as "one of the finest in the world" where as many as one hundred great ships docked at once.[3] Note his reaction to Chinese ship-

ping, which represented the most advanced maritime technology of the time.

Chinese seamen already used the compass and other modern navigational devices on the long and difficult run to India. And the Arabs, who introduced their innovations westward, regarded the Chinese ocean-going junks as the largest and safest ships of the time. Compare Ibn Batuta's description with the illustration in Source 10. Consider how much more such ships carried than the small dhows common in the western half of the trade realm or the carts and pack animals on overland routes. According to Marco Polo, who also praised Chinese ships, the largest had crews of three hundred men and carried "from five to six thousand baskets, or mat bags of pepper."[4] What does this suggest about the relative volume and wealth of trade within different parts of the system?

The huge ocean-going ships of China afforded its rulers unrivaled sea power. Kubilai Khan, the greatest of all the Mongol emperors, quickly grasped its potential, sending fleets of captured junks to invade both Japan and Indonesia at the end of the thirteenth century. Though the invasions failed, his armadas demonstrated the value of large, state-maintained navies. During the subsequent Ming dynasty, which restored native rule in China, the Yongle emperor thus revived an imperial fleet. Originally built for an invasion of Vietnam, this armada later projected

3. Quoted in *Travels of Ibn Batuta*, ed. and trans. Samuel Lee (New York: Burt Franklin, n.d.), p. 213.

4. These remarks appear in *The Travels of Marco Polo*, edited by Manuel Komroff (New York: Liveright Publishing Corp., 1953), p. 261.

Ming power far abroad when its commander, Zheng He, convinced the emperor to let him sail the convoy to the Indian Ocean on the seven voyages of 1402–1433 mentioned earlier.

The last document here, Source 11, gives the highlights of these voyages into the "Western" or Indian Ocean. Notice what it says about the motive behind the expeditions. Given this purpose, why do you suppose Zheng He made the Indian Ocean his destination? In thinking about this question, consider what ports he visited and what they collectively represented at the time of his voyages. In addition to the extent of their circuits, note the scale of these fleets. How do they compare with the later efforts of European states to send ships to the Indies? Think what outfitting fleets of this magnitude for voyages of several years must have entailed. Here again is some indication of China's economic stature at the time as well as its potential maritime power.

EPILOGUE

For reasons that remain unclear, this early world system, flourishing in the thirteenth century, began to disintegrate toward the end of the fourteenth. Various conjectures have been made about the possible causes, but much more study needs to be done before any conclusions can be drawn. Clearly the break-up and collapse of the Mongol imperium in the mid-fourteenth century were important contributing factors. A vast state, the Mongol Empire at its height foreshadowed the later Western empires of the modern world system in both its transcontinental size and its pluralism. It not only unified Inner Asia politically, making overland travel and trade across the whole breadth of the continent relatively safe, but stimulated new levels of interaction among the peoples all around its periphery. One unfortunate result of this heightened contact, however, was a diffusion of diseases. Mongol invaders appear to have spread bubonic plague to China and the Crimea, from which places it spread to the rest of Asia and Europe during the mid-fourteenth century. Decimating whole cities, particularly in Europe where it was known as the Black Death, this devastating disease not only weakened Mongol power but speeded the decline of Central Asia and its ancient trade centers.

Changes in China, too, contributed to the fragmentation of the system. Perhaps the wealthiest of its regions and its largest source of trade, China may well have been the single most crucial component in the trans-Asian system. Because of internal economic changes and Ming policies, however, Chinese trade and contact with the rest of the system declined dramatically in the second half of the fifteenth century. The Ming decision to abandon its fleets may have been decisive in this regard. The lure of unprotected shipping and rich ports

Chapter 12

Trans-Asian

Contacts:

The Basis of a

World System

(1200–1450)

along the China coast attracted huge bands of international pirates. Rather than build another navy to police its off-shore waters, the Ming regime decided to close its ports, fortify the coastline, and withdraw into semi-isolation to discourage pirate attacks. Along with shifts in domestic markets, this closure policy drastically cut back Chinese foreign commerce, capital, and shipping, depriving the Indies trade of key components without which it probably could not continue as before.

Despite these changes, interregional trans-Asian trade and relations did not end abruptly in the fifteenth century. India still remained an important heart of widespread commerce. But the intensity as well as the frequency of economic, political, and cultural contacts across Asia evaporated. As traditional connections weakened or shifted to new alignments, the network of trade and travel centered around Central Asia and the Indian Ocean slowly dissolved. When Vasco da Gama's two Portuguese ships appeared in the Indian Ocean in 1498 after rounding Africa from the west, the process was already well underway. By then, of course, Christopher Columbus's misguided attempt to reach the Indies by sailing westward from Spain in 1492 had put Europeans in contact with the Americas. In the age of European colonialism that followed, a new world system straddling the North Atlantic soon emerged, gradually displacing the older trans-Asian one. Its once thriving cities were relegated to peripheral status in emergent empires centered in Atlantic ports like Lisbon, Amsterdam, and London. Yet in the early stages of building their own modern empires, Portugal, Holland, and Britain all coveted control of the Indies, attesting to the value of this once great hub even in its decline.

CHAPTER THIRTEEN

THE COURT CHRONICLE: THE MAKING OF

OFFICIAL HISTORY (800–1400)

On February 15, 1990, historian Warren I. Cohen resigned as chair of the U.S. State Department's advisory committee on the publication of official documents concerning United States foreign relations. "The State Department," Cohen charged, was "playing games with history." He believed this was particularly significant because his committee had been instructed to assure the historical accuracy of the official history of American foreign policy. That record, Professor Cohen argued, was being altered by American officials who insisted on removing important documents that might suggest the United States was less than honest and forthright in dealing with other countries. "I could not protect the integrity" of the official history, Cohen argued when he resigned.[1]

1. The immediate issue concerned documents relating to U.S. involvement in the 1953 *coup d'état* in Iran. Professor Cohen explained his position in an opinion column in *The New York Times*, May 8, 1990, p. A29.

That an official version of history should be completely honest and accurate, no matter how it might reflect on its sponsor, might at first seem unusual. After all, as Professor Cohen also noted, "contempt . . . has long greeted most of [the] foreign equivalents" of the State Department's documentary official history. Indeed, skepticism about any official history is often great. During the Cold War Americans came to distrust any historical account published in the Soviet Union and frequently those prepared by other governments as well.

Yet official histories—of many individuals and institutions beyond governments—have long been recorded in a wide variety of societies. Apart from political disagreements with particular governments and personal rivalries with other groups and individuals, is there any reason to be cynical about official histories? There are many motivations for creating such accounts, and many ways to do so. These records also serve a variety of purposes. Certainly modern historians want to look for the

Chapter 13
The Court
Chronicle:
The Making of
Official History
(800–1400)

truth in the sources they use, attempting to find all the facts—pleasant or not—concerning the people and societies they are writing about. Can they find that truth in official histories? Should they expect to?

In this chapter you will be looking at a variety of official histories written many years ago about a number of governments and rulers from various countries and cultures. Many of these take a form known as "court chronicles," formal records of the accomplishments of particular rulers and the people around them who comprised their governments. Why and how were these histories created? What was their intended function without the societies that created them? And in what ways do they represent the truth about the past of the societies that created them?

BACKGROUND

Human groups have long sought to understand and explain their past, to shape a collective consciousness of their common existence. Myths, legends, and folktales have all been a part of establishing this sense of historical place in all societies. Only gradually, though, have attempts been made to create formal accounts of the past, what we are more likely to call "history" in the modern sense. These efforts have occurred in societies with strong oral traditions as well as in those with long-established written traditions.

Among the former, the nature of oral traditions has largely been determined by the social and political structures of the societies in which they develop. In small villages and extended family groups, growth of historical traditions has been minimal. The small scale of these societies—in terms of both geography and population—limited the historical depth possible, or even necessary, in their oral accounts. Only as larger societies and states developed among peoples having no writing systems did oral traditions of full historical importance appear. Few of these traditions, however, initially had the force of official history.

Among peoples having well-developed systems of writing, the situation is somewhat similar, although historical writing often emerged from the literary traditions of such societies. In western civilization, for example, the Greek writer Thucydides is generally viewed as one of the originators of historical writing. However, neither Thucydides nor any of his Greek successors were writing what we would call official history. Indeed, Thucydides—an Athenian—had a much broader historical design than simply narrating the past of his native city. Rather, he saw history unfolding along the careful patterns evident in Greek drama. Frequently he molded the words of various people in his histories, transforming what he had heard them say or had been told about their views into the rhetorical patterns of a classic Greek tragedy. In this way Thucydides shaped his accounts of the past into a uniquely Greek understanding of history.

For many centuries after Thucydides, other European writers of history followed similar patterns in their work. Among these was the Roman historian Tacitus who, like his Greek predecessor, was most interested in shaping the past into a distinctly Roman history. For Tacitus, however, it was not a literary tradition, but rather the political values of the Roman republic, that shaped his historical accounts. This change in emphasis, though subtle, would help set a tone for the development of later official histories.

In both oral and written traditions, many early accounts of the past took the form of stories, a kind of entertainment as much as history, which also was intended to have important social and political purposes. Indeed, some of the accounts that we will consider here as court, or royal, chronicles have been described by some historians as legend or even as the work of the storyteller's art. Yet other evidence—from archaeology, ancient coins, inscriptions, accounts from other peoples—has frequently made it clear that at least some portions of these chronicles represent what we might call historical truth.

The transformation of these accounts—from story to chronicle to a kind of official history—is what you will be trying to understand. Many of the societies from which we derive such court chronicles were growing much more rapidly than their own people had anticipated, frequently through the conquest of other peoples. In such situations, it became vital to have a record of how this expansion came about. As these societies grew, some of them into states, many of the inhabitants lived farther and farther from the centers of political power and the creators of social norms.

This distance was frequently physical. The more people who lived in the society, the greater the geographic area over which they were spread; access to political and social centers was necessarily limited. Perhaps more importantly, the remoteness people felt from such centers was often related to the fact that these states and societies included peoples who were ethnically different, frequently spoke different languages, and sometimes practiced different religions. For many of these peoples it was extremely hard to feel close to the centers of social and political power as well.

It is also important to remember that for the whole of Afro-Eurasia (or what is sometimes called the Old World), the era beginning in the ninth or tenth century was a time of increasing interactions between peoples. There had long been contact between different cultures and peoples, but following the century of Islamic expansion, such meetings between various groups increased dramatically. Initially, these contacts may have involved the exchange of ambassadors or the extension of economic relationships and, as a result, greatly expanded trade. Frequently the parties later became less than friendly, and strained relations often led to extreme hostility and even warfare.

All of the chronicles you will read in the Evidence section come from this period, and all reveal a good deal about the changes taking place both inside and outside the societies that produced them. Some of these ac-

Chapter 13
The Court
Chronicle:
The Making of
Official History
(800–1400)

counts were built from oral traditions and were only later committed to written form; others were initially produced as written documents. All of them were intended not as accounts to be preserved in libraries for scholarly historians and their students, but were instead produced for public consumption, at least at home.

Needless to say, the continued growth of states and societies led to a proliferation of such chronicles, representing both the histories of new political units and alternate versions of the past in some large empires and kingdoms. Many contain what we might best call competing truths, different versions of the same events.

Increasingly these overlapping chronicles served their subjects and sponsors less and less well, requiring further forms of verification. In this environment, many rulers turned to keeping a host of records to document the conditions and accomplishments of their reigns. These collections, frequently written but always larger and more complex than the original chronicles, may be seen as ushering in a new development in the study of the past, the beginning of modern history as we know it. Yet even in those circumstances, as we noted at the beginning of this chapter, the idea of an "official history" has never quite been lost.

THE METHOD

The first source you will read, and one of the first historical accounts we might properly consider a court chronicle, was the work of a man known as Einhard, the private secretary to Charles, King of the Franks. Einhard was born in 770 in a region along the River Main and educated at the monastery at Fulda, in present-day Germany. He served King Charles, whom we also know as Charlemagne or Charles the Great, in several political offices, including director of public works. Perhaps most important, he became the king's private secretary, preparing correspondence and keeping records in Latin. He also served Charles's successor and, during his final years prior to his death in 830, served as abbot of

several monasteries within the Frankish kingdom.

The chronicle Einhard produced concerning Charlemagne (Source 1) is an excellent example of the form and an important, but by no means the only, source concerning the many achievements of that king. Charles successfully consolidated a number of peoples who had once been united under the Roman Empire into a fairly large empire in Western Europe. He saw himself as not only a political ruler, but also as a servant (at least in the religious sense) of the church and a patron of education and other cultural activities within his kingdom. That such a ruler might inspire an "official history" such as Einhard's chronicle is not extraordinary.

About two centuries later another political figure, Duke William of Normandy (in what is now western

France), also embarked on a campaign of political consolidation, reinforcing his claims for control of England from his base on the French mainland. His successful efforts are known as the Norman Conquest and resulted in a new government and vastly altered social and political system for England and subsequently the other peoples of the British Isles. His conquest—and most especially his spectacular victory at the Battle of Hastings in 1066—though known from a variety of sources, has but one complete chronicle, that of William of Poitiers. Source 2 consists of excerpts from that chronicle.

William, the chronicler, was Norman by birth but was educated in the monastery at Poitiers south of his native Normandy, where he learned to read and write Latin. Returning to his homeland, he served as a soldier and later became a priest. He was appointed as Duke William's personal chaplain but, despite his military background, did not accompany the duke's forces on their famous expedition to England. He was nonetheless an eager student of that campaign and certainly discussed it with many of the participants. He completed writing his chronicle about five years after the events he describes.

It took much longer for the stories of Mongol leaders in eastern and central Asia to find their way into written form, sometimes into Mongol script, but always into the language of their perpetual adversaries, the Chinese. The emergence in the twelfth century of the renowned Mongol leader Temujin—better known as Chingis Khan—elevated many of

these stories to the level of chronicle, outlining the life and many of the early achievements of the great leader. These accounts were clearly intended to inspire Temujin's successors; in this sense they became a kind of official history, helping to unite the sometimes fractious Mongol clans. Just as certainly, these accounts were *not* meant for other peoples, particularly the Chinese, who undoubtedly would have scorned the Mongol culture revealed in these stories as uncompromisingly barbaric. Hence, this account has become known to us as *The Secret History of the Mongols*, Source 3.

In a similar vein, the traditional chroniclers of West Africa—known as *griots*—have a saying: "All true learning should be a secret."[2] African accounts of the lives of kings were nevertheless well known as official histories, and the epics they told and retold during impressive performances on virtually every important occasion were very much like the royal chronicles of the European rulers. To some extent, they may have been even more significant, for in the societies of West Africa the accounts of *griots* served not only as chronicle, but also as the sum total of all official record-keeping for the societies and states of the region. Their spoken accounts were handed down from generation to generation, frequently with a precision that amazes those not accustomed to this form of recording the past.

As is the case elsewhere, the greater and more important the subject of

2. Quoted in D. T. Niane, *Sundiata: An Epic of Old Mali* (London: Longman, 1979), p. viii.

Chapter 13

The Court

Chronicle:

The Making of

Official History

(800–1400)

these spoken royal chronicles, the more likely the account would have survived into the present. That is surely true regarding Sundiata, one of the great rulers of the West African kingdom of Mali and the architect of its initial rise to prominence during the early thirteenth century. His story, recounted in Source 4, provided a kind of founding history for Mali and its successors. It has also become a folk legend throughout West Africa, embodying elements of traditional African culture and the more recent allegiance to Islamic values. And Sundiata himself has come to be regarded by many historians as comparable to Charlemagne in his political and cultural contributions to the consolidation of peoples in West Africa.

On the other hand, the outstanding achievement of another important African ruler—the fourteenth-century Ethiopian emperor, Amda Seyon (meaning "pillar of Zion")—was not in creating and consolidating his power, but in protecting his people from continuing Islamic attacks. Ethiopia, a Christian state since the fourth century, had become increasingly isolated from the rest of the Christian world following the Islamic conquest of Arabia (across the Red Sea) and North Africa in the eighth century. In addition, various non-Christian elements thrived within Ethiopia despite efforts of the church to suppress them. This situation had reached a crisis point during the twelfth century, and the defense of the kingdom that followed, inaugurated by Amda Seyon, is known as the heroic age of Ethiopian warfare.

That spirit is certainly conveyed by the unknown chronicler who produced a record of Amda Seyon's reign, probably the first contemporary court chronicle of any Ethiopian monarch. We know very little about the circumstances surrounding the origin of this account (Source 5). It was almost certainly written by a clergyman, since almost no one outside the church was at that time able to write (as was also true in Europe). The vivid detail and personal comments of the chronicler have led some modern historians to insist that it must be the creation of a participant in the events, or at least a person, like William of Potiers, with immediate access to eyewitnesses. The importance of this chronicle, and of its subject, are certainly evident in the pattern of subsequent Ethiopian official records, many of which were kept by leaders of the Ethiopian church rather than within the court itself, probably because they were written in Ge'ez, the Ethiopian liturgical language, which served similar religious and political functions as Latin did in Europe.

Certainly you will notice a marked difference between these five chronicles, created over several centuries. Read all of them carefully and take note of all the differences you find, particularly in how and why they were created. In some ways, those differences may reflect the varied cultures from which the chronicles come. Try to distinguish between those cultural factors and matters of organization, presentation, and purpose. Of course, it is important to consider the similarities among the several accounts as well, and to identify the common features that place them all in the "official history" genre.

Modern historians, in evaluating any documents (but especially official histories), also try to determine the reasons why a particular document was created, by whom, and for what purpose. Keep those questions in mind as well during your reading. Some of the narrators are clearer about the reasons for undertaking their work than others, but are they genuine in their professions of their motives? Do any of them have personal interests at stake in the stories they tell about the past? On what sources do they base their chronicles? Understanding those issues may also

help you come to grips with the central question of this chapter: In what ways do court chronicles represent the truth about the past of the societies that created them?

Finally, think about the people, primarily the rulers, whom the chronicles were meant to glorify. Were they people of extraordinary standing? Why? Do they merit that standing in your mind because of the chronicles? Would others hearing or reading these accounts reach the same conclusions? What would be the effect of these chronicles upon audiences in their own cultures, at the time they were written? Consider what is more important to a society: telling a story based on truth, or creating an account that exalts a leader.

THE EVIDENCE

Source 1 from Einhard, The Life of Charlemagne, *trans. Samuel E. Turner (New York: American Book Company, 1880), pp. 11–13, 21–22, 40–47, 56, 58–59.*

1. From Einhard, *The Life of Charlemagne,* 9th century

Since I have taken upon myself to narrate the public and private life, and no small part of the deeds, of my lord and foster-father, the most excellent and most justly renowned King Charles, I have condensed the matter into as brief a form as possible. I have been careful not to omit any facts that could come to my knowledge. . . . I see no reason why I should refrain from entering upon a task of this kind, since no man can write with more accuracy than I of events that took place about me, and of facts concerning which I had personal knowledge. . . .

I would rather commit my story to writing, and hand it down to posterity in partnership with others, so to speak, than to suffer the most glorious life of

Chapter 13

The Court

Chronicle:

The Making of

Official History

(800–1400)

this most excellent king, the greatest of all the princes of his day, and his illustrious deeds, hard for men of later times to imitate, to be wrapt in the darkness of oblivion.

But there are still other reasons, neither unwarrantable nor insufficient, in my opinion, that urge me to write on this subject, namely, the care that King Charles bestowed upon me in my childhood, and my constant friendship with himself and his children after I began to take up my abode at court. In this way he strongly endeared me to himself, and made me greatly his debtor as well in death as in life; so that were I, unmindful of the benefits conferred upon me, to keep silence concerning the most glorious and illustrious deeds of a man who claims so much at my hands, and suffer his life to lack due eulogy and written memorial, as if he had never lived, I should deservedly appear ungrateful. . . .

It would be folly, I think, to write a word concerning Charles's birth and infancy, or even his boyhood, for nothing has ever been written on the subject, and there is no one alive now who can give information of it. Accordingly, I have determined to pass that by as unknown, and to proceed at once to treat of his character, his deeds, and such other facts of his life as are worth telling and setting forth, and shall first give an account of his deeds at home and abroad, then of his character and pursuits, and lastly of his administration and death, omitting nothing worth knowing or necessary to know.

[*The chronicle then recounts many of the
wars fought by Charlemagne and his
armies to secure his kingdom.*]

He so largely increased the Frank kingdom, which was already great and strong when he received it at his father's hands, that more than double its former territory was added to it. The authority of the Franks was formerly confined to that part of Gaul included between the Rhine and the Loire, the Ocean and the Balearic Sea; to that part of Germany which is inhabited by the so-called Eastern Franks, and is bounded by Saxony and the Danube, the Rhine and the Saale—this stream separates the Thuringians from the Sorabians; and to the country of the Alemanni and Bavarians. By the wars above mentioned . . . he vanquished and made tributary all the wild and barbarous tribes dwelling in Germany between the Rhine and the Vistula, the Ocean and the Danube, all of which speak very much the same language, but differ widely from one another in customs and dress. The chief among them are the Welatabians, the Sorabians, the Abodriti, and the Bohemians, and he had to make war upon these; but the rest, by far the larger number, submitted to him of their own accord.

He added to the glory of his reign by gaining the good-will of several kings and nations; so close, indeed, was the alliance that he contracted with Alphonso, King of Galicia and Asturias, that the latter, when sending letters or ambassadors to Charles, invariably styled himself his man. His munificence won the kings of the Scots also to pay such deference to his wishes that they never gave him any other title than lord, or themselves than subjects and slaves: there are letters from them extant in which these feelings in his regard are expressed. His relations with Aaron, King of the Persians, who ruled over almost the whole of the East, India excepted, were so friendly that this prince preferred his favour to that of all the kings and potentates of the earth, and considered that to him alone marks of honour and munificence were due. Accordingly, when the ambassadors sent by Charles to visit the most holy sepulchre and place of resurrection of our Lord and Saviour presented themselves before him with gifts, and made known their master's wishes, he not only granted what was asked, but gave possession of that holy and blessed spot. When they returned, he despatched his ambassadors with them, and sent magnificent gifts, besides stuffs, perfumes, and other rich products of the Eastern lands. . . .

This King [Charlemagne] who showed himself so great in extending his empire and subduing foreign nations, and was constantly occupied with plans to that end, undertook also very many works calculated to adorn and benefit his kingdom, and brought several of them to completion. Among these, the most deserving of mention are the basilica of the Holy Mother of God at Aix-la-Chapelle, built in the most admirable manner, and a bridge over the Rhine at Mayence, half a mile long, the breadth of the river at this point. This bridge was destroyed by fire the year before Charles died, but, owing to his death so soon after, could not be repaired, although he had intended to rebuild it in stone. He began two palaces of beautiful workmanship—one near his manor called Ingelheim, not far from Mayence; the other at Nimeguen, on the Waal, the stream that washes the south side of the island of the Batavians. But, above all, sacred edifices were the object of his care throughout his whole kingdom; and whenever he found them falling to ruin from age, he commanded the priests and fathers who had charge of them to repair them, and made sure by commissioners that his instructions were obeyed. He also fitted out a fleet for the war with the Northmen [Vikings]; the vessels required for this purpose were built on the rivers that flow from Gaul and Germany into the Northern Ocean. Moreover, since the Northmen continually overran and laid waste the Gallic and German coasts, he caused watch and ward to be kept in all the harbours, and at the mouths of rivers large enough to admit the entrance of vessels, to prevent the enemy from disembarking; and in the South, in Narbonensis and Septimania, and along the whole coast of Italy as far as Rome, he took the same precautions against the Moors, who had recently begun their piratical practices. Hence, Italy suffered no great harm in his time at the hands of the Moors, nor Gaul and Germany from the Northmen, save that the Moors got possession of the Etruscan town of Civita Vecchia by treachery, and sacked it, and the Northmen harried some of the islands of Frisia off the Germany coast.

[355]

Chapter 13
The Court
Chronicle:
The Making of
Official History
(800–1400)

[*Here the chronicle discusses many of Charlemagne's "great qualities."*]

He liked foreigners, and was at great pains to take them under his protection. There were often so many of them, both in the palace and the kingdom, that they might reasonably have been considered a nuisance; but he, with his broad humanity, was very little disturbed by such annoyances, because he felt himself compensated for these great inconveniences by the praises of his generosity and the reward of high renown.

Charles was large and strong, and of lofty stature, though not disproportionately tall. . . .

He used to wear the national, that is to say, the Frank, dress . . . and he always had a sword girt about him, usually one with a gold or silver hilt and belt; he sometimes carried a jewelled sword, but only on great feast-days or at the reception of ambassadors from foreign nations. . . . On great feast-days he made use of embroidered clothes, and shoes bedecked with precious stones; his cloak was fastened by a golden buckle, and he appeared crowned with a diadem of gold and gems: but on other days his dress varied little from the common dress of the people.

Source 2 from David C. Douglas and George W. Greenaway, eds., English Historical Documents, 1042–1189 *(New York: Oxford University Press, 1953), pp. 218–219, 223–225, 227–231.*

2. From William of Poitiers, *The Deeds of William, Duke of the Normans and King of the English,* late 11th century

[*King Edward of England had named William, Duke of Normandy, as his successor. The chronicle records that Edward, nearing death, sent his subject Harold to Normandy to confirm William as heir to the throne. Harold, having delivered the message and then sworn loyalty to William as the future king, returned to England.*]

There came the unwelcome report that the land of England had lost its king, and that Harold had been crowned in his stead. This insensate Englishman did not wait for the public choice, but breaking his oath, and with the support of a few ill-disposed partisans, he seized the throne of the best of kings on the very day of his funeral, and when all the people were bewailing their loss. . . . Duke William therefore having taken counsel with his men resolved to avenge the insult by force of arms, and to regain his inheritance by war. This he determined despite the fact that some of the greatest magnates of Normandy sought to dissuade him from the enterprise, considering it to be too difficult and beyond the resources of Normandy. . . . "God gives wisdom to the pious" has said one skilled in divinity, and the duke had acted piously since his childhood, so all obeyed him in whatsoever he ordered unless they were reluctantly forced to admit an overriding necessity. It would be tedious to tell in detail how by his prudent acts ships were made, arms and troops, provisions and other equipment assembled for war, and how the enthusiasm of the whole of Normandy was directed towards this enterprise. . . .

[*The chronicle then records that, while preparing for war, Duke William also sought a peaceful solution with Harold. When his entreaties for peace were ignored, William led his Norman forces across the Channel and invaded England.*]

The duke ordered a certain monk of Fécamp to carry this message forthwith to Harold: "It is not with temerity nor unjustly but after deliberation and in defence of right that I have crossed the sea into this country. My lord and kinsman, King Edward, made me the heir of this kingdom even as Harold himself has testified; and he did so because of the great honours and rich benefits conferred upon him and his brother and followers by me. . . . He acted thus because among all his acquaintance he held me to be the best capable of supporting him during his life and of giving just rule to the kingdom after his death. . . . He sent me Harold himself to Normandy that in my presence he might personally take the oath which his father and the others had sworn in my absence. While he was on his way to me Harold fell into a perilous captivity from which he was rescued by my firmness and prudence. He made himself my man by a solemn act of homage, and with his hands in mine he pledged to me the security of the English kingdom. I am ready to submit my case against his for judgment either by the law of Normandy or better still by the law of England, whichever he may choose; and if according to truth and equity either the Normans or the English decide that the kingdom is his by right, let him possess it in peace. But if it be decided that in justice the kingdom should be mine, let him yield it up. Moreover, if he refuses these conditions, I do not think it right that either my men or his should perish in conflict over a quarrel that is none of their making. I am therefore ready to risk my life against his in single combat to decide whether the kingdom of England should by right be his or mine."

We have been careful to record all this speech in the duke's own words rather than our own, for we wish posterity to regard him with favour. Anyone may easily judge that he showed himself wise and just, pious and brave. . . .

[357]

Chapter 13

The Court

Chronicle:

The Making of

Official History

(800–1400)

When Harold advanced to meet the duke's envoy and heard this message he grew pale and for a long while remained as if dumb. And when the monk had asked more than once for a reply he first said: "We march at once," and then added, "We march to battle." The envoy besought him to reconsider this reply, urging that what the duke desired was a single combat and not the double slaughter of two armies. (For that good and brave man [Duke William] was willing to renounce something that was just and agreeable to him in order to prevent the death of many: he wished for Harold's head, knowing that it was defended by less fortitude than was his own, and that it was not protected by justice.) Then Harold, lifting up his face to heaven, exclaimed: "May the Lord decide this day between William and me, and may he pronounce which of us has the right." Thus, blinded by his lust for dominion, and in his fear unmindful of the wrongs he had committed, Harold made his conscience his judge and that to his own ruin. . . .

The duke summoned to arms all those within the camp, for the greater part of his host had gone out foraging. . . .

Although no one has reported to us in detail the short harangue with which on this occasion he increased the courage of his troops, we doubt not it was excellent. He reminded the Normans that with him for their leader they had always proved victorious in many perilous battles. He reminded them also of their fatherland, of its noble history, and of its great renown. "Now is the time," he said, "for you to show your strength, and the courage that is yours." "You fight," he added, "not merely for victory but also for survival. If you bear yourselves valiantly you will obtain victory, honour and riches. If not, you will be ruthlessly butchered, or else led ignominiously captive into the hands of pitiless enemies. . . . Men, worthy of the name, do not allow themselves to be dismayed by the number of their foes. . . . Only be bold so that nothing shall make you yield, and victory will gladden your hearts.". . .

It is not . . . our purpose, or within our capacity, to describe as they deserve the exploits of individuals. Even a master of narrative who had actually been present that day would find it very difficult to narrate them all in detail. For our part we shall hasten to the point at which, having ended our praise of William the count, we shall begin to describe the glory of William the king. . . .

Evening was now falling, and the English saw that they could not hold out much longer against the Normans. They knew they had lost a great part of their army, and they knew also that their king with two of his brothers and many of their greatest men had fallen. Those who remained were almost exhausted, and they realized that they could expect no more help. They saw the Normans, whose numbers had not been much diminished, attack them with even greater fury than at the beginning of the battle, as if the day's fighting had actually increased their vigour. Dismayed at the implacable bearing of the duke who spared none who came against him and whose prowess could not rest until victory was won, they began to fly as swiftly as they could, some on horseback, some on foot, some along the roads, but most over the trackless

[358]

country. Many lay on the ground bathed in blood, others who struggled to their feet found themselves to weak to escape, while a few although disabled were given strength to move by fear. Many left their corpses in the depths of the forest, and others were found by their pursuers lying by the roadside. . . .

It would have been just if wolves and vultures had devoured the flesh of these English who had rightly incurred their doom, and if the fields had received their unburied bones. But such a fate seemed cruel to the duke, and he allowed all who wished to do so to collect the bodies for burial. Then, having arranged for the honourable interment of his own men, he left Hastings in charge of a brave commander. . . . The duke then proceeded on his way and when he was in sight of London the principal citizens came out to meet him. They surrendered themselves and their city into his hand, like the citizens of Canterbury before them, and gave him such hostages as he asked. Further, the bishops and the lay magnates begged him to assume the crown. "We are accustomed to obey a king," they said, "and we desire to have a king as lord."

The duke therefore took counsel with those Normans who were of proven wisdom and fidelity, and explained to them why he was reluctant to accede to the demand of the English. Whilst the country was still unsettled and so much resistance remained to be crushed, he would prefer the peace of the kingdom to his crown. Besides, if God were to accord him this honour, he would wish to be crowned with his wife. It therefore seemed foolish to him to show undue haste in reaching for the peak of achievement. In short, he had no lust for dominion, and cherishing the sanctity of his marriage vows he desired to keep them holy.

His familiar counsellors, however, although they respected his motives and his wisdom, none the less urged him to take the crown, for they knew that this was the fervent desire of his whole army. . . . The duke, therefore, after further consideration, yielded to their fervent wishes in the hope that after he had begun to reign, men would hesitate to rebel against him, or if they did so, would be more easily crushed.

Source 3 from Arthur Waley, The Secret History of the Mongols and Other Pieces *(New York: Barnes and Noble, 1964), pp. 223–225, 227–232, 234–235, 237, 239–240, 245, 275–277, 279–280, 285.*

3. From *The Secret History of the Mongols,* early 13th century

During battles with the Tartars Yesugei [the father of Chingis Khan] took prisoner from among them two Tartars called Temujin-uge and Khori-bukha. At that time Yesugei's wife Ho'elun was with child and beside the Onan river

Chapter 13

The Court
Chronicle:
The Making of
Official History
(800–1400)

under the Deli'un-boldakh mountain,[3] she bore Temujin [the future Chingis Khan]. When he was born, he was grasping in his right hand a clot of blood in the shape of a knuckle-bone playing piece. It was because he was born at the time his father captured Temujin-uge that he was given the name Temujin. Ho'elun bore four sons, Temujin, Khasar, Khachi'un and Temuge, and one daughter called Temulun. When Temujin was eight Khasar was six, Khachi'un was four and Temuge was two. The girl Temulun was still in the cradle.

When Temjuin was eight his father . . . Yesugei said, "I am very ill. Who is at hand?" Old Charakha's son Monglik was there. Yesugei sent for him and said, "My sons are still young. . . . I was secretly poisoned by the Tartars. I am very ill indeed. I want you to see to it that your 'brothers' and 'sister-in-law' [Yesugei's sons and his wife Ho'elun] are properly looked after." No sooner had he said this than he died. . . .

Some time afterwards the Taichiu'ut Tarkhutai-kiriltukh said, "What about Temujin, his mother and her other children . . . ? No doubt by now, quick as the chicks of flying birds, they have grown their wings, quick as the young of running beasts they have filled out." He went with his friends to look at them, and when Temujin and his mother and brothers saw them coming, they were afraid. . . . The Taichi'uts shouted, "Bring your elder brother Temujin. We do not want any one else." This frightened Temujin. He got on to his horse and galloped off into the mountain woods. The Taichi'uts saw him go and caught up with him at the mountain called Tergune. Temujin bored his way into a thicket. The Taichi'uts could not get in, so they surrounded the wood and mounted guard. He spent three nights in the thicket and then, while he was dragging his horse out of it, his saddle fell to the ground straps and all. When he went back and looked at it both the breast-strap and the girdle-strap were still fastened. He said, "It is possible for a saddle to come off even if the girdle-strap is still fastened. But how can a saddle fall off if the breast-strap is fastened? Surely this must mean that Heaven does not want me to go on?" So he went back into the wood and stayed another three days. When he once more came out he found that a huge white boulder as big as a tent had toppled down and was blocking the way out of the thicket. "Surely this must mean that Heaven does not want me to go on," he said, and he went back and stayed another three days. Altogether he stayed there nine days with nothing to eat. He said, "How can I bear to die ingloriously like this? I had far better leave the wood." With the knife he used for sharpening arrows he cut a way through the trees at the side of the rock that blocked the entry into the wood and led his horse down the hill. The Taichi'uts who were mounting guard at once seized him.

When Tarkhutai-kiriltukh took Temujin prisoner he gave orders to his people that he was to pass one night in each group of tents. While he was being passed round in this way the sixteenth day of the fourth month came, when the

3. Very few of the place names (apart from some of the large rivers) are identifiable today.

Taichi'uts hold their feast on the banks of the Onan river, not returning to their tents till sunset. At this time Temujin's gaoler was a young weak man. When Temujin saw that the Taichi'uts had scattered, he knocked down the young weak man, hitting him on the head with the cangue[4] he was wearing, and escaped. When he reached the woods on the bank of the Onan he lay down. But he was afraid some one might see him, so he went and lay on his back in the shallows of the river, with his body in the water and only his face showing.

The young man who had let him get away shouted, "The prisoner has escaped!" and at once all the Taichi'uts who had gone back to their tents arrived in a throng. The moonlight was so strong that one could see just as in the daytime, and helped by it they searched in one place after another in the woods by the Onan river. While Temujin was still lying in the water, Sorkhanshira of the Suldus clan who was one of the search-party passed close by and saw him. "It is because you think of such clever ruses that the Taichi'ut brothers are envious of you. Do not do anything rash. Just lie where you are. I will not give you away." So saying he went on his way.

After the searchers had scattered, Temujin thought to himself, "Recently when I was being passed round to be guarded in one group of tents after another, the night I was in Sorkhanshira's tent his sons Chimbai and Chila'un took pity on me and during the night took off my cangue so that I might sleep in comfort. And now when Sorkhanshira saw me he told no one at all and once again just went on his way. If I were now to go to his tent he would certainly help me." So he went down the Onan river to look for Sorkhanshira.

He knew how to find the tent, for from nightfall to dawn mare's milk was beaten there. He listened for this sound as he went and when he heard it, he went into the tent from which the sound of mare's milk being beaten was coming.

Sorkhanshira said, "I told you to go and look for your mother and brothers. Why have you come back here?" But his sons Chimbai and Chila'un said, "When a sparrow is chased by a sparrow-hawk into a thicket, the thicket saves the sparrow's life. If even a thicket can do so and we fail to save a man that comes to us we are not so good as a thicket." So they took off Temujin's cangue and burnt it. Then they hid him in a cart the back part of which was loaded with wool. They told their younger sister Khada'an to look after him, saying, "On no account tell anyone, whoever he may be."

On the third day the Taichi'ut brothers said, "It looks as though someone were hiding him. We had better do a bit of searching among our own people." The search brought them to Sorkhanshira's tent. They looked everywhere they could think of, in the tent itself, in the other carts, under the bed. Last of all they searched the cart loaded with wool, raking out the wool that was at the door of the cart and finally getting to the wool that was in the back part of it. At this point Sorkhanshira said, "In such hot weather as this, if there was

---

4. **cangue:** a large collar, 3 or 4 feet square, used primarily in Asia to confine prisoners.

Chapter 13

The Court

Chronicle:

The Making of

Official History

(800–1400)

any one in the wool, how could he endure it?" Whereupon the people who were searching came down from the cart and went away.

After they had gone Sorkhanshira said to Temujin, "You very nearly brought me to my end, 'smoke scattered, fire put out.' Now go and find your mother and brothers." He gave him a liquorice-coloured mare with a white mouth, that had never borne a foal, but gave him no saddle. He cooked for him a lamb that had been fattened by the milk of two ewes, he gave him mare's milk in a leather pail, one bow and two arrows, but no fire-making gear, and so set him off on his way.

Temujin started on his way and reached a . . . mountain called Beder, at the foot of which there was a hill standing by itself called Khorchukhui, and here he met his mother and brothers. . . . Temujin, . . . taking his brother Belgutei with him, went down-stream along the Kerulen river. . . . When they reached a point between the two mountains Chekcher and Chikhurkhu they found Dei-sechen's home. He was very glad indeed to see Temujin, and said, "I had heard that the Taichi'ut brothers were envious of you and I was very sorry about it, and was indeed in despair. But here you are at last!" So saying he gave his daughter Borte to Temujin to be his wife. . . . Lady Borte, . . . in order to perform the rite of giving a ceremonial present to the parents-in-law on first seeing them, had brought with her a black sable overcoat. Temujin said, "In old days my father Yesugei Khan became the bond-brother of the Ong Khan, ruler of the Kereits, and consequently he counts as my father. He is now living beside the Tula river, in the black forest. I shall take this overcoat and give it to him." Upon this Temujin and his three brothers took the overcoat with them and came into the presence of the Ong Khan. Temujin said, "In old days you and my father became bond-brothers; so you count as my father. I have now brought to you the present that my wife brought as the ceremonial gift given to parents-in-law on first seeing them." So saying, he handed over the black sable overcoat. The Ong Khan was delighted to get the sable overcoat and said, "I will bring together again your people who have deserted you; your people who have scattered in all directions to the last man I will unite. That promise shall remain inscribed under my heart." When he had said this, Temujin went home. . . .

[*Later, three rival Merkit clans abduct
Borte, Temujin's wife.*]

Temujin . . . went to see To'oril the Ong Khan, ruler of the Kereits, who was living in the black forest beside the Tula river. Temujin said, "Taking me by surprise the chiefs of the three Merkit tribes have captured and carried off my wife. How, I wonder, will the Khan my 'father' rescue and restore to me my wife?" So he said and the Ong Khan answered, "Last year when you gave me the sable overcoat, I said I would gather together for you your people who were scattered, and that promise has remained always inscribed in my heart. Now I will carry out my words by destroying the Merkits and by rescuing your wife Borte and restoring her to you. You can tell my 'brother' Jamukha so. He is now at the Khorkhonakh valley. I here will raise twenty thousand horsemen, to be the right wing; Jamukha will raise twenty thousand more, to be the left wing."

Starting from Botokhan-bo'orji they came to the side of the river Kilkho, bound together logs to make rafts and crossed the river. . . . Accordingly Tokhto'a, Dayir-usun and a few others, taking nothing with them, went downstream along the Selenge river and fled to the region of Barkhujin. All night long the Merkit people fled in panic down the Selenge closely pursued by our soldiers who were managing to do a lot of pillaging, though it was still night. As he went Temujin, in the midst of these fleeing people, kept calling out the name of his wife Borte. Borte, who was indeed among those people, heard him and recognized the voice as that of Temujin. She jumped down from her cart and along with the old woman Kho'akhchin ran up to Temujin's horse and seized the bridle. There was bright moonlight at the time and each was now sure that it was the other. . . . Such is the story of how Lady Borte was recovered.

[*The chronicle continues with other early exploits of Temujin, along with those of his growing number of followers and warrior companions.*]

All of them, after consulting together, said to Temujin, "We appoint you as our Khan. If you will be our Khan, we will go as vanguard against the multitude of your enemies. All the beautiful girls and married women that we capture and all the fine horses, we will give to you. When hunting is afoot, we will be the first to go to the battue and will give you the wild beasts that we surround and catch. If in time of battle we disobey your orders or in time of peace we act contrary to your interests, part us from our wives and possessions and cast us out into the wilderness." Such was the oath they made to serve him. They made him Great Khan, with the name Chingis.

[*The chronicle then recounts many of Chingis Khan's conquests, among which the following is typical.*]

On the sixteenth day of the fourth month of the Rat year [1204] Chingis sacrificed to his battle-standards and went off to fight against the Naimans, going up stream along the Kerulen. He sent Jebe and Khubilai ahead as scouts and when they got to the Sa'ari Steppe they met some Naimans scouting on the Khangkha-khan heights. While the scouts of both sides were chasing one another this way and that, the Naimans captured one of our people, who was riding a white horse with a broken saddle. They said to one another, "True enough, the horses of the Mongols are lean." Afterwards Chingis with his main army reached the Sa'ari Steppe and camped there. Dodai-cherbi

Chapter 13

The Court

Chronicle:

The Making of

Official History

(800–1400)

said to Chingis, "We are few in number and have travelled a long way. We had better turn out our horses to graze and establish decoy troops in large numbers all over the Sa'ari Steppe. [That is, people of all kinds, other than combatants, were to be disguised as soldiers.] At night every one should light five fires. The Naimans are in great force, but their ruler is timid and weak. He has never been far from home and will certainly be bewildered and deceived. Then when our horses have had their fill we will press back their scouts, make straight for their main camp and fall upon them before they have time to draw up in battle-order. In this way we should be sure to win." Chingis took his advice.

The Naiman scouts did indeed look down from the hilltop and say, "If the Mongols are really so few as we thought, how is it that the fires they have lit are numerous as the stars?" When sending the man and horse they had previously caught to Tayang Khan they said, "The Mongol armies fill the whole of the Sa'ari Steppe. They seem to be increasing every day. One can judge this by the fact that the fires they light at night are numerous as the stars."

When his scouts went out, Tayang Khan was on the bank of the Khachir stream at Khangkhai. When he heard what the scouts reported he sent a messenger to his son Guchuluk saying, "The horses of the Mongols may be lean, but the fires they light are numerous as the stars, and they must certainly have a very large army. I have been told that the Mongols are very tough; you may prick them in the eye and they do not blench, you may prick them on the cheek and they do not wince. If we became too closely involved now, it would afterwards certainly be difficult to disengage. I am told that the horses of the Mongols are lean. The thing for us to do is to move our people across the Altai Mountains, then marshal our armies and lure the Mongols on. By the time they reach the Altai their lean horses will be exhausted, whereas our fat horses will just be at the top of their form. Then we can turn round and fight with them successfully."

When Tayang's son Guchuluk heard these words, he said, "There's that old woman Tayang, frightened again! If the Mongols are really so numerous, where can they all have come from? A good half of them have ranged themselves with Jamukha and are with us here. My father Tayang has never in his life been farther away from home than the place where the pregnant women urinate or the calves eat their fodder. No wonder he is now afraid!" Having said this he sent a messenger to repeat it to his father. When Tayang heard that his son had called him "an old woman," he said, "Let us hope that when it comes to the actual fighting Guchuluk 'the strong and brave' won't let down his reputation!" . . . When his scouts saw the Naiman army, Chingis drew up his own forces in battle-order and with them formed the vanguard. He put the central army under the leadership of his younger brother Khasar and put Temuge in charge of the reserve horses. Upon this, the Naimans retired to a point in front of the cliffs of Mount Nakhu and halted along the fringe of the mountain. The scouts of Chingis then threw back those of the Naimans and pursued them to the foot of the mountain. . . .

Chingis saw that it was getting late, so he surrounded Mount Nakhu and prepared to spend the night thus. During the night the Naimans tried to escape. Many of the horses and their riders fell over precipices in the darkness, and the dead lay heaped upon one another. Next day Tayang was captured. His son Guchuluk was not at hand and managed to escape. He had a few followers with him and when he saw that his pursuers were catching up with him, he tried to fortify and hold a position on the Tamir river. But he did not succeed and continued his flight. At the foot of the Altai mountains, his situation became more and more desperate and all his people were captured. . . .

After Chingis had made subject to him all the many tribes he set up at the source of the Oman river a white banner with nine pendants and became Great Khan. This was in the year of the Tiger [1206].

Source 4 from Sundiata: An Epic of Old Mali, *edited by D. T. Niane and translated by G. D. Pickett (Harlow, Essex: Longman, 1965), pp. 1, 41, 60–65, 70, 72–75, 81–82.*

4. From the *Epic of Sundiata of Mali*, as Narrated by Mamadou Kouyaté, 13th century

I am a griot. It is I, Djeli Mamoudou Kouyaté son of Bintou Kouyaté and Djeli Kedian Kouyaté, master in the art of eloquence. Since time immemorial the Kouyatés have been in the service of the Keita princes of Mali; we are vessels of speech, we are the repositories which harbour secrets many centuries old. The art of eloquence has no secrets for us; without us the names of kings would vanish into oblivion, we are the memory of mankind; by the spoken word we bring to life the deeds and exploits of kings for younger generations.

I derive my knowledge from my father Djeli Kedian, who also got it from his father; history holds no mystery for us; we teach to the vulgar just as much as we want to teach them, for it is we who keep the keys to the twelve doors of Mali.[5]. . .

I teach kings the history of their ancestors so that the lives of the ancients might serve them as an example, for the world is old, but the future springs from the past. . . .

Listen to my word, you who want to know; by my mouth you will learn the history of Mali. . . .

Other peoples use writing to record the past, but this invention has killed the faculty of memory among them. They do not feel the past any more, for writing lacks the warmth of the human voice. With them everybody thinks he knows, whereas learning should be a secret. The prophets did not write and

5. **the twelve doors:** the twelve original provinces in the Mali federation.

[365]

Chapter 13
The Court
Chronicle:
The Making of
Official History
(800–1400)

their words have been all the more vivid as a result. What paltry learning is that which is congealed in dumb books!

I, Djeli Mamoudou Kouyaté, am the result of a long tradition. For generations we have passed on the history of kings from father to son. The narrative was passed on to me without alteration and I deliver it without alteration, for I received it free from all untruth.

Listen now to the story of Sundiata, the Na'Kamma, the man who had a mission to accomplish.

At the time when Sundiata was preparing to assert his claim over the kingdom of his fathers, Soumaoro was the king of kings, the most powerful king in all the lands of the setting sun. . . .

Soumaoro advanced as far as Krina, near the village of Dayala on the Niger and decided to assert his rights before joining battle. Soumaoro knew that Sundiata also was a sorcerer, so, instead of sending an embassy, he committed his words to one of his owls. The night bird came and perched on the roof of Djata's tent and spoke. The son of Sogolon in his turn sent his owl to Soumaoro. Here is the dialogue of the sorcerer kings:

"Stop, young man. Henceforth I am the king of Mali. If you want peace, return to where you came from," said Soumaoro.

"I am coming back, Soumaoro, to recapture my kingdom. If you want peace you will make amends to my allies and return to Sosso where you are the king."

"I am king of Mali by force of arms. My rights have been established by conquest."

"Then I will take Mali from you by force of arms and chase you from my kindgom.". . .

Thus Sundiata and Soumaoro spoke together. After the war of mouths, swords had to decide the issue. . . .

Sundiata wanted to have done with Soumaoro before the rainy season, so he struck camp and marched on Krina where Soumaoro was encamped. The latter realized that the decisive battle had come. Sundiata deployed his men on the little hill that dominates the plain. The great battle was for the next day.

In the evening, to raise the men's spirits, Djata gave a great feast, for he was anxious that his men should wake up happy in the morning. Several oxen were slaughtered and that evening Balla Fasséké, in front of the whole army, called to mind the history of old Mali. He praised Sundiata, seated amidst his lieutenants, in this manner:

"Now I address myself to you, Maghan Sundiata, I speak to you king of Mali, to whom dethroned monarchs flock. The time foretold to you by the jinn is now coming. . . .

"You, Maghan, you are Mali. It has had a long and difficult childhood like you. Sixteen kings have preceded you on the throne of Niani,[6] sixteen kings have reigned with varying fortunes, but from being village chiefs the Keitas

6. **Niani:** the original capital of Mali and home to its early kings, including Sundiata's father.

have become tribal chiefs and then kings. Sixteen generations have consolidated their power. You are the outgrowth of Mali just as the silk-cotton tree is the growth of the earth, born of deep and mighty roots. . . ."

At break of day, Fakoli came and woke up Sundiata to tell him that Soumaoro had begun to move his sofas [Malian warriors] out of Krina. The son of Sogolon appeared dressed like a hunter king. . . . He gave the order to draw up the sofas across the plain. . . .

He unhooked his bow from the wall, along with the deadly arrow. It was not an iron arrow at all, but was made of wood and pointed with the spur of a white cock. . . .

The sun had risen on the other side of the river and already lit the whole plain. Sundiata's troops deployed from the edge of the river across the plain, but Soumaoro's army was so big that other sofas remaining in Krina had ascended the ramparts to see the battle. . . .

With his powerful voice Sundiata cried "An gnewa." The order was repeated from tribe to tribe and the army started off. Soumaoro stood on the right with his cavalry. . . . Manding Bory [Sundiata's half-brother and best friend] galloped up to announce to Sundiata that Soumaoro, having thrown in all his reserve, had swept down on Fakoli and his smiths. . . . Already overwhelmed by the numbers, Fakoli's men were beginning to give ground. The battle was not yet won.

His eyes red with anger, Sundiata pulled his cavalry over to the left in the direction of the hills where Fakoli was valiantly enduring.

Sundiata's presence restored the balance momentarily, but Soumaoro's sofas were too numerous all the same. Sogolon's son looked for Soumaoro and caught sight of him in the middle of the fray. Sundiata struck out right and left and the Sossos scrambled out of his way. The king of Sosso, who did not want Sundiata to get near him, retreated far behind his men, but Sundiata followed him with his eyes. He stopped and bent his bow. The arrow flew and grazed Soumaoro on the shoulder. The cock's spur no more than scratched him, but the effect was immediate and Soumaoro felt his powers leave him. His eyes met Sundiata's. Now trembling like a man in the grip of a fever, the vanquished Soumaoro looked up towards the sun. A great black bird flew over above the fray and he understood. It was a bird of misfortune. . . .

The king of Sosso let out a great cry and, turning his horse's head, he took to flight. The Sossos saw the king and fled in their turn. It was a rout. Death hovered over the great plain and blood poured out of a thousand wounds. . . .

Sosso vanished from the earth and it was Sundiata, the son of the buffalo, who gave these places over to solitude. After the destruction of Soumaoro's capital the world knew no other master but Sundiata. . . . The arms of Sundiata had subdued all the countries of the savanna. From Ghana in the north to Mali in the south and from Mema in the east to the Fouta in the west, all the lands had recognized Sundiata's authority. . . . Sundiata wended his way to Ka-ba, keeping to the river valley. All his armies converged on Ka-ba and . . . entered it laden with booty. Sibi Kamandjan had gone ahead of Sundi-

[367]

Chapter 13

The Court

Chronicle:

The Making of

Official History

(800–1400)

ata to prepare the great assembly which was to gather at Ka-ba, a town situated on the territory belonging to the country of Sibi. . . . Even before Djata's arrival the delegations from all the conquered peoples had made their way to Ka-ba. Huts were hastily built to house all these people. When all the armies had reunited, camps had to be set up in the big plain lying between the river and the town. On the appointed day the troops were drawn up on the vast square that had been prepared. . . . Sundiata had put on robes such as are worn by a great Muslim king. . . .

Everything was in position. The sofas, forming a vast semicircle bristling with spears, stood motionless. The delegations of the various peoples had been planted at the foot of the dais. A complete silence reigned. . . .

Kamandjan, who was sitting close by Sundiata, stood up and stepped down from the dais. He mounted his horse and brandished his sword, crying, "I salute you all, warriors of Mali, of Do, of Tabon, of Mema, of Wagadou, of Bobo, of Fakoli . . . ; warriors, peace has returned to our homes, may God long preserve it."

"Amen," replied the warriors and the crowd. . . .

"It is to you that I now address myself, son of Sogolon, you, the nephew of the valorous warriors of Do. Henceforth it is from you that I derive my kingdom for I acknowledge you my sovereign. My tribe and I place ourselves in your hands. I salute you, supreme chief, . . . I salute you, Mansa!"[7]

The huzza that greeted these words was so loud that you could hear the echo repeat the tremendous clamour twelve times over. With a strong hand Kamandjan stuck his spear in the ground in front of the dais and said, "Sundiata, here is my spear, it is yours."

Then he climbed up to sit in his place. Thereafter, one by one, the twelve kings of the bright savanna country got up and proclaimed Sundiata "Mansa" in their turn. Twelve royal spears were stuck in the ground in front of the dais. Sundiata had become emperor. . . .

. . . Every year, Sundiata gathered about him all the kings and notables; so justice prevailed everywhere, for the kings were afraid of being denounced at Niani [Sundiata's city].

Djata's justice spared nobody. He followed the very word of God. He protected the weak against the strong and people would make journeys lasting several days to come and demand justice of him. Under his sun the upright man was rewarded and the wicked one punished.

In their new-found peace the villages knew prosperity again, for with Sundiata happiness had come into everyone's home. . . .

There are some kings who are powerful through their military strength. Everybody trembles before them, but when they die nothing but ill is spoken of them. Others do neither good nor ill and when they die they are forgotten. Others are feared because they have power, but they know how to use it and

---

7. **Mansa:** a royal title meaning emperor, or paramount ruler.

they are loved because they love justice. Sundiata belonged to this group. He was feared, but loved as well. He was the father of Mali and gave the world peace. After him the world has not seen a greater conqueror, for he was the seventh and last conqueror. He had made the capital of an empire out of his father's village, and Niani became the navel of the earth. In the most distant lands Niani was talked of and foreigners said, "Travellers from Mali can tell lies with impunity," for Mali was a remote country for many peoples.

Source 5 from The Glorious Victories of Amda Seyon, King of Ethiopia, *trans. and ed.* G. W. B. Huntingford (Oxford: Clarendon Press, 1965), pp. 53–54, 60–61, 63–65, 83–84, 87–92, 109.

5. From the Royal Chronicle of Emperor Amda Seyon of Ethiopia, 14th century

Let us write, with the help of our Lord Jesus Christ, of the power and the victory which God wrought by the hands of 'Āmda Ṣeyon king of Ethiopia, whose throne-name is Gabra Masqal [meaning "servant of the cross"] in the eighteenth year of his reign [1329]. . . . Let us write then this book trusting in the Father who helps, in the Son who consoles, and in the Holy Spirit who guides and seeks help from the Holy Trinity, "for," says the Apostle James, "if any one lacketh wisdom, let him ask from God, who giveth generously to all, and he shall not be spurned" [James 1:5]. And so we also seek help from the Father, the Son, and the Holy Spirit, that they may guard us for ever. Amen.

Now the king of Ethiopia, whose name was 'Āmda Ṣeyon, heard that the king of the [Muslim] Rebels had revolted, and in [his] arrogance was unfaithful to him, making himself great, like the Devil who set himself above his creator and exalted himself like the Most High. The king of the Rebels, whose name was Sabradin, was full of arrogance towards his lord 'Āmda Ṣeyon, and said: "I will be king over all the land of Ethiopia; I will rule the Christians according to my law, and I will destroy their churches." . . .

Now when the king (of Ethiopia) heard of the Rebel's insults to him, he was very angry. . . .

. . . And obeying the king, a detachment from the corps called Takuelā marched out joyfully and in five days came to the headquarters of that Rebel. . . . And they fought with him and forced him out of his residence; and he fled before them. . . .

Then the army of the king set forth and attacked the camp of the Rebel. They looted the [Rebel] king's treasure houses and [took] gold and silver and

Chapter 13

The Court

Chronicle:

The Making of

Official History

(800–1400)

fine clothes and jewels without number. They killed men and women, old men and children; the corpses of the slain filled a large space. And those who survived were made prisoners. . . . Then they sent word to the king saying, "[There is] good news for you, O king, for we have defeated your enemy who set himself up [to rule] over your kingdom.". . .

[*The chronicle continues to describe Amda
Seyon's conquests until, ill and separated
from the bulk of his armies, he faced the
forces of another Muslim rebel, Gemaldin.*]

King 'Āmda Ṣeyon was in his pavilion, lying sick upon his bed; he was very ill and ate no food and drank no water for seven days. He had told one of his officers named Zanā Yamānu, chief of the pages, who was in charge of the hounds, to go hunting; [and this man] while on his way came upon the rebel army. He abandoned the hunt, and sent word to the king, saying, "The army of the rebels is approaching, and it is larger than the whole of your army; we are returning to you that we may die with you." On hearing this, the king sent mounted scouts to reconnoitre the rebels' camp, [to see] whether it was large or small. And when [these] servants saw how many the rebels were, like a great cloud which hid the sky, or like a swarm of locusts which covered the whole earth, their eyes were darkened and their hearts failed them; they returned to the king and told him, saying, "The whole earth is not enough to contain all these peoples; and if they come, and all the troops of Ethiopia great and small are brought together to the frontier, we shall not be able to overcome them." And when the king heard these words he rose from his bed and wished to leave his tent, though sick and weak; but he could neither gird himself nor stand upon his feet owing to the force of his sickness; and he fell [back] upon his bed. And his servants raised him up and girded upon him his equipment; and he came out of the tent, falling from side to side, and followed by the two queens, who said to him, weeping bitterly, "O our lord, how [can] you go forth to war? Is your foot swift as before, when it was healthy? Is your hand strong to draw the bow and hold the shield and spear? Have you strength to mount the horse? For your spirit is weakened by sickness." And speaking thus they wept many bitter tears. The king answered them saying, "Shall I die the death of a woman, I [the king]? I will not die the death of a woman, for I know the death of a young warrior.". . .

And he went forth putting his trust in the Lord his God, who kills and gives life, punishes and forgives, takes away and grants, impoverishes and enriches, abases and elevates, weakens the strong and strengthens the weak. . . .

The king was strengthened by God, and forgetting his sickness and weakness, girded himself with the two-edged sword, which is Prayer and Intercession; and put on the breastplate of victory, which is Belief and Faith. And he said, "Help me, O God of Moses and Aaron," and to the priests he said, "Pray and intercede [for me] before God, and forget me not in your prayers."

And having said this, the king went out from the gate of the camp and remained for a time alone. The queen also went out after the king, accompanied by the other queen and concubines; and while they were watching him, the king looked once towards the door of the tabernacle. Then the younger queen said to the elder queen, "What shall I do with my children?". . .

When they saw that the king remained there by himself, the queens and concubines wept bitterly and cried, "Woe unto us! misery unto us! For our lord will be destroyed!". . .

Then advanced the multitude of the rebels, their swords gleaming like lightning, their bows strung, the iron spear, the wooden lance, and the . . . iron staff, in their hands. They were as numerous as locusts or as the stars of heaven or the sands of the seashore or the rain-clouds which cover the sky. Their sound was like the roaring of the waves of the sea raised by the wind; their voice was like the voice of the lightning and thunder during the rain; their clamour shook the mountains and hills, and the resounding of their steps made the earth quiver.

Listen once more, friend, to what I shall tell you, and liken not my story to a parable. When they were running, [it was] as if [they had] with them tall trees, mountains, and hills, as if the moon and stars were travelling with them, for so it seemed to me when I saw the countless host of the rebels which covered the earth. [It was a sight] hard to describe; the senses could not comprehend it, nor could the lips and tongue tell of it.

. . . His friends kissed his hands, his feet, his eyes, his breast, and his shoulders; and with one accord they left him to [his] death. But the king stood alone like a firm foundation, like a wall of hard stone, and called out to his soldiers, "Stand in patience for a time, and see how I fight and how I die, and [see also] what God will do to-day by my hand." But none was there to hear his words, for all had fled. When I say that all had fled, I do not mean [that it was] from fear . . . all the armies of Ethiopia joined together could not stand against them except through the power of God.

When the king saw them fleeing, he called with a loud voice to his soldiers saying, "Whither are you fleeing? Do you think that to-day you will reach your own countries? Do you not know that it is I who brought you up, made you grow by means of fat cattle, honey-wine, and grain, and decorated you with gold and silver and fine clothing?" So saying, he bounded like a leopard and leapt like a lion, and mounted his horse whose name was Harab Asfarē. And he told one of his attendants named Zana'as-farē, the commander of the young horsemen, to go by the right into the midst of the rebels. And he obeyed the order and went among the rebels and passed through them, followed by five horsemen. . . . The king went against the left wing where the rebels were numerous; he did not flinch nor turn his back when arrows rained upon him like rain and spears and javelins of iron and wood like hail. They

Chapter 13

The Court

Chronicle:

The Making of

Official History

(800–1400)

surrounded him with their swords and he, his face set hard like stone and his spirit undaunted by [the prospect of] death, clove the ranks of the rebels and struck so hard that he transfixed two men as one with a blow of his spear, through the strength of God. Thereupon the rebels scattered and took to flight, being unable to hold their ground in his presence, [for he was] an old and experienced warrior; and none could stand against him in battle.

The six horsemen of whom I spoke before struck at the rebels from the rear, and when the king had put the [other] rebels to flight, his troops which had fled returned and forced the rebels into a ditch which God had prepared, and a countless number [fell into it]. Then the king dismounted from his horse, took his shield, and struck the rebels; and when his right hand was tired he struck them with his left hand; and when his left hand was tired he struck with his right hand [again]. . . . 'Amda Ṣeyon prevailed against them and totally destroyed them through . . . his trust and faith.

Then the king mounted his horse and pursued the fugitives, accompanied by a few of his soldiers, saying, "Take no trophies from the dead, but pursue the living and kill them, and let the women take the spoils of the dead." And the king found one of his soldiers in the act of taking the clothes from a dead body, and struck him with his spear from behind; and the soldiers were afraid and did as he commanded them. . . .

Now listen while I tell you again about the battle on that day. None of the former kings of Ethiopia have been like him, for this king made war in all the provinces belonging to his kingdom. None willingly made war on him, but the rebels deliberately attacked the king when he was alone without his army, for it had gone to another country, that by the will of God He might reveal His strength, wisdom, and power, that the army of the king should not say, "We have conquered by our own strength.". . . 'Amda Ṣeyon had only ten thousand, but he destroyed and exterminated the rebels in one [battle]. He trampled on them like the dust, he crushed them like corn, he broke them in pieces like reeds, he scattered them like leaves, he consumed them like the fire which burns the grass or the flame which scorches the mountains.

[*Again, the chronicle continues with accounts of Amda Seyon's many military victories.*]

Much remains to be written about the war [carried on] day and night throughout the land of the Moslems by the king and his army. We have told [only] a little; we have not added [more], that the story might not be [too] long, and that it might not frighten the readers.

King 'Amda Ṣeyon, gentle and humble like Moses and David; discerning, merciful, and patient; caring for the aged like his father, the young like his brother, the poor like his mother, and priests and monks like his Lord. Though king, he humbled himself before all like a poor man. He gave alms to the poor and needy, to widows and orphans; offerings to churches of gold and silver in abundance, and also ornaments. May God give him a reward on earth and in heaven, lengthen his days on earth, and save him from sudden death. May He give him a place in the kingdom of heaven with the good kings, for ever and ever.

As for me, miserable sinner that I am, who wrote this book, do not forget me in your prayers, [O my readers]. May God lengthen your days, both great and small. May He bring safety and peace to your country. May He give your king power over his enemies.

QUESTIONS TO CONSIDER

Because all of these chronicle selections are in some ways very similar, at least in their intended purpose, it may at first seem difficult to approach them with a critical eye. Perhaps the easiest way is to begin by comparing and contrasting them, trying to identify what is similar and what is decidedly different about them. You may wish to compile a kind of chart as you try to sort out these similarities and differences. One way to do this would be to make three-column notes, one column each for similarities and differences, with the sources listed in a smaller column on the left. Leave several lines open for each of the documents. Then as you read and reread the selections, you can mark the items you notice in the appropriate open blanks in each column.

Try to discover if some share certain characteristics that the others do not. For example, compare the two chronicles that began as oral accounts, the epic of Sundiata and *The Secret History of the Mongols*. Focus not only on the reasons for their creation and the method of their transmission, but also on the explanatory devices used by the authors to account for the achievements of their subjects. Are they alike in any way? Do those similarities bear any resemblance to the nature of explanations in the other accounts? You might also examine the issue of sources. How were those used by Mamadou Kouyaté different from those available to Einhard hundreds of years earlier? Of what significance is the change in the sources themselves, and the chronicler's use of them, to your understanding of the development of official history?

Similarly, reexamine those extracts that emphasize the military achievements of the rulers they are extolling, particularly Duke William, Sundiata, Temujin, and Amda Seyon. Consider whether personal military glory seems most important, or if association with wartime victories was sufficient to establish the importance of the particular ruler. Also examine how rulers were contrasted with their enemies in these chronicles. What other sorts of achievements, besides military glory, are important to establishing the authority of each leader?

Finally, return to the issue of comparisons. Are these court chronicles,

Chapter 13

The Court

Chronicle:

The Making of

Official History

(800–1400)

representing a variety of official histories from societies throughout Afro-Eurasia, similar? Or do they represent totally different cultural efforts to explain the past? Answering these questions again, with the insights you have gained in carefully examining each chronicle, should make it easier to develop a position on the central question of this chapter: In what ways do court chronicles—and official histories—represent truth concerning the past of the societies that created them?

EPILOGUE

In many ways, court chronicles may be seen more as public relations efforts than as history. Certainly they were intended to present the rulers and their governments in the most favorable, if not flattering, manner. Understood in this way, it may be easier for us to see the way selective historical memory in these chronicles served a particular purpose. That purpose, while unchanged, has resulted in differing approaches to this type of official history through the centuries. This is particularly true with the growing reliance on collections of documents to represent official history, especially as European nations came to dominate the writing of world history after the successes of their fifteenth- and sixteenth-century naval expeditions around the globe.

The proliferation of documents, however, may not have lent any greater credibility to official histories. As practiced in the twentieth century, such accounts of the past all too often are intended to paint countries, governments, and frequently other institutions (even businesses!) in the best possible light. The realization that the *intent* of a history, perhaps even more than its form or its sources, is the most telling barometer of its accuracy should be a cautionary lesson for all students of the past. That was precisely what Professor Warren Cohen had in mind when he urged Americans to be wary of the official histories created by their own government.

CHAPTER FOURTEEN

THE FAMILY IN MEDIEVAL ENGLISH

VILLAGES (1350–1500)

THE PROBLEM

If one were to judge from most portrayals on television or the speeches of contemporary politicians, the family of the past was one of two types: either (1) a married couple and their children whose most important bonds were emotional—a nuclear family; or (2) a large extended clan of multiple generations, bound together by economic ties and respect for elders.

Until about thirty years ago, it was possible to hold either position with little concern for what the historical record actually revealed, for the family—other than very prominent families who were the subject of extensive records—was not a normal topic of historical inquiry. This apparent neglect is rapidly being reversed, both because the interests of historians have changed and because new techniques are available for delving into family life, particularly the use of computers to handle and sift large amounts of quantitative data. Questions that were regarded as unanswerable for those

not among the elite—When did people marry? How many children were they likely to have? How did they feel about their children? their spouses? How did families respond to change or crisis? What did they do to improve their situation?—are now being researched for ever earlier time periods, with an entire journal, *The Journal of Family History*, devoted to the field. Though historians do not always agree about the answers, they see such questions as an important part of our understanding of the past.

Some of the most intriguing questions being asked by historians of the family may best be answered cross-culturally and comparatively, but cross-cultural work always begins with intensive local studies of the way that families behaved and operated in one particular time and place. Our focus in this chapter will thus be narrower than in our other chapters, for we will be using a variety of types of records to look at families in villages and small towns of late medieval England, with sources dating from the 1340s to the 1490s. This is, in fact, a broader focus than many studies of premodern families, which by and large look at only one village, and we will rely on such studies to provide the context for our investigation. Your task in this chapter is to explore the actions of family members in medieval English villages and small towns in relation to one another and to the world beyond the family. How did common people in medieval England seek to strengthen the economic and social position of their family? How did they define *family* and relate to those they saw as members of this group?

BACKGROUND

The vast majority of people in late medieval England lived in villages or small towns and made their living predominantly by raising crops and animals. Most of these villages were nucleated; that is, the houses were clumped together with the fields stretching out beyond this compact center. Most houses sat in the middle of a *toft*, a yard with pens for animals and storage sheds, and many also had an adjacent *croft*, or garden, which they cultivated by spade and hoe rather than by plow. In many parts of England, the fields of the village were farmed in what is termed open-field agriculture, a pattern that differs sharply from modern farming practices. In open-field agriculture, the village as a whole decided what would be planted in each field, rotating the crops according to tradition and need. Some fields would be planted in crops such as wheat or rye for human consumption, some in oats or other crops for both animals and humans, and some would be left unworked, or *fallow*, to allow the soil to rejuvenate. The exact pattern of this rotation varied from location to location, but in most areas with open-field agriculture the holdings farmed by any one family did not consist of a whole field but of strips in many fields. These strips were traditionally measured in widths a team of oxen (or oxen and horses, for these animals were often yoked together) could plow, and in lengths called *furlongs*; between the plowed strips a *balk*, or unplowed ridge, was left as a dividing line or stones were used for this purpose, and at each end there was an unplowed *headlong* for turning the plow team around. The boundaries between fields were marked by hedges or ditches. In parts of England with heavy clay soil the plow-team might consist of eight animals, too many to be owned by any but the richest villagers, so although families held their strips separately, they often worked them together. Most families were also allowed to run some animals in the woods or meadows outside the cultivated fields.

The open-field system and many other local issues were largely handled by the village itself, but much of the economic and political life of the village fell under the jurisdiction of lords, members of the nobility or gentry who might live in a large house in the village but often lived elsewhere. The territory controlled by a lord, generally termed a *manor*, might consist of one village, a number of villages, or even only part of a village. Within each manor, the lord established the duties each villager owed and occasionally took surveys, termed *extents*, that listed what services or rents were due him from each head of household and how much land each household held. The lord also directly controlled some of the land of the village—his *demesne*—which he could rent out, hire workers to farm, or demand that the villagers farm as part of their obligations to him. Villagers whose land carried heavy labor obligations are generally termed *serfs* or *villeins;* in theory, villeins were required to remain on a manor forever in order to fulfill their obligations to the lord, so that they were personally unfree. Villagers with few or no labor obligations were regarded as free, though they still had obligations to the lord, which they generally paid in cash or in goods such as wheat or animals.

Though we might think that the distinction between serf and free would be the most important distinction between villagers, by the time our sources begin, wealth mattered more than personal status, and it is often difficult to tell from the records if a person was serf or free. Serfs did have labor obligations, but by 1330 they were often paying these off in money rather than in labor and using any extra money they acquired to buy more land rather than their freedom. In fact, their obligations might actually be lower than those of free

peasants because their rents were set by custom. Based on studies of many villages, historians have found a more useful division to be between what we might call well-off, middle-rank, and poor villagers. Though the classification differed somewhat from place to place, well-off villagers were those families who farmed about 25 to 30 acres or what is often termed a *virgate* or *oxgang*. (The size of the acre and the number of acres in a virgate varied throughout England, so that it is hard to compute exactly what medieval measurements mean in modern terms.) These families often had some disposable income left once their taxes and rents were paid, so we might expect this group to be those most able to pursue activities and acquire property that furthered their own interests. Middle-rank village families were those that farmed about a *half-virgate*, about 10 to 15 acres. Historians estimate that this was the minimum needed to sustain a family, and left it susceptible to hunger and poverty in times of poor harvests. Poor villagers, often termed *cottars* or *cottagers*, were those who held less land than this, and were dependent on activities other than farming to survive. In many villages and small towns, individuals and families belonging to all three groups also carried out craft or retail activities in addition to farming, such as brewing, blacksmithing, baking, or selling food.

Lords generally appointed officials termed *bailiffs* and *reeves* from outside the village to oversee the legal and business operations of their manors, but because the village itself attended to many local economic and legal issues, additional officials were chosen by the village residents themselves. We do not know how these were chosen or elected in many cases, but we do know that they were always adult men and generally heads of households. Women had no voice in the running of the village, though they did hold land independently and, especially as widows, headed households; of course, land-holding women were required to pay all rents and taxes. Women could, with some limitations, buy and sell land and execute certain financial transactions, but in general they appeared in court much less often than men and so are also less visible in the types of legal records that appear in the Evidence section. Female and male servants who often worked for and lived with wealthier village families had no political voice.

Several times a year in most English villages, and in some places even more often, the villagers, or at least some of them, gathered for court proceedings during which the legal and financial affairs of both the lord and village were handled. These courts, sometimes termed *hallmotes,* began keeping formal records in the thirteenth century. The records were written on pieces of parchment that were stitched end to end and then rolled up; they were generally made while the court was in session, not written up afterward. Such court rolls are the most important type of documents surviving for exploring the lives of medieval English villagers and their families. Most of the sources we use here are court rolls, and the quantitative charts we include in the last two sources are based on court rolls.

Manorial courts collected fees due the lord, such as *chevage,* a payment to the lord from a serf for permission to live off the manor; *merchet,* a fee paid by a bride, her father, or the bridegroom in order to receive a marriage license; *heriot,* a fee due on the death of a tenant, usually the best animal owned by the family, although this later changed to a cash payment; a *gersuma,* or entry fine, due when someone other than the widow took over land on the death of a villager. They also handled breaches of the peace such as fights, assaults, or robberies, litigation between villagers, and infractions of laws or customs regarding the fields, roads, or public places. The courts often went beyond what we would recognize as judicial activities and issued new ordinances, which historians now term *by-laws,* to regulate activities in the village or its fields and forests. Generally these by-laws were passed not out of theoretical reflection or long-range planning, but as constraints against certain activities already being carried on to some degree, but deemed harmful to the village. By-laws are thus an accurate reflection of what individuals or families might be doing on a small scale to improve their economic position.

In addition to their legislative function of issuing by-laws, many other concerns and actions of medieval manorial courts are foreign to modern courts. The medieval village had no police as we know them; instead, if villagers saw a crime or infraction, they were expected to chase the perpetrator themselves and yell to others to join in. Witnesses could be fined for failing to "raise the hue and cry," or for doing so when it was unwarranted—the original false alarm.

This idea of community responsibility for law and order may be traced in a number of other court activities as well. Each male villager over the age of twelve was expected to enroll in a *frankpledge* or *tithing,* a unit of ten or so men who were responsible for one another's behavior. Each tithing was headed by a so-called capital pledge, usually a villager from a more prominent family who also often acted as a juror on cases brought before the manorial court. The village jurors rendered judgments as a group and were also expected to bring cases to court. The manorial courts relied more on the collective memory of village traditions and customs than on written laws; thus jurors—or some group of responsible adult men—were often asked to decide issues, such as who

had the rights to a certain piece of land, simply by talking among themselves or to others who might know. Because of this reliance on expert knowledge, jurors were chosen from among those most familiar with the facts of the case, the opposite of modern jury selection. Both plaintiff and defendant often brought in others who would swear to their view of the case or their good character, with the jurors deciding in hotly contested cases to ask the whole village to back their judgment. Punishments were generally fines or occasionally banishment, with imprisonment and corporal punishments quite rare. (Serious criminal cases were not handled by the manorial courts but by the royal courts.) Villagers were expected to bring cases against each other to court and could be fined if the jurors learned about violations such as debt or trespass they had not brought to court.

THE METHOD

One of the reasons most studies of premodern common people focus on one village or small town is the difficulty of tracing large numbers of people over time in an era before birth, marriage, or death records. Historians must thus creatively use the records they have to try to determine the make-up of families and households, and to trace the ways family members related to one another. Researchers often begin simply by listing in a computer file every time a name is mentioned in court records

or elsewhere, and then gradually grouping together all references to a single individual, then all records of how that individual was linked to others with the same name or described as relatives, then how those family groupings were linked to other family groupings through marriage or legal transactions. The end result is an extremely complex picture of at least some of the village residents, with reasonable conclusions or speculations about factors such as age, number of children, or number of marriages based on various references.

Deciding when entries refer to the same person is not always easy, however. In fact, before the fourteenth century this process was extremely difficult as people often had no surnames but might be referred to merely as "John" or "Agnes." In England, surnames gradually became more common in the thirteenth century, based usually on a father's or mother's name, an occupation, a place of origin, or a physical characteristic. By the time our sources begin, most men, though not all, had surnames that stayed with them their whole life, and identification problems come primarily from numbers of people having the same first name and surname—John Miller, for example, or Richard Smith. This problem is exacerbated by the fact that first names varied little; in one fifteenth-century English village, for example, 90 percent of the men were named John, Thomas, Richard, or Robert. At this time married women in England usually adopted their husband's surname; tracing a woman's identity, therefore, can be more complicated, though eased somewhat by references to male members of her birth family that show up in the sources. We will not be carrying out the tracing of individuals to the extent that village historians do, but we will still use this method as we investigate people's activities through the court rolls.

Once historians have identified individuals, they can begin to count them and arrange them in groups to note trends and changes. To do this, they need to correct for various types of deficiencies in the records. When using any type of record to count people, whether medieval court rolls or the modern census, historians must determine whether certain groups were likely to be underrepresented, or inadequately counted. In the modern census, underrepresented groups include illegal aliens, who for obvious reasons avoid the census taker. In medieval court records, underrepresented groups include those who are less likely than others to appear in court—children, those too poor to have engaged in any financial transactions, and women, who did not serve as jurors and were much less likely than men to bring cases to court.

In this chapter you will be using four types of sources: court rolls, bylaws, wills, and quantitative tables recently compiled by historians from medieval court rolls. The original documents are, of course, all in Latin and all handwritten; Source 1 shows what a court roll actually looks like. Unless your Latin and paleographic skills are superior, you will find this 1492 manuscript from the village of Gnossal impossible to read, although you can probably tell that it is arranged in groupings with headings at the left. The third grouping down lists the jurors by name.

Source 2 includes selections from one sitting of a manorial court from the small town of Ramsey in 1460. Because many of the items refer to similar issues, we have chosen to edit it selectively. With this source, your first task is to read it and the notes carefully to make sure you understand what is being discussed and ruled on. What types of problems are the focus of items 9 and 11? How does the bylaw passed by all household heads ("the whole homage") in item 11 seek a resolution? What penalty does

Thomas Tyler incur in item 14? If this situation had not been discovered, how would his actions have improved his family's situation? What types of problems are the focus of items 17–32? From the description of the actions, can you recreate what might have gone on? What information does item 22 give us about relations between spouses? about the way villagers expected these relations to be? What does item 31 tell us about relations between siblings? Why might the town choose to pass the new ordinance noted in item 35? Items 36 through 50 concern activities other than farming that residents of Ramsey engaged in. How might these have improved a family's economic position? What do you notice about the surnames of some of the artisans? If you were beginning a study of individuals and families in the town of Ramsey, you would now note each instance in which an individual is mentioned. Try it here for these five individuals: William Wayte, John Newman, William Clerk, John Water, and Katherine Love. (All the entries that mention these people are included in Source 2.) Note carefully the circumstances with which each person's name is connected. Do any of the combinations of circumstances surprise you?

The next two pieces of evidence are selections from court rolls that describe legal agreements between family members, Source 3 from the village of South Elmham in 1408 and Source 4 from the village of Wymondham in 1421. Read Source 3 carefully. What does the younger Henry Pekke gain from his grandmother? What

does he agree to do in return? What provisions are made if he does not carry out this maintenance agreement? In Source 4, what do John and Joan Notte receive from John's father William? What do they agree to do in return? What do these sources tell you about relations between parents and children? between grandparents and grandchildren?

Source 5 is a translation of a brief court roll from the small village of Winterborne in Lancastershire from 1494. What concerns of the village and the lord are addressed in items 3 and 4? Read items 5 and 6 carefully, for they discuss related matters. What provisions are made for the young daughters of William Barcoll? Why might William Webbe wish to do this? What assistance does he provide for his own sons?

Source 6 is a selection from the court rolls of Bromsgrove and King's Norton, a small town in Worcestershire, from 1496, concerning conflicting claims to the same piece of land. In order to untangle the confusion and understand the debate, it will be useful for you to do what medieval historians do as the second stage of tracing families: draw a family tree linking the parties to the dispute. In item 1, what does Henry Banard ask the twelve tenants to decide? Who owned this piece of land originally? Who were his children, according to Henry's claim? How did Henry Banard inherit what he sees as his rights to the land? In item 2, do the jurors agree with Henry Banard's assertions? Items 3 and 4 concern Peter Parre's claim to the same land. How does he say the original owner disposed of the land? How did he inherit what he sees as *his* rights to the land? Why might Henry Banard have neglected to mention that William had given the land to his brothers Richard or Robert, or even that Richard and Robert (who appear to have been his uncles) existed at all? Why might William have given the land to his two brothers when it was really for the work and use of one of them? (Here you will have to speculate about motivation, which is something historians of the premodern period often have to do.) Look at the lists of jurors in items 2 and 4. Why do you think none of the men are the same? Based simply on the evidence here (and there are no more records about this case, nor do we know who got the land in the end), can you judge which man has the stronger claim to the land? What does this case tell you about family land transactions?

Sources 7 and 8 are by-laws, Source 7 from the village of Wistow in Huntingdonshire from 1410 and Source 8 from the village of Hitchin in Hertshire from 1471. Like the by-laws contained in Source 2, they address— and seek to restrict—activities some villagers were probably already engaged in. Why might people let their animals loose in the meadows or stubble? Why might this be a problem? Why would people dig pits in the road? Item 6 in Source 7 and all of Source 8 concern *gleaning,* or picking up loose heads of grain that fall off when the sheaves are gathered. Villages generally tried to reserve this privilege for those who were very old, very young, or physically infirm, who could not work a normal day

helping with the harvest; however, by-laws about gleaning (here, item 6 in Source 7 and item 1 in Source 8) occur frequently enough to suggest that able-bodied people consistently took advantage of the system. Why might people choose to glean instead of working for wages in the harvest? According to item 2 in Source 8, what opportunities could gleaning provide? What does item 3 in Source 8 tell you about the legal responsibilities of a head of household? How might this have affected relationships within the family?

Sources 9 through 11 are wills recorded in the small town of Cranbrook in Kent from the late fifteenth century, the earliest time period from which many wills of common people survive. Just as they do today, people in medieval England used wills to dictate how their property and possessions were to be divided and handled after their deaths. Once a number of wills survive from any one area, historians can use them quantitatively to trace such variables as religious and charitable donations, kinship and family networks, the role of professional lawyers, the relative wealth of a region or group of people, remarriage of widows and widowers, changing patterns of investment or book ownership and literacy. We will not use enough wills to make a large-scale study, but the amounts mentioned in some of the bequests can help us answer our questions for this chapter. Again it will be helpful if you make a family tree for each will, to see who the person making the will—the *testator*—decides to include and to make comparisons within a family; alongside this, keep a chart of all gifts bestowed outside the family to help you assess the relative importance of other concerns, such as the church. When you make these charts, you will want to translate all amounts into the same type of money in order to make comparisons. The English monetary system in the fifteenth century was not a decimal one: the basic unit was the penny (Latin *denarius*, abbreviated d.); 12 pennies made a shilling (Latin *solidus*, abbreviated s.) and 20 shillings or 240 pennies equaled a pound (Latin *libra*, abbreviated £); a mark was 6 s. 8 d., or two-thirds of a pound. Amounts were often written simply as numbers without the abbreviations; thus 2/13/6 means £2, 13 s., 6 d. and 13/6 means 13 s. 6 d.

Read Source 9 carefully, making your chart. Which family members does the testator, John Jalander, mention by name? Who are his executors? What does this role entail? Although at the beginning of the will it is not clear what relation Richard Crysp is to Jalander, whom does he turn out to be? How would you compare the inheritance of the two brothers, Robert and William? (This is not possible to do with complete assurance because we do not know the value of Jalander's land, but you can still get some impression of this from other aspects of the will, such as the distribution of animals and the instructions about what to do should Robert die without issue, that is, childless.) Based on this will, how would you judge the importance of godchildren to people in late medieval England? of their own siblings or nieces and nephews? Along

with Jalander's family, who else benefits from the will? How would you assess the relative significance of these bequests outside of the family?

Now go on to Source 10, and make another chart. What special provisions does the testator, John Lurker, make for his wife? How do these compare with those of the previous testator to his wife? How would you compare the inheritance of Lurker's son William (presumably the eldest) with that of his other sons and daughters? How would you compare the inheritance of the younger sons with that of the daughters? Analyze Source 11 the same way. How do the inheritances of the two sons and daughter of the testator, Thomas Herenden, compare? How would you compare Herenden's donations to the church for his funeral expenses and for his own memorial ceremony with his gifts to his children?

You can discern in these three wills a high degree of economic stratification in English villages and small towns. Learning how these economic differences might have affected family strategies is difficult to do by reading only a few sources; this next step of investigation is best done quantitatively. Sources 12 and 13 are charts for the period 1350 to 1400 made by the medieval historian Zvi Razi. They are based on his study of the village of Halesowen in Worcestershire, with the bulk of his information coming from court rolls. Razi carried out the laborious task of identifying individuals and determining family connections to arrive at the figures tabulated here. Look carefully at Source 12, which gives the adjusted mean (that is, average) number of offspring over the age of twelve for rich, middling, and poor village families. (The "adjusted" annotation refers to the fact that Razi had to add daughters to arrive at an accurate count because girls and young women were so much less likely to appear in the court rolls than boys and young men. If he had not corrected the figures, it would have appeared as if all families were bearing twice as many sons as daughters, which is not biologically possible.) Why do you think the numbers are what they are? (Remember these are offspring who lived to age twelve.) In a largely agrarian economy such as medieval England's, what are the advantages and disadvantages of having more surviving children?

Source 13 traces the sales and leases of land in the same village. What differences do you see in the ability of rich and poor families to improve their economic status through buying or leasing land? From the chart, does it appear that economic differences among families were increasing or decreasing during this period? How might the differences in number of children who survived have affected this trend? Add up the columns of lessor, lessee, vendor, and buyer in Source 13; how many families were involved in land transactions during this time? Source 12 calculates that there were 253 families living in Halesowen during this period. What percentage were involved in land transactions of some type?

Having examined the thirteen sources, you may seem to have a wealth of absolutely random information about how families and family members acted and related. Before you try to answer the central questions for this chapter, we recommend turning to the Questions to Consider section, which offers some suggestions for tying all this data together.

THE EVIDENCE

Source 1 from Nathaniel J. Hone, The Manor and Manorial Records *(Port Washington, N.Y.: Kennikat Press, 1971; first published, 1906), p. 183.*

1. Court Roll, Village of Gnossal, England, 1492

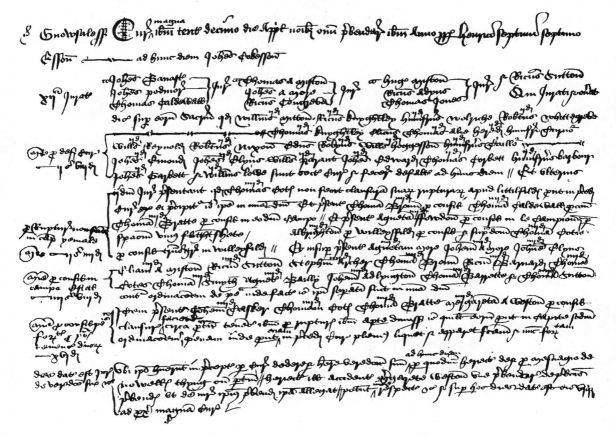

Source 2 from Edwin B. DeWindt, The Court Rolls of Ramsey, Hepmangrove and Bury, 1268–1600 (Toronto: Pontifical Institute of Medieval Studies, 1990), pp. 833–838.

2. Court Roll of Ramsey, 1460

RAMSEY. VIEW OF FRANKPLEDGE[1] WITH COURT HELD THERE ON MONDAY AFTER THE FEAST OF ST. ANNE, IN THE THIRTY-EIGHTH YEAR OF THE REIGN OF KING HENRY VI AND THE TWENTY-FIFTH YEAR OF THE LORD ABBOT JOHN STOWE.[2]

1. (ESSOINS:[3]) None.

2. [JURORS:] Thomas Cok, John Baker, Thomas Plomer, Henry Brampton, Philip Aleyn, John Browse, Richard Baker, John Fen, William Abbot, Richard Toute, John Ridman, Thomas Vigerous, William Clerk, John Betcod, Robert Stone, William Wayte.

3. 3 d. from John Newman for not prosecuting a plea of debt against William Freman of Upwood. . . .

8. 2 d. from John Newman for having a dung heap too near the common lane, opposite his tenement[4] in the Wyght, to the nuisance of all passers-by.

9. 2 d. from John Thomas, 1 d. from Alice Shelford, [no amercement[5]] from John Bryan (beggar), 2 d. each from John Kent, Richard Glasyer and William Wayte for not cleaning their ditches at the end of their orchards towards Little Wyght. . . .

11. Ordinance by the whole homage that each tenant sufficiently clean his ditch opposite his tenement and make brinks[6] with piles and undergrowth before the next feast of All Saints[7] after this view, under an individual penalty of 40 d. . . .

14. 12 d. from Thomas Tyler, tenant of the Cellarer,[8] for making an encroachment by ploughing at the land he holds from the Cellarer, [appropriating] 24 feet from the common balks[9] leading towards the pond upon Pilcham. Order to correct before the feast of St. Michael[10] next, under penalty of 40 d.

---

1. **view of frankpledge:** inspection of all those sworn in to the frankpledge.
2. July 28, 1460.
3. **essoins:** people's excuses for not appearing in court, brought in by others.
4. **tenement:** house.
5. **no amercement:** no fine levied, usually because the defendant was too poor.
6. **brinks:** banks.
7. **All Saints:** November 1.
8. **Cellarer:** steward of the lord or a local monastery.
9. **balks:** ridges of land left unploughed between fields.
10. **Feast of St. Michael:** September 29.

15. 6 s. 8 d. each from Thomas Porter, John Bothby, John Whytwell and Peter Marche for putting dung near the Chapel of St. Thomas, contrary to the ancient ordinance. . . .

17. 6 d. from John Faukes for assaulting Matthew Kelew Wever and attempting to strike him, against the peace.

18. 6 d. from the same John Faukes for similarly assaulting Richard Merwyk and attempting to stab him with his dagger and for knocking him down and throwing him into the river, against the King's peace. . . .

20. 3 d. from John Kent for similarly assaulting Thomas Wode and striking him with a cudgel and drawing blood from him, against the King's peace.

21. 6 d. from William Stedeman for assaulting Thomas Wode and drawing blood from him by fracturing his skull.

22. 6 d. from Thomas Wode for unjustly raising the hue and cry on (his) wife, and [no amercement recorded] from his wife for unjustly raising the hue and cry on him, to the serious nuisance of their neighbors, which is something they do regularly, both day and night. . . .

25. 6 d. from John Water for assaulting Thomas Baker Junior and slightly wounding him in the chest with his dagger, against the King's peace.

26. 4 d. from John Water for assaulting Thomas Rolf and his wife, against the King's peace.

27. 1 d. from the same John for entering the lord's park and carrying off wood and undergrowth.

28. 6 d. from William Clerk for assaulting John Love, against the peace.

29. 6 d. from the same John Love for assaulting the said William, against the peace.

30. 6 d. from Thomas Love for assaulting William Clerk by shooting arrows at him and mistreating him, against the peace.

31. 12 d. from Robert Love, chaplain, for assaulting Thomas Love, his brother, with a drawn knife, against the King's peace.

32. 1 d. from Katherine Love for unjustly raising the hue and cry on William Clerk, to the nuisance and annoyance of their neighbors.

33. A half-mark from William Warde for regularly having diverse men within his dwelling playing tennis, contrary to the decree concerning this. . . .

35. A new ordinance: If anyone within the precincts of this leet[11] has pigs, piglets and sows wandering regularly in the street, the Bailiff, through his servant or deputy, is permitted to drive them and impound them in the lord's park, charging 1 d. for each pig or sow and 1/2 d. for each piglet, to the use and profit of the lord, and charging for his labour 1 d., as often as it happens that they have to be impounded.

---

11. **leet:** court.

36. 8 d. each from Joan Overton and Mariot Amy, 6 d. from Agnes Depyng, 8 d. each from Alice Couper and Agnes Faunt, 6 d. each from Marion Baveyn, Katherine Love and Joan Filhous, and 8 d. each from Agnes Symmes and Audrey Cooke, common brewers, for selling ale contrary to the assize.[12] . . .

38. 1 d. each from Joan Brampton, Isabelle Stedeman, Agnes Gelam, Margaret Baker, Juliana Baker, Joan Shirwode and Agnes Webster for not bringing their gallons and pottles[13] before the steward of this leet on this day. . . .

40. 16 d. from Thomas Plomer and 20 d. from John Asplond, bakers of bread, for selling bread contrary to the assize. . . .

42. 20 d. from William Faunt, 40 d. from Thomas Cokk, 20 d. from John Awbys and 8 d. from William Warde Sadeler, butchers, for charging too much in selling meat. . . .

44. 4 d. each from Thomas Cok, William Faunt and John Hunt, [no amercement] from John Berforth (because he is dead), 2 d. each from John Awbys and Marion Amy, 4 d. each from Walter Pamlion and John Asplond, 2 d. each from Alice Keteryng and John Whete, 1 d. each from John Treygo and Finetta Water, and 4 d. from Thomas Plomer, common victualers,[14] for charging too much in selling victuals.

45. 6 d. each from John Brouse and William Wayte, ale-tasters, for not performing their office.

46. 3 d. from William Wayte, 2 d. from Richard Wayte, 1 d. from Robert Grene, 2 d. from John Sowle, 12 d. from Richard Toute, 2 d. from Robert Tayllor, 3 d. from John Wryght Tayllor, 3 d. from John Hyll and 1 d. from Thomas Bonfaye, tailors, for charging too much in their art.

47. 6 d. from Richard Geyte, 2 d. from John Missangle, 6 d. from William Geyte (dead), 1 d. from John Boller (dead), and 3 d. from John Denby, cobblers, for charging too much.

48. 3 d. from John Webster, 6 d. from John Faukes, 2 d. from Richard Faukes, and 3 d. each from Robert Hyde and Matthew Kelew, weavers, for charging too much.

49. 3 d. from Roger Glover and 2 d. from John Pecok, glovers, for charging too much in their art.

50. 3 d. from Robert Skynner and 6 d. from Gilbert Skynner, skinners, for charging too much in their art. . . .

52. Election and swearing-in of William Wayte and Richard Baker as Constables.

53. Election and swearing-in of William Clerk and John Fen as ale-tasters.

12. **contrary to the assize:** against the ordinances regulating weights and measures.

13. **gallons and pottles:** measures for ale, which the steward must regularly inspect for accuracy.

14. **victualers:** food-sellers.

Sources 3 and 4 from Elaine Clark, "Some Aspects of Social Security in Medieval England,"
Journal of Family History, 7 (1982), p. 318; pp. 318–319.

3. Court Roll of South
Elmham, 1408

The jury presented that Henry Pekke died seised[15] of 1 messuage,[16] 10 acres,
½ rod of customary land. His grandson, Henry Pekke, is his heir and is of legal
age. He requests admittance to the tenement. But Joan Recher, the late
Henry's widow, requests half of the tenement as dower.[17] She is admitted.
Henry is admitted to the other half with reversion of dower etc. to hold to
himself and his heirs for services etc. Henry surrenders his half to the use of
Joan for life. She resurrenders the entire tenement to him and to his heirs, but
reserves 1 lower room (*camera*) and 1 upper room (*solar*), also a parcel of land,
with free entry and exit for herself and her friends for life. Conditions: she is
to receive yearly at 30 November 1 quarter of faggots[18] valued at 12d.; yearly
for life, 8s. paid in quarterly installments at 30 November, Easter, 24 June, 29
September; Henry to keep her 2 rooms fully repaired; he is to provide her
with the same food and drink that he himself has, and if she is not pleased
with this fare, she is to have 12d. yearly on account of her displeasure; entry to
the main house whenever she wishes.

4. Court Roll of Wymondham,
1421

From William Notte to John, his son, and Joan, his wife, and their heirs and as-
signs 1 messuage, 10 acres of the tenement "Banymouth," 4½ acres of the
tenement "Rewald," 1 rod of the tenement "Hardened," ½ acre at Shirwod,
½ acre called "Qwythed," and 1 property with appurtenances[19] in Watt. Conditions: reservation of 1 room with solar at northern end of hall; food and clothing; William to warm himself at their fire and to have a horse, a saddle and
a bridle in order to ride whenever he wishes; annually they will plow and
seed 4 acres of his in a field called "Kalleye"; they will maintain 24 ewes.
Entry fine £3.

15. **seised:** in possession of.
16. **messuage:** land surrounding a house, also called a croft.
17. **dower:** right of a widow to a portion of an estate.
18. **faggot:** bundle of sticks for firewood.
19. **appurtenances:** that which belongs to the property, such as buildings.

Source 5 from Nathaniel J. Hone, The Manor and Manorial Records *(Port Washington, N.Y.: Kennikat Press, 1971), pp. 164–166.*

5. Court Roll of Winterborne, 1494

Court held there the 18th day of April the ninth year of the reign of King Henry the Seventh.

1. Essoins—none.
2. The homage there come and are sworn. And they present that all things are well.
3. A penalty is imposed upon all the tenants there that they shall well and competently make all repairs of their tenements, under penalty for each one of them not doing so 20ˢ.
4. The suitors[20] there come and are sworn, and present that Thomas Hatt hath overburdened the common pasture there with his sheep, therefore he is in mercy.[21] And so it is commanded him for the future not to do so under penalty of 10ˢ.
5. Also they present that William Barcoll, freeholder, hath closed his last day, who held of the lord certain lands by knight service. And they say that Alice and Sibell are daughters and next heirs of the said William. And that Alice is five years of age and not more. And that the aforesaid Sibell is three years of age and over. And upon this comes William Webbe[22] and gives to the lord of fine for the minority of the aforesaid heirs 3ˢ4ᵈ.
6. Also they present that the said William Barcoll held of the lord, according to the custom of the manor there, 3 messuages with their appurtenances, after whose death there falls to the lord by way of heriot, a horse of a roan colour value 10ˢ. And upon this comes the aforesaid William Webbe, and takes of the lord the aforesaid 3 messuages with all their appurtenances. To have and to hold to him, and Thomas, and John, sons of the said William for the term of their lives, or of the one of them longest living, according to the custom of the manor there, by rent and other services therefrom aforetime due and of right accustomed. And moreover it was granted to the aforesaid William, Thomas, and John, that each of them shall have a sufficient deputy dwelling in the said 3 messuages with their appurtenances, during the term aforesaid. And he gives to the lord of fine for entry, and for possession of his estate, 6ˢ8ᵈ. And further, the tenants shall give to the lord by way of heriot 10ˢ.

---

20. **suitors:** those bringing cases to the court.
21. Thomas Hatt has placed more sheep there than he is entitled to do by his tenancy.
22. William Webbe seeks the wardship or custody of the children till they come of age.

Source 6 from A. F. C. Baber, The Court Rolls of the Manor Bromsgrove and King's Norton, 1494–1504 *(Kineton, Warwick, England: Worcestershire Historical Society, 1963), pp. 84–85.*

6. Court Roll of Bromsgrove and King's Norton, 1496

1. To this court came Henry Banard and paid 12d as a fine to the lady[23] to have an inquest of office[24] according to the custom of the manor of Bromsgrove and King's Norton to enquire on the oath of twelve of the tenants of the said manor as to what legal right Richard Sharpe had to grant any estate to Peter Parre and to enquire whether Giles Sharpe had issue[25] William and Elizabeth and whether the said William died without issue or not and to enquire whether the said Elizabeth married a certain William Banard or not and to enquire whether the said William Banard and Elizabeth his wife had issue Henry Banard and whether the said . . . Henry . . . is the true heir of the said Elizabeth or not. And he asked that the next steps might be taken according to the custom of the manor and Roger Bydell the bailiff of King's Norton was ordered to summon twelve of the tenants of King's Norton by good summoners to be at the next court at Lykehay that is on Monday (4 April) next ready to make an examination in the said inquest of office and the same day was given to the said Henry.

2. At this court the jurors empanelled, charged and sworn for the inquest of office of Henry Banard appeared that is William Benton, Thomas Reynold, Thomas Grene, Humphrey Rotton, Thomas Blyke, Richard Slough, Baldwin Sye, John Holyok junior, Thomas Holme, Thomas Byssehill senior, Baldwin Feld of Geyhill, Richard Lette and Thomas Lee and each of them say on oath that a certain William Sharpe gave an estate in the land to Richard Sharpe and they say that Giles Sharpe had issue William and Elizabeth and that the said William died without issue and they say that the said Elizabeth married a certain William Banard and that the said William Banard and Elizabeth had issue Henry Banard and that the said Henry Banard is the true heir of the said Elizabeth.

3. To this court came Peter Parre and paid 12d as a fine to have an inquest of office according to the custom of the manor to enquire on the oath of twelve of the tenants of King's Norton as to whether William Sharpe son and heir of Giles Sharpe at any time was seised of a tenement in Wrednale with

---

23. The domina or lady of the manor was the widow of the previous lord.
24. **inquest of office:** official inquiry.
25. **issue:** children.

appurtenances . . . and thus seised whether by charter he gave the said tenement to Roger Sharpe and Richard his brothers in fee and whether the said tenement was only for the work and use of Richard Sharpe and not of Roger Sharpe or not and whether the said Richard Sharpe after the death of the said William Sharpe his brother by virtue of the said charter entered alone into the whole of the said tenement and occupied the tenement throughout his life taking for himself all the profits without claim or blame from Roger Sharpe or not and if the said Richard Sharpe during his life time gave the said tenement with its appurtenances to Peter Parre and Alice his wife daughter of the said Richard Sharpe in fee[26] or not and if the said Peter and Alice by virtue of the said gift were alone peaceably seised of the said tenement . . . taking the profits thereof or not. And he asked that the next steps might be taken according to the custom of the manor of Bromsgrove and King's Norton. Therefore Thomas Reynold the under-bailiff of King's Norton was ordered to summon twelve of the tenants of King's Norton by good summoners according to the custom of the said manor to be at the next court at Lykehay on Monday (23 May) to make an examination in the said inquest of office and the said Peter has the same day.

4. At this court Roger Bedull the under-bailiff of King's Norton as ordered at the last meeting of the court appeared with the men empanelled to make the inquest of office of Peter Parre that is Roger Norton, John Feld in le hole, Baldwin Feld senior, John Freth, John Greve, Edward Kyteley, John Lyndon, William Hawkes, William Oldenhale, John Vitter, Richard Marten, John Feld of Gorshaw, William Halle, Robert Taillor, John Sergeaunt, John Chamber and John More junior and each of them sworn and charged of and in the said premises say upon oath that William Sharpe son and heir of Giles Sharpe was seised of the said tenement with its appurtenances in Wrednale . . . and thus seised by his charter gave the said tenement to Roger Sharpe and Richard Sharpe his brothers . . . and that the gift of the said tenement was for the work and use only of Richard Sharpe and not of Roger Sharpe and they say that Richard Sharpe after the death of the said William his brother by virtue of that charter himself entered into the whole of the said tenement with appurtenances and occupied it peaceably all his life taking the profits thereof to his own use alone without claim or blame from Roger Sharpe and they say that Richard Sharpe (gave) the said tenement . . . to Peter Parre and Alice his wife daughter of the said Richard and they say that the said Peter and Alice by virtue of the said gift are alone peaceably seised of the tenement in their demesne . . . taking the profits thereof etc.

26. **in fee:** with the rights to pass it on to heirs.

Sources 7 and 8 from Warren O. Ault, Open-field Farming in Medieval England: A Study of Village By-Laws *(London: George Allen and Unwin, 1972), p. 117; p. 133.*

7. Bylaws of Wistow, 1410

1. It is ordered by the lord and the whole homage that each tenant shall fill the pits which he made in the low way [*loway*] under pain[27] for each one of 12d.

2. Item that no one shall let his colts go loose so they are taken in the grain from the Feast of St Peter in Chains (August 1st) to the Nativity of the Blessed Mary (September 8th) under pain of 7d.

3. And that no sheep shall be allowed in the meadow at Wyldbrigg next to the meadow of the rector before the Feast of the Nativity of the Blessed Mary under pain each one of 4d.

4. And that each tenant of Wistow shall mend the road next to his land with stone before the Feast of St. Michael under pain each one of 12d.

5. And that no one shall mow or dig in the fen near the boundary ways by a width of three acres under pain each one of 40d.

6. And that no one shall glean in autumn who is able to earn 1d. a day and food under pain each one of 12d.

7. And that no one shall tether or pasture beasts in the wheat stubble this side the Feast of the Nativity of the Blessed Mary under pain each one of 12d. The jury of Wistow elect Robert Waryn, John Randolf, William Becker and Thomas ffraunces reeves of autumn and they were sworn.

8. Bylaws of Hitchin, 1471

1. It is ordained by the assent of the lord's council and of his tenants that none shall enter the sown field in autumn time to gather grain or spears[28] with rakes or by hand if they are capable of earning 2d. a day, under pain for each one doing contrary to this ordinance of 3s. 4d.

2. Those who are not capable of earning 2d. a day shall not enter or cross through the sown fields until the sheaves have been gathered, removed and carted from a space of four acres of land under the aforesaid pain.

3. And if they be boys and under age or someone's servants who are not able to satisfy the lord in respect of the aforesaid pain then their masters who have these persons in governance shall answer to the lord for the aforesaid pain.

27. **pain:** fine.
28. **spears:** stalks of grain.

Sources 9, 10, and 11 from Jules de Launay, Abstracts of Cranbrook Wills Proved in the Diocesan Courts of Canterbury *(Canterbury, England: English Records Collection, 1984), pp. 28–29; p. 30; p. 39.*

9. Will of John Jalander, Cranbrook, 1476

JALANDER, John
18 Apr 1476

To the High Altar of Cranbrook for tithes forgotten, 6d.
To the construction of the new chapel of the Blessed Mary, 6/8.
To my godson Nich. PEND, 6d.
To each each godchild, 4d.
To the repair of the way, where most needed, between the Cross of Hertle and Turneden, 40d.
To my wife Alice, my best cow.
To Rich. CRYSP, another cow.
To my son Robt., a cow & a calf.
RESIDUE of my goods, to my wife Alice and Rich. CRYSPE.
EXECS:[29] my wife Alice and Rich. CRYSPE.

WILL:
FEOFFEES:[30] Stph. CRAKREGE, Laur. TAYLOR, John KYTT, & John NETTAR son of Rich. NETTAR.
To my wife Alice, all my lands & tenements for life.
After her dec., my feoffees shall deliver to my son Robt. the sd. property in fee simple[31] on condition that the sd. Robt. my son pay his brother Wm. 18 marks within 6 yrs. after the death of my wife, at the rate of £2/yr.
To be sold to pay my debts and bequests: a garden with a passage to it, called Smythisfeld.
Should my son Robt. die before age 22 and without lawful issue, then I will that my dau. Alice CRYSPE have a croft of land called Loggecroft, in fee simple. And should my dau. Alice die without legitimate heirs of her body, then I will that the sd. croft be sold and the money be used for charitable works.
And if, as just said, my son Robt. should die before 22 without lawful issue, all my lands and tenements (except the croft bequeathed to Alice) shall be sold. The money therefrom shall be distributed as follows:
    to my son Wm., 26/8;

29. **execs:** executors.
30. **feoffees:** persons acting as trustees.
31. **in fee simple:** as a free holding, that is, with no labor obligations attached to it and able to be handed down to any of his own heirs.

to a suitable priest to celebrate in the church of Cranbrook for a year, for my soul and the souls of the faithful departed, 10 marks;

the remainder of the money shall be used to buy a chalice for the church of Cranbrook.

Robt. shall pay Mgt., the dau. of my dau. Alice 26/8 towards her marriage.

10. Will of Robert Lurker, Cranbrook, 1477

LURKER, Robert
30 Mch 1477.

To the High Altar of Cranbrook for tithes forgotten, 6d.

To the parish chaplain there, 2d.

To the parish clerk there, 1d.

To the Light of St. Christopher there, 4d.

To the repair of the foul ways from my mansion[32] to the messuage of Rich. BENETT, 12d.

To my wife Agnes, a bed and bedding, including a mattress and undercloth; also to her, a pan.

To my sons and daus., the RESIDUE of all my utensils, to be distributed among them at the discretion of my execs. and feoffees.

To my son Wm., all my instruments pertaining to his trade of wheelwright. I give to my son Wm. 800 felloes (felloe = the rim or part of the rim of a spoked wheel) and 1000 spokes.

RESIDUE of my goods, to Simon LYNCH & Wm. BASSOK, and they are my EXECS.

WILL:

FEOFFEE: Wm. BALDEN, enfeoffed in my lands in Cranbrook.

Wm. BALDEN shall deliver to my son Wm. in fee simple, my messuage in which I now dwell, and a garden thereto, & a croft called Blakland, on condition that my son Wm. pay my wife Agnes 40s within 2 yrs. after my dec.

My feoffees shall deliver to my son Alex., a piece of land called Derbers (?), (2 acres), to hold forever.

To my sons John and Simon, 2 pieces of arable land[33] and 3 pieces of grazing land called Stonerok, the Pucell, & the Wodes (27 acres), forever, on condition that John & Simon pay to the marriages of my daus. Margery, Petonille, & Agnes, 13/4 each.

---

32. **mansion:** house.

33. **arable:** land that can grow grain crops.

If my wife, who is pregnant, gives birth to a son, then this son shall share the 2 pieces of arable land and 3 pieces of grazing land with his brothers John & Simon.

My wife shall have her quarters in my messuage, and a solar, and a fire in the hall, and her easement there, and the use of the bakehouse, for 8 years.

11. Will of Thomas Herenden, Cranbrook, 1483

HERENDEN, Thomas
6 Jul 1483

To the High Altar of Cranbrook for tithes forgotten, 12d.

To the Light of the Blessed Mary, 4d.

To the chaplain of Holy Trinity of Milkhouse in the parish of Cranbrook, 2s, of which 12d immediately after my dec. and 12d later.

To my wife Eleanor, all the utensils now in my house.

EXEC: my son John HERENDEN, and to him the RESIDUE of my goods. . . .

WILL:

My son John shall have my messuage lying in the parish of Cranbrook upon the den of Hesilldenwode, with my lands, except 2 pieces of land with a garden called le Graunge, forever.

To my son Jas. (Jacobus), the 2 pieces of land with the garden called le Graunge, forever, he releasing and acquiting[34] the property of the feudal lord for 6/8.

My son John shall pay my wife Eleanor 16s.

I will that after the death of my wife, my son Jas. shall have 2 pieces of land called le Joyfeld and Bachell, he acquiting this land of the feudal lord for 3/4.

To my dau. Joan BARGH, after the dec. of my wife, 6/8, out of these last 2 pieces.

My wife Eleanor shall have a room in the southern part of my messuage, for life.

Also to her, fire, a cow with its pasturage on my son John's land summer and winter.

My sons John and James (Jacobus) shall pay 13/4 for my funeral expenses and 13/4 for my month's mind.[35]

---

34. **releasing and acquiting:** paying the fees necessary to the lord to inherit the property.

35. **month's mind:** memorial service held one month after an individual's death.

Sources 12 and 13 from Zvi Razi, Life, Marriage and Death in a Medieval Parish: Economy, Society and Demography in Halesowen 1270–1400 *(Cambridge, England: Cambridge University Press, 1980), p. 142; p. 148.*

12. Average Number of Offspring over the Age of Twelve in Halesowen Families, by Economic Status, 1350–1400

Economic Status	No. of families	Adjusted mean no. of offspring
Rich	60	3.0
Middling	89	2.0
Poor	81	1.4
Unidentified	23	—
Total	253	2.1

13. The Socioeconomic Status of Lessors, Lessees, and Buyers of Land in Halesowen, 1350–1400

	No. of Leases (32)			No. of sales (81)		
	No. of lessors[36]	No. of lessees	Excess of lessees	No. of vendors	No. of buyers	Excess of buyers
Members of rich families	12	16	+4	17	25	+8
Members of middling families	11	8	−3	25	21	−4
Members of poor families	9	4	−5	30	9	−21
Total	32	28	−4	72	55	−17

36. **Lessors** leased or rented land to **lessees; vendors** sold land to buyers.

QUESTIONS TO CONSIDER

Both central questions for this chapter center on medieval family relationships, the first on relationships between families and the second, on relationships within families. The first is in some ways easier to answer because of the nature of our sources, for economic transactions and other interactions *between* family members often left a historical record only if they were unusual or contested. The case referred to in Source 6, for example, would never have come to court if distant cousins Henry Banard and Peter Parre had not both claimed the same piece of land; ordinarily the land would have been transferred from generation to generation without much notice. The maintenance agreements found in Sources 3 and 4 probably were entered into the court rolls because there was some doubt that the younger people mentioned in them would actually support their elders; most such agreements were either understood or, at most, oral and never made it into the records. Court records thus offer a picture of familial relations that is skewed toward the negative and disputatious.

To answer the first question, you need to gather your evidence about specific actions. Look again at Source 2, item 14. Why is Thomas Tyler fined? How would you compare his fine with those assessed for other types of infractions? What might account for the difference? Look at Source 5, item 4; what is Thomas Hatt fined for? Keeping these actions in mind, look at the by-laws in Source 7, especially items 2, 3, 5, and 7. How would you generalize about people's attempts to improve their economic position based on these sources? Why do you suppose the fines are so high? What do your calculations regarding Source 13 tell you about additional ways that families improved their position?

Go back to the charts you made tracking certain individuals in Source 2. What did William Wayte and William Clerk do to improve their lot? How might their actions have helped or hurt their whole family? How might the nonfarming activities of various men and women mentioned in items 36 through 50 have strengthened their families' economic position? What other nonfarming activities are mentioned in the sources, and how might these have shaped a family's social and economic position? (Include activities that would have worsened a family's position as well as those that would have upgraded it.) How were a family's opportunities for improving their position determined by the amount of wealth or land they already held?

To answer the second question, you need to assemble information from many sources. What evidence have you found about relationships between spouses? between siblings? between parents and children? What differences do you see in the treatment of daughters versus sons? older versus younger sons? Do the sources present a uniform picture, or do you see contradictions? What might be some of the reasons behind these contradictions? Have you found any sign of an extended family, or do people tend to think of their family as a more or less nuclear unit? (Here the wills in Sources 9, 10, and 11 are your most important resource.)

One of the central issues debated among historians of the premodern family is the depth of people's loyalty to family interests as opposed to self-interest, or what is usually termed individualism. Based on the sources you have read in this chapter, do loyalties to family come first; that is, are there signs of people doing things against their own interests for the good of their family? Do people appear to be more individualistic when engaging with their own family members or with unrelated villagers? Based on the sources, how would you assess the relative importance of economic need and emotional ties in holding medieval families together? What other factors seem to reinforce this bond?

You are now ready to answer the central questions for this chapter: How did common people in medieval England seek to strengthen the economic and social position of their families? How did they define *family* and relate to those they saw as members of this group?

EPILOGUE

Because we have only been able to see their reflection in official legal documents, the medieval families we have observed in this chapter might strike you as rather cold. Private sources such as letters or diaries that flesh out our picture of family relationships in later periods simply don't exist for villagers in medieval England. Added to this is the unfortunate fact that court records from any period pertain only to matters of discord or disagreement. Just imagine what a future historian might conclude about twentieth-century American families if all he or she had to go on were divorce court proceedings.

When used carefully, however, official legal documents can often reveal intimacies of normal, as well as extraordinary, family life. One medieval historian, Barbara Hanawalt, has used English records of coroner's inquests into accidental deaths to trace the movements of children and adults in their daily round of chores and activities. She finds, for example, that even at a very young age girls were more likely to die accidentally in the house and boys outside, and that the holes in the roads, dung-heaps, and uncleared ditches—which our sources in this chapter lament—could be very dangerous for people, especially those who were very old, very young, or drunk. Other historians have used the language of wills—of which we have a small sampling here—to trace the opinions of men about the intelligence and competence of their wives, which no doubt had some bearing on day-to-day life in the household. Doing this kind of digging is hard, but the results are often fascinating as historians gain surprising insight into the everyday lives of ordinary people. (We might think, for example, that rules about building a tennis court on one's property were a result of modern zoning restrictions, but our sources here demonstrate that this was a concern more than five hundred years ago.)

Though in this chapter we have investigated family relationships and activities in only one time and place, when we combine our findings with those from other cultures and periods, we can begin to make comparisons and trace changes. We could do this with cultures closely connected—say, England before the Black Death, the period immediately preceding the one we've studied here—or far removed— say, West African villages in an era before urbanization and industrialization—or even extremely remote—such as the late-twentieth-century family in Los Angeles. Each of these comparisons will reveal differences and similarities, but the most important result of any of them may be an affirmation of the historical nature of the family, and the recognition that the family's structure and function, even the very meaning of the word *family*, have changed many times in the past.

CHAPTER FIFTEEN

CONCEPTUALIZING THE

MODERN WORLD (1500s)

A revolution in the way Europeans envisioned the world helped to launch the modern age of global interaction and interdependence. Renaissance scholarship, which altered so much of Western thought during the *Quattrocento,* or 1400s, changed the way in which Europeans understood and mapped the earth. They began to picture the earth on a new scale and to regard it as a global whole between whose parts long-distance maritime travel seemed not only conceivable but practical. Inspired by this vision, European captains like Columbus ventured out beyond familiar waters, exploring the entire globe and drawing its once separate regions and people into a single integrated world. More than anyone else, it was a Flemish mathematician and chart maker, Gerhardus Mercator (1512–1594), who helped express this new conception. In 1569 he won renown for a world map whose "projection," or way of translating the curved surface of the earth to a flat plane, solved a key

technical problem among cartographers and made a better map for navigators. First hailed as a practical navigational tool, Mercator's map later gained popularity among Europe's academic circles during the Scientific Revolution in the seventeenth century. With Europe's rise to global mastery, westernizing people everywhere adopted the map, making it the standard image of the modern world.

Though often associated with a modern, scientific point of view, the Mercator Projection Map does not provide an accurate picture of the earth's actual surface. In fact, it seriously distorts a number of features. For this reason, it has always drawn criticism of some sort. Recent critics, however, object to the perspective of the map, which they find highly ethnocentric. They argue that the map presents an image of the world shaped by Western values rather than scientific principles. Some opponents have even called upon international agencies to reject Mercator-style maps in favor of other depictions of the world. But the choice of alternatives creates fresh controversy because to one extent or another all world maps distort reality.

Of course professional map makers, or cartographers, have long been aware that mapping the globe inevitably entails distortion. More than anyone else, they realize that only on a sphere can the earth's curved surface accurately be duplicated: all efforts to depict it on a flat map require alteration of its shape. The logical solution would be to draw all maps on globes, but practical considerations make this difficult to do. Any large map of the world with a scale sufficient to show significant detail, particularly the kind of detail a navigator needs, would require a huge globe. Thus cartographers have always accepted the drawbacks in the nearly impossible task of projecting a spherical reality onto a flat plane to produce inexpensive and manageable maps.

In addition to this fundamental distortion, cartographers have often simplified or changed elements of their maps to help users find what they want to know more quickly or easily. The use of different-sized circles to show cities of varying population or the superimposition of colored lines to indicate elevations represent distortions of this sort. Besides these features, which result from conscious decisions, still other distortions may

arise from unconscious choices. How a cartographer orients a map, frames it, and selects what to include in it, for example, may reflect prevailing beliefs of the time rather than specific cartographic needs. Maps thus cannot be viewed as simple depictions of geographic facts; often they reflect intellectual and cultural landscapes as well.

Accordingly this chapter looks at how maps present mental as well as geographic realities. It treats them like any other historical document and studies the way they reflect the values and outlook of their makers. Some of these reflections may be highly personal, but because map makers generally work in the context of established conventions, they more often project cultural rather than individual visions. Maps thus offer historians an important means of studying the perspectives of the past. And this chapter asks you to consider the Mercator Projection Map in this light. After reviewing the evidence, ask yourself, what cultural conventions helped shape the Mercator map? And what are the implications of such a culturally informed, scientific work? Doing so will not only show how cultural factors affect the way people see reality but offer insights into the way we have visualized the modern world.

BACKGROUND

The Mercator Projection Map derives from a long tradition of Western cartography, or map making. Begun in ancient Greece, it initially reflected

an interest in cosmology or the nature of the universe rather than practical travel. Fascinated with ideal systems, the Greeks believed that a rational and harmonious order underlay the natural world, patterning it in perfect, geometric forms. This belief led the Pythagorean school of the fifth century B.C.E. to envision the world mathematically and to depict it as a sphere, the shape they deemed most nearly perfect. This vision reflected cosmological assumptions rather than empirical study. Greek thinkers believed the earth nestled at the core of a series of concentric, transparent orbs that rotated around it at varying rates, carrying with them the sun, moon, and planets. Calling this system the Celestial Sphere, they claimed its rhythmic motions gave visible proof of nature's harmony. Early Greek map makers thus looked to the sky and abstract mathematics when charting the Earth.

This approach led them to develop a gridwork-like system of imaginary lines to locate places on a map. One of the first Greek cartographers, Eratosthenes (276–195 B.C.E.), arbitrarily drew nine north-south lines, or *meridians,* through what he judged to be well-known or important cities. He located most of his east-west lines, or *parallels,* with equal arbitrariness but tried to relate them to celestial order by basing some of them on the *klimata,* imaginary lines associated with the sun's apparent seasonal movement, which we know as the equator and the tropics of Cancer and Capricorn. Unaware that the seasons resulted from a tilting of the earth's axis, the Greeks attributed them to an annual north-south shift of the sun across the globe. They thus named the paths that the sun appeared to trace across the sky at its most extreme summer and winter positions "tropics," meaning a "turning." Because the sun "turned" in its extreme summer path when the constellation Cancer dominated the sky, the Greeks termed this path the tropic of Cancer. And they named its opposite path after the constellation Capricorn, which formed the backdrop for its winter "turning." Though visualized in the sky these paths could be mentally projected on the earth.

Hipparchus, an astronomer of the second century B.C.E., favored a more mathematically precise system with all parallels equally spaced and perpendicular to the meridians. The latter he envisioned as great circles, evenly located around the equator and convergent at the poles. His system appealed to Claudius Ptolemy, a Greek scholar of the second century C.E., who used it for a world map in his *Geographia,* a treatise on the nature of the earth. Ptolemy tried to align his gridwork even more closely with celestial order by deriving its measurement from the "equinoctial hour," or time of the equinoxes when the daylight and darkness are equal. Thus he laid out parallels so that each one marked a point where at the time of the equinox the length of the day would be fifteen minutes longer, obtaining regularly spaced lines that seemingly reflected cosmic intervals. He located meridians similarly, spacing them out evenly along the equator at intervals of "the third part of an equinoctial hour."

Ptolemy also grappled with the problem of distortion. Noting the need for a "certain adjustment" to allow a spherical surface to be depicted on a flat plane, he represented the meridians as straight lines at the equator but made them converge toward the poles and drew the parallels as arcs sharing a common center along the earth's axis. He claimed his approach succeeded in representing a curved surface on a flat plane. But as he openly admitted, this compromise was problematic, "since it is impossible for all of the parallels to keep the proportion that there is in a sphere."[1] His adjustment produced what modern cartographers term a conic projection, which distorts details in the polar regions but depicts mid-latitudes well. On this abstract grid, well-suited to a Mediterranean based map, Ptolemy laid out his conception of the world.

He put North at the top, a convention followed by modern Western cartography and one of its most obvious hallmarks. As he lacked information about the northern polar region and most of the southern hemisphere, he left out these areas, claiming that "the extent of our habitable earth from east to west all concede is much greater than its extent from the north pole to the south." His world map—to judge from surviving copies—included only twenty-one parallels north of the equator and one south of it. Like most Greeks of his time, he assumed that the equatorial zone must be uninhabitable due to its heat. He also ignored the Pacific side of the world about which he knew nothing, a factor that led him to inflate Eurasia while reducing the apparent diameter of the earth. Therefore, although called a world map, Ptolemy's work showed only a segment confined to Europe, North Africa, and parts of western and southern Asia.

Though Ptolemy's map became the standard world map during Roman times, it fell out of favor following the fall of Rome in the first centuries of the common era. As Rome declined, Hellenistic culture derived from Greek roots waned with it. Christianity, however, thrived, and around its beliefs a new mentality began to form. Christian thinkers deemed the natural world an imperfect reflection of a higher, divine reality. In their view, physical things merely obscured divine truth, which revealed itself directly to intellect through the spirit. Thus, they had little motive to study the natural world much less to model the earth with mathematical precision or to map its actual contours. More important to them was a symbolic map showing spiritual landmarks to divine grace. A new tradition of *mappæ mundi*, or world maps, thus evolved to meet this need in the sixth and seventh centuries. Though derived from diagrammatic Roman maps, they defined a new, medieval vision of the world quite unlike the older Hellenistic conception.

Because these maps show the earth as a perfect circle divided into three parts by a T-shaped confluence of waters, scholars today generally term them T-O maps. Its exact origin remains uncertain, but the T-O map had assumed its essential form by the seventh century. An early example appears in an encyclopedic work of that century, called the *Etymologies*, written by Isidore of Seville. Many subsequent variations survive. Highly influenced by passages in the Chris-

1. For Ptolemy's remarks, see *The Geography of Claudius Ptolemy,* trans. and ed. Edward L. Stevenson (New York, 1932), bk. I, chaps. XXI–XXIII, pp. 41–42.

tian Bible, all typically portray the world as a circle ("the circle of the earth" in Isaiah 40:22) surrounded by an encircling *Mare Oceanus,* or Ocean Sea. From this flow the waters that meet in the center to divide the land into the three continents of Asia, Africa, and Europe.

Unlike Ptolemy's map, T-O maps put the East at the top, giving prominence to paradise, which Genesis (2:8) located "eastward in Eden." This convention explains why *orientation,* or "eastward pointing," means taking correct bearings. Thus Asia appears above the other continents, separated from them by the rivers Tanais (the modern Don) on the left and the Nile on the right. The Mediterranean Sea, drawn as a simple perpendicular bisecting these two rivers and forming the stem of the T, occurs as a central feature partitioning Europe from Africa. Most maps also indicate a few important cities, particularly Jerusalem, which they symbolically place near the center of the map. Few actual geographic features appear, though these maps depict many sites of religious significance to Christians.

The medieval iconographical approach to cartography, like the Greek cosmological approach, produced maps for intellectual contemplation but of little practical value. Throughout ancient and medieval times in the West, however, travelers needed maps to help them find their way across land and sea. Hence a quite separate tradition of practical route maps developed to serve their needs. The Romans had a tradition of road maps that dated back at least to the time of Julius Caesar who ordered his son-in-

law, Marcus Agrippa, to chart imperial highways. No actual Roman versions of this map, which was engraved on a marble slab in the Forum at Rome, remain, but its appearance may be duplicated in an eleventh- or twelfth-century copy of a late Roman road map of the empire known as the Peutinger Table (*Tabula Peutinger*). It shows highways together with sufficient schematic renditions of towns, rivers, and mountains to help a traveler maintain proper bearings. But it grossly distorts landforms, and the overall effect is that of a cartoon. Nonetheless, maps of this sort, like the Ebstorf map of Germany, continued in use during the European Middle Ages to illustrate routes of pilgrimage in guidebooks. Because texts provided most information, these maps merely showed towns, abbeys, crossroads, and so on as stylized icons.

European seafarers, however, needed more accurate maps. By late medieval times, they used two types, both of which were essential navigational aids. One was a partially blank map of open waters upon which navigators could lay out new courses; the other was a commercial chart of common coastal areas. The latter, sold in bound sets called *portolani* (Italian for "harbor books") in Mediterranean waters, provided navigators with detailed information on how to pilot ships using coastal landmarks. Devised for seamen, both represented an empirical approach to cartography unlike those used by earlier scholars whose world maps were tailored to suit abstract mathematical or theological principles. Most had a very limited focus. But an eight-panel work known as the Catalan Atlas, created by Abraham Cresques for King Charles V of France in 1375, shows the sea lanes from Britain and the Canary Islands in the west to the coast of India. Such *portolani* sets attest to a growing interest among Europeans in visualizing a larger world in more practical terms. The way navigators charted courses also began to reflect this interest.

Pilot maps gave landmarks from which a position might be taken by sight, but sailing charts used an abstract system of lines to help sailors keep their bearing when sailing out of view of land. This system had nothing to do with the old Greek gridwork of meridians and parallels. It was based instead on a web-like pattern of "lines of rhumb" (from the Spanish word *rhumba*, meaning a "ship's heading") upon which courses could be laid out. These lines indicated hypothetical bearings leading off to a number of abstract points, or "quarters," equally distributed around the world's edge—envisioned as an encircling Ocean Sea. The points to which the lines radiated were named after conventional "winds," or storm fronts, thought to originate near them. By the late Middle Ages, this device, which went back to Roman days, evolved into a system of eight primary points, four full and four half-winds, that could be expanded further by the addition of quarter- and eighth-winds. When all thirty-two such points were drawn, the resulting figure looked like a many petaled flower; and so it was called a "wind rose."

By drawing the points of the wind rose out into radiating lines of rhumb,

chart makers created a basic star-shaped design, which could be repeated regularly on a blank map to create an overlapping webwork of lines. Upon this webwork they then drew in coastlines and seas so that navigators could plot courses between landfalls parallel to the imaginary lines of rhumb. This system was so well established that Europeans adapted it for use with the compass when they obtained that device from the Arabs in the early 1300s, simply realigning the lines of rhumb to the cardinal compass points. By the 1500s, Flemish cartographers, then the leading chart makers of Europe, replaced the traditional names of the winds with the French terms for the compass points and used the fleur-de-lis, the French royal symbol, to mark North, the key point.

Like so many other aspects of European culture, map making changed with the fifteenth-century revival of classical Mediterranean learning. New interest in Greek thought rekindled speculation about the nature of the world and brought a shift in cartography. Ptolemy's world map, rediscovered in Byzantine copies, became popular again, as the development of the printing press in Germany allowed relatively inexpensive editions of his *Geographia* to circulate widely. Though underestimating the circumference of the earth and filled with errors, Ptolemy's map broadened European horizons. Unlike *portolani* and course-plotting charts, which remained too localized to inspire ventures into the unknown, the Ptolemaic map, as a theoretical construct, indicated uncharted areas as well as known regions. When redrawn with the system of rhumb line coordinates superimposed upon it, it offered mariners a global context in which to project new sailing routes. Thus the merger of the old, Greek cosmological style of cartography with medieval navigational conventions created a new, practical map of the world that promoted exploration.

Fifteenth-century Portuguese captains used updated versions of the Ptolemaic map to plot their voyages around Africa to India, and Columbus based his belief in the feasibility of sailing westward to Asia on them. Columbus's letters, in fact, clearly show that he obtained Ptolemaic-style charts from Paolo da Pozzo Toscanelli (1397–1482), a leading Florentine scholar and map maker who also advised King Alfonso of Portugal on sea routes around Africa. Though none remain, we know what Toscanelli's charts looked like because they were based on a world map that *has* survived. Known as the Martellus map after the name of its maker, Henricus Martellus, who drew it in 1489 on the eve of Europe's age of exploration, this map also inspired the Flemish chart maker Gerhardus Mercator.

Mercator's goal was not only to make an up-to-date world map but to create a better navigational tool for those sailing in unfamiliar waters far from Europe. Like most world maps of the mid-sixteenth century, it tried to show the Americas and Pacific Ocean in proper relationship to the Old World of Eurasia and Africa. But what really made it innovative was Mercator's effort to depict the earth's curved surface on a flat plane in a way that allowed mariners to plot more accurate courses. As European sailors ventured on long voyages that eventually took them around the world, they found that plotting courses on a global map like Ptolemy's using conventional rhumb lines led to problems. The lines that appeared to be straight on the maps actually represented courses arching over the curved surface of the earth. On short voyages such as those in the Mediterranean, the discrepancy proved insignifcant. But on long voyages, ships on headings plotted as straight lines strayed far off course, and if sailing in uncharted regions without known landmarks by which to correct the error, they became hopelessly lost. True lines of rhumb, known as *loxodromes* (from the Greek words for "oblique running"), must take this curvature into account. But if drawn as curved lines on a flat map surface, they do not intersect meridians in the identical oblique angles that mariners needed to check their course bearings with a sextant.

Mercator wanted to solve this problem by making a world map that compensated for the curvature of the earth but allowed navigators to plot courses as straight lines intersecting meridians at constant angles. He did so, as he noted on the face of his 1569 map, by devising "a new proportion and a new arrangement of the meridians with reference to the parallels." His method was simple. It merely required drawing meridians parallel rather than convergent at the poles. Made this way, meridians and parallels coincided exactly with the north-south and east-west axes of the conventional wind rose pattern, and all the lines of rhumb radiating outward maintained constant angles with respect to them. Of course, this created another distortion, since true meridians form great circles around the earth that *do* converge at the poles.

This distortion, though barely noticeable at the equator where meridians almost parallel one another, becomes extreme near the poles. There, where they should converge, Mercator's meridians remain apart, grossly distorting all features. They make east-west distances near the poles appear much greater than they are and skew alignments out of proportion. To compensate, Mercator spaced the parallels or lines of longitude ever farther apart toward the poles so that their spacing increased in exact measure to the progressive spread of the meridians. By thus making a mile at the equator much shorter than a mile at the poles, Mercator minimized the way his projection contorted shapes near the poles. But this compensation makes landforms toward the polar regions appear much larger than they really are. Mercator, who was himself aware of this problem, found a partial solution by simply leaving the polar regions off of his map. Because nothing was

known about them in his time and most important sea lanes lay closer to the equator than the poles of the earth, gross polar distortion seemed a small price to pay for a very practical new kind of map.

Mercator's method of mapping caught on in Europe. Mercator himself won it acclaim through a three-volume set of maps that he and his son published from 1585 to 1595, coining the term *atlas* to designate a comprehensive cartographical survey of the world. But other Flemish map makers helped to popularize it. A fellow Fleming, Abrahim Ortel, used it to prepare maps for a book published in 1570 under the name *Theatrum Orbis Terrarum*. Soon others followed suit, most notably Jocondus Hondius who kept various versions of Mercator's map in print until 1637. Because of the high regard enjoyed by Flemish map makers at this time, European cartographers elsewhere followed their lead. Mercator's approach thus became the map on which explorers charted their findings and through which the image of the modern world first emerged. But, as recent critics charge, that image was far from objective.

THE METHOD

The task of determining the cultural perspective of the Mercator map, as you might guess, requires you to deal with cartographic materials. Therefore, maps make up the primary material presented in the Evidence section. Some illustrate the Western map-making tradition that formed the background of Mercator's work, whereas others depict alternate ways of portraying the globe. Comparisons between these materials and Mercator's map should help you detect the special features of the Mercator Projection Map and determine what elements it emphasizes at the expense of others.

Sources 1 and 2 show Mercator's original world map of 1569 and a standard modern map based on his projection. These are followed by reconstructions of two ancient maps from the classical Mediterranean world, Sources 3 and 4, illustrating the Greek tradition of cartography. Sources 5 through 7 present three examples of the diagrammatic and T-O shaped *mappæ mundi* produced in Europe during the Middle Ages. By way of contrast, Sources 8 through 10 display how differently people in some other cultures saw the world: Source 8 reproduces a twelfth-century Islamic map, and Sources 9 and 10 demonstrate the perspective of traditional Chinese cartographers. A fourteenth-century Catalan sea chart, Source 11, and a Florentine world map of 1489, Source 12, give some indication of the shift that came in Western map making with the Renaissance and created the immediate cartographic context in which Mercator worked. Finally, Source 13, a contemporary equal-area map, shows an alternate vision of the world advocated by those favoring a more global perspective.

An analysis of these different maps should allow you to uncover the conceptual framework of Mercator's map and recognize the cultural conventions reflected in it. Such an approach does not demand great expertise with the technical details of cartography. It does, however, ask you to consider the Mercator map as a cultural artifact and to approach it as a cultural historian would, view-

ing it not so much as a device showing what the world actually looks like but as an abstraction reflecting the outlook of its creators. In other words, it requires you to "read" Mercator's map as a cultural document rather than a statement of geographic fact. To do so, you will have to look beyond its geographic details for clues to the values and assumptions that helped to shape it. Of course, to distinguish these elements in the first place, you need some awareness of the basic conventions of traditional map making.

Unfortunately, we do not have a lot of maps from which to reconstruct those conventions. Usually designed to be portable, most were made of lightweight, fragile materials that did not survive for very long. Until the start of the modern age of printing in the West during the fifteenth century, maps tended to be rare, handmade objects. Only a few, therefore, have come down to us from earlier times, particularly from the ancient world and distant cultures. And those that have are almost all handmade copies fraught with the errors and variants common to copies. So our understanding of old maps remains sketchy, and many questions plague efforts to study them. Nonetheless, enough survive for us to see that different cultures had unique ways of translating three-dimensional space and complex geography into visual conventions.

Without knowing these conventions, you often cannot make sense out of a map. As with any other document, you have to learn the "language" in which maps are written before you can read them. You will thus probably find some of the examples that follow totally confusing. Do not let this circumstance deter you. If nothing else, this bewilderment ought to convince you just how much conventions of this sort affect the way we envision reality. Our own maps today would seem just as confusing to people of other cultures as some of these do to you. Yet you can read them without trouble. With a little effort and some guidance, you will discover how to read the less familiar ones presented here, too, or at least how to interpret enough of their major features to make general comparisons possible. Moreover, in making the attempt you will, we hope, come to see familiar maps in a fresh light. For you will have learned to notice things you might otherwise take for granted.

Begin by simply looking carefully at each strange map and systematically noting what it shows. A threefold approach may help you search for clues to an understanding of its larger significance. First, note what devices, if any, each employs to orient the user and to locate points in relationship to each other. Most maps use a set of coordinates or some sort of framework from which an observer is expected to construe the reality represented. So look especially for signs of such devices. Often they involve explicit symbols like the compass points, grid lines, and mileage scales on modern maps that stand out clearly as unnatural features. Second, consider how each map frames a field of vision and thereby implies some coherence or unity to what it

shows. Ask yourself what the map defines or implies by this framing. What sort of entity does it visualize? Does it evoke a whole world, a specific region, a country, a community, or merely a network of connections like roads? This question leads to a related third and last consideration. What kinds of individual features appear on the map and how do they correlate to each other? Does it, for example, highlight some over others by making them larger or placing them in a prominent position?

Note, of course, that most of these components probably do not reproduce natural features. Lines of latitude, political boundaries, and "centers" exist in peoples' thoughts as abstractions rather than as elements of an actual landscape. They, like the maps that illustrate them, help us to visualize space and make sense of it in social terms so that we can talk about it coherently and direct one another around in it. For that very reason, of course, maps tend to reveal how we regard a space—that is, what we value most about it or want to do in it. Once you have identified the three types of information listed above for a given map, therefore, ask what this information tells you about the interests of the people who made and used it. How, for example, did they define or bound their world? What did they value enough to represent within it? And finally, what purpose or activity would the information presented serve?

In reaching some conclusion about these broad questions, you should begin to glimpse something of the overall "slant," or cultural perspective, that shapes a map. Using this insight, revisit the Mercator map with great care and try to detect elements that you might have otherwise ignored or that you might have considered too obvious to notate. Be just as systematic and ask the same questions of it as you did of the strange maps. What do your conclusions suggest about the way in which Europeans conceptualized the modern world and their place in it? Why might the perspective reflected in this map seem odd or even disturbing to some people, particularly now that European nations no longer dominate the world and we seem to be entering a new global age of interdependence?

THE EVIDENCE

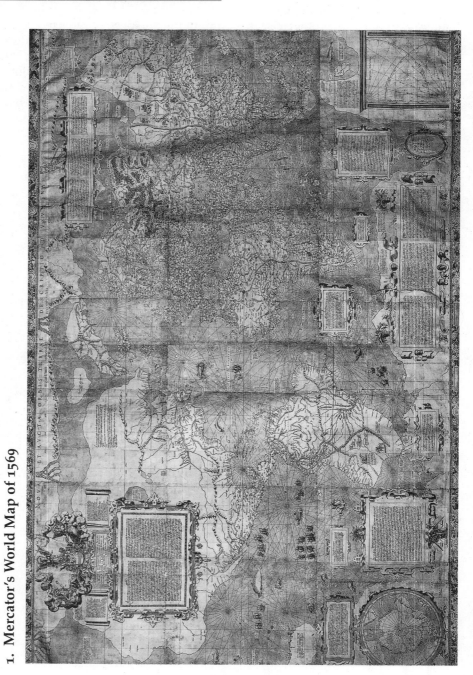

Source 1 from the Bibliothèque nationale de France.

1. Mercator's World Map of 1569

Source 2 from William R. Shepherd, Historical Atlas, 8th edition (New York: Barnes and Noble, 1956), p. 176.

2. Map of the World Based on Mercator Projection, early 20th century

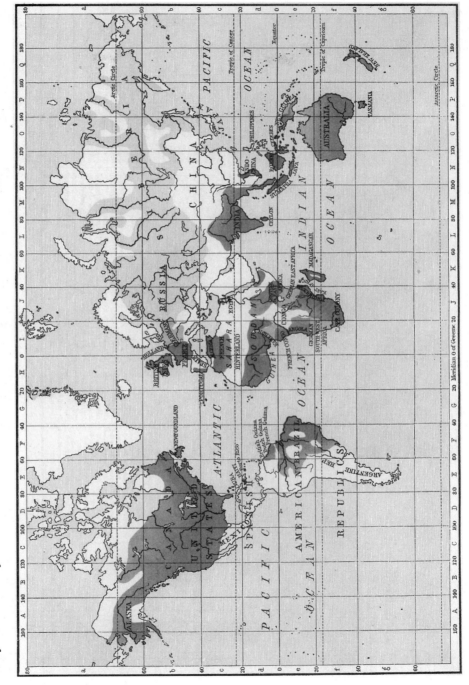

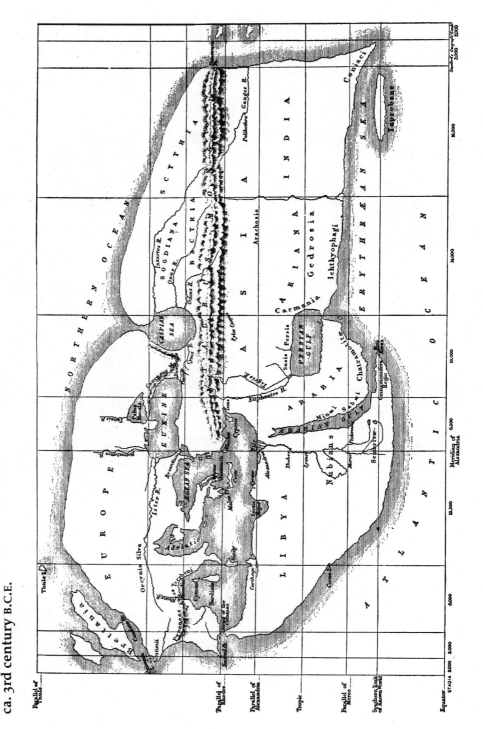

Source 3 from John Onians, Art and Thought in the Hellenistic Age (Thames and Hudson, 1979). Reproduced by permission of Thames and Hudson.

3. A Modern Reconstruction of Eratosthenes' Map of the World, ca. 3rd century B.C.E.

4. A Renaissance Reconstruction of Ptolemy's Map of the World

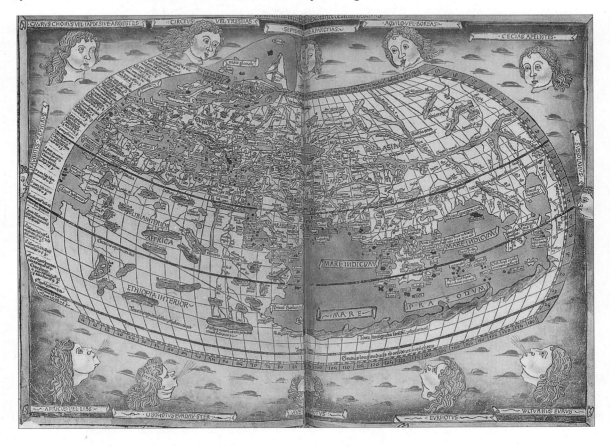

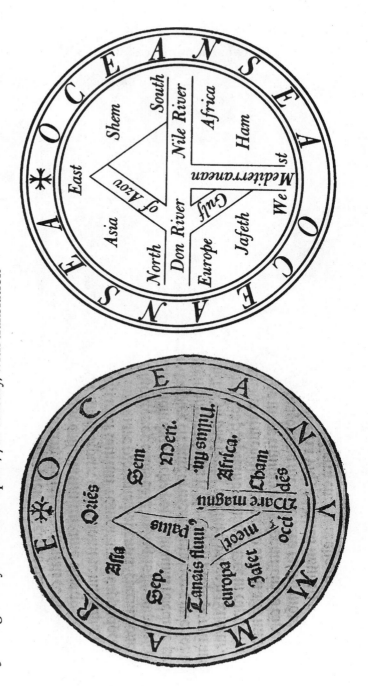

Source 5 from the Walters Art Gallery, Baltimore. Translation from Lloyd A. Brown, The Story of Maps (Boston: Little, Brown, 1950), opp. p. 103. Reproduced with permission.

5. Diagram by Isidore of Spain, 7th century, with translation

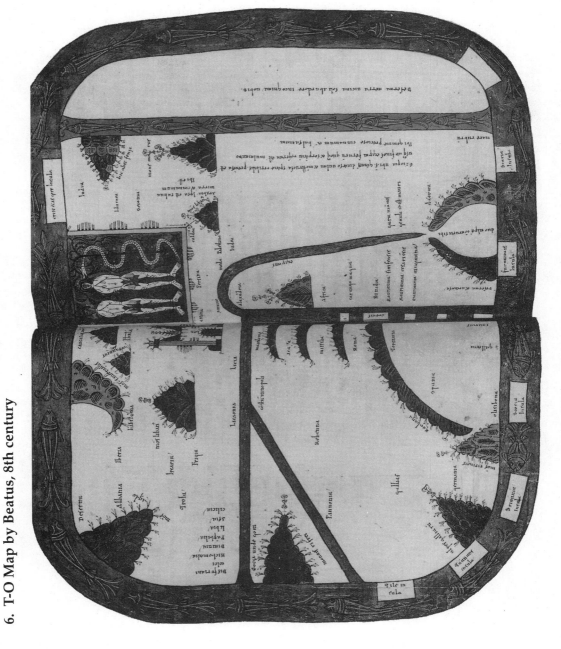

Source 6 from the British Library.

6. T-O Map by Beatus, 8th century

Source 7 from the Niedersächsische Landesbibliothek, Hanover.

7. Medieval Map of the World from Ebstorf, Germany

Source 8 from the Bibliothèque nationale de France.

8. The Islamic World Map of Al Idrisi, 12th century

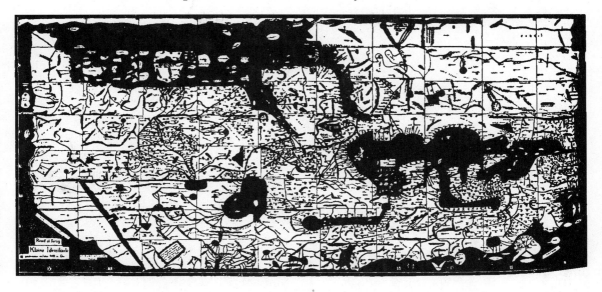

9. Korean Version of Chinese Cosmological Map, 17th century

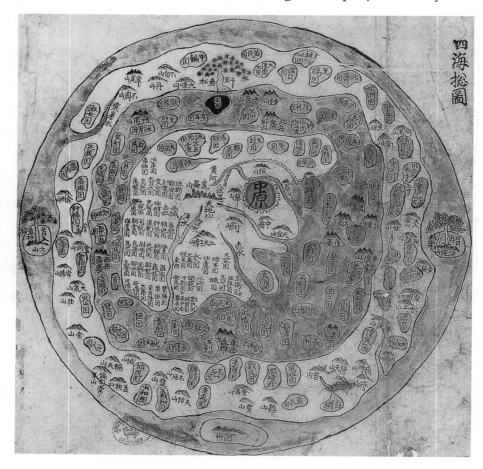

10. Ancient Chinese Mirror with TLV Cosmological Pattern, ca. 1600–1200 B.C.E.

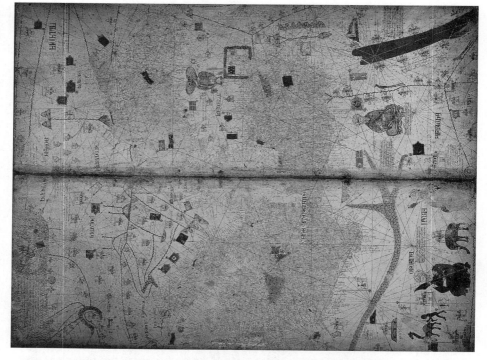

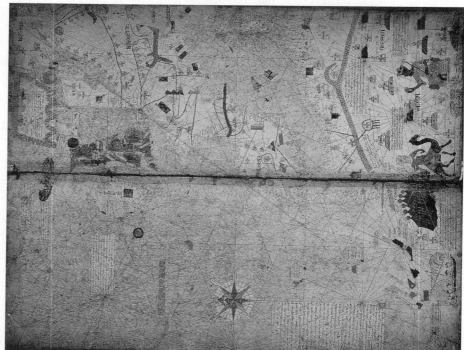

Source 11 from the Bibliothèque nationale de France.

11. From the Catalan Atlas, 1375

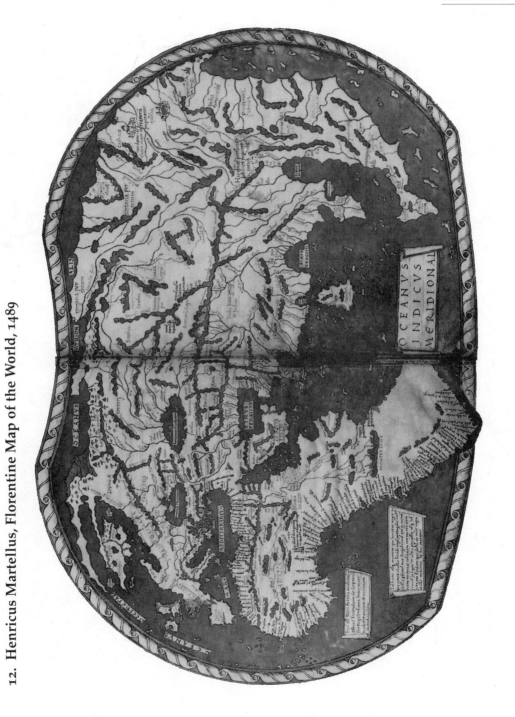

Source 12 from the British Library.

12. Henricus Martellus, Florentine Map of the World, 1489

Source 13 from Which Map Is Best? © *1988 by the American Congress on Surveying and Mapping. Reproduced by permission.*

13. Modern Equal-Area Map

QUESTIONS TO CONSIDER

The obvious first step in any attempt to read the Mercator map as a cultural document reflecting the perspective of its time is to familiarize yourself with the map itself. Spend a few minutes, therefore, going over Source 1, the reproduction of Mercator's original world map of 1569. As you can see by comparing this reproduction with the more recent map in Source 2, standard modern world maps looked remarkably similar to Mercator's map, at least in their general outline and focus. Details, of course, vary a great deal, and at first glance you may find all the lines and drawings on the Mercator map more confusing than informative. Rather than trying to make sense of them now, turn to the reconstruction of the ancient Greek map of Eratosthenes that appears as Source 3. It offers an easier starting point for learning how to read maps. Like most ancient Greek maps, it is not only simpler but probably seems familiar, because so many modern Western maps share its conventions. Yet its details remain different enough that we have to observe them carefully to make sense of them.

Look, for example, at the way Eratosthenes framed and focused his "world" map. He clearly regarded the conjunction of western Asia, northern Africa (known to him as Libya), and Europe as the center of the world. Note how he laid out his map with North at the top and a strong horizontal axis running from the Mediterranean Sea to the Taurus Mountains on the Iranian plateau. This approach no doubt reflected an effort to depict the broader Greco-Persian world revealed through Alexander the Great's conquests. But look at the way he set up the abstract gridwork through which to locate places in relationship to one another. Both a key meridian and the midmost parallel run through the great Hellenistic city of Alexandria, making it the central point of reference. He also seems to have ignored the Southern Hemisphere, which he dismissed as too hot for human habitation, and let the edges of his map fade off into vague bodies of water. Though we cannot identify all the features included in his map, it apparently included mainly geographical elements—rivers, mountains, seas—as well as the location of important regions and cities. But could a traveler use this map to plan a journey?

Ptolemy adopted a similar focus and orientation in his famous world map. As you can see from one of the surviving copies reproduced as Source 4, he, too, centered it around the eastern end of the Mediterranean, a sea whose assumed centrality led the Romans of his day to give it its name, which means "middle of the earth." But Ptolemy considerably enlarged its scope, expanding the margins to include more of Asia and Africa and filling in more geographical details. He also clearly tried to show that the area depicted forms part of a much larger, and spherical, world. Despite his suggestion of a greater world, Ptolemy abandoned the old device of showing an encircling ocean to mask ignorance of unknown regions. Note, however, the curious land connection he posited between Africa and Asia. On the whole, his more regular gridwork of cosmologically determined meridians and parallels allowed him to locate places and natural features in fairly accurate relationships if not distances. As you can see, he made his map much more wide than tall, a fact that forced him to lay out eleven meridians of longitude but only nine parallels of latitude. Moreover, his use of icons for the twelve winds provided an additional frame of reference. Whom do you think would make use of such referents—and for what purpose? Current viewers often find Ptolemy's map remarkably "modern" in its focus and orientation despite its antiquity, and many deem it naturalistic in appearance. Why might this be so?

A comparison between these ancient Greek maps and medieval European T-O maps quickly shows the uniqueness of their features. Both focus on the eastern Mediterranean. But, as you can see from Source 5, a map attributed to a seventh-century Spanish bishop named Isidore of Spain, many medieval maps were so highly schematic that they seem to us more like diagrams. Note, for example, how Isidore abandoned efforts to suggest a spherical earth in favor of a flat, circular field. As even more diagrammatic versions show, this shape derived from the letter O and probably represented a symbolic rendering of the medieval concept of an *orbis mundi,* or "world orb." This schematic approach equally characterized the way medieval map makers treated geographic elements. As in the case of the encircling ocean sea, natural features were generally simplified into decorative details.

More significantly, T-O maps shifted the field of view of world maps. Look at Source 6, a more complex T-O map of the eighth century made by the Benedictine monk Beatus. Beatus put East rather than North at the top, making the Holy Land the central feature. This shift created an interesting hierarchical effect that had little to do with actual geography. For these maps usually located Eden, the Biblical paradise, eastward *above* Jerusalem, the holy city of Christianity. Both sites thus symbolically tower over the more worldly areas of early Christendom, which make up the bulk of the map. To allay any doubts about the spiritual symbolism of this orientation, most maps include an image of Christ at their apex. Look at this feature in Source 7, the Ebstorf German map of the world. Clearly East was uppermost here in more than a geographical sense. This scheme puts the Christian Holy Land in the place of honor at the top, with Europe relegated to a secondary spot in the lower left-hand quadrant on a par with Africa to its right. As all the pilgrimage sites and other iconographic details further show, these maps portray a distinctly Christian vision of the world.

The full implication of this reconfiguration may best be seen by comparing the T-O maps with the twelfth-century world map prepared by an Arabic cartographer, named Al Idrisi which appears as Source 8. Al Idrisi obviously still knew and followed the Ptolemaic tradition without any of the Christian changes, for his map incorporates both its framework and general outline. It, too, focuses on the eastern Mediterranean and uses

Ptolemy's system of meridians and parallels to locate places. But Al Idrisi reoriented his version so that South appears at the top, thereby giving North Africa more prominence and shifting Europe down into the lower right-hand corner. Consider the effect this change produced. It is also worth observing how this shift subtly made the Arabian peninsula and the Mesopotamian plain central features on his map. What city does this map highlight instead of Jerusalem?

An even clearer indication of the way in which cultural values affect the perspectives of maps may be seen by looking at examples from traditions not influenced by the Greeks. In such maps, few conventions will seem normal or natural enough to be decipherable on sight. Look, for example, at the seventeenth-century Korean copy of an old Chinese-style world map that appears as Source 9. Like the T-O maps of the medieval West, this work presents a highly schematic vision of the world. Here, too, the world appears as a disk encircled by the ocean. But within the world disk, shown with North at the top, a vast outer square of unknown land, marked with legendary sites, frames the Eurasian continent. Note how the latter appears as a rounded mass whose principle rivers all radiate out from a great central mountain, known as *Kunlun*, which supposedly stood under the palace of the god of Heaven and marked the axis of the earth. At either extreme to the right and left, two trees locate legendary sites where the sun and moon began and ended their daily course. What kind of landscape do these features evoke?

Some scholars think these maps duplicate a cosmological pattern found on implements associated with ancient Chinese cosmology, such as the mirror back depicted in Source 10. As you can see, both share a common design in which a circle encloses a square and a central boss. Thus an ancient cultural pattern, as symbolic in its own world as the T-O schema in the West, may have shaped this conception of the world. Yet the underlying paradigm did not prevent its makers from also recording actual geographic information. For lack of adequate information, they depicted western Asia as a vague realm filled only with the names of fantastic kingdoms, but they represented East Asia fairly well. The crenelated circle to the right of center marks the "Central" Plain of northern China, locked between the arms of the Yellow and Yangtze Rivers; like the Mediterranean in the West, this feature was deemed the center of the globe by the ancient Chinese, who thus called their homeland *Zhung-guo,* or the "Middle Land." To the north curves the Great Wall, which arcs toward the Korean peninsula and the Japanese archipelago lying just offshore. Nonetheless, a cultural image clearly underlies and shapes the geographic view.

Keep that possibility in mind as we turn back to the way in which Europeans began to map their expanding world on the eve of the modern period. Note how the makers of the Catalan Atlas, Source 11, rejected the usual medieval T-O scheme and revived the basic focus and orientation of the old Ptolemaic approach. The many diagonal lines of rhumb overlaid upon the segments of the Catalan Atlas, of course, provide clear indication of the new use for which such charts were intended. Yet the northward orientation and the wide but vertically flattened field focused on the eastern Mediterranean, equally demonstrate general familiarity with the perspective of old Ptolemaic maps. The Florentine Martellus world map, Source 12, shows how interest in this approach increased during the Renaissance as copies of Ptolemy's work began to circulate widely. Martellus expanded the edges of his map a bit, shifted its center to the Indian Ocean, and abandoned the land bridge between Africa and Asia, but the underlying image still reveals the Ptolemaic conception of the world. Here is graphic evidence of the impact of ancient thought on early modern Europe.

Now compare this early Renaissance vision of the world with the one presented in Source 1, the Mercator map of 1569. To incorporate the many new discoveries that explorers had reported back to Europe by his time, Mercator vastly expanded the scope and details of his map. For the moment, ignore the details and pay particular attention to the way in which he focused and framed his map. Although he continued to orient the field of his map to the north, note how he dramatically shifted its framework. The old Ptolemaic world image remained almost intact within his new map but scaled down and shifted off to the upper right-hand quadrant. Older European maps based on the Ptolemaic model generally position Eurasia so that western Europe and eastern Asia appear at opposite ends of the earth. Mercator, however, edged Eurasia off to the right to make room for the Americas. In his new view, what now replaces the eastern Mediterranean as the center of the world? Note Asia's small overlap on the left near the North American coast and the implied size of the Pacific. What does this shift suggest about Mercator's viewpoint on the world?

After you have analyzed the framework of the map, look closer at the details. What system did Mercator use to locate places on his map? What do his choices intimate about his relationship with older cartographic traditions? And what do they imply about who he expected would use such a map? In this context, take time to locate the equator on Mercator's map and compare his treatment of this key coordinate with that in other maps. What factors might explain why Mercator did not center it between the top and bottom? Perhaps even more important, given the sliding scale of his projection, how did this skewing of the equator affect the appearance of other portions of the globe, particularly toward the poles? Compare the size of Africa and South America on his map with their counterparts on the equal-area map included as Source 13. Now reexamine the places and geographical features on Mercator's map. What natural features did he include? What regions, states, or cities seem to merit attention? Do these details provide any further clues about who would find his map useful and what they might do with it? Who would view the world from this perspective—and why?

EPILOGUE

In the centuries following Mercator's first publication of his map, Western cartographers devised many other ways to render the earth's surface on flat maps, including some that preserved equivalence of area. But because of the inherent problems involved in transposing a curved reality onto a flat representation, all such projections distorted some feature or another. Thus no alternate approach has ever proved fully satisfactory. More by default than design, therefore, the Mercator map retained its popularity in the West, often influencing the frame and focus of other maps if not always their method of projection. So it survived to attain the stature of a modern classic, conveying its image worldwide—until in recent decades it has come under increasing criticism for alleged ethnocentrism.

By this point you should have some insight into the reasons. To some it seems to incorporate vestiges of an old Mediterranean concept of a concentric world order in which a central region holds a superior position over the periphery. Certainly the vision it gives of the world is one centered around the North Atlantic region. Western Europe and North America dominate the field of view, and the rest of the globe seems marginalized, a position made worse by areal distortions. This pattern, of course, coincided with the actual international order created by Europeans during the heyday of their power. It also reflected a measure of truth during most of the twentieth century, when many people in the West talked about the dawn of a new Atlantic century in which the United States would join Western Europe in directing world affairs. And it offered a comforting picture of the democratic "West" throughout the Cold War era—despite its gross magnification of the Soviet "East." But to what extent does the image of the map symbolically convey a cultural hierarchy?

Non-Western people have always been chagrined by the way in which the map seems to depict their homelands as marginal places. During the period of decolonization following World War II, however, discontent with this vision mounted as Europe's patent decline called into question its centrality in world affairs. Representatives of newly emerging nations openly criticized its vision, particularly in the proceedings of the United Nations. Criticism of this sort has intensified recently as many of these nations now see themselves generically as a less-developed South in competition for scarce global resources with the more economically advanced countries of the North. In their eyes, the foreshortening of the Southern Hemisphere and the resulting diminishment of Africa and South America relative to northern landmasses have unpleasant, insulting connotations. How valid do *you* find these concerns? What might be a better image for the multicentered contemporary world?

[429]

TEXT CREDITS

Chapter 1   Page 15: From Richard G. Klein. *The Human Career: Human Biological and Cultural Origins,* 1989, p. 419. Reprinted by permission of the publisher, The University of Chicago Press. **Page 19:** From Rick Gore, "Neandertals," *National Geographic,* 189, 1, January 1996, pp. 25, 28–29. Copyright © 1996. Reprinted by permission. **Page 27:** "Anthropological Description of the Early Discovery and Use of Fire" from *The Emergence of Man,* 3rd edition by John E. Pfeiffer. Copyright © 1978 by John E. Pfeiffer. Reprinted by permission of Addison-Wesley Educational Publishers, Inc.

Chapter 2   Page 44: From Joseph Needham, *Science and Civilization in China,* Vol. 4, Part 3. Reprinted with the permission of Cambridge University Press. **Page 45:** From *Roman Civilization* by Naphtali Lewis and Meyer Reinhold. Copyright © 1955 by Columbia University Press. Reprinted with permission of the publisher. **Pages 46; 48:** From Cho-yun Hsu, *Han Agriculture: The Formation of Early Chinese Agrarian Economy.* Copyright © 1980. Used with permission of the University of Washington Press.

Chapter 3   Page 64: From *The Torah: A Modern Commentary.* Copyright © 1981. Reprinted by permission of The Union of American Hebrew Congregations. **Page 68:** From Baynes, Cary F. (trans.), *The I Ching (Yijing) or Book of Changes,* 3rd Edition. Copyright © 1967 by Princeton University Press. Reprinted by permission of Princeton University Press.

Chapter 5   Page 111: From *The Persian Wars* by Herondotus, translated by George Rawlinson. Copyright © 1942 by Random House, Inc. Reprinted by permission of Random House, Inc.

Chapter 6   Page 135: From *Historical Records* by Raymond Dawson. Copyright © 1994 by Raymond Dawson. Used by permission of Oxford University Press, Inc. **Page 142:** From *Sources of Chinese Tradition* by William Theodore de Bary. Copyright © 1960 by Columbia University Press. Reprinted with permission of the publisher. **Pages 143; 146:** From *Roman Civilization* by Naphtali Lewis and Meyer Reinhold. Copyright © 1955 by Columbia University Press. Reprinted with permission of the publisher. **Page 151:** "Edict and Speech of Nero to the Greeks" from David C. Braund, *Augustus to Nero: A Sourcebook in Roman History.* Copyright © 1985. Reprinted by permission of the University Press of America/Barnes & Noble.

Chapter 7   Page 168: From *The Edicts of Aśoka,* edited and translated by N. A. Nikam and Richard McKeon, 1959, pp. 27–29, 30, 34, 51–52, 58, 66, 67–68. Reprinted by permission of the publisher, The University of Chicago Press. **Page 172:** From John S. Strong, *The Legend of King Aśoka: A Study and Translation of the Aśokāvadāna.* Copyright © 1983 by Princeton University Press. Reprinted by permission of Princeton University Press. **Page 174:** From Maude Aline Huttman, "The Establishment of Christianity and the Proscription of Paganism," *Columbia University Studies in History, Economics, and Public Law,* 147, 1914, pp. 152, 154, 161–162, 163, 164. **Page 180:** From A. J. Arberry, *The Koran Interpreted.* Copyright © 1964. Reprinted by permission of HarperCollins Publishers Limited. **Page 180:** From Al-Khatīb al-Tibrīzī, "Niches of Lamps," in John Alden Williams, ed., *Themes of Islamic Civilization.* Copyright © 1971. Reprinted by permission of John Alden Williams. **Page 184:** From Abu Yusuf, *Kitāb al-Kharāj,* in John Alden Williams, ed., *Themes of Islamic Civilization.* Copyright © 1971. Reprinted by permission of John Alden Williams.

Chapter 8   Page 201: From *Contemporaries of Marco Polo* by Manuel Komroff, editor. Copyright © 1928 by Boni & Liveright, Inc., renewed © 1955 by Manuel Komroff. Reprinted by permission of Liveright Publishing Corporation. **Page 203:** From *The Conquest of Constantinople,* by Robert of Clari, translated by Edgar Holmes McNeal. Copyright © 1936 by Columbia University Press. Reprinted with permission of the publisher. **Page 207; 208:** From Deno John Geanakoplos, trans., *Byzantium: Church, Society, and Civilization Seen Through Contemporary Eyes.* Reprinted by permission of the publisher, The University of Chicago Press.

Chapter 9   Page 229: From Usamah ibn-Munqidh, *An Arab-Syrian Gentleman and Warrior in the Period of the Crusades,* translated by Philip K. Hitti. Copyright © 1987 by Princeton University